Bc

Best Sermons

1944 Selection

Best Sermons

1944 Selection

EDITED BY

G. Paul Butler

CHICAGO • NEW YORK

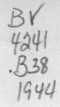

To

THREE GENERATIONS

OF BUTLERS:

WILLIAM A. BUTLER,

PAUL,

and

ERIC and PAUL NATI;

and

To

the men fighting
to win the war, the peace,
and a better world.

Foreword

SOME MONTHS AGO I HAD THE UNUSUAL EXPERIENCE OF being in a new community which does not yet have a church. It has a school, adequate for intellectual interests. It has a neighborhood center, devoted to social and cultural pursuits. It has a park and an athletic field, which provide for recreation. The community already seems to be well equipped—what more is needed? One of the citizens stated it rather naïvely, but pointedly, "We don't want our children and youth to grow up without seeing a building with a spire." A spire, thrusting itself upward, would remind them of something above themselves, on which everything else in the community would depend for its final meaning.

The deepest need of man is a sustaining faith that our human existence has ultimate significance and value. Without that we become, soon or late, the victims of a haunting sense of the futility and emptiness of everything. For if our existence is, in the last analysis, devoid of moral or spiritual meaning, it really makes no difference what we do about anything. In that event we are reduced to the cynical philosophy which Dorothy Parker describes in her sardonic lines:

> There's little in taking or giving,
> There's little in water or wine;
> This living, this living, this living
> Was never a project of mine.
> Oh, hard is the struggle and sparse is
> The gain of the one at the top,
> For art is a form of catharsis
> And love is a permanent flop,
> And work is the province of cattle
> And rest's for a clam in a shell,
> So I'm thinking of chucking the battle,—
> Would you kindly direct me to Hell?*

The sermons in this volume, although they come from men who differ on many points, are united in their witness to the high significance of life as the creation and gift of God. They lift our vision to a level where we see our existence in terms of a redemptive purpose that sheds light on the otherwise dark riddle of life and affords guidance in the human struggle.

A visitor to Sulgrave Manor, the ancestral home of the Washingtons in England, has reported that for many years a splendid upper room had a low ceiling which once made the place seem cramped and oppres-

* From *The Viking Portable Library, Dorothy Parker,* Copyright 1928, 1936, 1944 by Dorothy Parker. By permission of The Viking Press, Inc., New York.

sive. But one day it was discovered that the original structure had been different. The removal of the low ceiling disclosed a lofty, raftered roof that made the room spacious and glorious. The building, the guide explained, had been designed to be a Benedictine abbey, but later generations, turning it to what seemed more "practical" uses, had put in the temporary ceiling of lath and plaster—with the result that men's vision no longer soared upward to the Eternal. What a parable of many lives!

It is the vision of the Divine which alone gives ultimate significance to the human. Faith in God is the necessary condition of faith in man. If man is what certain superficial scientists say—a mere bundle of automatic physical reflexes; or if man is only what the Marxists say—a being whose status in life is determined wholly by economic processes; or if man is what the Nazis say—a creature in whom the decisive thing is the racial chromosome—then no high estimate of the worth of personality or of human destiny is plausible. Against any such devaluation of man the sermons in this volume are a noble testimony.

There are many indications that our generation is ready to listen to such a witness. We begin now to see that something more than our boasted achievement in the material realm is necessary if civilization is to endure. All our progress in the mastery of nature is impotent to save us from ruin; it may only mean a vaster ruin. Of what avail to have a machine that can fly three hundred miles an hour if its chief use is to spread deadlier destruction? Of what avail to have the miracle of radio if it is to be used only to propagate a narrow nationalism?

In the marvelous structure of Radio City in New York you see an impressive symbol of the physical achievement of man. Its towering buildings are a triumph of his engineering skill. It houses great commercial enterprises, great marvels of modern invention, great shipping concerns that span the seven seas, great diplomatic offices representing mighty governments, great publishing houses, great agencies of secular education. It is a concentrated picture of what man can do. Nestled in this vast aggregation of human handiwork is a little building with a spire —a symbol of the fact that life has a dimension other than size and wealth and power and knowledge. It declares that all these proud accomplishments are unable in themselves either to satisfy the human spirit or to make a decent civilization. What that spire does at Radio City, these sermons also do in their own way.

Faith in God is necessary not only to any worthy conception of human individuality but also to any achievement of world community. Universal brotherhood is the most splendid of goals, but much talk about it is unconvincing and romantic. As a result most people would probably agree with Marshal Pétain's remark that "fraternity is a magnificent ideal but only in natural groups such as the family and the fatherland." But we cannot have a dynamic hope for human unity across the chasms of nation, race and class unless we can have faith that mankind has the ultimate source of its being in a Reality that transcends all these earthly divisions. It is only a common origin in God and a common relation to Him that can afford an adequate basis for the binding of mankind together in one community.

The sermons in this volume all contribute to such an understanding of life. They are outstanding examples of great preaching and of the spiritual insight which our generation needs.

SAMUEL MC CREA CAVERT

Acknowledgments

THIS BOOK WAS MADE POSSIBLE BY THE CO-OPERATION and participation of thousands of ministers, priests and rabbis who gave their sermons, their advice and their friendship. To all I am sincerely grateful.

The preliminary selections were made by the editor from the 6,146 sermons received for possible inclusion, but the final selection was made with the assistance of the Advisory Committee members, who gave their time and effort in the midst of their own busy careers.

The fifty-two sermons presented in this collection were all chosen for their religious message, their homiletic qualities, and their insight into the needs of men in our day. I would like to emphasize that this was in no sense a contest but a wide search for the best sermons preached during 1943 and 1944.

Each sermon represents the distinct opinions and convictions of the clergyman who delivered it. Thus, Father Gannon's message has a Catholic flavor; Rabbi Mann's discusses spiritual problems and beliefs of the Jewish people; Dr. Moldenhawer's is Presbyterian; Bishop Tsu's has the feel of the Orient about it; and Kaj Munk's brings the problems of Denmark and the war before the reader. Yet, each sermon approaches the universal in its religious message, and each is as the preacher gave it.

The Protestant sermons were selected with the advice of Dr. Joseph R. Sizoo, Dr. Paul Scherer, Dr. Ralph W. Sockman, and Dr. Jesse M. Bader. Their balanced judgment, insight and impartiality were invaluable.

The Very Reverend Ignatius Smith, O.P., helped with patience and skill in choosing the Catholic sermons. The Reverend Gerald G. Walsh, S.J., generously gave his scholarly abilities to other Catholic details. The Reverend John F. Cronin, S.S., was prevented by illness from completing all the Catholic co-operation he had planned.

My Jewish advisors, Dr. David de Sola Pool, Dr. Israel Goldstein, and Dr. Israel Bettan, were gracious in helping to select the Jewish sermons.

To all of these Advisors I wish to express my deep appreciation. Without their help the book could not have had the truly representative character I believe it possesses.

At the special request of the editor, several members of the Advisory Committee consented to have their sermons included, and he assumes the responsibility for their selection. These sermons are indicated by an asterisk.

Just as the book was nearly completed, several unusual sermons were received, three from Europe (two via the Underground) and one from the Orient. Believing that they merited a place and would afford real inspiration to the readers of the book, they were included. To do this, several other excellent sermons had, unfortunately, to be omitted.

So many helped with the book that it is impossible to list all of them, but I must, at least, express my obligation to a few who were unusually helpful: To Edward J. Heffron of the National Council of Catholic Men for special assistance, to the Right Reverend Monsignor Arthur J. Scanlan for reading the Catholic parts of the manuscript, and to the Right Reverend Monsignor Francis X. Shea for counsel and advice; to Dr. J. V. Moldenhawer, Dr. Harold Cooke Phillips, and Dr. J. Quinter Miller for assistance in securing some of the outstanding sermons in the volume; to Monsignor Joseph F. Flannelly of St. Patrick's Cathedral for his kind advice; and to the Very Reverend Monsignor John J. McClafferty for his recommendations concerning outstanding Catholic preachers. Other acknowledgments are made in the book itself to the Macmillan Co., Viking Press, *Saturday Review of Literature, Catholic World,* William Rose Benét, and others for permission to use quotations.

To Warren Kelly and other friends on the New York *Mirror* who gave encouragement and helpful suggestions, I am happy to acknowledge my appreciation. And to Erica Butler for her constant loyalty and help I am also grateful.

G. P. B.

Contents

Christmas

Charity

The Church

The Church and War

The Church in the Country

Devotional Study

Easter

Faith

History

Immortality

The Intellect

The Jewish New Year

Missions

The Social Gospel

Social Service

Vision

* Sermons by members of the Advisory Committee were contributed at the request of
the editor and are included on his responsibility.

Advisory Committee

PROTESTANT

DR. PAUL SCHERER
DR. JOSEPH R. SIZOO
DR. RALPH W. SOCKMAN
DR. JESSE M. BADER

CATHOLIC

THE VERY REVEREND IGNATIUS SMITH, O.P.
THE REVEREND JOHN F. CRONIN, S.S.
THE REVEREND GERALD G. WALSH, S.J.

JEWISH

DR. DAVID DE SOLA POOL (ORTHODOX)
DR. ISRAEL GOLDSTEIN (CONSERVATIVE)
DR. ISRAEL BETTAN (REFORM)

Introduction

The Perspective of Preaching

The Burden of the Valley of Vision. Isaiah 22:1

PREACHING HAS A LONG HISTORY. FROM EARLY HEBREW times to the present it has held its unique place because it takes to men the message of religion—of God and Christ and the Holy Spirit, of sin and salvation, of the brotherhood of man, and of social justice and personal daily religious life. If preaching in any period fails in this, it misses its great function. As Kaj Munk said, "That the Church is ignored by so many as something that doesn't concern them, is often because preachers speak of things that seem absolutely useless to them."

Through wars, pestilence, suppression, plagues, and imprisonment, the Church has carried its message and worship to the people. In times of war churches have been stripped of their altars, lands, and buildings and deprived of their prerogatives; the clergy have been forced into hiding, but continued to give counsel and spiritual guidance to their followers in the face of death. It was thus that Peter spoke to the Christians in Jerusalem, Paul in Rome, and men of God through all the ages and nations in times of persecution and adversity.

Historically, preaching has always been important in making religion a reality. It carries the Word of God to the people and has held a vital place in Synagogues and Churches for centuries. The preacher opens the spiritual understanding and fortifies men for the problems of life. Thus men of God in every age have worked with the tools available to extend the Kingdom of God in their own time, and, despite tragic retrogressions, man has, on the whole, advanced—spiritually—generation by generation, sometimes so slowly as to seem to be standing still, and then again, by great forward strides.

Through the preaching and teaching of the rabbis, the tradition of the prophets has lived and developed uninterruptedly. By this continuous tradition of Jewish preaching, the rabbi of our day is the lineal follower of Elijah and Jeremiah, Amos and Hosea. For two thousand years the rabbis by this leadership have kept alive the highest ideals of their race, the faith of their people, their institutions of mercy and enlightenment, and the hopes of their children.

The preacher of the Christian Church is the inheritor of the inspired words of the Hebrew prophets and is the follower of John the Baptist, Paul and Peter, Jerome and Augustine, and the long line of Churchmen in every generation since Christ brought salvation to the world. This Hebrew-Christian tradition of preaching has been an ever-increasing stream flowing into new lands and to new peoples each generation.

Christ Himself was the world's greatest preacher, great in His simplicity and power and divinity and understanding of God and men. His own Sermon on the Mount has never been equaled, and it is to Him that all Christian preachers look for their spiritual commission.

The Apostles called by Jesus—after Pentecost—carried forward by their preaching the Church whose foundation He was. And the early church grew rapidly under the leadership of Peter and Paul, Timothy, Barnabas, and Matthias, and a steadily enlarging circle. The prophets and the disciples and the Church Fathers preached the message of God; their successors in the Church today proclaim the same God and His way of life. Century by century, Christianity made progress, softened the shell of humanity, made its way into the law codes, and tempered the daily life of men. Where the Christian religion has penetrated, justice, mercy, education, protection for women, care for children, hospitals, homes for the aged, food for the hungry, and relief for the oppressed, have been woven into the fabric of living.

The Christian Church has grown most rapidly under the inspiration of great preachers like Ambrose, Augustine, or Paulinus, men who carried Christianity farther in one lifetime than ordinary men did in a hundred years. Urban II and Peter the Hermit precipitated the Crusades by sheer eloquence; there is still need for such eloquence—there are still crusades to be preached. In the 13th century the tradition of preaching was kept alive by the popular talks of the Franciscans and the more theological sermons of the Dominicans. In the Middle Ages, it was the Church which kept learning and faith and culture alive for a thousand years.

Although John Wyclif set off the signal fires of the Reformation, probably without realizing it, it was not until a hundred and fifty years later that Beza, Zwingli, Luther, Melanchthon, Farel, and Knox proclaimed the Protestant and Lutheran Reformations. The Saintly Bishop Fisher and Hugh Latimer made preaching an event in sixteenth-century England. Fisher's funeral sermons for Henry VII and Lady Margaret in 1509 are noble examples of the funeral oration in English. Latimer won great fame by his fearless attack on abuses, his homely anecdotes, and commonplace allusions. He was successful as no other English preacher before Wesley and Whitefield. When he was burned at the stake with Ridley, he said, "We will light a fire today that will not soon be put out."

With the Protestant Reformation preaching was exalted by making it an essential part of the church service. The reformers gave their views in long sermons on theology and morals. Luther and Calvin tapped the springs of religious thinking which influenced thousands of other preachers. To Martin Luther the function of the sermon was the exposition of the Scriptures, but his enduring monument in the Lutheran faith is his Small Catechism. His emphasis upon singing was a deliberate attempt to give the people a part in the church service.

The Reformed Church organizations in several districts of Switzerland were founded by Zwingli and still exist. But John Calvin's more ordered theology made him the intellectual and religious leader in Switzerland. His influence rapidly spread to France, England, Holland, and Scotland and his *Institutes of the Christian Religion* became the source book of Calvinistic preaching and is the masterpiece of strictly Protestant theology. His preachers founded Presbyterian and Reformed churches, and later greatly influenced the development of the Congregational Churches. John Knox in Scotland was so imbued with Calvinism that his preaching won the entire country. The Baptists made preaching important; Hubmeier influenced the Baptist movement, while Menno Simons and John Smyth were among the first Baptist preachers in Holland and England. In America, Roger Williams was the great Baptist.

The Catholic or Counter Reformation inspired renewed great preaching in Spain, Italy, and France. Ignatius of Loyola founded the famous Society of Jesus and sent his followers all over Europe to preach. The Jesuits raised Catholic preaching to a new point of greatness. In the late Middle Ages Saint Vincent Ferrer of the Order of Preachers (Dominicans) and Bernardine of Sienna, the Franciscan, were the two great preachers of the Catholic Church.

Thus, in the sixteenth century, the Catholic Reformation, the Lutheran Reformation, and the Calvinistic Movement all made for increased and improved preaching—definitive, argumentative, and inspirational.

Seventeenth century France gave birth to three great Catholic orators, Bourdaloue, Bossuet[1], and Fenelon. The funeral orations of Bossuet are among the greatest in the world. In Italy in the same period, Paolo Segneri stirred the people with his powerful and beautiful Lenten sermons. The nineteenth century saw a revival of great preaching in France with the establishment of The Conferences of Notre Dame, which brought the greatest preachers of France to Paris for a course of sermons. These were made famous by the Jesuits, de Ravignan and Félix, and the Dominicans, Lacordaire and Monsabré.

English preaching reached its zenith with Lancelot Andrews, Dr. Reynolds, John Donne, Jeremy Taylor, Richard Baxter, and John Bunyan in the seventeenth century. The Wesleys and George Whitefield were the great preachers in the eighteenth century. John Wesley's preach-

---

[1] Cf. *Selections from Bossuet,* New York and London, 1930, for a current English edition.

ing, according to one historian,[2] saved England from horrors similar to those which occurred during the reign of terror in the French Revolution. Religion was a major factor in the American colonies from their foundation and preaching was the great event of the week. Jonathan Edwards, Increase Mather, and Francis Asbury were among the leading preachers of America in the colonial period. In the nineteenth century Cardinal Newman, Charles Kingsley, and Benjamin Jowett were great voices in England while Henry Ward Beecher, Phillips Brooks, Cardinal Gibbons, T. De Witt Talmadge, and Russell H. Conwell were some of the outstanding American preachers.

Ministers, priests, and rabbis still have courageous preaching to do to bring men to the practice of faith in God. Dictators found their citizens ready for the materialism of Hegel, Nietzsche, and Marx and the militarism of Gneisenau and Von Clausewitz and the politics of Machiavelli because the people did not accept the Fatherhood of God and the brotherhood of man. The totalitarian states reveal what government, education, and production without God can do.

The Church has many tasks in the world: preaching is one of its greatest. During this war the Church and the Chaplains must hold spiritual values before men, uphold moral standards, and help establish the ideals in men's minds which will enable us to win the war quicker and assure enduring peace. Monsignor Flannelly recently said, "The peace acceptable to God" must "join our . . . implements of war with law—God's law—the eternal principles that we should love one another. . . . Hatred cannot establish peace." When the four horsemen finish their ride in this Second World War the Church will be called upon for a ministry of compassion for those who have lost loved ones in the war, to be the moral guide in the reconversion from war to peace, and to work reverently for the rehabilitation of those wounded in body or spirit. Preaching can help in all of these problems, but the basis of all such preaching must be the Bible, and for the Christian minister, especially the Gospel of Christ. Evangelism and reform and socialization come to the world in ever-recurring cycles—perhaps we shall yet teach men and nations to apply the teachings of Christ in their relations with one another to the end that feuds and wars may cease.

Our preaching must have eloquence, contact, and content. True "eloquence," Bishop Kelley has said, "is conviction setting itself on fire." Dr. Kirkpatrick recently wrote, "In inspired preaching the Divine Reality

[2] Cf. W. E. H. Lecky, *A History of England*, Vol. 2, Ch. IX; F. J. McConnell, *John Wesley*; J. W. Funston, *The Wesleys in Picture and Story*. Wesley is credited with preaching 25,000 sermons in England, Ireland, America, and Scotland; Lecky puts the figure at 40,000. He spoke in Churches, and the streets, and even to miners in the coal pits; at eighty-five he delivered more than eighty sermons in eight weeks, and for fifty years he preached every day at five in the morning for working people.

finds a perfect, or well-nigh perfect, channel of expression,"[3] while Dr. Sockman, one of America's truly great preachers insists that "if the spark fails to flash between pulpit and pew, the power is wasted."[4] Every age of religious revival has been an age of great preaching. Are we, even now, at the beginning of another time of religious revival? Even now "the burden of the valley of vision" appears to men whose lips, like Isaiah's, have been touched by the Seraphim with the fire from the altar of God.

[3] R. W. Kirkpatrick, *The Creative Delivery of Sermons*, Macmillan, New York, 1944, p. 230.
[4] Ibid., Foreword by Ralph W. Sockman.

G. PAUL BUTLER

New York City

In This Thy Day

REVEREND HENRY SLOANE COFFIN, D.D.

*President of Union Theological Seminary, New York,
and Moderator of the Presbyterian Church, U. S. A.*

DR. COFFIN is one of the foremost ecclesiastical statesmen of our time. He is outstanding as a preacher, administrator, teacher, scholar, and leader in the ecumenical movement. Since 1926 he has been president of Union Theological Seminary, and at the 155th General Assembly of the Presbyterian Church, U.S.A., he was elected Moderator.

In addition to a penetrating intellect, Dr. Coffin has a warm evangelical passion and believes wholeheartedly in the power of the Christian Church and in the potential of the individual church member. Above all, he has the courage to speak frankly and forcefully on critical issues many men avoid. As a result he has the respect both of leading businessmen and of the humblest citizens of the community.

His reputation as a preacher is based on the work he did in his two influential pastorates in New York City—the Bedford Park Presbyterian Church (1900-05) and the Madison Avenue Church (1905-26) —and on his annual visits as guest preacher to the chapels of many leading colleges.

In this sermon, preached at St. Bartholomew's Church, New York City, on March 19, 1944, Dr. Coffin raises the questions, "What is the meaning of human history? What is the living God saying to us through the events of our day?" He discusses in answer three of the most important issues: international co-operation and war, economic injustice, and race discrimination.

The printed sermon retains the oral style of its original delivery, as it was taken down stenographically. Though necessarily sacrificing the forceful, convincing personality which his hearers experience, this sermon has the full rich flavor of Dr. Coffin's language, thought, and feeling.

REVEREND J. CHAPMAN
BRADLEY, D.D.

Sermon One

TEXT: *If thou hadst known, even thou, in this thy day. . .* LUKE 19:42

N A TIME WHEN NEWS OF SHATTERING EVENTS constantly assails the mind, thoughtful people cannot help asking, "What is the meaning of human history?" A generation arrives on the scene to find blunders of the past and contemporary forces which it did not produce, facing it with a tragic situation where its young men are claimed for tasks of destruction, its resources are diverted from productive uses, and millions of unfortunate men and women are in exile, or slave labor, or bitter imprisonment, or are suffering wounds, death, or tortures worse than death. What is the meaning of human history?

The Bible does not gratify our curiosity, but it asserts that the God of the universe appoints to individuals and nations their days, some calm, some tempestuous; and that these days contain encounters with God. Each is a "time of visitation." He may arrive as quietly as dawn steals over the earth. He may arrive like a storm on a sultry day, with clouds, wind, lightning, thunder, sheets of blinding rain. And when He confronts men, all that matters is that they recognize Him and perceive His will. Their day is momentous for them and for generations unborn. It may be filled with inestimable blessing or with incalculable misery. It is a *day,* and vastly much can be achieved in it, or pathetically much may be lost in it. It is only a *day* and passes irrevocably. "If thou hadst known in this thy day."

Our day has brought unwelcome war. Reluctantly and penitently—for we realize that by her selfish refusals and blind follies, our country had helped bring on the disaster—we have devoted our all to resist brutal oppressors. We hope to justify present appalling agonies and sacrifices by a better world for ourselves and mankind. The oppressors, thank God, seem destined for defeat. But that defeat will not create the better world. This must be born of changed thoughts and consciences; and it must be born now, in the time of our visitation, or our day will close and darkness will cover the earth.

What, then, is the living God saying to us through the events of our day?

Plainly He is saying that no nation can live to itself alone. Even in the churches many thought a nation could. There were small minds who never took in the wide world or felt any obligation for all of it. As children they had repeated, "God so loved *the world* that He gave"; they heard the words at the communion table. But it never occurred to them to give themselves or any sizable part of their means to make the world Christian. They have been startled to see what a pagan world is and does. To them it was unpractical politics that our country should involve herself to protect liberty and foster well-being in far-away lands. Why should we be taxed and our minds troubled to serve them? If they were wronged or distressed, what business was it of ours?

A profound thinker, half American, half Spaniard, who lived and taught many years among us, George Santayana, sums up the American character: "If it were given to me to look into the depths of a man's heart, and I did not find good will at the bottom, I should say without any hesitation, 'You are not an American.'"

But he goes on; and, remember, he had taught many college students: "If you try to pour instruction into him on matters that do not touch his own spontaneous life, he shows the most extraordinary resistance and forgetfulness."

And he concludes: "The American has never yet had to face the trials of Job."

In this our day the God of Job is putting us through a trial perhaps sorer than any we have so far known. He is showing us that what we thought practical politics and shrewd business land us in calamity. A foremost historian, Professor Carl Becker, entitles an article, "What we didn't know hurt us a lot." But is it certain that the hurt, the trials, have changed minds and stretched consciences to take responsibility for a world? And the time in which change and stretching must occur is swiftly passing.

The fighting will cease; keyed-up peoples will relax and settle back; nations which in peril planned and fought side by side will indulge in envies and squabbles, and fall apart. The war may have forced unconditional surrender on our foes; but if minds have not surrendered to the inclusive obligation, no just peace will have been won. Our young men will have endured homesickness, boredom, hardship, danger, disease, wounds, captivity, death—for what? The chance accorded our generation by the Lord of history will be gone. The lamentable cry may sound for us: "If thou hadst known, even thou, in this thy day, the things which belong unto peace."

Again, what is God saying to us through a disturbing accompaniment of the war, both in Britain and here—the constant tension between groups in our industries, with now and again a breakdown in a strike? Stop pages of labor and mutual recriminations between those engaged in doing the world's work do not occur where burdens and gains are felt to be adjusted fairly. Further, men in our armed forces and in the war industries are haunted by the specter of being left unemployed when present tasks cease. A current magazine entitles a suggestive article, "The New Fear"—fear not of war, but fear of what peace may bring. There are painful memories of desperate years not so far past.

Anyone who has seen the magnificent achievement of business, labor, and agriculture in making over our economic enterprise in brief months, so that we have become the unprecedented source of supplies in ships, planes, mechanized vehicles, weapons, food, and much else, cannot help believing that, could the same ingenuity, daring, and public devotion be roused to a like effort to prepare our economy for peace, so that every reasonably competent worker is assured a job at a return which would enable him and his to live decently, it might be done. Such justice for all is manifestly the will of Him who taught us to pray: "Give *us our* daily bread," and to include every child of His, both in our land and the earth over, in that prayer. If groups among our own people feel deprived of their rightful share in the national heritage, or if there be nations who feel themselves doomed to relative poverty, we shall not have stable order and peace.

In the postwar world two contrasting economic systems will confront mankind: that of Russia, which has captured imaginations by the heroic devotion and unguessed energy of its people; and that of our western democracies. It is evident that the Christian Church can exist under either system. But we Americans cannot help believing that the Church, education, and all spiritual institutions do best where there is a maximum of liberty. But liberty may seem to distressed and chaotic peoples too costly a luxury, and it might not appear desirable even here, should millions again look vainly for employment.

The two systems are already being assessed in millions of minds across the earth: Communism holding out the common good as the main goal and an assured place for every individual in the body politic; ours stressing freedom and initiative. Our day—the day when leaders in finance, labor, management, farming, can voluntarily get together and, pooling their wisdom, provide such adjustments as will make clear that the mass of plain folk can enjoy ampler life under free enterprise than under regimentation—is passing. An unprepared-for crisis, with widespread want abroad or here, would imperil this way of life. Now is the time of our visitation by the God of justice. Will the various groups in our industrial order become companions to render our freer system as just to all and more enriching than its rival? Or is our free system to pass, as other orders have passed, and a Voice say regretfully: "If thou hadst known in thy day"?

4

There is still another alarming accompaniment of this war all over our land—enmity between races. In some sections of the country it is the Japanese, in others the Jew, in still others the Mexican, in others again the Negro, against whom there is feeling. War brings to the surface and intensifies latent prejudices. We have had much to say of the hideous Nazi dogma of the "master race." Their retort has been: "Look at yourselves." The Japanese have dinned into Asiatic ears that Anglo-Saxon whites never treat colored peoples—yellow, brown, or black—as equals.

Among ourselves representatives of the Negro are vocal in protest that the freedoms for which we allegedly battle, and ask them to battle, are denied to them. They point out that there is a caste system in jobs—negro jobs and white jobs—and, no matter what skill or education the Negro acquires, a barrier hems him in. In an Ohio city recently, high school students competed for a prize in an essay on: "What punishment should be meted out to Adolph Hitler?" The contest was won by a Negro girl of sixteen, the thesis of whose essay was: "Give him a black skin and put him down in any American community." What experiences had that sensitive girl or her family and friends undergone to give birth to that essay!

The relation of races to each other is difficult and delicate, complicated by a great mass of emotions. It was the first big issue before the early Christian Church. Let us not forget that St. Paul dealt with it in six of his letters and declared that Christ had broken down "the middle wall of partition": "There cannot be Greek and Jew, barbarian, Scythian, bond nor free, but Christ is all and in all." If in our time we in the Church be true to our heritage, must we not take the lead in seeking a fair deal in employment and in education for folk of every race and in standing for such sane and reasonable relations between the races as shall enable each to contribute its God-assigned gifts to the commonweal and to the Church of God?

There is a growing sense of solidarity among colored races which may easily issue in a racial war against snobbish and oppressive whites; and we white folk are less than a third of the world's population. The eyes of the colored peoples are especially on the Christian Church because of our profession of brotherhood in Christ. The Church today has rivals for spiritual leadership in advocates of revolution by violence who claim to make no racial distinctions. If the Church loses the respect and confidence of these many millions the world over, who feel themselves held inferior—and loses to such rivals—what catastrophe may be in store for our children! How urgent is the call that every Christian take this issue on his heart and conscience. It comes home personally along various lines to every one of us and often finds us just a bundle of unreasoned emotions. National unity, world order, above all, the sincerity and consequent appeal of the Church of Christ, hang on the decisions of our

5

generation. Shall the voice of the Master of history be compelled to pronounce in sorrow: "If thou hadst known, even thou, in this thy day"?

When one looks squarely, as I have tried to do, at the big issues before the Christian Church—and I have only discussed three: the achievement of fellowship among nations, fellowship in the distribution of spiritual and economic goods, fellowship among races—how irrelevant seem the questions of Church government, or forms of worship, or the minor elaborations of doctrine which have divided her members into many communions! In the perspective of the colossal tasks immediately facing us, tasks for which our common Christian heritage plainly unites us, it would seem possible, with variety in forms and methods, to arrive at a unified organization of almost all non-Roman Christendom, which would enable us to bear a united witness and to exert a solid impact upon the world. Not only does it seem possible, but to those who know at first hand how hampering, how wasteful, how ineffective for the real job our inherited divisions prove, how meaningless and repellent they appear to outsiders, and to that large mass of indifferent nominal Christians whom the Church must recapture, it seems imperative.

The Church, in which God has set you and me, has her day of visitation. Down the centuries she has faced decisive days, sometimes magnificently, sometimes with tragic blindness. In our day how can she witness for fellowship on the world scene where the nations lie in pieces, or where antagonistic groups bedevil industry and business, or where racial animosities divide the family of God in bitterness and suspicion, unless she demonstrate, and demonstrate dramatically so as to catch public imagination, the power of her crucified and risen Lord to bind in one those who trust Him? Here and there leaders are trying to end the divisions of past centuries. What is wanted is an intelligent, insistent, clamant lay backing. Otherwise traditionalism and inertia will block every effort. The divisions will be handed on to our children, and we shall have missed our God-given chance to repair the breaches and transmit a Church worthier of and more serviceable to her Lord. Some future generation looking back on our obtuseness and pettiness, and what these did to obscure the Church's witness and impede her work, will lament: "If thou hadst known in thy day."

Fellow Christians, what a momentous day ours is in which to live, charged with such responsibilities for all nations, for the world's work, for races, for the Church of God. And what cogent incentives are ours from men giving their lives the earth over for a peace which will not be won if we fail them!

William Rose Benét puts on the lips of these millions of inarticulate youths questions addressed to us, their elders at home:

6

What did you do with the world that you bade us to bow
to anew?
With the strength and the beauty of life, and its valor, what
things did you do?
Did you lead out of bondage the captives, or fetter Mankind
for the few?
Did you shine for example, till all men declared for the
right and the true?

Did you plant on the mountains, for Youth to aspire to, a
fire and a star?
Did you lift a great song for a chant on the march to the
feet going far?
Did you kindle our pride in a wide smiling country where
under the sun
There was scorn for the liar and scorn for the cruel, and
justice was done?

By the horrors we have faced, by the carnage and pain . . .
we cry . . .
Our shuddering, urgent, ultimate desire:
Build in the spirit again—create, create—
*Lest, at the last, it prove too late, too late.**

LET US PRAY: *Righteous God, in whose hand are the times of men and
of nations, open our eyes to Thy will for us in this our day, and by all
the pain of myriads of innocent sufferers and by the valiant offering
of those who hazard themselves on the high places of the field to
achieve a juster world, dedicate us to seek righteousness in our land
and fellowship in Thy Church, through Him who laid down His life
for us all, even Jesus Christ our Lord. Amen.*

* Lines selected from "Arraignment," by William Rose Benét, which appeared in *The
Saturday Review of Literature*, March 11, 1944.

Conversation with an Electric Fan

THE MOST REVEREND FRANCIS C. KELLEY, D.D.

Roman Catholic Bishop of Oklahoma City and Tulsa

BISHOP FRANCIS CLEMENT KELLEY of Oklahoma is one of America's great preachers. His whole career has been marked by greatness. After having served in the Spanish-American War as a Captain and Chaplain, he was Pastor of a very poor little parish in Lapeer, Michigan. It was here that he dreamed the dream of the Catholic Church Extension Society, which he founded and directed for nineteen years. This Society helped to build five thousand Catholic Churches all over America.

From his important work with Extension, he went to Oklahoma twenty years ago to become Bishop. His untiring work, his kindness, his leadership, his preaching, and his writing have made him one of the leading churchmen and citizens of the state.

When Pope Pius XII sent his congratulations to Bishop Kelley on the occasion of his Golden Sacerdotal Jubilee last year, he recognized the Bishop's "greatness of soul and character, his faithfulness as a pastor of many, his ability as a writer, but most of all," he recognized Bishop Kelley's "eloquence in preaching." Bishop McGuiness said, "He above all others has expanded the horizon of the cross, for he has, in truth, dotted the hillsides with crosses," and his great mission has been "that the Gospel be preached to the neglected throughout this land."

They say of the Bishop, "if you have ever heard him preach, you will want to read one of his books. As you read, you will recall the speaker as he came smilingly out on the platform, paid his felicitations to the chairman and the audience, settled them into a happy mood and kept that mood happy for perhaps two hours. One often hears of tireless speakers and tired audiences. Bishop Kelley, as a speaker, is tireless, and his audiences are likewise." And, when one has read one of his books, he wants to hear the author preach!

Though he speaks with eloquence, no one refers to Bishop Kelley as an orator because he does not orate, but seems when preaching to be conducting a one-way conversation with his hearers. His sermons are heart-warming and you immediately warm to the man and his message. The following sermon-lecture has the fire and stimulation of his intellect and enthusiasm, the wit and bite of his thinking, the penetration of his criticism, and his insistence upon the spiritual as the greatest factor in education and life. It created a

8

sensation at the University of Oklahoma when it was delivered there. It is lighted by fantasy, fired with imagination, yet balanced with solid facts and truth. One can see the Bishop as an educator and man of God in this unusual sermon.

REVEREND GAVAN P. MONAGHAN, PH.D.

Sermon Two

TEXT: *Who makest the clouds thy chariot: who walkest upon the wings of the winds. Who makest thy angels spirits and thy ministers a burning fire.*   PSALM 103:3, 4 (Douay Bible)

OUR DISTINGUISHED PRESIDENT TELEPHONED ME an invitation to come here tonight and make trouble for myself. I thoughtlessly accepted, thoughtfully repented, and retired to pray. My favorite form of prayer is the Rosary which, in case you do not know about it, is the chain of matched prayer-pearls which our separated brethren—that means most of you—left behind on the mantle above the fireplace in the old spiritual home when you got things wrong and stamped out.

The Rosary calls for repetition. Some people think that too monotonous for them. A French orator, Henri Lacordaire, thought otherwise. "Love has but one word," he said, "which, though ever spoken, is never repeated." But the Rosary in sleepy hands sometimes plays a harmless little trick. It becomes a Catholic match for the Protestant devotion to slumbering during long sermons. With the prospect of trouble before me—but knowing the other prospect too—I sat down, Rosary in hand, to worry as well as to pray; careful to switch on an oscillating electric fan for coolness and company.

It was an old friend, that electric fan, usually quite reliable about its duty of sweeping breezes half-way around my study; all the while keeping its single bright round eye fixed on me. As a rule, it sticks to its business, but this time I saw that it wanted to talk. Being a celibate and having no other talking machine around but myself, I let it have its way; even gave it a start.

"Are you tired?" I asked. "You must be, for I had you on me all night and now have put you to work again."

"Not a bit tired," said the Fan. "Wind never gets tired. Of course the machinery I am now using for your comfort wears and sometimes breaks down. But that is not me. Go to sleep. I'll stay on the job."

"Thanks," I said. "In the future I won't feel that I am imposing on

9

you. But you do seem to be working hard and using up a lot of energy on my account."

"A lot of energy?" The Fan put on a pitying smile. "I'm only using a modicum of energy in comparison with all the energy there is. Did you ever hear of the amount of energy contained in an atom?"

"When I went to college, physics hadn't got quite that far," I answered.

"It has now," said the Fan. "You could light Oklahoma for a day at least with the energy contained in a tiny atom that can be seen only as a group of molecules through a microscope multiplying size fifty thousand times."

"You don't say," I remarked. "Well, well, we have advanced, haven't we?"

"Advanced?" sneered the Fan. "You admire yourself, don't you? Better go on sleeping."

"Pardon a correction," I suggested. "I am praying."

The Fan seemed to take on a smile of superior tolerance like the one quite generally used by candidates for office. It also changed the conversation.

"Was that Norman you had on the phone just now?" it asked.

"Yes, President Brandt."

"Nice chap that," said the Fan.

"Yes, I like him too," I returned. "Have you met him?"

"I've met everybody," said the Fan. "I would be glad to give President Brandt the air any time, as the saying goes; not speaking politically of course. I am no politician, as you know; I temper myself to the shorn lamb."

"I know."

"So do I. Presidents also need coolness and comfort. I wasn't born yesterday, though this metal suit of mine is fairly new. I was around in the old days when there was nothing to rely on for coolness but natural changes of temperature." It sighed. " 'Them was the days,' as Plato or somebody said—in Greek you know."

"Yes, in Greek," I remarked severely. "I think, however, that Plato would have been a bit more grammatically precise in his diction."

"That's true," agreed the Fan. "But consider the company I have to keep in these days; nothing personal intended, of course. But who studies grammar in school any more? Grammar is called antiquated; a relic of long-gone-by instructional inefficiency which passed with the Little Red Schoolhouse. Grammar doesn't fit into an integrated, consolidated, and up-to-graded new brick school with all the luxuries of a swimming pool, a gym, moving pictures, and teachers awaiting payment of their back salaries."

"Wait a moment," I said. "We were talking about a university president. That would naturally lead us to converse on the higher educational plane. What have you to remark about higher education? But perhaps you were mostly in the business of keeping bishops cool in the old days, and didn't bother about universities."

"I bothered about them all right," sighed the Fan, "though it was hard enough to keep bishops cool at the end of the Dark Ages when they were hot on founding schools. Yes sir, I have very decided and clear opinions on education—modern style. And my age ought to put force behind them. Wind is air at work; and air is one of the oldest created things, coming right after light. I antedate the rise and fall of every nation, if not of even every planet. I saw the birth and passing of every bloom and bush and being. But, counting my years in billions, I, nevertheless, have not what you humans, born only yesterday and passing tomorrow, possess. I do not have intelligence and free will. My work is one of simple obedience to fixed laws. My merit is in dumb service. I cannot know anything about the Law-giver. But you? You can. It is within your natural powers to glimpse truth. God speaks to you through me and all nature, but He did more for you; He sent His Word to speak to you. If you humans realized your greatness, it would be reflected in your education. What is reflected now is little more than what I reflect or what any other unintelligent thing reflects."

"I know that it was not so in the old universities," I said, "but we think. . . ."

"You don't think," broke in the Fan. "You don't think and that's what's wrong with you. Educators thought in the old days. It was their thought that made education. Hitler had predecessors: Goths, Huns, Lombards and all the rest of them. They didn't do a thing to the old Roman Empire but burst it wide open, and there was no one around but the few thinking men to pick up the salvage. Ever hear of the Cathedral schools? They grew into colleges. Ever read up on the monasteries? They grew into universities. O boy!—Beg pardon—that slipped."

"You are pardoned," I said in the lofty manner befitting wounded episcopal dignity. "Cease the scolding and tell me more about those old days. I have to talk to a class of university graduates, you know. That's what the President asked me to do, but—I am a bit lazy. Listening is easier than reading."

"As it should be," said the Fan. "Listening is the true road to learning, for man primarily is a being subject to instruction. He has to be taught. I heard old Abelard say that, one windy day in the woods where he was lecturing."

"In the woods?"

"Sure Mike—I mean Doctor or Something. This modern slang will burn out a fuse in me yet. They didn't need Gothic towers for universities

11

then. All they needed was a teacher with a strong voice and a headfull of wisdom, plus a few kids—I mean students—to listen to him. It's the teacher and not the book that makes the scholar. See what I mean?"

"Perhaps."

"The old teachers had a philosophy of life. They didn't cultivate fads; couldn't afford to. They didn't believe in easy courses. They held education to be a process of gradual mental development through hard exercising. When a student got that kind of start, he finished the job himself. The schools gave him the taste, the desire; sort of mixed the ingredients, and the Church put in the yeast. Getting him ready was a kneading and slapping process. The old teachers tried the boys and girls out on what they called the Trivium—that was grammar, rhetoric, and logic. If they absorbed this, they were given the Quadrivium—arithmetic, music, geometry, and astronomy. Then they became masters and teachers themselves; founded schools and made new scholars. It was from them that your modern colleges and universities descended. I know, for the wind was always around, as I said, and I had to carry a share of the talking and teaching from professor to boy; from past to future."

"Do you find much difference between what you carried then and what you'll have to carry to the next generation after us?"

"Now listen here," said the Fan, earnestly. "I don't want to get in bad with the President. You are making me prepare your address for you, and if it does not go over, I'll get the blame."

"Don't worry about the President," I soothed. "He can put the blame on me. Being a bishop, I'm used to that."

"I don't get fair treatment from you humans anyhow," mourned the Fan.

"As wind," I replied, "you are not yourself very considerate of us. What a mess you made at Pryor! Why don't you go straight and not get so twisted; or, better still, take the pledge?"

"In the Ozark country?" it queried. "Say, don't you know what I have to blow over before I get out of the mountains?"

I ignored that question and hastened to speak of something else.

"How have we been annoying you?"

"Take your literary group for example," shot back the Fan, "your poets especially. What sort of picture of the wind did Shakespeare make? 'Blow winds, and crack your cheeks. Rage! Blow!' There's a caricature for you. Shelley, too, when he got ecstatic about a cloud:

> From my wings are shaken
> The dews that awaken
> The sweet buds every one.

"That's all right for the cloud, but who shook her wings? Me."

12

"Bad grammar again," I objected. "You had better stop breezing around the high schools."

The Fan ignored the suggestion.

"There are all kinds of poems about everything else in nature but mighty few about me," it complained. "All right, all right. Let bygones be gone with the wind. I'll talk, but you are sure to tell. The Irish can't keep their mouths shut."

"What do you know about the Irish?" I snapped.

"It's what the Irish know about me that's important, not what I know about them. I'm part of Irish history. Ever hear about the Night of the Big Wind?"

"I did. Was it you?"

"Me and three others. I'm ashamed of it now. I shouldn't have treated the Irish as I did. I was at the schools they founded all over Europe. I knew St. Gall and I filled the sails of St. Brendan when he discovered America. I knew Columba and Duns Scotus too. I blew into the Bobbio Monastery and had Irish friends at the University of Paris. The Irish did a grand educational job on Europe when fighting had all but put out its light. It may have to be done all over again if you humans can't learn to keep peace." He added that sadly.

"There were others than the Irish," I remarked magnanimously.

"There were," agreed the Fan. "But some were English—I didn't want to start a fight. By the way, did you ever take any interest in the guilds?"

"A passing interest only," I said.

"If it hadn't been for the guilds," said the Fan, "there wouldn't have been such schools. Professors can live only if there are students. The name, university, didn't indicate a group of buildings but a union of students modeled on their father's pious labor-union idea. Their sons had a special course made up for them in the schools the guilds founded: grammar, rhetoric, and dialectics. That would take in Latin and the vernacular prose and verse and logic. The old universities later supplied the liberal arts; then medicine, mathematics, astronomy, and architecture. A funny thought comes to me. Imagine Erasmus going into a shop to buy a pair of shoes and the son of the shoemaker saying: *"Quid vis, egregie Doctor?"*

"How could shoemakers' sons at that time be prepared for such studies?"

"Easily enough," said the Fan. "Many of the guilds had permanent chaplains who added to their religious duties that of running a school for guildsmen's children. There was little real illiteracy in the old-time cities and towns. How could printing have succeeded so quickly had there been no demand for books? Answer me that! The most beautiful printed book is still the first that came from the clumsy press of Gutenberg. Businessmen knew Latin and used it in trading with strangers. Thus it was a bond between nations. Before a guildsman could be declared a master of his trade, he had to pass examinations. Fancy John L. Lewis having to pass an examination. I wonder if he can speak Latin?"

"You seem to have gotten around quite a lot," I encouraged.

"Wind does, you know," said the Fan carelessly. "I have touched everything in my line of business, and you know how much wind there always is around colleges. Oklahoma was not the only university to graduate a speech professor into the Senate—and I'm not *joshing*. Wasn't Cicero a Senator? He was a master of eloquence. But you should read up on the first universities: Bologna, Paris, Coimbra, Padua, Oxford, Cambridge, Salamanca, Prague, Cologne, Louvain. They were the real McCoy, if you'll pardon another lapse into slang. They were all the work of Church and churchmen."

"Oh! I know about them," I put in.

"You do? Well, then you can't be ignorant of the fact that the Christian spirit kept founding universities in Spain even while fighting the Moslems for life and civilization. There's something," he said a bit ironically, "to be said for bishops."

"Thanks."

"Don't mention it. Say, would you be good enough to push that lever on my foot up to 'high'? I want to close this talk as it should be closed."

I got up and did as asked. The Fan seemed to take a deep breath and swung around like an orator in full broadside action.

"What modern educators need to know more about," he shouted, "is their ancestry. They think they *made* education when, as a matter of fact, they only inherited it and, apart from physical science, squandered a goodly part of it. You moderns think that it was *ignorance* you inherited. You inherited *light*—light, do you hear? Light, and lots of it. Know your ancestry and the distinction between education and instruction. The objective of instruction may be, for example, to make proficient engineers, but the objective of education is to make well-balanced men fit to be proficient engineers."

"Just a moment." I lifted my hand. "I seem to feel a presence. Do you?"

"It has been here all along," replied the Fan.

"Do you see it?"

"It can't be seen. It is a spirit; the spirit of the old masters, the spirit of Augustine, of Thomas Aquinas, of Bonaventure. It's never absent when Truth is declared."

"Can it speak?"

"It speaks as a spirit speaks; by influence and creative inspiration. Listen to it."

I heard no voice, yet I received the message.

14

"A fundamental mistake of the moderns," the Spirit said, "is in thinking that education begins in the school when it really begins in the
family. Education is the process by which the child is lifted out of the
vegetative and animal nature proper to it at the beginning and brought
up to the dignity and greatness of the life of the intellect and spirit.
Education is ascension to the perfection of the human person; to realization of the fact that man is the triumph of creation and its king. When
taken as less, the human person slips back, away from its true greatness.
The senses are not made for its pleasure but for its instruction, and the
earthly fulfillment of its high destiny. Free will is the mistress of our
faculties and directs our conscious activities toward the realization of
our high moral and eternal destiny.

"The foundations are laid in the family. The school, in all its degrees
from grade to university, must continue the building; not limiting it to
a room or a stairway, but finishing the whole palace. A clear intelligence
and a rightly directed will need everything; not 'more and more about
less and less.' The intelligence needs the culture of a true philosophy of
life. The will is never free and master of the passions without that discipline which was promulgated in the Decalogue centuries before the
foundation of the first university. The sensibility cannot bloom into full
beauty without artistic culture. The true, the beautiful, and the good
walk in its train and are the highest joy of the educated man. This is
the legacy we left you to develop. What are you doing with it?"

"I'll tell him," shouted the Fan. "You are trying to balance the man
by loading a heavy weight of instruction on the physical end of the rod
of his life and leaving the spiritual end with scarcely any weight at all to
carry. Then you push the rod off-center to find a spot where it will balance in spite of the difference in weight. But the rod is not of infinite
length. It has limits that stop you. Perfect balance is the true objective
of education. Man has a will as well as a mind, and a soul which is the
true center of the rod of his life. When you push the rod over to make
it balance where there is no balance possible, you not only move away
from the will but put the rod itself on a false center. If the weight of
instruction is all on the mental and physical, with nothing or little on
the spiritual end, there never will be a balance. Then you are too often
afraid to put on weights. A well-balanced man must carry them. Education is not a process of relieving the back of burdens but of imposing the
right ones. The more necessary developing burdens are lifted, the lighter
and more useless becomes the rod of life. The scales of education were
not made for trifles but to weigh the imponderable thing which is
Eternal Destiny. Tell your graduates that if you dare."

It quieted down a little and said: "Favor me again, please push that
lever back to 'low.' I got worked up too much."

15

I did as requested and, as the voice of the Fan gentled down, I felt easier.

"Man," it said, "comes to resemble and almost to be what he knows and loves. Tell that to the graduates."

I woke up. My Rosary had fallen to the floor. As I stooped to retrieve it, I saw a current magazine lying open on the rug beside it. I picked it up and read this contribution by John Edward Spear, a private soldier of the new army of the United States of America—your army:

> Professors, writers, learned men, what do
> You, faced with present circumstances, say
> About the things you taught us yesterday?
> For I remember clearly still how you,
> Enthroned upon the seats of wisdom, threw
> With pompous show and scholarly display
> The ancient laws God gave to man, away
> And introduced the lawlessness you knew.
>
> You taught us this in days before the war.
> What teach you now? There is no wrong or right?
> Truth is a myth? Man needs his God no more?
> You do not dare, for war has brought to light
> Your lies; so give us back the truth you swore
> Away, that we may honorably fight.*

* Private John Edward Spear, "The Guns Speak," *The Catholic World,* July, 1942, p. 468.

By Invitation of Jesus

Reverend Peter Marshall, D.D.
Pastor, New York Avenue Presbyterian Church, Washington, D. C.

Although Dr. Peter Marshall has been in the ministry only thirteen years, he occupies the pulpit of the New York Avenue Presbyterian Church, one of the important churches of Washington, sometimes called the Presidents' Church because it has been attended by many of our presidents since before the time of Abraham Lincoln.

Dr. Marshall was born in Scotland. He attended a technical college there, studying engineering, and was employed in a steel-tube mill for six years. He came to this country in 1927, where his experiences have been many and varied. He worked in a machine shop and became a foreman. Later, he was an accountant, a laborer, a timekeeper, and a newspaperman.

He held two pastorates in Georgia before going to Washington in 1937. The honorary degree of D.D. was conferred upon him by the Presbyterian College of South Carolina in 1938. It is easy to understand why his sermons appeal to rich and poor, workmen and executives: he knows what work is about. This sermon has beautiful simplicity and imagination. It reminds one of Dr. Charles M. Sheldon's *In His Steps,* which brought the question, "What would Jesus do?" into every act of daily life. "By Invitation of Jesus" is a moving parable of religion in modern life.

Sermon Three

> Text: *Then said he also to him that bade him, When thou*
> *makest a dinner or a supper call not thy friends, nor thy*
> *brethren, neither thy kinsmen, nor thy rich neighbors; lest*
> *they also bid thee again, and a recompense be made thee.*
> *But when thou makest a feast, call the poor, the maimed,*
> *the lame, the blind:*
> *And thou shalt be blessed; for they cannot recompense thee;*
> *for thou shalt be recompensed at the resurrection of the just.*
>   Luke 14:12, 13, 14

UPPOSE SOME ONE LIVING FAR OUT ON MASSAchusetts Avenue, or in Chevy Chase, happened one day to open a Bible, and by that mysterious process known only to angels, chanced to read these verses in the Gospel of Luke. Suppose the reader concluded that these words, probably spoken in Aramaic so long ago beneath a Syrian sky, were just as applicable in

17

twentieth-century society. Suppose that person believed that the blessings Jesus mentioned were worth having and decided to claim them. Suppose he had the courage and the love that would be required to take Jesus at His word. What do you think would happen?

One bitterly cold night, when Washington was covered with a blanket of snow and ice, a man sat in his home on Massachusetts Avenue. The house was very comfortable, a crackling log fire in the fireplace threw dancing shadows on the paneled walls, the wind outside was moaning softly like someone in pain, and the reading lamp cast a soft warm glow on the Book this man was reading. He was alone, for the children had gone to the Shoreham for supper and dancing, and his wife had retired early after a strenuous afternoon's bridge game. He read the passage of Luke which is our text, and then could read no more. Somehow, he could not get away from those simple words. He had read the Bible often, for he was a good man, but never before did the words seem printed in flame, never before did they seem to burn with such heat. He closed the Bible, and sat musing—conscious for the first time in his life of the challenge of Christ. He felt as though Someone were standing behind him; he knew he was no longer alone; but no one was there. What strange fancy was this? Why was it that he kept hearing, in a whisper, the words he had just read? "I must be sleepy and dreamy," he thought to himself; "it is time I went to bed."

But it was long ere he fell asleep, for still the voice whispered, and still he was conscious of a Presence in the room. He could not shake it off. Never before had he been so challenged. He thought of the dinners and parties that they had given in this beautiful home. He thought of those whom he usually invited. Most of them were listed in the *Who's Who in Washington;* and there were his own particular and intimate friends; and there were those whose names were household names in business, finance, clubs, and in government circles. There were men with the power to grant political and social favors; there were those who reciprocated his hospitality, and thus provided a round of gaiety and fellowship. But *they* were not poor or maimed or lame or blind. What a challenge it was! What had put this absurd thought into his head anyhow?

He tried to sleep, but somehow he could not close the door of his mind to the procession that shuffled and tapped its way down the corridors of his soul. There were beggars with trembling lips, there were sightless eyes that stared straight in front and faces blue with cold, there were sticks tapping on the pavement, there were crutches that creaked with the weight of a twisted body. As he watched them pass, his own lips quivered, his eyes moistened, and his heart was touched. He whispered a prayer that if the Lord would give him courage he would take Him at His word and do what He wanted him to do. Only then did he find peace and fall asleep.

When the morning came, his determination gave him new strength and zest for the day. He must begin his preparations, and he was impatient to go downtown. His first call was on the engraver's to whom his name was quite familiar. At the counter he drafted the card he wished engraved, chuckling now and then as he wrote, his eyes shining. The clerk who read the card looked somewhat puzzled but made no comment, although he stood watching the retreating form swing down the street. The card read:

JESUS OF NAZARETH
Requests the honor of your presence
at a Banquet honoring
The Pilgrims of Pain
The Sons of Want
and
The Casualties of Cruel Circumstance
on Friday evening, in a home on Massachusetts Avenue
Cars will await you at the Central Union Mission
at six o'clock
*"Come unto me, all ye that labor and are heavy laden,
and I will give you rest."*

In the engraving room, they did not know what to make of it; but the conclusion they reached was that someone had more money than sense, that someone was crazy, but that it was none of their business.

A few days later, with the cards of invitation in his hand, he walked downtown and gave them out, and within an hour there were several people wondering what could be the meaning of the card that a kindly, happy, well-dressed man had placed in their hands. There was the old man seated on a box trying to sell pencils, another on the corner with a racking cough and a bundle of papers under his arm, there was the blind man saying over and over to himself "Jesus of Nazareth requests the honor of your presence." A fellow who was fingering a gun in his pocket and bitterly thinking of suicide, wondered whether he should wait until night.

Because he had a sense of humor, this good man called the newspapers and was connected with the writers of the society column. To them he announced the banquet that was to be given in his home that night, and asked if perhaps they would like to make mention of it, or have some pictures made. Because his name was an impressive one, because he was rich and influential in Washington business and politics, he met with an enthusiastic response. When he was asked the names of his guests, he simply said: "I do not know their names; I never asked them." Somewhat puzzled, the editor of a society column laughed, thinking that he was joking, but he was even more puzzled when this man laughed and said, "If you care to come out tonight, I promise you a unique experience."

At six o'clock, a strange group of men stood waiting in the vestibule of the Central Union Mission, talking softly together. "What is the catch in this, anyhow?" asked one fellow with a cynical expression on his face. "What's the game?" "Who's throwing this feed? Anybody know the bird wot gave out the tickets?" "Well, what difference does it make? Who cares? I'd stand almost anything for a feed." And the blind man, with the little boy at his side, ventured to remark: "Maybe it's a part of the government relief program, maybe the W.P.A. has taken over this house." And the cynic was saying, "Aw, somebody's kiddin' us, as if we weren't wretched enough already." Just then someone came over and announced that the cars were at the door; without a word, they went outside. Perhaps there was something incongruous about it all—seeing these men, clutching their thin coats tightly around their thin bodies, huddling together; their faces pinched and wan, blue with cold and unshaven; their toes sticking out of their shoes, climbing into two shiny limousines. It was touching to see the lame get in, dragging one foot behind the other, swinging up with a twitch of pain, and to see the blind man fumbling for the strap. At last they were all inside, and the cars glided off with the strangest and most puzzled load of passengers they had ever carried.

When they dismounted, they stood gazing at the house, its broad steps and lamps, its thick-piled carpets; they entered slowly, trying to take it all in. They were met by the host, a little nervous but smiling. He was a quiet man, and they liked him—these guests of his whose names he did not know. How strange it was that no names were given at all! He did not say much, only, "I am so glad you came."

By and by, they were seated at the table. They had looked at the tapestries that hung on the walls. They had seen the illuminated pictures in their massive frames and the giant crystal chandelier, the concert grand piano that stood across the hall, the spotless linen and the gleaming silver on the table. They were silent now; even the cynic had nothing to say. It seemed as if the banquet would be held in a frozen silence. The host rose in his place, and in a voice that trembled slightly said: "My friends, let us ask the blessing. If this is pleasing to Thee, O Lord, bless us as we sit around this table, and bless the food that we are about to receive. Bless these men. You know who they are, and what they need, and help us to do what you want us to do. Accept our thanks, in Jesus' name. Amen." The blind man was smiling now. He turned to the man seated next to him and asked him about the host. "What does he look like?" And so the ice was broken; conversation began to stir around the table, and soon the first course was laid. "My friends, I hope you will enjoy the dinner. I would suggest that we waste no time, for I have no doubt that you are hungry. Go right ahead." It was a strange party, rather fantastic in a way, thought the host, as he surveyed his guests. There they were—men who otherwise might be still loitering on the back streets of Washington, crouched in doorways; or huddled over some watchman's fire. What an amazing thing that he didn't even know the name of a single man! His guests had no credentials, no social recommendations, no particular graces, so far as he could see. But my! they were hungry!

It was funny, as he sat there talking, how the stories in the Gospels kept coming back to him, and he could almost imagine that the house was one in Jerusalem. It seemed to him that these men would be the very ones that Jesus would have gathered around Him—the legion of the world's wounded, the fraternity of the friendless, pieces of broken human earthenware. He remembered what the family had said, how they had insisted on demanding, "Why? Why are you doing such a thing?" Well, why was it anyway? Wasn't it plain? His reason was the same old glorious reason that Jesus had for every miracle, for every gesture of love, for every touch of healing. *It was simply because he was sorry for these people,* and because he wanted to do this one thing on an impulse of love.

Yet there was not a trace of condescension in his attitude. He was treating them as brothers, talking to them as though they had a right to be sitting where they were. It was a grand feeling, a great adventure. Never before in his life had he felt this thrill. These men could not pay him back! What had they to give him?

He watched each plate and directed the servants with a nod or a glance. He encouraged them to eat; he laughed at their thinly-disguised reluctance, until they laughed too. As he sat there, it suddenly occurred to him how different was the conversation! *There were no off-color stories, no whisperings of scandal, no one saying, "Well, I have it on good authority."* They were talking about their friends in misfortune, wishing they were here too—wondering whether Charlie had managed to get a bed in the charity ward, or whether Dick had stuck it out when he wanted to end it all, and whether the little woman with the baby had got a job. Wasn't the steak delicious! And they marveled that they still remembered how different foods tasted; they wondered, most of all, who this man was, and why he had invited them all here.

When the meal was over, there was music. Someone came in and sat down at the piano. He began to play softly, familiar melodies, old-fashioned songs, and then in a soft, but understanding voice, he began to sing. They listened to "Love's Old Sweet Song," "Silver Threads among the Gold," then a march by Sousa, and "Traumerei," and "The Sidewalks of New York." Someone else joined in, a cracked wheezing voice, but it started the others. *Men who had not sung for months, men who had no reason to sing;* there they were, joining in. Now some old favorites:

21

"Daisy," "A Bicycle Built for Two," "Swanee River." Soon they began to request this and that, and before they knew it they were singing hymns: "What a Friend We Have in Jesus," "The Church in the Wildwood," "When I Survey the Wondrous Cross."

The pianist stopped, and the guests grouped themselves in soft, comfortable chairs around the log fire; some of them smoked. The host moved among them, smiling, his eyes shining. Then when he had settled himself again, and his guests were comfortable, he said, "I know you men are wondering what all this means. I can tell you very simply. But, first, let me read you something." He read from the Gospels stories of One who moved among the sick, the outcasts, the despised and the friendless; how He healed this one, cured that one, spoke kindly words of infinite meaning to another, how He visited the ostracized; and what He promised to all who believed in Him.

"Now I haven't done much tonight for you, but it has made me very happy to have you here in my home. I hope you have enjoyed it half as much as I have. If I have given you one evening of happiness, I shall be forever glad to remember it, and you are under no obligation to me. This is not my party. It is His! I have merely lent Him this house. *He* was your Host. *He* is your *Friend.* And He has given me the honor of speaking for Him. He wants you all to have a good time. He is sad when you are; He hurts when you do; He weeps when you weep. He wants to help you, if you will let Him.

"*I'm going to give each of you His Book of Instructions. I have marked certain passages in it that you will find helpful when you are sick and in pain, when you are lonely and discouraged, when you are blue and bitter and hopeless; and when you lose a loved one. He will speak a message of hope and courage and faith.* Then I shall see each one of you tomorrow where I saw you today, and we'll have a talk together to see just how I can help you most. I have made arrangements for each one of you to get back to your homes, and those who have nowhere to go, I invite to spend the night here."

They shuffled out into the night, a different group than they had been. There was a new light in their eyes, a smile where there had not been even interest before. The blind man was smiling still, and as he stood on the doorstep, waiting, he turned to where his host stood, "God bless you, my friend, whoever you are." A little wizened fellow who had not spoken all night paused to say, "I'm going to try again, mister, there's somethin' worth livin' for." The cynic turned back, "Mister, you're the first man who ever gave me anything. And you've given me hope." "That is because I was doing it for Him," said the host and he stood and waved good night as the cars purred off into the darkness. When they had gone, he sat again by the fire and looked at the dying embers, until the feeling became overwhelming again that there was Someone in the room. He could never tell anyone how he knew this, but he knew that he was smiling and that He approved. And that night, on Massachusetts Avenue, a rich man smiled in his sleep. And one who stood in the shadows smiled too, because some of the least of these had been treated like brothers for His sake.

Of course, that never happened. It is only a piece of imagination. But why shouldn't it happen . . . on Massachusetts Avenue? on Connecticut Avenue? in Chevy Chase? in Spring Valley? I wonder what would happen if we all agreed to read one of the Gospels, until we came to a place that told us to do something, then went out to do it—and after we'd done it, begin reading again? Why don't we do what Jesus says? How exciting life would become were we to begin living according to His way of life! Friends would say we had lost our minds—perhaps. Acquaintances would say we were "peculiar." Those who dislike us would say we were crazy. But Someone Else, who had these same things said about Him, would smile, and the joy and peace in our own hearts would tell us who was right.

There are aspects of the Gospel that are puzzling and difficult to understand. But our problems are not centered around the things we don't understand, but rather in the things we do understand—*the things we could not possibly misunderstand.* This, after all, is but an illustration of the fact that our problem is not so much that we don't know what we should do—we know perfectly well—but that *we don't want to do it.*

The Man Who Lost His Soul

Reverend Ferdinand Q. Blanchard, D.D.

Pastor, Euclid Avenue Congregational Church, Cleveland, Ohio,
and Moderator, Congregational-Christian Churches

Pastor of the Euclid Avenue Congregational Church in Cleveland, Dr. Ferdinand Quincy Blanchard still finds time to live in the realm of the spirit and create sermons that paint lasting spiritual impressions on the mind and heart. Moderator of the Congregational-Christian Churches for the past two years and interested in the social agencies of his city, he does not lose sight of the real job of the Protestant Minister—to preach and care for the souls in his congregation.

He was ordained as a minister of the Congregational Church in 1901 and has been at the Euclid Avenue Church for the last twenty-nine years. Twenty-five years ago Amherst and Oberlin recognized his work with the honorary doctorate.

His writings reflect a combination of the imaginative, the spiritual, and the uplifting. Among his books are *For the King's Sake, The Authority of Jesus, How One Man Changed the World,* and *Jesus and the World's Quests.* He wrote the hymn, "O Child of Lowly Manger Birth."

"The Man Who Lost His Soul," given at Euclid Avenue Congregational Church, April 11, 1943, may be an answer to Anatole France's short story of Pontius Pilate, in which Pilate is asked about Jesus. Pilate replies, as only Anatole France in his satiric skepticism could have had him respond, "Jesus? Jesus? Who was Jesus?" Dr. Blanchard's message is distinctly different and stimulating. It certainly has more of lasting value than Anatole France's unbelief.

Sermon Four

IN THE ROADSTEAD OF JOPPA, A ROMAN GALLEY was moored at the end of a long pier built to enable the shallow-draft vessels of that day to embark passengers and cargoes directly from the shore. It was evidently ready to start its voyage. The lading was clearly completed. A young Roman officer of the rank of centurion paced back and forth, ever and again stopping to study the road leading to the pier. Another man in naval uniform nearby revealed a like impatience with the delayed arrival of someone or something upon which the vessel's departure depended. "We had definite word, captain, that our man would be here this morning," remarked the officer. "It is too bad to lose this off-shore breeze, but what can we do? Pilate insisted by the messenger of a day or so ago that it was very important for his report to go by the first vessel leaving Joppa. Ah," he suddenly interjected, "here he is now."

Through the dust raised by the rushing feet of his horse a man was seen coming at full gallop. He clattered up the stone pier and pulled up short.

"Delayed by a crowded road, sir," he said, with a salute. "Here is your packet."

"So be it." The centurion hastily wrote a receipt which he handed the messenger. "All aboard at last, captain."

Three hours later, well beyond the jagged rocks which mark the entrance to Joppa's open harbor, the galley sailed westward, the wind relieving the oarsmen of their tedious labor. In a comfortable spot at the stern was the young centurion. He was reading a long letter which accompanied the report of the procurator of Judea and which was entrusted to his hands for delivery to the old emperor. It gave an account of his stewardship in imperial affairs. Let us then look over his shoulder and read what he found there.

"Lucullus, my friend, all too brief was your stay in Jerusalem, for even in this city good companions may find pleasure together. I am giving you the official report for delivery to the emperor, but let me tell you, because it is a strange story, something more than is there set down.

"It was the day after you left that early in the morning, before I had had time even to finish breakfast with due leisure, my captain of the guard came to me and said that a great rabble was in the street outside the palace. It seems that they had a man whom they had arrested the night before. The pestiferous group of the Sanhedrin had been sitting in judgment upon him and found him guilty. They wanted him put to death and had come to get me to carry out their plans, since they could not do it themselves.

"Anything hatched in that nest of politicians would naturally look bad to me. However, they had the right to state their case. I found, when I went into the hall where I give public audience, that their prisoner was there with the guards; but the rascally priests, and the crowd they had stirred up, were outside. The prisoner was a young man—about thirty, I should judge. He had evidently been treated pretty roughly, and showed his weariness plainly enough. But he was offering no resistance and seemed to me strangely quiet. What surprised me was a sort of dignity, a cool courage, if you please. He made none of the noisy protest I had expected from him.

"I immediately went outside and ordered someone to act as spokesman and tell me what was their charge. As nearly as I could judge, they were holding him for some disturbance of the public peace, and I sensed immediately that he had run afoul of the leaders on some point of their religion. This looked so clear to me that I thought at once to wash my hands of the business, and I thereupon told them to take their prisoner and deal with him according to their own foolish laws. But not so. They were out after blood, and only my judgment could give it to them.

"So there was nothing for it but to deal with the man. I went back to the audience room and had him brought up before me. I give you my word, Lucullus, I did not like the business. I have put enough of these Jews out of the way to feel no compunction over another. That is, in an ordinary case. But this, you see, was not ordinary. At least the man was not. He was calm, faced me steadily, never showed insolence, but apparently was not in any panic. He moved me. I never had met a Jew like him before. I confess to you, my friend, I had never met any man like him before.

"Picking up the charge as I had caught it outside I asked him, 'Do you claim to be the King of the Jews?'

"He replied to me very quietly, 'Am I answering your charge, or that of my accusers?'

"Of course I told him that I knew nothing of the disturbance he seemed to be involved in. He was turned over to me. What had he to say for himself? Then he made a strange statement: 'My kingdom is not of this world.' There he went out of my depth. I tried to bring him back to plain facts by repeating my query, 'Do you claim to be the King of the Jews?'

" 'Yes,' he said, 'I am a King.' But he went on, 'I came into the world to bear witness to the Truth.'

"What do you make of that, Lucullus? Here was a man charged with a crime for which, if he was guilty, he could be put to death, and he tells me he is a witness to the truth.

"There was nothing to say. I knew, however, that he was not what the rascally priests pretended. Then I bethought me. They had dropped the word that he had come from Galilee. So I said to myself, 'Galilee is Herod Antipas' territory. I'll let him deal with this matter.' So I thought to get rid of the vexatious question. Herod, you well know, is not only unscrupulous but cruel. I never thought he would lose the chance to vent his mean spite on the defenseless peasant. But he took it by making brutal sport of Jesus. And an hour or so later, the crowd was back with the man. Herod declared the trouble occurred in Jerusalem, and it was therefore my trouble.

"Then I thought of another way out. There was a prisoner in the dungeon, picked up a few days before in a revolt against our authority. These Jews have been permitted a privilege in their period of the feast. They

26

can ask for the release of some prisoner held for punishment. 'Give them,' I thought, 'a choice between Barabbas and Jesus, and between the latter and the brigand taken in his crimes, the decision is sure.' But will you believe it, the crafty priests so worked on them that they shouted with almost a single voice, 'Barabbas.' Well, Lucullus, there I was. I knew by this time the man might be, probably was, only a dreamer, a sort of visionary. But he was no menace to the public order. The case had been plainly framed against him. But if I let him go, you know what would have happened. Somehow these Jewish troublemakers would get word to Rome that I was careless of the need to keep order. Unfortunately, as you also know, we have had several recent outbreaks. I crushed them without mercy, but the plain fact was that they implied disorder in the province. Too much harshness then, too great leniency now. You can imagine what that would mean, with a dozen fellows at Rome eager to grab for my office.

"Did I have any choice? I concluded I could not afford to practice abstract justice. There was nothing for it but to sacrifice this young Jew. And so, Lucullus, I went through with the business. I had him scourged, and on that same day he was crucified with two robbers who had been condemned and were awaiting execution.

"He had no followers apparently, for no resistance was offered. And now the noisy festival of the Passover is ended, and the city has sent home its crowds. I have set down all the details for Tiberias. I hope all goes well. For I cannot get the young man out of mind. 'To stand for the Truth,' he said. And I ask you, Lucullus, What is Truth? What we have to deal with in this hard world is what pays, what gets us ahead, what puts cash in our pocket and power in our hands.

"But now if Truth is real it would mean what lies beyond today. It means acting as if justice, goodness, loyalty, kindness were the ultimate things, the things that are going to win at last. It means that they pay in the end, if you please. But whether they pay or not, only they will satisfy. If a man had a soul, a something that does not consist of things that we have, then we could satisfy the soul only with what is true and honorable and of good report. Then one would say I had sold my soul for this place, and I might wonder if the gain were worth the price. What a strange letter, you are saying, Lucullus. But it is a relief to write. I cannot forget the man's face, nor put out of mind his words.

"If we have souls, if only truth can satisfy them, then this man, who knows, might have had word for them. If he had had a chance, many might have followed him. There would have been no disorders growing out of his words—of that I am sure. But there might be a better world than this hard one of ours today. Then it would have been well to have done him justice.

"And just suppose, Lucullus, that the wild rumor going about in Jerusalem were true. He is not dead, but is risen. If, somehow, the truth he believed in endures defeat and triumphs. Where, at the last, are those of us who say, take your chance at any cost? What will be said of me by any who remember this young man, Jesus Christ? Foolish speculation, you say. But if I were wrong? What if my question did not, as I meant it, blow away a foolish fancy, but raised the query upon which all life turns?"

There followed the signature, "Pontius Pilate." And the young officer stared at it, lost in thought. What if to know Truth were freedom, light, life? What if this Jesus Christ had known and given the Truth?

The Reversal of Human Values

REVEREND HUGH T. KERR, D.D., LL.D.

Pastor, Shadyside Presbyterian Church, Pittsburgh, Pennsylvania

WHEREVER GOOD PREACHING and leading preachers are known, the name of Hugh T. Kerr is familiar. Successful pastor of the famous Shadyside Church in Pittsburgh since 1913, Dr. Kerr has been honored with the D.D. from the College of Emporia, Kansas, and Lafayette College, and with the LL.D. from Washington and Jefferson, the University of Pittsburgh, and the University of Toronto.

He was ordained in 1897 and became pastor of Oakland Church, Pittsburgh; from 1901 to 1907 he served the First Church in Hutch-inson, Kansas, and then became pastor of the Fullerton Avenue Church, Chicago, and lecturer on systematic theology and religious pedagogy at McCormick Theological Seminary. He returned to Pittsburgh in 1913.

He has written many successful books, among them several for children, including, *Children's Story-Sermons, Children's Missionary Story-Sermons, The Highway of Life, My First Communion, Children's Nature Story-Sermons, After He Had Risen, A God Centered Faith.*

Sermon Five

TEXT: *He taught them, saying, Blessed. . .* MATTHEW 5:2, 3

HE BEATITUDES ARE THE TEN COMMANDMENTS of the New Testament. There are differences, however. The Ten Commandments have to do largely with actions, with deeds. The breaking of this and that Commandment may bring one before the judge. The Beatitudes, however, have to do with attitudes. You can never be brought before the judgment for the breaking of a single Beatitude. They have to do with motives, with atmosphere, with the way we think. There is this difference, too, that the Ten Commandments are negative—"Thou shalt not," "Thou shalt not," ten times the hammer falls "Thou shalt not." The Beatitudes, on the other hand, are positive. They contain promises and they imply something that is constructive. There is this difference, too, that the Commandments are commands. They are mandatory. They speak with authority; while the Beatitudes are invitations. They graciously invite to something that is

29

better and higher. They present the case of blessedness, which is an elusive word. We understand it but find it difficult to interpret.

Blessedness is something higher than and different from happiness. Happiness usually relates to circumstances and "no list of circumstances will ever make a Paradise," said George Eliot. No matter how we may dream about the postwar world it could never come about that the arrangement of circumstances could guarantee happiness. Perhaps Thomas Carlyle has given us the distinction: "There is in man a higher love than love of happiness," he says. "He can do without happiness, and instead thereof find blessedness." Blessedness is inner satisfaction. It was blessedness that came to Peter on the Mount of Transfiguration when he said, "It is good for us to be here." Blessedness is that state in which the mind finds what the engineers call "the angle of repose," in which desire is satisfied and life finds itself poised and happily adjusted.

The question, therefore, is, what is it that will satisfy? What is it that we seek? What is it men most eagerly desire? When we answer that question we find that the Beatitudes contain the very reversal of the values which we most cherish.

What is it men most eagerly desire? We would agree that men desire wealth. They seek money. There are multitudes who are absent from the church service who are in pursuit of wealth. The modern world has been knocking at the door of the Sabbath quite largely in the interests of money. The excuses that the managers of sports and the movies make are largely because of money. From the beginnings of history men have thought in terms of money; and people uniformly think that the man who has money, who has achieved wealth, must inevitably be satisfied and must have attained blessedness. And because men fail to get money and to acquire wealth they are unhappy. There are probably more unhappy people in the world today than ever before in history. The hardest thing for people to bear is the loss of money. They can lose their health or their friends, but when they lose money they go mourning all their days. *Jesus says No,* "Blessed are the poor in spirit: for theirs is the kingdom of heaven." St. Luke gives us the words more abruptly and from an economic point of view, "Blessed be ye poor." But doubtless Matthew has recorded the inner meaning which was in the mind of Jesus. The benediction is pronounced upon those who are free from acquisitiveness and are not devoted to the accumulation of wealth. The love of money is the root of all kinds of evil. We must have studied the Gospels and the teachings of Jesus to little effect if we have not discovered that the desire, the straining after wealth, shuts men out of heaven—which after all is blessedness. Wealth in itself is a neutral thing; but the passion to obtain, the desire to acquire, the urge to get, poisons life. *Do you think this will ever be the world's ideal?* Do you think that we will ever have a society in which money is not king? Do you think we will ever have a civilization in which the drive to acquire, to accumulate for its own sake, will take second place and the desire to serve will be our first aim?

What is it men most eagerly desire? Money? Yes! And then perhaps pleasure. Pleasure takes second place, probably first place in the minds of youth. What a blow it is when the mandate goes forth that there shall be no pleasure driving! The longing to have a good time holds high place in the minds of many people. Glance at your newspaper and see how much space is given up to the presentation of opportunities for pleasure. Young people, and often older people, must make their plans for the evening in the pursuit of pleasure. Indeed pleasure has been reduced to a world-encompassing philosophy expressed in the adage, "Take thine ease, eat, drink, and be merry." *Jesus says No,* "Blessed are they that mourn: for they shall be comforted"—that is, made strong, not merely consoled. No wonder people shy away from the teaching of Christianity. No wonder young people look askance at the pulpit that proclaims such a doctrine as this. Surely no one can get far with a crying religion. Jesus, of course, is not talking about crying and weeping and wailing. He is saying that life is serious business. He is saying that there are big issues at stake before our very eyes and if we can go through life seeking pleasure in the presence of sorrow and pain and tragedy, then we are far from entering into blessedness. Jesus is saying to all of us that we are not here "to dream, to drift. We have hard work to do and loads to lift." There was a king in olden times who did not let anyone in mourning come near him, and we take our place with that sort of royalty when we hide our eyes from the tragedies that take place in the world about us. *Do you think this will ever be the world's ideal?* Do you think that people will ever take life seriously and look facts in the face? When they do there will be no more slums, no more undernourished children, none of the brutality and cruelty of war.

What is it men most eagerly desire? Money? Yes! Pleasure? Yes! And next to money and pleasure perhaps position, or a better word is probably recognition. People like to be recognized. They like to find themselves in the society of important people. They like to have on their mailing list names that are prominent in the social world. An invitation from the President or from the Governor gives them a sense of distinction. They are unhappy when they are overlooked and when their names are omitted from the list of prominent guests, or when the society editor forgets to mention that their daughter was a bridesmaid at a New York wedding. People do not like to be slighted or overlooked or passed by. Ministers in particular are guilty in this respect, and perhaps women fall before this temptation more than men. People like recognition. *Jesus says No,* "Blessed are the meek: for they shall inherit the earth." Blessed

31

are the people who are not pushers, shovers, but who do obtain recognition because of their humility. I have met a few really great men, and I have been impressed by their naturalness, their humility, their modesty, their willingness to take a back seat or to take second place or to substitute when some lesser person has failed at his task. "Blessed are the meek." That is not the way the world thinks. *Do you think this will ever be the world's ideal?* Do you have any hope that we will have a society or a civilization or even a church where people are eager to take the lowest seat?

What is it men most eagerly desire? Wealth? Pleasure? Recognition? Yes! And they desire contentment, they want to let well enough alone, they do not want to be disturbed or agitated. They wish to enjoy security, comfort, peace. The thought that is in their minds is expressed in the words, "Oh, that I had wings like a dove! for then would I fly away, and be at rest." The words of the prophet agree with their inner state, "Oh, that I had in the wilderness a lodging place of wayfaring men, that I might leave my people, and go from them!" They long for a balcony view of life, that is, a place of security where they can watch the turmoil and the confusion that goes on in the street below. They would build for themselves a place of retreat where the storms of life would never touch them. *Jesus says No,* "Blessed are they which do hunger and thirst after righteousness: for they shall be filled." In other words, blessed are the dissatisfied. Blessed are the restless who are seeking a better world and a better life, who hunger and thirst after justice and honesty and righteousness. They do not cry "Peace, Peace" where there is no peace. There is nothing the devil loves so much as peace. He is the father of all those who are satisfied to let well enough alone. The war-maker in the person of Hitler cried out to the nations for years, "Let us alone! We want peace." The liquor-makers are constantly crying out, "Let us alone! We are satisfied." The gamblers throughout the land are heard saying, "Let us alone!" Jesus, however, demands a divine discontent, a dissatisfaction, which refuses to be satisfied with things as they are and which calls upon all that is within us to set things right. *Do you think this will ever be the world's ideal?* Do you think we will ever attain unto the place where we will not be satisfied to have a dirty city or a dirty civilization? Do you think the time will ever come when we will have a people who are hungry after the things of God and the way of righteousness?

What is it men most eagerly desire? Wealth? Pleasure? Recognition? Contentment? Yes! The list grows and still our desires are not satisfied. Men want to dominate. They wish to possess authority. They wish to be able to say to this man "Go!" and to another man "Come!" That is what is wrong with our world today. All around us we see big and little dictators who like to feel that they have authority over others. We see bureauc-

32

racy growing in our own land, and a bureaucrat is an official who moves in a narrow and arbitrary routine. The politician does not wish to retire to private life because he misses the sense of authority. The dictator wants men to march to his command, and we all in lesser ways like to command. *Jesus says No,* "Blessed are the merciful: for they shall obtain mercy." Mercy does not speak hard words even to the lowest servant. There is no mistrust, no arrogance, in mercy. Mercy is kind and generous. Mercy is the ability to put one's self in the place of another. *Do you think this will ever be the world's ideal?* Do you think that our social life will ever be guided by those who speak kindly and think mercifully concerning others?

What is it men most eagerly desire? Wealth? Pleasure? Recognition? Contentment? Authority? Yes! And they also desire popularity. They want to be secure in their reputation. They want to be spoken well of, which after all is not a bad thing. They are satisfied, however, to keep up a good front, to be respectable, to make a noise in the world, to present a fine appearance. *Jesus says No,* "Blessed are the pure in heart: for they shall see God." He demands utter sincerity, not merely respectability but personal purity. It is not purity in a narrow sense about which Jesus is speaking but singleness of heart, purity of motive, sincerity of purpose. It was said of a good man of olden times that he walked before God with a perfect heart. That is what Jesus means. It is to live in the altitude of clear and high ideals. We are told that the bees and butterflies of Switzerland will leave the valleys and the lower slopes, and take themselves far up to the glaciers of the Alps and to the rare sweetness of the flowers that they find there, and that no honey can match the honey drawn from those Alpine flowers. It is the life of the heights concerning which Jesus is speaking. "Blessed are the pure in heart: for they shall see God." *Do you think this will ever be the world's ideal?* Do you think there will ever be a civilization or a social order where people will be sincere and pure in heart, trustworthy, with their eyes unclouded by the fogs of the valleys?

What is it men most eagerly desire? Wealth? Pleasure? Recognition? Contentment? Authority? Popularity? Yes! And they also want what they call independence. They want to have a free hand. They want to live and let live, and they are willing to fight for their rights. They are ready to do battle for what they consider to be theirs. It is natural for them to resist, to retaliate. The mind of man is aggressive and is ready constantly in business, in society, in education, in politics, to take up arms. We stand upon our rights. *Jesus says No,* "Blessed are the peacemakers: for they shall be called the children of God." And let us remember that He is speaking of peacemakers and not of peacelovers. We have plenty of peacelovers and there are plenty of people who talk peace and who are ready to make plans for the postwar world, all of which is good. But

Jesus is speaking of people who make peace in homes, in churches, and in the world. He is speaking of people like Abraham who said to Lot in the midst of a heated controversy, "Let there be no strife, I pray thee, between me and thee, and between my herdmen and thy herdmen; for we be brethren." *Do you think this will ever be the world's ideal?* Do you think there will ever come a time when we will be peacemakers? Do you think we will ever settle the question of harmony in labor circles, in the business world, and in the political arena?

Now I know perfectly well what you are thinking about and I am thinking the same thing. We are thinking that this ideal which Jesus has set before us is so high, so ethereal, so impossible, so unworldly that it is beyond us. It is indeed the reversal of human values, and we are not surprised when people say that it presents an ideal out of touch with reality, an impractical ideal which cannot be put into operation in our workaday world. Nevertheless, there it stands and you must confess, as I must confess, that it holds our heart and challenges our conscience. Has anyone ever lived in accordance with this ideal? In all your reading of history and biography have you come upon anyone who has embodied these Beatitudes in his life? Let us call the roll of the saints and prophets and martyrs who have lived and died and written their names on the world's roll of honor, and ask if any of them measures up to this ideal of Jesus? I must answer No. What do you answer? Have you met with anyone in all your experience concerning whom you could say, "Yes, he was the Beatitudes alive." You answer No. And then you call the roll again and answer Yes. Yes there was one. He who spoke the Beatitudes, and stood uncondemned before them. He was their living embodiment. Did not John Stuart Mill, who shied away from the Christian faith, say concerning Him, "Not even now would it be easy, even for an unbeliever, to find a better translation of the rule of virtue from the abstract into the concrete, than to endeavor so to live that Jesus Christ would approve our life." Let us admit that, and then let us ask the further question, Does that mean anything for us in our hard-pressed situation today? Does His ideal and His life count for anything in a world such as ours? Some time ago George Bernard Shaw was asked that question by a newspaper reporter. Now I know all about George Bernard Shaw. I know that he is a cynic and often a scoffer, but for that very reason his answer to the question that was put to him is all the more impressive. The question that was asked him was this, "Do you think that Christ is a living influence in the present day?" He replied, "The wholesale rebellion against His influence which culminated in the war has turned out so badly that just at present there are probably more people who feel that in Christ is the only hope for the world than there ever were before in the lifetime of men now living." Now that is a wonderful thing to say, and it is true. It ought to be something of high encouragement to everyone of us who believes in the Christian faith. It ought to lure us on, for there is lots of time, there is all eternity itself, for us to follow after if we may attain to the stature of the perfect life in Christ Jesus.

One of Them

REVEREND RAY FREEMAN JENNEY, D.D., LL.D.
Minister, Bryn Mawr Community Church, Chicago, Illinois

DR. JENNY is a strong preacher, an able pastor, and a splendid church executive. The qualities of a fine mind, a friendly nature, a sympathetic spirit, and driving power plus wide experience enable him to proclaim with clarity, conviction, and prophetic insight the great truths of a complete gospel of individual and social redemption.

Dr. Jenney was born in Meriden, New Hampshire, in 1891. He took his theological training at Union Theological Seminary and did graduate study at Columbia University. He was ordained in the Presbyterian ministry in 1917. Following a pastorate in Faith Church, New York City, from 1919 to 1922, he was called to the pulpit of the First Presbyterian Church, Galesburg, Illinois, where he served four years—and at the same time helped coach the football team at Knox College. Then he went to the University of Pennsylvania as Head Minister and General Director of the United Religious Work. In 1929, he was called to the Park Central Presbyterian Church of Syracuse, New York; during his ministry that Church increased in membership from seven hundred to over fourteen hundred. Late in 1942, he became the Minister of Bryn Mawr Community Church, which was composed of thirty-seven denominations and had a membership of over two thousand. In the last year and a half, Dr. Jenney has received over three hundred and thirty people into the fellowship of this Church.

During World War I, he served as chaplain with the 59th Infantry, A.E.F., and was wounded in action. In 1933, he spent three months in Europe and Russia, studying social, religious, economic, and political conditions. In 1936, he spent the summer in England as an exchange preacher. He was Vice-Moderator of the General Assembly of the Presbyterian Church in the United States of America in 1940 and 1941. Knox College recognized his ability with an honorary D.D., and James Millikin University honored him with an LL.D. He has done much radio work, has written numerous sermons and articles for magazines. He is the author of *Speaking Boldly*.

Sermon Six

TEXT: *Is it I?* MARK 14:19

ECENTLY I CAME ACROSS A LETTER WHICH I should like to share with you. It is a very old letter which was written some seventeen hundred years ago in Carthage, North Africa, by a Christian leader, Cyprian, to his friend Donatus. Listen to these significant lines:

This seems a cheerful world, Donatus, when I view it from this fair garden under the shadow of these vines. But, if I climb some great mountain and look out over the wide lands you know very well what I would see—brigands on the roads, pirates on the high seas, in the amphitheaters men murdering each other to please applauding crowds, under all roofs misery and selfishness. It is really a bad world, Donatus—an incredibly bad world. Yet, in the midst of it, I have found a quiet and holy people. They have discovered a joy which is a thousand times better than any pleasure of this sinful life. They are despised and persecuted—but they care not. These people, Donatus, are the Christians and I am one of them.

Could you and I write such a letter today? Yes, I am confident we could, at least the first part of it. For that old, old letter is very timely and gives us a most accurate description of the day in which we live. Granted we could easily write the first part of the letter, I wonder if you and I could in truth write the last part and end it with the proud claim, "I am one of them." Well, we had better try to write it and ask in earnestness: "What does it mean to be one of the Christians?"

We have failed to be one of them. Our age is "red of tooth and claw." Mass murder is claiming its high toll every day and gives proof that "The night rolls back upon the West, and the night is solid." In his poem "The Litany for Dictatorship," Stephen Vincent Benét pictures the brutality of our time: the ruthlessness of the totalitarian state, the bitterness of the class struggle. Our day is summed up with the intensity of a poet's insight in these telling words:

> We thought we were done with these things,
>   but we were wrong.
> We thought because we had power, we had
>   wisdom.
> Now the night rolls back upon the West,
>   and the night is solid.

It is not so important to be serious as it is to be serious about the important things. In the Upper Room Jesus made the startling statement,

"One of you shall betray me." One by one the disciples asked "Is it I?" "Is it I?" Betrayal was a terrible thing where loyalty was everything. These humble, honest, searching words "Is it I?" test a Christian and give proof of his integrity more than would an abstract and pious boast. You and I must ask this question "Is it I?"

This question as to whether one really can lay claim to the fact that he too belongs to a continuing fellowship that enables one, in spite of everything, to overcome the world, is not an academic one. It is raised by all sorts of folk around the world. To be sure the answers are many, but the one which above all others holds in this desperate, demanding, and despairing hour is the ultimate question that Browning has asked:

> What think ye of Christ, friend?
> When all's done and said?
> Like you this Christianity or not?
> It may be false, but will you wish it true?
> Has it your vote to be so if it can?

Browning's question is ours. It is a question of the deep wish, and of the vote and venture of one's life. Certain ruling ideas or basic principles will serve as tests to enable us, in true humility and with unvarnished honesty, to consider this question: Are we "one of them"—one of the Christians?

First: Our religion must be a faith that we affirm; a positive, radiant, confident, contagious faith; an affirmation, not a negation. Listen to the Psalmist sing of his faith, *"Yea,* the Lord is my *strength* and my *song."* Or again in the Shepherd Psalm: *"Yea,* though I walk through the valley of the shadow of death, I will fear no evil." Here religion is pictured in words of sustaining power and singing confidence, as a positive force in life.

The advertisement of our spiritual need is this: "Wanted—Faith in Something"; something to believe in, something to hold to, something to give purpose and meaning to life. That is religion's specialty. Is that what religion does for you?

Even more than "faith in something" is required faith in *Someone.* Religion is not primarily doing something, however good; religion is not alone a matter of believing something, however orthodox; religion is being in fellowship with Someone whom we call God. For we have observed how it is possible for one to do all the ceremonial acts and repeat the creeds without coming into conscious and vital relationship with God and with His purpose for our lives.

There was never a truer word than that of Carlyle when he said that the religion of a man is the chief fact concerning him. By religion he meant, as he went on to explain, not the creed to which he subscribed or otherwise gave his assent—not that necessarily, often not that at all, since we see men of all degrees of worth and worthlessness singing all manner of creeds. This is not what he calls religion, this assertion which may come from the outworks of a man, if even so deep as that. No! By religion he meant that which a man practically believes, lays to his heart—often enough without asserting it to himself—and acts upon, and therefore knows, concerning this mysterious universe and his duties and destiny in it. That is in all cases the primary thing in him and it creatively determines his life—that is his religion. If you know that about a man, you know what he is and what he will do.

There is no one route which the trudging feet of the Christian must travel if he would go up to the City of his God. There is no one way to find God or be found of Him. Michael Fairless, in *The Roadmender*, tells of a child from the slums, who, after listening to the spell of music made by the hand organ, put up his face to be kissed by the hardened old organ-grinder. But he swore at the child and struck him a blow, at which the child ran away in fear. A few days later the organ man met with an accident and lay for days in a hospital, where he was all the time haunted by the memory of that upturned face. As soon as he was well again he went in search of the child that wanted to be kissed, playing the tunes he knew would draw the children out of the streets and alleys. He never found the child whom he had repelled, but in his loving search for him he became kind and gentle, loving and noble in spirit. Fairless says of the organ-grinder: "He saw the face of a little child and looked on God." Ah, yes!

It is not easy to find God. There is no clear voice from behind saying, "This is the way: walk ye in it." The note of the trumpet is lacking in our confused and demanding age. That was the state of affairs in the days which are depicted in Isaiah, some six hundred years before Christ. The Hebrew people had been beaten and cowed into silence. Then it was that the author of the fortieth chapter of Isaiah gave his thrilling exhortation: "Lift up thy voice with strength; . . . be not afraid. . . . Behold your God!" The same idea is reiterated in the fifty-eighth chapter of Isaiah: "Cry aloud, . . . lift up thy voice like a trumpet!" The author speaks boldly to the people about their transgressors and what is more, about that which will enable them as a nation to walk in the ways of righteousness. Then they will be able to "mount up with wings as eagles, they shall run, and not be weary; and they shall walk, and not faint," because they "wait upon the Lord."

Second: If we are to be "one of them," we must remember "we are members one of another." That statement needs to be written large in our day. Jan Smuts has said, "The disease of the world is fragmentation; the cure of the world is holism, and that is God." He called his theory "holism" from the Greek word for "whole." The main trend of evolutionary development, he contends, is the building of more complicated wholes. "Ours is a whole-making universe. We are all interrelated." Dr. Paul Tillich has expressed the same idea. He says that "the disease of the world is brokenness; the cure of the world is unity." E. Stanley Jones is right, "It is time that the Church and Christians cease being a part of the disease and become a part of the cure."

We will never be able to feel a sense of "oneness" with mankind until we are able to look on life with eyes of compassion. Then, sympathy becomes "your pain in my heart." Sympathy is demanded, not pity but fellow suffering, which is what the word "sympathy" by derivation means. Shared suffering is the binding force of this hour. The Arabian parable illuminates that truth: "I complained because I had no shoes, until I met a man who had no feet." When we have our eyes opened to our interdependence, then we can comprehend the "glory of the lighted mind," and acknowledge our kinship with all mankind. No man can long stand up to life alone. "Robinson Crusoe was bound for madness until he discovered Friday's footprints."

One of the "best sellers" not so long ago was a book called *For Whom the Bell Tolls,* by Ernest Hemingway. The scene of the book is the civil war in Spain, which took place in the middle thirties. Unfortunately, when this book was filmed much of this splendid story was lost. The title of this book and its theme were taken from one of John Donne's famous sayings: "No man is an island, entire to itself; every man is a piece of the continent." If any part of the continent is "washed away by the sea," then every man is a loser by just that much. "Any man's death," says Donne, "diminishes me, because I am involved in mankind." Therefore one never really knows "for whom the bell tolls," as it tolls for all and "it tolls for thee." How true it is that we live in and through every man's life. We die in and through every man's death. We are in deed and truth "members one of another." A common need and a common destiny bind us together.

Finally, if we would be "one of them" we must remember that life is an entrustment. An entrustment not alone from the past, or from our family, or from our country, or even from our church, but from our God. "For this cause was I born into the world." History acclaims those who have "forgotten themselves into immortality." They are they to whom life was indeed an entrustment from God. Thus David Livingstone was motivated with his three-fold program of evangelization, exploration, and emancipation of a continent. A sense of entrustment sent Wilfred Grenfell to Labrador to redeem the least and last and lost people of that bleak country. It was the motivation that made possible the epic saga of George Washington Carver, a slave who became a scientist of world-wide

40

acclaim and helpfulness. These valiant comrades of the quest all looked upon life as an entrustment from God, and thus became "one of them."

It violates good taste to tell stories about heaven and hell, yet such a story, patterned after Dante's *Inferno*, illustrates a basic truth and, therefore, should be told. A man died and awoke in hell. There he saw men and women gathered around tables which were heavily ladened with food and drink, yet all were starving and thirsty. None could feed himself, for on each one's arms there were fastened long metal implements that kept his arms straight and prevented him from lifting the food and drink to the mouth. Later, this same man was transported from hell to heaven. There he saw the same scene enacted. There men and women were gathered around tables on which there was an abundance of food and drink. The same long implements were strapped to their arms, yet all the people were well fed—for each one was feeding his neighbor. This is a modern parable of significance. The cry of hunger is heard from despairing people in Europe, China, and India. What must we do to be one of the witnessing Christians who feeds his neighbor?

We too must look upon life as an entrustment from God. Paul Hutchinson, in his most able book, *From Victory to Peace,* has rightly reminded us that the "real problems of our generation are the problems of victory, even more than the problems of war." It is not enough to win the battle of arms. We did that in the First World War. We won the battle of arms, but our ideas and ideals were defeated. Today we appreciate only too well the truth of Clemenceau's words: "Our difficult time is just approaching." The Premier made this statement to a group of French senators who had waylaid him with congratulations a few days after the Armistice was signed. He went on to say, "It is harder to win peace than to win war." A bankrupt world testifies eloquently to the tragic truth of this statement. Those of us who believe in a moral universe see clearly that war is not in the program of God. It is one of the problems of men of God.

From our responsibility for the vexing problems of the postwar world we cannot escape. It is an entrustment from which we cannot, must not, shrink. It calls for the investment of our time, thought, money, and lives. Aye, we must wage peace as men wage war.

One of the questions, among many, which we must face and answer is this: "What shall we do with our enemies after the Victory?" That is a question we cannot brush aside. Now is the time for the people of the church to confess and then confer, to think and then act. We are united during war by fear, coercion, and singleness of aim. After the war, disunity comes through lust for power, greed, war weariness, and the unexploded hatred that will seek expression and thus make the postwar problems titanic ones.

In the planning of postwar reconstruction, the church must exercise the function of moral judgment. To this question of the treatment of our enemies must be summed our clearest powers of reason and of conscience, brought to the test of the justice of God and the redemptive love of Christ. Only thus can we become the salt of the earth and the conscience of a better world order.

A consideration of three schools of thought should help us in making our moral judgment.

First: The "Never Again Movement" in England under Lord Vansittart demands consideration. The founder and disciples of this "movement" rest their case on the premise that the Germans are inherently, biologically brutal; that they are a nation of barbarians; that they are "dangerous paranoids"; that they are "impervious to reason, generosity or even fair play." They should, therefore, be crushed, Lord Vansittart contends, pulverized, and flung beneath "the iron plowshare of implacable retribution." Is Edmund Burke's statement that "You cannot draw up an indictment against a whole people" obsolete?

Second: The second school of thought finds its best expression in Dr. William Temple, the Archbishop of Canterbury. His major thoughts are set forth in his little book *The Hope of a New World,* and his principles enunciated in the Malvern Manifesto. Dr. Temple's ideas deserve careful consideration, both because of the influence of his position and the vigorous quality of his mind.

Third: This school of thought has as its competent expositor, Dr. Edward Hallett Carr, the professor of International Politics in the University College of Wales. He has written a book called *Conditions of Peace.* His varied experience as a member of the British Foreign Office staff, as a journalist, and as an able student in the field of economics and politics compels us to weigh with care his conclusion that "no policy ultimately incompatible with reconciliation can endure, for it will be found morally unbearable." We are not here contending for a "sobsister" sentimentality, but that impartial justice may prevail, that order may be established out of chaos, and that a more enduring peace may be achieved.

"If you could choose one page," asks Dr. Paul Hutchinson, "that you would like to see blotted out of the history of the United States which page would it be?" He answers his own question that most thoughtful Americans would wish to blot out the record of the Reconstruction years after the Civil War. That was the time when unbridled vengeance, retaliation, and retribution were meted out to the conquered. We must not write another page like that in the history of the world. Not in weak sentimentality but in seeking for a just and humane treatment of our enemies after the war, that World War III may not be fought at the end

42

of another twenty-five years, let us lift up our voices with the clearness and power of a trumpet.

Four things we would do well to remember. "Whom the gods would destroy they first make mad"—mad with anger and vengeance. "Vengeance is mine; I will recompense, saith the Lord." We "cannot cast out Satan with Satan." "Overcome evil, not with evil, but with good." That is the message of the prophets and of Christ that will redeem the world. With the voice of a trumpet let us proclaim, both by our talk and our works, that we are "one of them."

This Is a Year for Greatness

REVEREND OSCAR FISHER BLACKWELDER, D.D., LL.D.

Pastor, Lutheran Church of the Reformation, Washington, D. C.

DR. OSCAR FISHER BLACKWELDER, known as a speaker at educational, youth, pastoral and religious conferences throughout the country, is pastor of the Lutheran Church of the Reformation in Washington, D. C., to which he came in 1933. Before this appointment, he had been pastor of the Virginia Heights Lutheran Church, Roanoke, Virginia, and Christ Lutheran Church, Baltimore, Maryland. He also served in the National Preaching Mission under the Federal Council of Churches, speaking in about two-thirds of the cities the Mission visited.

Dr. Blackwelder was born in Newbury, South Carolina, and was graduated from Roanoke College, Virginia, and Southern Lutheran Theological Seminary, Columbia, South Carolina. For twelve years, he was a member of the Board of Publication of the United Lutheran Church in America. He is at present a member of the Council of Washington Cathedral, a member of the Board of Trustees of American University, a life member of the Kiwanis Club, and his term as President of the Washington Federation of Churches has just expired.

He has written numerous articles and pamphlets, and is the co-author of *Epistle Messages, A Faith for These Times, The Parable of the Empty Soul,* and *It Was for You.*

Sermon Seven

TEXT: *But he that is greatest among you shall be your servant.*
MATTHEW 23:11

My grace is sufficient for thee. II CORINTHIANS 12:9

THIS IS A YEAR FOR GREATNESS—AND MEN CAN BE great by the grace of Christ. There are perhaps three outstanding dreams for which most men live. There are those who live to be secure. There are those who live to be loved. There are those who live to be significant. I've thought a long time about those three longings of the human heart, and I have come to one conclusion. A man will never be secure in this kind of world until he fulfills the conditions of security. A man will never be loved until he fulfills the conditions of being loved. A man will never be significant, surely within the

Christian framework of personality, until he fulfills the conditions of significance. All three of these add up to the same total. That total reads: A man must be truly great if he is to be secure, if he is to be loved, and if he is to be significant.

But what is a great man? Let's draw a sharp distinction between a great man and a famous man. Many great men are famous, but most great men are not. A moron, for example, thanks to high-powered advertising, can have a national reputation in thirty days. But that will not make him great. And, further, notice that greatness does not mean a difference in kind, but in degree. Thus a man may be great on a one-talent pattern or a five-talent or a ten-talent. You see, all true greatness is cut off the same cloth.

I am indebted to a friend for three words by which to describe, it seems to me, a truly great person.

The first of these three words is *GOOD*. A man must be good if he is to be great. Before a man can be professionally great or intellectually great or politically great, he must be a great person. In other words, greatness is moral before it is social, intellectual, or professional.

And now comes one of the hardest questions in the world: What is a good person? There is perhaps more unanimity of opinion on the make-up of the stars than on what constitutes a good life. How is this for a practical, working answer? A good man is one who deserves to be trusted. He may not be trusted, but he deserves to be. That's the fundamental mark of a good man. So that a much more essential word than love is confidence. It is the root from which love grows, blossoms, and blooms. Let's illustrate this idea.

A famous queen is said to have made this prayer, "O God, keep me innocent, make others great." The queen evidently forgot that innocence is impossible, and that greatness includes goodness as its first constituent. What I think she really said was, "O God, keep me good, make others great." But she overlooked the fact that greatness includes goodness as its first ingredient.

One of my Washington parishioners said to me, "I would have more confidence in my surgeon if I did not know so much about his personal life." Precisely. It is often tragic that many public characters are, in their private lives, not so well balanced as they are in their public performances.

I am thinking of another Washington friend who is able to do his work in about eight languages. A young lady said to me recently, "My, he's a great man. He can read eight languages." To which I replied, "Yes, he is a great fellow, but not because he can speak eight languages, for you see he could be a liar in all eight." In like manner, the test of a man is not whether he can do higher mathematics, but whether he is honest in simple arithmetic. Thus, professional skill must be preceded by personal integrity and character, if a man is to be truly great.

Well, here is where Jesus comes in. You remember the line in the old hymn, "He died to make us good." I believe it is fair to say that no other person or influence in history has produced so many dependable people as has Jesus. From a social point of view alone He justifies Himself by the production of dependable men and women, people you can trust.

One day Simon Peter had a moment of special penitence and unworthiness, and cried out to Jesus, "Depart from me for I am a sinful man, O Lord." And, of course, that is exactly what Jesus would not do. He stayed by Peter, started a private revolution in Peter's life, and out of it came a character of rock. He can do that for us, too.

The Psalmist prayed, "Create in me a clean heart, O God, and renew a right spirit within me." That prayer was never really answered until Jesus came. He pulls triggers in men's consciences. He gives them sharpness of moral judgment. He makes men good. Therefore, a man must be good in order to be great, and he really can be good only by the help and grace of Christ.

But a man may be good for nothing, so that as we try to analyze a great man there is a second word to describe him. He must be good for something, that means he must be *useful*.

These are days of adversity, especially for young people. They are the chief sufferers of the world. And such days of adversity for every one of us are times to examine our motives, our ambitions, and our desires. What are you and I living for? In days when so many are giving their lives and their health and their future for others, the question must come home to every one of us. What are we living for? What is the meaning of life, anyhow? Let's try to get at that question.

The first purpose of an education is to enable a man honestly to earn a living. For those of us with normal health and strength, the first description of a useful man is one who is able to carry his own weight and pull his own load. Who, except a weakling, wants to be guaranteed security from cradle to grave? But the test of usefulness is not simply to carry our own load. We must carry it with a margin. Tell me how much you can do and are doing beyond actually supporting yourself and your family, and I will tell you how useful you are. The world goes forward only upon the shoulders of men and women who support themselves, plus. Isn't that the principle of Jesus? "Except your righteousness shall *exceed* the righteousness of the scribes and Pharisees, ye shall in no case enter into the kingdom of heaven . . . What do ye *more* than others?"

I want to enter here a word of reserve. There are many people with physically frail bodies, known to society as shut-ins, whose beds of affliction have become community and family altars. We light our torches at their candles. We refresh our spirits at their springs. They may seem a burden and a liability, but I am personally acquainted with so many of the sick and of the shut-ins that I know they often render a spiritual, an inspirational, a courage-building contribution to all who meet them. Even though they are physically frail, they share that intangible something which moves men's hearts. Shut-ins are not exceptions to the principle I am pleading for—they illustrate it.

There is a prominent inscription in Washington that reads, "Justice is the foundation of society." I don't believe it. Men who do justice only meet their fellow men half way, but they don't build a better world. Men who bless society—the discoverers, the inventors, the pioneers, the creative spirits, the saints—don't stop with doing justice. The clash of mutual self-interest doesn't make the world better. The kinds of people by whom this world progresses are those who do justice with a great big plus.

Suppose everybody in the world was able to carry his load unaided, and did just that, do you think the world would get anywhere? I don't think so. I believe it would simply mark time. Indeed, the world advances upon the shoulders of people who do carry their load with a margin.

There are some outstanding illustrations, of course—men with great margins who illustrate the principle. Take Thomas A. Edison. I suppose he could have supported his family with an hour's work a day, but the world is richer because he often worked, as I understand, twenty hours a day. Dr. George Washington Carver, the great Negro scientist, could have met his simple wants with a few moments work each day, but the world is far richer because he toiled on and on in his laboratory. Well, that's the principle which every one of us must seek to follow. Carry your load with a margin. And that measures our usefulness. How useful are we?

These are days that compel us to get our thinking straight. Consciences will haunt us, when we think of the suffering and sacrifices of others, if we do not "come clean" with life.

May God save us from being minimum persons. And what is a minimum person? He is one who lives for food, shelter, sex, and position. He is the boaster, the bully, the easily angered and the self-seeker. You see that the business of Christ is to make maximum persons.

I believe the following formula will prove true. Assuming that a man is normally healthy, if he is lazy, indifferent, and selfish, it is proof that he is out of touch with Christ. No man can be in touch with Christ and lose his initiative. Christ sharpens a man's personality. He puts a cutting edge on his talents. If you want to see a glorious example of what I am trying to plead for, take a look at Mme Chiang Kai-shek. Read her confession of faith. You simply don't produce people like Mme Chiang Kai-shek apart from Christ. That's Christ's mission in the world.

There are those who hold that the unstable ages are the creative ages.

May this be an age like that. And a man cannot be a creative thinker unless he begins with his own motives, ambitions, and desires.

> Rise up, O men of God,
> Have done with lesser things.

Lesser themes for lesser days—let's be big. And I ask you, how big is your margin? To be useful by the grace of Christ is to be great.

But there is at least one more word to say. A man may be *good* and he may be *useful,* yet have only a present tense. But a great man has, also, a future tense, for he has achieved the sense of destiny. That means he must be *courageous.*

You may know the story of that little group of travelers who were huddled around a campfire on one December 31, as they watched the old year pass. One of them lamented his vanished gold; another, his faded honors; a third, his false friends; and the fourth, his lost loved ones. But the last one told his story in a verse:

> Sad losses ye have met
> But mine is sadder yet—
> The believing heart
> Is gone from me.

May I tell you why that is the greatest loss in life? The outstanding need of us all today is courage without hate. And how are we going to get it? By whistling in the dark? I don't think so. By clenching your fists and determining to see a hard job through? That helps. By the cocktail hour? I don't think so. Here is the real secret of courage. Tell me what and Whom you believe in, and I will tell you your courage. Let's see how that works.

Opinions are ideas men hold, but convictions are ideas that hold men. Great ideals, great ideas, eternal principles, convictions based on these principles are the hands of God by which He holds men and makes them brave. Tell me what and Whom you believe in, and I will tell you your courage.

A little while past I heard Stanley Jones use words like these: "I don't know how this old world is coming out but I believe that the future belongs to those who belong to Christ." The poet was right, "Till Thou hast bound me fast I am not free"—nor brave.

Every night in these times, before I go to sleep, as far as I can control my last fading thought, I try to say this over to myself:

> Change and decay in all around I see,
> O Thou who changest not, abide with me.

The man whom Christ holds has the secret of abiding courage. When a man is thus held, he can believe in the high and eternal when the low and tragic are around him everywhere. He is sure that something eternal is being accomplished in the midst of this painful and difficult world, and he is struggling to find out what is going on and to share in it to the full. He believes each man has his part to do in history, assigned by Him who presides over all history.

For ten years I have worked on Capitol Hill in Washington. Next in my affections to my own study, my favorite spot on the Hill is the lighted dome of the Capitol building. Since Pearl Harbor, the dome has been dark. Frequently I work at my church late in the evening. A few months ago, on a particularly dark night, as I rounded the Capitol near midnight with the sky as black as ink, one glorious star hung o'er the Capitol dome. I got out of my car. That star seemed to say to me, "You love this dome?" And I answered, "I certainly do." The star seemed to reply, "I am only part of the light that never will be blacked out. I am part of the light that the darkest night cannot put out. Follow my light, and Him of whose light I am only a part, and find as many others as you can, to follow, too. Then some day this dome that you love may be relighted again."

So may we be great—great by the grace of Christ. That will mean: To be good, to be useful, to be courageous.

A Good Word for Jesus Christ

REVEREND EDGAR DeWITT JONES, D.D., LL.D.

Pastor, Central Woodward Church, Detroit, Michigan

EDGAR DeWITT JONES abandoned the study of law for the ministry and was ordained as a minister of the Disciples of Christ in 1901. From 1920 until 1926 he was pastor of Central Church, Detroit, Michigan, and has been pastor of Central Woodward Church since 1927.

Dr. Jones was born in Hearne, Texas, in 1876. He studied at the University of Missouri and Kentucky University (now Transylvania). He has received the honorary D.D. from Kentucky University and Illinois Wesleyan University; LL.D. from Lincoln Memorial University; and Litt.D. from Culver-Stockton, Bethany, and Texas Christian.

His life and career have been full and varied. In 1910 he was a delegate to the World's Missionary Conference, Edinburgh. For six years he was on the editorial staff of the *Detroit News,* then on the staff of *The Christian* from 1926 to '32, and he has been on the staff of *The Christian Century* since 1927. In 1932 he was an exchange preacher to Scotland. He has been on the Judicial Council of Michigan since 1933, and was appointed to the Michigan Corrections Commission in 1941. He was a delegate to the 1937 Oxford and Edinburgh Conferences and has been active with the Federal Council of the Churches of Christ in America.

He is the author of *The Inner Circle, The Wisdom of God's Fools, American Preachers of Today,* and *The Dogs of War.* He toured Europe and the Near East as correspondent for the *Detroit News.* He is a student of Americana; a lecturer on Lincoln and Jefferson, and the winner of the W. J. Long prize for the best Lincoln sermon in 1939.

"A Good Word for Jesus Christ" represents Dr. Jones' intense devotion to Christ and his belief in the Gospel as the way of salvation.

Sermon Eight

TEXT: . . . *Jesus of Nazareth, a man approved of God.* ACTS 2:22

IN THE MIDDLE OF THE 1890'S, NEARLY EVERYBODY was talking about a little book entitled *Beside the Bonnie Brier Bush.* Especially was this true in church circles, and among ministers. Sermons were adorned with references to the book; and the author, Ian Maclaren, the pen name under which Dr. John Watson wrote, became famous almost overnight. The story is of the

Scottish church people in a quaint little village far removed from the great cities, and is filled with humor, pathos, and the sturdy beliefs of that rugged race.

Perhaps the most notable chapter in the book is the one entitled "His Mother's Sermon." It tells the story of a rare Scottish lad, whose decision for the ministry gladdened the heart of his saintly mother, who, just before she died, bade him be sure when he went into the pulpit to speak a good word for Jesus Christ. Her son went to the university and completed his course at the seminary. He was a lad of parts and won distinction. His teachers and fellow students prophesied great things for him. Now he was in his first parish, from which kirk had gone out so many gifted preachers of the Word. The first Sunday of his ministry was at hand, big with expectations for him, and for the maiden aunt with whom he made his home.

All week this young minister had been at work on his sermon. He meant that it should show something of his modern scholarship. There were a number of big names that he felt sure he should mention. So he wrote out his sermon with scrupulous care, and with a vast deal of pride he read it to his auntie. She listened patiently, but he knew that it did not wholly please her. "Out with it, Auntie," he said, "tell me, what is the matter with it?" Reluctant and humble, she pressed his hand and took courage. She said that it was not for her to criticize, but that he must remember that they were a humble people and that they needed comfort, for their lives were hard and acquainted with privations. And she concluded by saying, "Oh, laddie, be sure you say a guid word for Jesus Christ."

Well, you know, or can imagine, what followed. Her words brought up the dying counsel of his dear mother; his face whitened, and he went to his room to be alone. Yes, you know what happened; or if you do not know, your conjecture is likely to be correct. He cast his carefully prepared scholarly discourse into the fire and watched it burn. And then, he prepared a wholly different sermon, one that set forth that life of lives, so that the people saw Jesus as he went about his ministry, putting his hands on the heads of little children, speaking comfort to the distressed and heartbroken, and dying at last on the central Cross with a prayer of forgiveness for his enemies on his lips. And that morning in the kirk, in that quaint little town, young and old saw the Lord and were glad.

On this, the first Sunday of the New Year, I want to say a good word for Jesus Christ. And first, let me say a good word for his race. Jesus was a Jew. He came of a race with a genius for religion, whose conception of God, the one holy and righteous God, was such as to single them out from other peoples, making them a peculiar people, chosen of God, through whom he spoke not only to their race but to all the world. From this race came that lawgiver and leader of his people from Egyptian bondage, the renowned Moses—statesman, pathfinder, liberator. His was the race that produced the long line of prophets, such noble personages as Isaiah, Jeremiah, Ezekiel, Amos, Micah, and Hosea. This is the race from which stems Christianity, and of the sixty-six separate writings that compose our Bible, all of the thirty-nine of the Old Testament and all but two of the twenty-seven of the New Testament were written by members of the race that gave us Jesus Christ.

The story of the Jewish race is one in which commingle joy and sorrow, victory and defeat, grandeur and degradation, mountain-top and valley experiences, such as no other race has known. From the day the kingdom divided, in the days of Jeroboam, later exiled to Babylon, the Jewish people have never had a country they could call their own. Their bones have bleached on almost every battlefield; with no nation of their own to fight for, they have at one time or another fought in the ranks of every nation on the face of the earth. They are still a people set apart, in a sense, by racial characteristics, religious devotion, extraordinary success in business, persistence, perseverance, ambition to excel. Nearly everywhere they have been persecuted, oppressed, knocked from pillar to post, deprived of their possessions, exiled and enslaved, yet they have refused to be exterminated, and they hold together tenaciously through good and evil. At this present time their sorrows are as the sorrows of no other people because of bitter, brutal persecution in the lands of the dictators. Jews have perished by the millions since this present war engulfed the globe.

Prejudice against the Jewish race is present practically everywhere. Some of it is based on certain types who are said to be obnoxious; some of it may originate in envy. But, however we account for it, this prejudice and spirit of intolerance against the Jew is real, not imaginary. When we think of what individuals of this race have contributed to the world of science, literature, music, art, and statesmanship, we are moved to expressions of praise and wonder, unless blinded by bias and misled by propaganda. Think of Disraeli, prime minister of Great Britain. Remember Louis D. Brandeis, gifted member of the Supreme Court of the United States. Recall Judah P. Benjamin, bright, particular star in the Cabinet of the Southern Confederacy. Bear in mind Julius Rosenwald, merchant prince, who gave away a fortune to better the Negro race in this country. But time would fail me if I would call the names of even a small number of men and women who have blessed the world, and who were of the same race that gave us Jesus Christ.

Now, I hold no brief for the Jews, any more than I hold one for other peoples and other races, save as this particular race that has given so much to the world needs some of us, of the Christian fellowship, to protest against bias, prejudice, and intolerance directed toward Jews, just because they are Jews. I make no apology for any excess or extravagance in the characteristics, or eccentricity, of the Jewish people. There are high-minded Jews and there are Jews who are rogues. But the same can be said of Gentiles; and we who wear the name of Christian do not always live up to it, nor behave ourselves as men and women should, who own a magnificent obsession in behalf of the spirit and the teachings of him whom we call Master, Savior, Teacher, and Divine Companion. This is an imperfect tribute to an illustrious race of history—a race that should receive if not abundant praise at our hands, at least justice. How can we consistently belittle a race that gave us our Scriptures, begat the Hebrew prophets as spokesmen of God, and in the fullness of time gave us Jesus Christ our Lord?

In the second place, I wish to say a good word for Jesus' Bible. His Bible is what we call the Old Testament. It was practically completed in his day, although the Canon of the Old Testament was not officially established until about 90 A.D. There is nowhere in the world such a literature as the Old Testament, slowly produced through a long stretch of time, presenting writings unique and of varying values. There is the majestic account of creation, terse, almost laconic. "In the beginning God created the heavens and the earth." The stories of the patriarchs are incomparable. They deserve to be capitalized thus: The Story of Abraham and Sarah; The Story of Isaac and Rebecca; The Story of Jacob, Leah, and Rachael; The Story of Joseph and His Brethren; The Story of Gideon and His Fleece; The Story of Samson, the Playboy. The Story of Ruth and Naomi belongs to a later period, but who can forget its beauty and oft-quoted declaration: "Intreat me not to leave thee, or to return from following after thee; for whither thou goest, I will go; and where thou lodgest, I will lodge: thy people shall be my people, and thy God my God." There, too, is The Story of Samuel, his boyhood in the house of the Lord, his career as judge and prophet, the unselfish way in which he stepped down from high office and made room for Saul, Israel's first king. The Story of David lingers in memory with its commingled beauty and blight, its victories and defeats, so vivid and so memorable. Vivid also is the record of King Saul, and the sorrowful twilight of his kingship; the rise and fall of Israel, and the division resulting in the Northern and Southern Kingdoms; the emergence of the great Hebrew prophets; the sweet singers of Israel, who gave us the glorious Book of Psalms; the sages and the seers, who produced the sparkling Book of Proverbs and Ecclesiastes—how arresting the changing scenes! And that unnamed poet, and his masterpiece, the sublime drama of Job. What a book!

Jesus was familiar with his Bible. He quoted from it often, and quotations were to the point. In that period when he was so sorely tempted, just before his public ministry, he met the three testing experiences with as many quotations from the Scriptures. On that occasion he quoted twice from the Book of Deuteronomy and once from the Psalms. Close students of the fourfold Gospel narrative have observed that Jesus often quoted from Deuteronomy, which in some respects seemed to be his favorite section of the Scriptures. On that memorable day when he went back to his old home town, and as his custom was, went to the synagogue on the Sabbath day, he stood up to read from the Prophet Isaiah a notable passage which, he declared to his astonished hearers, was being fulfilled that day. He loved to quote from the Psalms, and it is worthy of note that, on the Cross as the end drew near, he cried out with a loud voice, saying, "Father, into Thy hands I commend my spirit." This is a quotation from the thirty-first Psalm, the fifth verse. It is said to be the goodnight prayer the Jewish boys and girls offered before they slept. "Father, into Thy hands I commend my spirit." A tender and comforting committal.

Jesus puts his stamp of approval on the Holy Scriptures of his day. It is well that we remember this, for there are those who in their zeal for the New Testament have slighted and possibly belittled the Old Testament. Some of the values of the Old Testament are peculiarly its own. It speaks directly to the human heart and misses none. It seems to say, "Thou art the man," even as the prophet Nathan spake to David and reminded him of his great sin. Its realism is stark and terrible. If you or I had been writing about Abraham, we would have left out the story of a falsehood that he told. We certainly would not have told all the truth about Noah or David or Absalom. We would have touched lightly upon the seamy side of their lives and glorified the virtues of the most eminent characters; and in the case of those where we could have found little to praise, we would have been loath to criticize. As literature alone, the Old Testament deserves to be known by everyone who would consider himself educated. And, as a book of life, with the Spirit of God brooding over its pages, it is supreme. There is much, very much good to be said for the Bible that Jesus knew.

I wish also to say a good word for Jesus' church, and I mean now by this term, the church that grew out of his life and ministry; the church that had its beginning on the Day of Pentecost. I remember once hearing a brilliant theologian say that Jesus did not found the church, that the church founded him. There is truth in that statement, but not all the truth. Even if it be conceded that the church of Christian history was not in his mind, it was inevitable that there should grow out of that nucleus of his followers and, in particular, the intimate group whom he so carefully selected, an organism which should in time become an organization. However, be it remembered that his great commission which is

54

thrice repeated, seems to require a body, a movement, a society. And we have his own words in reply to Simon Peter: "On this rock I will build my church." That is the truth just confessed by Simon—the Christhood of Jesus. And so it came about that these Christian groups, companies, organizations, of which we read in the Book of Acts and the Epistles, came to be known as churches and are referred to in such eloquent figures as his "body" and his "bride." How many times we have sung with the spirit, if not always with complete understanding, that grand hymn, "The Church's One Foundation Is Jesus Christ, Her Lord."

Of course, being made up of human beings, the church—and I employ the term here to include all the various communions which seek his mind and to do his will, no matter by what name they are known—is imperfect, has not lived fully up to its ideals, or carried out courageously the program which he announced that day in the synagogue at Nazareth when he read from the Prophet Isaiah. Yet when all concessions possible have been made to the critics of the church, and its mistakes and failures realistically appraised, it remains the one institution that we have in this world that provides for public worship of God and has, as its main business, the building of spiritual and moral fiber in human beings, and the leavening of the lump of the community with the yeast of Christ's spirit and teaching. Somebody has said the church is all-knowing, and that is true; almost everywhere there is a church. Driving along the highways one glimpses what our fathers loved to call "the meeting house" at many a crossroad and tiny hamlet. Coming into cities aboard a train, or by automobile, there is always a church spire on the horizon. And when the pioneers blazed paths where highways never ran, along with their cabins and the little schoolhouse, they built the church in the wildwood.

That we so often confine our thinking of the church to the local congregation where we hold membership, or the communion with which our local church is identified, is to be deplored. It would be as reasonable to think of humanity in the terms of ourselves and our immediate family and friends, and to forget or ignore the human family as a whole, with its company of great hearts, its heroes, sung and unsung, its victories and defeats, aspirations, dreams, yearnings. The church is greater than the churches, however great they may be; the churches are but broken lights of the church; I mean the church universal, the spiritual commonwealth, the company of those who walk by faith the world over. We say that we belong to this or that church; what we should say is that the church and all the churches belong to us, and the prophets, pathfinders, preachers, and evangels, of whatever groupings, denominations, or communions—all belong to us because we are of the church and in the church. St. Francis of Assisi is ours; Bernard of Clairvaux is ours; Wesley, Luther, Calvin, Campbell—all are ours, for they are in the same continuity of that body which began on that first day of Pentecost after the victory of Christ over the grave.

A congregation is not the same as an audience, nor is a platform or stage the same as a pulpit. Here is a bit of personal history, which I have not so much as whispered to a living soul. Perhaps I do well to mention it now. It is in keeping with the subject I am discussing. Some years ago, no matter how many, the suggestion was made to me here in Detroit that I would have a larger hearing and could find support from men and women who were friendly to me, but were not in any church in this city, if I separated myself from organized Christianity and spoke on Sundays in the largest auditorium available, with orchestral music preceding the address, lecture, sermon, the same to be widely publicized by trained advertising men. I suppose if I had been favorably inclined to this suggestion, something definite would have resulted. I never for a moment considered it. Quite apart from my duty to this particular church at that time, I felt then, and I feel now, that I would have stepped down rather than stepped up. It is possible that I might have had a much larger audience, but I would not have had a congregation. I might have had an attractive platform from which to speak, but I would have lost my pulpit as part of world Christianity, and my place in the long line of those who have gone before and who will come after me. Perhaps I may be wrong in this viewpoint. Better men than I am have taken a different attitude; but at any rate, I kept faith with my conscience.

In *The Atlantic Monthly* for January, 1943, appeared an engaging anonymous article entitled "We Build a Church." The concluding paragraphs I quote with relish:

There is romance in building a bridge, a factory, a department store, a school, anything which develops a community and helps humanity on. But the romance of building a church is greater still. Not many months ago, there was a tract of bare ground with a blank wall at one end of it. The stone was still in the quarries. The wood was standing timber. The glass was in neat piles of tiny panes in the cubbyholes of a faraway shop. The tin, copper, and brass of the organ pipes had not yet been so shaped that they could sing. Now these various fabrics have been fashioned into a shrine beneath whose high and hospitable roof men engage in the highest act of which men are capable, communion with the infinite and eternal Creator Spirit to whom our spirits are akin.

Already its walls are bathed in the atmosphere of prayer and praise. To it through the years young men and women will come to plight their marriage vows. To it little children will be brought to be dedicated to God in the beautiful rite of baptism. To it our dear dead will be borne for the tender offices of faith and hope and love. From its pulpit the good news of a gracious God will be proclaimed. From its altar will be distributed the sacred symbols of God's grace, validated by a love of which the Cross is the measure and the sign. We who built it dare to hope that our children and children's children will gather in it long after we are gone, to pledge their allegiance to the ancient loyalties which alone can transform this beautiful but shadowed world into a family of God, wherein men know and feel themselves brethren because of their common origin and destiny in Him.

How appropriate now to quote from that hymn beloved by the church the world around:

> I love thy Church, O God!
> Her walls before thee stand,
> Dear as the apple of thine eye,
> And graven on thy hand.
>
> For her my tears shall fall,
> For her my prayers ascend;
> To her my cares and toils be giv'n,
> Till toils and cares shall end.

Having said a good word for Jesus' race, for his Bible, and for his Church, I want now to say a good word about Jesus Christ himself, his character, and his teaching, his ways of looking at life, and the supreme sacrifice he made on the Cross. Whatever I say will be inadequate and fall far short of what he deserves. I have been reading books about Jesus Christ, it seems to me, for two-thirds of my life. I began with those standard books on the life of Christ which had their great day, nor has that day wholly ended: Farrar and Geikie, the first-named published in 1874, the second in 1877. These books make Christ live, and contemporary thought and customs are attractively presented. I came to know Andrew's *Life of Our Lord* early in my ministry and also *The Incarnate Savior* by Robertson Nicoll. I think I owe more to these biographies than to any others on our Lord and Savior, though I have read numerous more modern works, some good, others not so good; yet, perhaps, all of them possessing certain values. Since all of these "lives" are based on the four Gospels, there is all the more reason for knowing Matthew, Mark, Luke, and John as we know no other books. Beginning with Mark, because his is the earliest and the briefest, we should go on to Luke, then Matthew, and last of all the narrative attributed to John, the beloved disciple.

I say a good word for the teaching of Jesus. Thomas Jefferson, who was a libertarian in both theology and politics, held that the purest code of morals the world knows came from Jesus. They are high, so exalted that they seem out of our reach. On the other hand, they are simple and practical. If we lived according to the Golden Rule, that is, Do unto others as we would have them do unto us, the result would be not a little bit of heaven here on earth, but a great deal of heaven. Jesus also said, "I am among you as one who serveth," and if the other rule is golden, this one is diamond. No, we haven't tried out his teachings save in spots and in fragments; but wherever they have been tried, they have wrought wonders. It is humbling when we think of the vast discrepancy between our glib talking about these teachings of Jesus, and our putting of them into practice. I have a good word for his world view and world program, his whole family-of-God idea. It is difficult to see how those who claim to follow him can be sectional and partisan, prejudiced and intolerant of spirit and outlook. He essayed the stupendous task of attempting to captivate and transform his earliest followers with this world view. They were slow to understand it and slow to accept it; but it finally won them completely.

I want also to say a good word for the mind of Jesus, by which I do not mean simply his intellect, but in addition to his mental processes which were so clear and penetrating, I would include his spirit and purpose. There have been renowned scholars whose stock of knowledge was vast, yet they lacked considerateness and sympathy, being impatient with "the little people." That passage of St. Paul's in Philippians, the second chapter, is one of the most profound of all his writings: "Have this mind in you," he urges, "which was also in Christ Jesus." And what does the Apostle say of what the mind of Jesus consisted? In substance this: that though he existed in the form of God, he was not eager to grasp being on an equality with God; that he took upon himself the form of a servant, was found in fashion as a man, became obedient unto death, yea, the death of the Cross. Now, all this was his mind, or was part of it, namely: humility, obedience, renunciation, even the degradation that the crucifixion exacted. His mind was saturated with love, a love that will not let us go. Yes, I would speak a good word for the mind that was in Jesus Christ, knowing that if we seek his mind, the endeavor, even though we do not attain fully, will be worth all that it costs.

I would say a good word for Christ's remarkable understanding of our human lot. Never was it necessary to explain to him the conditions and circumstances that bring human beings to the places where he found them. Very few of us understand many of us. We are seldom interested, for one reason; for another, it requires putting one's self in another's place, nor is that easy. Ponder the words, "He knew what was in man"; recall his friendly approach to Zaccheus, the publican, who was used to rebuffs and had probably become hardened. Who but Jesus could have answered, as he did, the brazen accusers of the woman taken in adultery? That dinner party at Bethany, in the home of Martha, Mary, and Lazarus would have been a failure and the ending most unhappy had it not been for his understanding heart and his boundless sympathy. Someone has called Jesus "the first great gentleman," for there is a chivalric quality in his mercy, sympathy, and understanding.

I must say a good word for the Cross of Christ, for its meaning and its Gospel of redemption. No thoughtful person wishes to be glib or voluble when he talks of the Cross, or speaks of the crucifixion. One touches mystery here, just as he touches mystery on the occasions of birth or death. Something happened at Calvary different from anything else that happened before or since. It was not merely the death of a good man. It was that, of course, but more than that. He who died there that day was a revealer not only of the nature of God but also of the nature of man. He mirrored God's true self. The Cross is both the center and the climax of that Life of lives. To quote one of our most thoughtful modern Christian scholars, Charles Clayton Morrison: "The veil was withdrawn and God showed Himself as the eternal Sufferer, crucified by man's sins, saving men by His forgiving grace. This is the everlasting Christian Gospel— the good news which no materialistic interpretation of the Cross must be allowed to hide," to which I most heartily subscribe.

That was a good word that the Scotch poet-preacher said for Jesus Christ in one of his finest poems, which the church has rightly set to music and incorporated into the Christian hymnal:

> O Cross, that liftest up my head,
> I dare not ask to fly from thee;
> I lay in dust life's glory dead,
> And from the ground there blossoms red
> Life that shall endless be.

On Setting Christianity Right-Side-Up

REVEREND PAUL E. SCHERER, D.D., LL.D.*

Pastor, The Evangelical Lutheran Church of the Holy Trinity, New York

THOSE WHO KNOW him best believe that Paul Scherer has a genius for preaching. He himself insists that it is mostly a matter of hard work in the preparation of each sermon. But his sermons of the "Great Preacher Series" in Reading, Harrisburg, and other cities; his Lenten and Easter sermons in Detroit, and his sermon on the 400th Anniversary of Martin Luther have the elements of greatness.

Born in Mt. Holly Springs, Pennsylvania, in 1892, Dr. Scherer studied for his B.D. at the Lutheran Theological Seminary, Mt. Airy, Philadelphia, and was ordained a minister of the Lutheran Church in 1916. He taught at the Mt. Airy Seminary for ten years—from 1919 to 1929—and has been pastor of Holy Trinity Church since 1920. In addition he has preached frequently at colleges and universities along the eastern seaboard, in England during the summers of 1930 and 1931, and on NBC's Sunday Vespers program. At the August Conference in Northfield he has served as Vice-Chairman since 1937 and as Dean since 1942.

This sermon is an excellent example of Dr. Scherer's style, which emphasizes "preachability." He knows what he wants to say, and he says it in a way that reaches each hearer. (Note Bishop McConnell's sermon on this text.)

---

* Sermons by members of the Advisory Committee were contributed at the request of the editor and are included on his responsibility.

Sermon Nine

PRAYER: *Grant us, O God, to be mindful now of Thy presence that what we think and say, and all we do, may learn to arrange itself as before Thy face; through Jesus Christ our Lord. Amen.*

TEXT: *And, behold, a certain lawyer stood up, and tempted him*—tempted him out, really; if Jesus had given him the wrong answer, the indications are that he wouldn't have been excessively worried about it, or lost any sleep: he might have been very well satisfied with himself—*tempted him, saying, Master, what shall I do to inherit eternal life?**   LUKE 10:25

S YOU READ THE BIBLE, IF YOU WANT TO ENJOY it and profit by it, stop long enough to see, not just what the words mean, but what they reveal about the people who utter them.

This text, for example, carries a revealing question. It was asked, you see, by a learned person; not one of the babes and sucklings Jesus had been talking about a moment before, the simple folk who know so little and understand so much, but a scholar. That may be partly why it wasn't completely honest. Scholars have such a hard time being honest. They have to turn so many more corners than plain people! Not quite honest, then; but interesting and thoroughly important. It was an important question in itself, because of its subject matter: it had to do with this critical business of making the most out of life, both here and hereafter. But it was almost equally important, maybe more so, by reason of its phrasing. The bare wording of it is proof enough to anybody who will look at it twice that the questioner had ideas of religion that were all topsy-turvy—wrong-side-up.

Here's the suggestion that religion is altogether a matter of doing. He knew better himself, as we shall see; but never mind that. What shall I *do . . .?* Then, not content with getting off on the wrong foot, he insists on getting off wrong with both feet! He thinks he must have something in view. Nothing childish and crude, like golden streets and pearly gates, but it's fairly clear that his eye is on some kind of main chance. It wasn't enough to do this or that, you had to do it in order to arrive by that means at some end beyond the doing! "What shall I do—to inherit eternal life?"

I wonder if it strikes you that by the very nature of things *inside,* this scribe, or lawyer, as Luke calls him, could never himself have been the good Samaritan. It's unthinkable. The man who got down off his beast

* Note the form of interpolated text used by Dr. Scherer. It is one of the distinguishing marks of many of his sermons.

that day and knelt by the side of the road wasn't thinking about eternal life. He had no axe to grind and nothing to gain!

That's how it is, then, everything is wrong about this question that *can* be wrong. And Jesus so gently, with such good humor, sets it right. This is what *I* should like to do. I want to take at least two of the most popular notions we have about Christianity, notions quite prevalent in the Christian Church, and stand them up as they've *got* to stand, if you and I are to make any headway at all with our religion.

Let me begin with this. All of us know that there are just three factors in every man's universe. Think of them, if you will, as the three sides of a triangle: *himself*—that's one side, over here at the left, shall we say; *other people*—that's the second side, over here at the right; and *God*—that's the long side, at the bottom. Every man's universe is really constituted that way. Here are all his relationships. Nothing else of any great moment enters in. What I'm saying to you first of all is that it has to stand that way if it's going to stand at all. That's Christianity right-side-up. It has to stand on God!

The trouble with us is that we are forever trying to upend it, and get it to stand on one or the other of these two sides at the top. We upend it in our prayers for instance, and get ourselves at the bottom of it all. That's one of the most subtle of all our habits; and it makes the whole structure unstable. Take a casual journey through the hymn book some time. You'll see it there. "Jesus, Saviour, pilot me, Over life's tempestuous seas." "Hide me, O my Saviour, hide, till the storm of life be past." "When I tread the verge of Jordan, bid my anxious fears subside." It's all right, if that's your story—unless you get stuck with it! The only thing I'd like you to notice is, how often when I sing I seem to be fairly *obsessed* with what happens to *me!*

And the whole tenor and movement of the Christian gospel aims to get my mind off that! There was a man in Cromwell's time whose name was Praise-God Barebones. He had, I am told, a brother whose name was Jesus-Christ-Came-Into-The-World-To-Save Barebones. But that was nothing. There was a third brother whose name was If-Christ-Had-Not-Died-For-Thee-Thou-Hadst-Been-Damned Barebones. And that, writes Howard Robinson, of Oberlin, was just too much name. They called him Damned Barebones for short!

What intrigues me about that is this: all of it came out of one of those periods of history when human life had to discover all over again, as it's having to do now, the immense significance of the individual. It was necessary in those early days of Protestantism and Democracy. But everybody seemed to swing over at once into this ridiculous excess, until they had turned religion itself into a man-centered thing, with very little social conscience, with less and less emphasis on the fellowship of the Christian

62

Church, and with God more and more undertaking to run personal errands—His will and His very existence increasingly subject to every man's private judgment.

In our day we can't afford to lose sight of the fact that people matter. One by one they matter. That's what Fascism and Nazism and Communism want to cancel in the interests of this new and emergent fellowship of Society and the State. But these very movements themselves should serve to reveal the deadly peril into which we had fallen: the peril of forgetting, not that we count but that anything else *besides* us counted at all! Some of us may have been priding ourselves on the fact that we have tried to preach the Gospel where the Gospel has to be preached, to the separate lives of men and women, while a good many others were running around trying to get whole communities to act differently—Capital and Labor, Wall Street, Industry, and the Farm Bloc. Today it's even more vital to remind ourselves that the Christian gospel doesn't center in Tom, Dick, and Harry, or in you and me; it still centers in Christ, who is the judgment and the mercy of God!

Soberly I put it to you: unless we can get these selves of ours out of His way, all the religion that we have will topple over. You tell me you have certain difficulties with your faith; I tell you here's the nub of them. We've maneuvered ourselves into the middle of it! We've left out of the picture this word of Jesus, "whosoever loseth his life for my sake shall find it," while we go on praying for the old comforts. Macy's store had a whole-page advertisement in the New York *Times* some time ago telling us what we're fighting for. The four freedoms were in a tiny paragraph at the top; but the real spread was about the steaks in the frying pan, and the cars in the garage, and the bars of milk chocolate—eight or ten such items; I forget the rest.

We have taken to asking such questions as, Why do *I* have to suffer? I can understand *your* loss and your pain, but *mine!* Why should this happen to *me?* There's no justice in the world, no decency. God's a lie! It's *all* a lie! What do you suppose twists things like that but this self we carry about with us and shove into the forefront of our religion even, prodding it to its hind legs until it tries to whistle the whole creation to heel and to bend God Almighty to its will, in a world where God Almighty won't be bent!

It's this divine recklessness about Christianity that we've turned our backs on; a recklessness that counts the cost all right, but doesn't give the snap of a finger for it; sits down by its friend as *my* friend one night sat down by me. I had just been preaching a sermon on "Setting Your Life To Music." And he said to me, after a long silence, what I knew was true: "You tried, didn't you, Paul; but it didn't sing. And I know why. You got in its way." Then he laid his hand on my knee, and with deep emotion, because he was blind, gripped my leg, and whispered, "It doesn't matter a damn what happens to *us*." That was the most religious profanity I ever heard. It doesn't matter, you know. Not alongside of what happens to *God*. I shall take that with me through death, and it won't lose its luster.

But let me get on, because this isn't the really startling thing about Christianity—that you can't upend it and get it to stand on the "you" side—the really startling thing about Christianity is that you can't upend it and get it to stand on the "other people" side, either. Most of us who have quit thinking that it's altogether about us have taken to supposing that it's almost entirely about them. That's better, no doubt of it. Only see what happens: we take this parable of the good Samaritan, and we say, There now. Do you get it? That's Christianity. And it isn't. Not if you leave God out of it, which is precisely what we do. We're tired of worship. It's so futile. Let's just be kind to one another. We don't need all this doctrine business. Let's have a Good Neighbor Policy. Don't you see that's what it is that damns it? Simply that it is a policy? Figuring on some likely return, or on some imminent danger! If *God* were still in the middle of it, it would be just our way of feeling about the Mexicans and the South Americans, because He made them too, strange as they seem. We wouldn't be elaborating policies on the basis of it! In one of his columns, Mr. Sokolsky, who is so often right, said that love is a weapon that might at least be tried. But it isn't. I hope to heaven you don't brandish it over your wife and children. You've got to leave God out of it to make it a weapon!

The parable of the Good Samaritan isn't Christianity. Neither is the Sermon on the Mount. It's tragic to hear people discover the Golden Rule, and say, "Now surely this is what it means to be a Christian." Then they pile up on it their social programs. They're going to make the thing work. They give advice on economic problems. They plan the postwar world, hysterically. Sometimes I think we've gone completely haywire on that subject. Nothing else occupies our thought any more. We're going to pay attention now to religion, we say, because we're going to need it in that world. Mr. Lionel Curtis, in Britain, has rediscovered Christianity for himself and written a book about it, as "the only possible foundation of a stable political order." We're going to need it to buttress our own Democracy here at home. We're going to need it if we mean to provide any machinery for the prevention of these constantly recurring wars.

What I'm afraid of is that a good deal of this is the devil's own device to keep our eyes off the thing that matters. Christianity has to stand on God, and keep standing there. On our knowledge of Him in Christ. On our passion for His will instead of our own. On these deep indicatives He has laid down under our common life, these things that *are so*, treat them as you like; only, don't whine when they begin treating you as God likes! Listen to Jesus coming back to that, there in the wilderness. "You're hungry, aren't you?" asked the Voice. "Why don't you give yourself a break? Man shall not live by bread alone." All right. All right. But how about these others? That crowd in the Temple. Think of what it would mean to them if you'd only prove what you're talking about by throwing yourself off this pinnacle, and turning up down there among them quite unhurt! That wouldn't be hard for you to do. You might very well win them at a single stroke. Why deny them this thing that would be for their good? "Thou shalt not tempt the Lord thy God." Oh very well; very well. Then this is the subtlest of all: he tries to get Jesus interested in a Cause, instead of about the God whose Cause it is. Why on earth don't you keep your eye on what you're after—the kingdoms of this world, and the glory of them? "Here," says the devil, "I'll get out. You take them over. All you have to do is to admit that I'm actually in control of them. You do that when you consent to take them over from me! What earthly difference would it make? What does it matter how you get them, if you only get them?" Only this—and the answers are like the ringing of a huge bell in the lofty tower of a vast cathedral, a deep bass note: "God, *God*, God! Thou shalt worship the Lord, thy God, and Him only shalt thou serve."

Shall we start right, then? Whatever else Christianity is, it's concerned about Him first. After that, this second point: its concern doesn't stop with what we think of Him, or what we do for Him; Christianity is agonizingly eager to know whether or not we love Him. There's a sort of triangle again, if you see what I mean. The first was self and others and God; and it had to stand on God. This is mind and will and heart; and it has to stand on heart.

Now that's embarrassing to some of us. We like to believe that the most important business on earth is this business of thinking. The Jews were great for that. They were orthodox, and had all the right answers. This scribe got farther. He had got around to *doing* something, at any rate. And Jesus seems to have agreed with *that* much of it—that thinking straight wasn't enough, because He picked out a Samaritan for his story, and the Samaritans as everybody knew very well, didn't *think* straight at *all!* There seems to be something else about us that's even more important. I told a young college woman once, years ago at Northfield, that her emotions, from which she was doing her best to back off as thoughtful young women sometimes do (she seemed to have cultivated the most violent distaste for them; whenever she caught sight of anything that even looked like an emotion, she was bristling all over with suspicion), were far more important than her sophomore brains. It was a little wicked, perhaps, she looked at me as if I'd left my brains in the kindergarten!

But it was true, anyhow. Thou shalt *love* the Lord thy God. *He* got around from doing to loving right off, the minute Jesus threw his question back at him. This first and greatest Commandment was a sort of ghost, haunting the corridors of his memory. Somebody said the other day that a ghost is an idea that has never really been put to work. There are scores of such ghosts in the field of religion: ideas that all of us have, and we hardly ever put them to work. Here's one of them: we know that Christianity has to stand, not on its head, nor on its hands; it has to stand on whatever heart it has for God, for this face of Him, this hurt body of Him, which is Jesus!

But we don't put that to work! We try to come to the Bible so often for the answers it has; it has about the richest assortment you'll find. We say that, after all, it's the best way there is of looking at things. Sometimes it doesn't seem to make sense; but it makes more sense than anything else we know about—its assumption that there *is* a God, and that we are souls. Its insistence on the evil that lies down deep in human life. Professor Joad, of the University of London, has given up his agnosticism recently and has become pretty much of a Christian because he's face to face now in the world with that evil; it doesn't look like a theory any longer, it looks like a fact. But when we've got all the arguments and all the answers and all the facts together, we suddenly discover that the trouble is somewhere else! Everybody goes out and flies in the face of everything that's rational, because we aren't rational. If you have even the remotest idea that we are, look around. Human life is like a crazy old hag sitting on an ash heap, ripping to pieces the costly fabric that she herself has been at infinite pains to weave! It isn't reason that drives us. That's why Christianity can't stand on its head. We know it.

And it can't stand on its hands. All societies for ethical culture are dedicated to the task of perpetuating this positive cause. It can't be done; we know that. Christianity isn't what thousands of us keep saying it is, a way of life—not down at bottom. Yet we go on undertaking to do the right things just because we are sure that's what's required of us. We go on watching our step, lest we stumble over the wrong things. And, too often by half, we get out of it a kind of self-conscious piety that rarely does us much good and makes other people tired, if not sick. Worse than that, some of us acquire in the process a conscience that grows weary of operating at home where it belongs, and after rubbing its hands a while and looking around, begins to operate on the neighbors. We go up to somebody one day and we say to him, "Now look here. My conscience compels me to tell you"—then you just listen how nasty it turns out to be! The queerest, ugliest things happen to us sometimes when we clench our teeth like that and strike our forehead with the palm of our hands and start out grimly to do our duty.

Because it's love—some kind of love—that stands at the bottom of human life to hold it up and make things go. Gregory Zilboorg has found it out from his study of psychoanalysis, and has written it up in his book, *Mind, Medicine, and Man.* Here's the ghost of our Christian religion, the idea we've never really put to work: Thou shalt *love* the Lord thy God. Things won't hold together on any other basis. They won't hold together on the basis of what we were taught as children. They won't hold together on the basis of what we believe is decent behavior. *God* put something at the bottom of Christianity—and we'd better quit up-ending it.

I can hear you say, right off, that this business of loving God is a bit vague. How are we supposed to go about it? Well, the New Testament thinks we can at least keep the channels open: "He that loveth not his brother, whom he *hath* seen, how can he love God, Whom he hath *not* seen?" Maybe there are some things in the way; things that go on between you and the Negro or the Jew, the German or the Japanese. That might at least *explain* a little of the difficulty we have in loving God, when all He has ever done He has done because He loves *us.* What else was all the turmoil in heaven about? Taking His mind off the stars to fasten it on Abraham, whispering His promise; then because everybody was so wilful, writing His law; getting into it so far that at last there was no way through but a cross, and a man there that you can't make out to this day, except that he was the trouble Love went to—not even to win *our* love, but just for its own sake, because it was eternal and altogether reckless and wouldn't spare itself a bit, not a single thorn, not one nail.

If that doesn't kindle anything in us that can answer to it, I'm afraid we simply haven't any religion. One thing I know: all that we *do* have is groundless and rootless, unless this word and deed of God in Jesus of Nazareth has laid siege to something inside of you that's deep, deeper than anything. That's why we come here to bow our heads and sing our hymns together. That's why we read and study these words of Scripture, graven far and away into human life, like the lineaments of a Father's face against the sky, if perchance the embers of our dull hearts might glow once more, and a flame burn again on this sad earth. Shall we at least get it right-side-up?

Let's not go into it this year to save our own skins, nor anybody else's, for that matter. There is a threat in the Christian gospel. It's the threat of a God Who is just. You can't offer excuses to Him or to life. But I don't want to operate under the threat! There is a promise in the Christian gospel. It's the promise of a God whose mercy always does somehow outrun His justice. But I don't want to operate under the promise. I want to be in this thing because, loving Him just a little for His love, I'd like to be as He is.

That's why this good Samaritan got down off his beast. It wasn't a policy with him, figuring out which neighbor might best be able to return the kindness. It wasn't a weapon, this compassion of his, bent on winning friends and influencing people. He wasn't just determined to do his duty that day, nor set on going to heaven, nor on improving the condition of the poor, nor on establishing a durable peace, nor making the world safe for travelers. There was just something in him, by the grace of God, that was this much like God Himself. You couldn't have argued him into it. You certainly couldn't have argued him out of it. It had rubbed off on him. He had caught it. He was that sort. So he knelt there by the side of the road. Not a priest. Not a Levite. Somebody who was little better than the cur in the street, with its nose in a heap of refuse. But he lifted that poor soul, half dead, and walked off with him toward an inn—until all you can hear in the story, as you lay your ear against it, is the "heart of the Eternal, most wonderfully kind."

That's what Christianity is when it's right-side-up, a sort of creative fellowship. A fellowship with this Love, "broader than the measure of man's mind," stands waiting in the middle of its own strange universe, holding things together with its own scarred hands—looking at ours now and then to see if we have yet any of the marks about us to show whose we are, and whom we serve!

LET US PRAY: *Lead us more and more, O God, into the secret place of Thy presence, that having seen Thee in Christ we may love Thee; and having loved Thee may fashion after Thy mind this place where Thou has set our feet; for Jesus' sake. Amen.*

The End of the Beginning

REVEREND RALPH W. SOCKMAN, D.D., PH.D.*
Minister, Christ Church, Methodist, New York

IF ROBERT BROWNING was "the poets' poet," then Ralph Sockman is "the preachers' preacher," yet he speaks the language of the multitude.

In any fair estimate of contemporary American preaching, Dr. Sockman must be included as one of the great preachers. Each Sunday morning at ten, he has a vast radio audience on the National Radio Pulpit, a service he renders without compensation. Each Sunday at eleven, he preaches to a church filled with active members and visitors from all over the country. On Sunday afternoons at five, during certain seasons, he gives a series of sermon-addresses on "Religion and the New Books."

Born in Mt. Vernon, Ohio, Dr. Sockman first attended Ohio Wesleyan, then went on to graduate from Union Theological Seminary. He holds a Ph.D. from Columbia University and the honorary doctorate from Ohio Wesleyan, New York University, Wesleyan University, Dickinson College, Rollins College, Washington and Jefferson College, and Florida Southern.

While yet a student, he became associate minister of the Madison Avenue Methodist Church (now Christ Church), New York City, and has been minister of this church since 1917. In 1918, he served with the Army Y.M.C.A. From 1927 to 1929, he was president of the Greater New York Federation of Churches. He was the Lyman Beecher lecturer on preaching at Yale University, 1941, and the Fondren lecturer in 1943. At present he is a director of Union Theological Seminary, of New York University, of Drew University, and of New York Medical College. He is also a trustee of Ohio Wesleyan University, and has served on the Board of Foreign Missions of the Methodist Church.

Dr. Sockman is widely known as the author of many books, including *Suburbs of Christianity, The Unemployed Carpenter, Paradoxes of Jesus, The Highway of God,* and *Date with Destiny.*

At his great New York Church he knows nearly every member by his or her first name. He is each member's personal friend as well as his counselor and pastor. "The End of the Beginning" was preached on December 26, 1943.

---

* Sermons by members of the Advisory Committee were selected by the editor alone and he assumes responsibility for their inclusion.

Sermon Ten

TEXT: *I am the door.* JOHN 10:9

UCKED AWAY ON A BACK PAGE IN THE DAILY PAPER of December eighteenth was a little item which barely caught my eye. Its heading read, "Kitty Hawk Celebration Canceled by Blizzard." What does the name "Kitty Hawk" signify to you? Although I tried that question on two or three college students, without getting any answer, I am sure that most of you recall Kitty Hawk as the town in North Carolina where on December 17, 1903, Orville and Wilbur Wright made their first flight in a power-driven airplane. So unbelievable did their achievement seem, at the time, that most newspapers were unwilling to risk their reputations by publishing the report. Then the possibilities of aviation caught the imagination of the world, and its development has become probably the greatest wonder of our generation.

Yet the achievements of aviation have become so common that the wonder has faded, until the fortieth anniversary of its beginning draws only a little space on a back page of the daily paper, and the account reads as follows: "A few persons slipped over icy roads to the Wright Memorial on the tall hill to pay tribute to the inventors. But the formal program had to be canceled."

There are some wonders we outgrow; there are other wonders which grow up with us. Airplanes belong to the first group; stars, for instance, belong to the second. When we were children we learned the rhyme:

> Twinkle, twinkle, little star,
> How I wonder what you are!
> Up above the world so high,
> Like a diamond in the sky.

To be sure, I did look up at the stars when I was a lad. But I did not spend much time wondering about the stars. A new sled or a new bicycle could take my mind off the stars any time. But as I have grown up, I have discovered that the wonder of the universe has grown up so much faster. The heavens seem immeasurably vaster to me now than when I was a boy. When I read Dr. Harlow Shapley's estimate of the diameter of the Milky Way as one quintillion, 800 quadrillion miles, I am simply lost in wonder. Yes, there are wonders which grow up with us.

And Christmas, the event which we celebrated yesterday, is one of the wonders which grows. I confess that Christmas was the red-letter day of the year when I was a child. When the red bells and the green wreaths began to appear in the windows and shops, my temperature started to rise. The excitement, the expectation, the glow continued to mount as the day drew near, until the night before Christmas—well, that was the greatest night of the year.

The emotional excitement of Christmas has cooled with maturity, but the wonder of it has deepened and widened. Whereas, in my childhood I thought most about the presents to be received and given, now I think beyond the gifts to that tidal wave of good-will which sweeps up the coast-line of the world, even though the shores be studded with bristling battleships. What is the power that lifts the tide of the world's heart at Christmas time?

I know, of course, that Christmas is celebrated as the birthday of Jesus. But why is it so different from the birthdays of other great men? We Americans declare holidays on the anniversaries of Washington's and Lincoln's birth, but they pale beside Christmas. The memories of national heroes, however great, fade with the passing of time. The great figures of World War I are already dim, as the spotlight is turned on the leaders of World War II. But Christmas does not fade. More millions observe it each year. Can you imagine the daily papers this morning carrying a news item concerning Christmas similar to that a week ago concerning the observance of aviation's fortieth birthday? Can you imagine the papers saying "Christmas Observance This Year Canceled Because of Blizzard"? No, blizzards, battles, global wars do not cancel Christmas. It goes on growing. Why?

And then the wonder of Christmas grows still more, as I think that not only does the observance of it increase with time, but also that our time itself is measured from the Christmas event. Our calendar, of which we become especially conscious as the old year passes into the new, is a most eloquent reminder that the birth of Jesus was the turning point of history. The Hebrew ancestors of Jesus reckoned time by the reigns of Israel's kings. Read your Old Testament and see how it goes: "In the six and thirtieth year of the reign of Asa," "in the third year of his reign he sent Jehoshaphat"—thus go the recordings. But the Kings of Israel could no longer be used as dates when Jesus was born, because Palestine had been conquered by Rome, and Israel's kings were no more.

Hence the contemporaries of Christ calculated his birth according to the reign of the Roman emperors. It was a tax decree issued by Caesar Augustus which dated the Bethlehem event. But about five hundred years after Christ's birth, the Roman Empire collapsed and Rome's emperors were out of date.

Where, then, was there any fixed point universal enough for calculating time in the disheveled and leaderless Europe after the fall of Rome? Then it was that Diogenes Exigius started a calendar based on the birth of Christ, some 533 years after the event. The hinge of history was fastened to the door of the Bethlehem stable, and since that date time has been divided into B.C. and A.D.

Now it might have been expected that just as the Hebrew kings and the Roman emperors went out of date, so Jesus would be superseded. But has any event occurred since Christ's birth which could be seriously considered as the start of a new calendar for the world? Some seven hundred years ago Genghis Khan set up an imperial regime which stretched from the Yellow Sea to the Caspian, from the Indian Ocean to the Arctic. On his seal were these pompous words: "God in Heaven, The Kha Khan, the power of God, on earth, the Seal of the Emperor of Mankind." But ask the average man today what he knows about Genghis Khan and he will likely not know whether you are talking about a mountain peak or a race horse.

No, Asia has no date to offer which can supplant that of the birth of Jesus. In Europe, Charlemagne's victories and the signing of the Magna Charta were significant events, but they would not mean much in Asia. In America, the Fourth of July, 1776, marks the birth of a new nation, but even that would have little significance in Africa. Some twenty years ago Mussolini started a new calendar for Italy, dating his official documents from the founding of Ancient Rome. But pompous little Mussolini has now been bumped from his balcony, his official documents have become scraps of paper, and we doubt if he himself is using his calendar wherever he may be, and certainly his partner Hitler is not reckoning time by it—what little time he has left.

Nineteen centuries have passed since the Christmas event, but no other date can seriously be suggested to displace the birth of Jesus as the basis for the world's calendar. No other career has the universal appeal of Jesus'. No other figure in history could fitly apply to himself the words which Jesus is recorded as using when he said: "I am the door." Christ is the door that divides recorded time into before and after. On Christ the door is the hinge of history. That is the wonder which grows. With the birth of Christ something began whose end is not yet.

And what was it that came into the world with Christ? What was it that justifies Jesus in saying, "I am the door"? It was this: Christ is the door by which God comes to man.

Everywhere, and at all times, from primitive society to the most advanced stages of enlightenment, men have clung to the belief that there is an Invisible Power or Powers behind the walls of this visible world. Whether it be the savage groveling before a sacred stone, or a Phoenician woman flinging her child into the brazen arms of Moloch and the flames of devouring fire, or the cultivated Greek being initiated into the mystery cults, men have believed in gods that work them good or ill. The persistence of this belief in a divine being has convinced the world's greatest thinkers that there must be such a power. Otherwise, life mocks man in his highest motives, and we are like rats in a cage beating against the bars of an imprisoning world, which taunts us with hopes only to deny them. Such a conception of life as a cosmic jest is untenable.

But before Christ came, the conceptions of man's relation to God were, in general, pretty dark and dismal. When I try to comprehend the darkness of that pre-Christian world, a personal experience comes to mind. Some years ago when I was a seminary student, a slight operation which I had undergone took a sudden turn for the worse. It was after midnight, and the doctor could not be reached. The nurse exhausted all her known resources, and sent out for some medicine, only to find that the drugstores of the neighborhood were closed. Vividly do I recall the seemingly interminable experience of those few dark hours. The hands of the clock seemed paralyzed. Hungrily, my ears listened for the sounds of the city's waking life. Impatiently my eyes kept turning toward the eastern windows to catch the first signs of approaching sunrise. When the prosaic sounds of the milk wagon betokened the stirring of the city, it seemed heavenly music to me. And the first rose-tinted streaks of light reaching above the horizon looked like the fingers of a friendly hand stretched out to help me. I always think of that night when I hear the cry in Mendelssohn's *Oratorio*, "Watchman, will the night soon pass?"

The wise men of the world were looking for some star of hope to guide them through the darkness. The plain people, like the shepherds, were looking for a Savior to deliver them from the drabness and futility of existence.

Then Christ came. He made warmly personal the conception of God as a Father, a Father who cares for all his creatures, who notes the sparrow's fall and numbers the very hairs of our heads. Where the object of pagan worship was to placate the ill temper of the gods and get them to leave the worshipers alone, Christ taught that the object of worship was to find the way home to God—home to a Father who eagerly came forth to welcome the returning prodigal.

When Christ came, he gave a new worth to man as man. The late George Washington Carver, son of a Negro slave, was once asked by my friend, Dr. John Gross, what Simpson College had done for him while he was a student there. The great Negro scientist replied, "Simpson College made me realize that I was a human being." Well, Christ made men feel that they were human beings, beings with an immortal soul and a divine destiny, whether they were bond or free, male or female, white or black.

When Christ came, he gave love a new impetus. Whereas men had been taught to love their families and neighbors, Christ taught them to love their enemies and to pray for them that despitefully used them, that they might be children worthy of their Father in heaven, who made his sun to rise on the just and the unjust. And whereas in pre-Christian society under-par children were given little care and left to drop out and make room for the strong, Christ started a passion for healing that won for him the title of the Great Physician, and launched his followers on the road to modern medical science with its glorious record of hospitals, research, and the Red Cross.

When Christ came, he brought both life and immortality to light. He convinced men that our little and vexed life is not rounded with a sleep, but that in our Father's house are many mansions, and death is but the passing from one room to another. He made his followers feel that neither death nor life, nor things present nor things to come could separate them from the love of God which was revealed through him. Christ set us singing:

> This is my Father's world, O let me not forget
> That though the wrong seems oft so strong, God is the
>   ruler yet.
> This is my Father's world, why should my heart be sad?
> The Lord is king; let the heavens ring! God reigns! let the
>   earth be glad.

These are some of the convictions that Christ brought into the hearts of men. This is the light which he let in. Is it any wonder that his followers cried, "For God who commanded the light to shine out of darkness, hath shined in our hearts, to give the light of the knowledge of the glory of God in the face of Jesus Christ"? Christ could say, "I am the door," for through him God came to men in a new and personal way. That is what began on that first Christmas; and the end is not yet.

Ah, yes, and more. Christ could say "I am the door," because through him man comes to God, even as God comes to man.

The followers of Christ not only felt that they beheld the glory of God in the face of Jesus Christ, but they also said that "To as many as received him, to them gave he power to become the sons of God." It is power that man needs, power to press toward his ideals. Socrates said that if a man knew what is right, he could do it. But Socrates was wrong there. "The good that I would, I do not"—that was Paul's confession; and it is ours. We need a Savior who gives us power over our temptations. And Christ does that. He looks into the eyes of a Magdalene, and the purity in his eyes slays the dragon in her soul. We need a Savior who gives us power over our fears and frustration. And Christ does that. He imparts a strength to Paul which makes him shout, "I can do all things through Christ that strengtheneth me." We need a Savior who gives us power to face death itself. And Christ does that. He did it for the martyrs who died in the arenas of Rome. He is doing it today for brave souls on many a battlefield, and in many a hospital bed.

Christ causes men to feel that they are workers together with God in a winning enterprise. And thus he builds up morale—that subtle power of the spirit which is so important these days. Winston Churchill told of being at General Haig's headquarters in August, 1918, before the last great Allied drive against the Germans in World War I. General Haig pointed to the German fortifications, supposedly the strongest possible, and said, "Now we shall see how much such fortifications are worth when men no longer have the will to defend them." I often recall those words in these days, when I think ahead to the possible crumbling of the German spirit in the near future. Morale is a stronger factor than forts or bombers. And morale is what Christ gives in the whole battle of life.

We children of the machine age have so fallen under the spell of noisy, mechanical power that we misjudge the quieter personal forces of the spirit. Jesus looks so gentle in contrast to the dictators. The manger and the cross seem only kindling wood in the path of machine guns and tanks. But when the shouting and the tumult die, Christ still lives. He survived the Caesars of his time, He will outlive the dictators of our day.

> There was a Knight of Bethlehem whose wealth was tears
>   and sorrows;
> His men-at-arms were little lambs; His trumpeters were
>   sparrows;
> His castle was a wooden cross, whereon he hung so high;
> His helmet was a crown of thorns, whose crest did touch
>   the sky.

That Knight of Bethlehem is the leader of tomorrow, because he can impart to men the power to become sons of God. He is the door by which men get to God. That is what began on the first Christmas; and the end is not yet.

PRAYER: *Eternal and all-loving Father, grant unto us the glow and the radiance of great hours. May our gratitude for the gifts and good-will of yesterday strengthen us for whatever tests and struggles may be ours tomorrow. Let the assurance of Thy love fortify us for the uncertainties of a world at war. Be very near, O God, to those who are away from home at this holiday season, and lighten with hope the hearts that are heavy at home. Help us to follow Thee faithfully in the duties near at hand and to trust Thee confidently in the darkness where we cannot see. Speed the triumph of righteousness and the return of peace, through Jesus Christ, Our Lord. Amen.*

The Little Sisters of the Poor

THE REVEREND ROBERT I. GANNON, S.J.
President of Fordham University, New York

THE REVEREND ROBERT I. GANNON, S.J., was born in New York in 1893. He was educated at Loyola School, New York, and Georgetown University, Washington, D.C. In 1913, he entered the Society of Jesus. From 1919 to 1923, he was instructor of English and Philosophy at Fordham College. Soon he founded the "Play Shop" and in 1925 wrote *The Technique of the One-Act Play*.

After leaving Fordham, he made his theological studies at Woodstock and was ordained in 1926. After his ordination he was sent abroad for special studies, taking his S.T.D. from Gregorian University in Rome in 1927, and his M.A. from Cambridge (Christ's College) in 1930. Since then a shower of doctor's degrees has rained upon him, seven doctorates in five years— from Georgetown University, Manhattan College, Holy Cross College, Boston College, Columbia University, Bowdoin College, and New York University.

In 1930, Father Gannon reopened St. Peter's College, Jersey City, which had been closed during the war, and became its Dean. He opened Hudson College of Commerce and Finance, of which he was the first Dean from 1933 to 1935. He remained as Dean of St. Peter's until his appointment as President of Fordham University in June, 1936.

In 1937, he went to Venezuela on the invitation of President Lopez Contreras for consultation on school problems, and in 1942, received the Award of the New York Academy of Public Education for distinguished service in the field of Education. He is a trustee of Town Hall, an Elective Manager of the New York Botanical Garden, a trustee of the New York Zoölogical Society, a director of The Netherland-American Foundation, and a member of the Committee for International Economic Reconstruction.

Father Gannon's most interesting pulpit assignment was in air-raided London, where he preached the Lent in 1943 at Westminster Cathedral as the guest of the late Cardinal Hinsley.

This sermon was delivered at St. Patrick's Cathedral, New York, on the occasion of the celebration of the Centenary of the Little Sisters of the Poor. There is a gentle, wistful, almost whimsical note in this delightfully tender message to those the world has all but forgotten in its wild hurry. It has the simplicity of true greatness, and brings charity and religion into daily life.

Sermon Eleven

TEXT: . . . *just and devout, waiting for the consolation of Israel.*

LUKE 2:25

HE DEAR GOD HAS SUCH AN UNACCOUNTABLE WAY of doing things. His bookkeeping is completely upside down. As far as we can see, all His credits are debits and His debits are all pure gain. For His business deals with souls, where each item purchased is worth more than all the material equipment of His Corporation—the Church. As for His efficiency, it is more puzzling than His bookkeeping. For example, whenever there is some great project on hand, He usually overlooks the logical selection and picks somebody whom nobody has any confidence in. His first Pope, the foundation stone of His Church, was an ignorant fisherman who had already denied the Faith. Centuries later, when that same Church was beginning to crumble, the man He chose to serve it was just a harmless little fellow who was playing a guitar in Assisi. Moreover, the instructions He gave him at the time were just as impractical as his selection. "Come, Francis," said the dear God, "give away your fine clothes. Go down to the little chapel in the valley and repair the roof. It is leaking." Again, three hundred years later, when this Church of His was being rocked to its foundation by a new heresy—Protestantism—when whole kingdoms and races were being torn away from its eternal fabric; when intellectual bombshells were shattering its windows—who was the champion chosen to save the day? An ignorant young Spanish soldier with a limp. What were his instructions? "Go down to Montserrat, hang up your armor and keep an all-night vigil before Our Lady's Altar. As for the rest—love to be poor and pray."

It doesn't seem to make much sense, and yet, the first Pope was a perfect foundation stone; St. Francis actually did revive the Faith in the 13th Century, and St. Ignatius was the inspiration of the Counter-Reformation. Now, therefore, with all that history behind us, we may be less surprised to find that a hundred years ago God's ways were still inscrutable. He wanted, at that time, to call back modern society to an apostolic love of poverty. He wanted an example that would illumine once more the beauty of Christian charity. We should probably have advised Him to strike down the head of the House of Rothschild as He did St. Paul before Damascus, convert him by a miracle, and use all his countless millions in building homes for the aged poor. That would have been the smart thing to do. But His choice for the great apostolate fell, instead, on a servant girl with 120 dollars. Jeanne Jugan with her 000 francs! The instructions which He gave her from on high ran true to form: "Go out and find an old woman whom nobody wants and wash her feet, and love to be poor, and pray."

So Jeanne went out and rented two little rooms in a garret, shabby, gloriously shabby, like Bethlehem, and pretty soon, around the corner came Anne Chauvin, sick, deserted, old. And thus it was that the three of them, a servant girl, a helpless old woman, and God began a great movement whose centenary we celebrate this morning.

Step by step the work advanced, of course. Other simple, holy women joined Jeanne Jugan; more old people came to live with them. The little garret gave way to a larger house, and then to an abandoned convent. Before three years had passed, the outline of a religious institute was taking form, and soon the early companions in the work were full-fledged nuns—habits, vows, and all. Heaven, meanwhile, kept smiling on them, because they clung to poverty. Foundation followed foundation—St. Servan, Rennes, Dinan, Tours, Paris; and before long there were a hundred and one houses for the aged poor in France alone. So the Little Sisters and their old black wagon journeyed far along the apostolic highway into every country of Europe, Africa, Asia, and into our own United States, conquering the world by their unworldliness.

Meanwhile, we must not forget an unofficial member of the family who joined the Little Sisters the very first day they needed him. For like a great, big, good-natured, all-powerful uncle, St. Joseph has been taking orders from them for nearly a hundred years. They talk to him as if he were in the room with them, and expect miracles from him for the asking. If the coal is low, they put him in the bin and tell him he can't come out until the dear old people are warm again. So St. Joseph shrugs his shoulders, with a smile—and down the street come tons of anthracite. The angels, of course, are all cleverly disguised as truck drivers, but somehow or other the bins are filled again. He finds property for them, too, and puts up buildings, and pays their bills; but I am sure that part of each day he spends driving the old black wagon around the town—and I am equally sure he likes that best of all. For the wagon is not only a constant proof of the Sisters' childlike Faith and eagerness to be poor with a poor Christ, it is also proof of lingering grace in the hearts of men. Did you ever stand in the courtyard of a Little Sisters' convent about five o'clock in the evening and watch them unload the gifts that God has sent them through the day? A fine big ham, a little bunch of onions, a peck of potatoes, a single eggplant, a few bundles of kindling wood, a meat bone, a can of gasoline—and every blessed thing wrapped up in the love of God! This butcher and that baker, this big store and that rickety pushcart, sending in day by day some little symbol of their abiding goodness of heart. No one could unload a single wagon and remain a misanthrope. Of course, we may see in it a symbol, too, of inefficiency.

78

The Sisters would save a lot of time if they made a few judicious investments in Wall Street and had a dietitian lay out one uniform set of meals for the old folks and another for the Community. But then the home would be just another city institution, where age is the saddest thing in life. The reason why men and women are so happy and contented with the Sisters is precisely because there is never too much worldly efficiency in sight. They all know that every one, old people and Sisters alike, must reach directly every day into the hand of God for everything that they eat and wear and have; that nobody knows from day to day what is coming next, but that whatever it is, it is God's personal choice for them; that, best of all, they are poor not in a grudging, temporary sort of way, but by deliberate preference. For to them it is luminously clear that poverty makes it easier to save their souls, easier to be like Christ Himself.

For having had wealth set before Him, He deliberately chose to be poor. You know, for instance, how He planned His entrance into this world—His triumphal entrance into His Kingdom. An obscure little girl named Mary was married to a poor carpenter named Joseph and he took her to live in a poor old house on the edge of a poor little village. They had nothing but just what the husband could earn, and that wasn't much. For tradition says he was a poor carpenter in both senses of the word; he could do, that is, only poor rough work like making yokes for the farmers' oxen—heavy work, with very little pay. So even if Mary's Child had been born at home, there would have been little enough luxury around the cradle. But poor as it was, it was too rich for Our Lord. All He needed as a baby was swaddling clothes and a Mother's breast; all He needed at the height of His career was an alms for food and a hedge to sleep under; all He needed at the end was a loincloth and that was all He had. He always loved to be poor and to pray.

Evidently, then, there is no disgrace in being poor, and that is a lesson that most of us need. For usually shame, false shame though we know it to be, hurts more than an empty stomach, and an old hat or a worn coat often ruins our peace of mind, not because we are suffering from the cold, but from pride.

So even in our passing days of prosperity we can cultivate a new way of talking about poverty—the Little Sisters' way. If the man in the next house has been out of work for a year, we shall not say that "the Joneses are reduced to beggary." No, we shall say "they are as poor as the Holy Family." And if our own luck happens to be down at the moment, we can tighten our belts a bit and say "Thanks be to God, I am as poor as His Blessed Mother, now, and if things do not improve I'll have a chance to end my days with the Little Sisters of the Poor."

And that, my dear Brethren, is something to look forward to, for it means a sweet and peaceful twilight after the heat of the day. It means the escape from the only thing we all dread in a long life—the feeling of being in the way; because the old people are not in the way of the Little Sisters, and they know it. They are the Kings and Queens of the Home, and their physical and spiritual comfort is of supreme importance to everybody there. You should see them dance and hear them sing and tell tall stories about the past—when he was a famous athlete and she was the belle of the ball! It is fun to be with them at recreation, but if you could see them prepared for Heaven, you would most certainly envy them. Perhaps that is why St. Joseph is always so close. He knows a happy death when he sees one.

So thank God for the Little Sisters, and thank God for the aged poor. Together they have blessed the world for a hundred years. Let us in this world show our gratitude to them, and through them to the Sacred Heart of Jesus.

IMPRIMI POTEST: James P. Sweeney, S.J., *Praep. Prov.*
NIHIL OBSTAT: Arthur J. Scanlan, S.T.D., *Censor Librorum*
IMPRIMATUR: ✠ Francis J. Spellman, D.D., *Archbishop, New York*

By What Authority?

REVEREND J. V. MOLDENHAWER, D.D., Litt.D.
Pastor, First Presbyterian Church, New York

PRIOR TO HIS COMING TO HISTORIC First Presbyterian Church in 1927, Dr. Moldenhawer was, for twenty-two years, pastor of the Second Presbyterian Church in Albany, New York. Through the long years, he has always been a speaker of sincerity and deep insight.

Julius Valdemar Moldenhawer was born in Tavastehus, Finland, in 1877, was brought to America at the age of two, and naturalized in 1905. He received his college education at Southwestern (now at Memphis, Tennessee), and took his theological studies at Union Theological Seminary, New York. He was ordained in 1900, and his whole ministry has been in the Presbyterian Church in the United States of America. The honorary degree of D.D. was conferred upon him by Western Reserve University and by Hamilton College, and the Litt. D. by Southwestern University.

A man of many interests, Dr. Moldenhawer is a trustee of Mackenzie College, São Paulo, Brazil; a director of Union Theological Seminary; a member of the Board of Managers of the Presbyterian Hospital, New York City, and a trustee of Sailors' Snug Harbor.

He is deeply interested in books, is widely read, and is the author of *Fairest Lord Jesus* and *The Voice of Books*.

"By What Authority?" was given at Union Theological Seminary Commencement, May 17, 1943. He asks the question every minister must ask himself from time to time, "By what authority do I stand here and speak?" And unless he can find the answer in his heart, "God put me here," his preaching will lack conviction, be it ever so dramatic and polished. This veteran preacher speaks out of his long and successful experience, speaks to those who feel called to preach "the Word." It is a challenging sermon.

Sermon Twelve

TEXT: *By what authority doest thou these things?* MATTHEW 21:23

E MUST BE A SINGULAR MINISTER OF THE GOSPEL who does not at times pull himself up sharply with the question: By what authority do I stand here and speak? And he will be less and less content with any answer which is rooted in mere self-confidence. Of all the advice offered to youth in more optimistic times surely the most outstandingly dated is that which bade us

81

believe in ourselves. And the advice was never worse than when it was whispered in the ear of a man of God making ready his sermon for the coming Sunday or mounting the steps into his pulpit. It is indeed among the first lessons a young minister learns that his very appearance in the pulpit will quickly become an intolerable piece of presumption unless his utterance can throw off any possible likeness to a display of formal oratory. I remember one mistaken young parson who complained bitterly that he was not permitted to stand up and speak on a theme that appealed to him personally instead of being, as he somewhat shockingly phrased it, tied to a passage of Scripture. If I could remember who he was I should probably cherish an unseemly curiosity as to what finally became of him. What happened to most of us was the swift enlargement and deepening of our sense of working under the divine commission. So again and again we answer the re-emerging question, "How came I to this time and place?" by saying without equivocation, "God put me here."

It is a good and sufficient reply in any age or clime. But surely it is beyond all measurement good in such a time as this. In hours like these, anxious and sad with the sense of partaking in the world's pain and grief, its towering and heartlifting heroism, solemn with the heavy realization of deadly peril and an uncovenanted expectation of good to come, we wish to fix our minds more firmly than ever upon our vocation, upon the assurance, paradoxically comfortable and dreadful, that we are God's men, sent forth by him to speak his word.

Let this be my witness to the shape which this assurance has taken in the forty-odd years of my own ministry. And I do not hesitate to declare my conviction that my experience is common to most preachers of the gospel. All of us are the better fit for our work today by phrasing for ourselves some sort of clean-cut reminder of this essential fact and of its most characteristic manifestation. Thus then it stands. We get our divine authority by way of the Bible, the Christian Society, and the immediate voice of God. For that matter why should I not say it in words lively with the vitality of a great tradition, thus: "God's authority for my utterance comes to me through Holy Scripture, Holy Church, and Holy Spirit. What I thus hear will, when I speak it, be indeed the living echoes of his tone."

Concerning the authority of Holy Scripture, I can only confess with the utmost simplicity that I am more sharply aware of it and more profoundly thankful for it with every passing year. No small element in my acceptance of that authority is in my very blood—it was drawn into me with my mother's milk. That this no doubt conditions all that follows I acknowledge without apology. But the rest is a tough web of intellectual wrestling and spiritual experience with one after another of the books of the Bible that has resulted in placing that written word in its essential content quite beyond the range of hostile criticism. I have definitely made up my mind that if our critical and scientific re-examination of the Bible has resulted in reducing it to the status of one more source book in comparative religion we have indeed fed ourselves with what may have been sweet to the taste but is exceeding bitter to the stomach. This does not mean that I have cultivated a carefully blind eye to the difficulties that for the past hundred and fifty years have caused so many headaches and heartaches to the faithful and so much malicious delight to the scornful. It means only this: that one-time uneasiness about the fate of Jephtha's daughter and about the divine choice of an unspeakable ruffian like Jehu to carry out Jehovah's will, those and others, for all their power to trouble my sense of Biblical authority, have gone to that very quiet limbo where they snuggle down for long slumber side by side with that ancient puzzle propounded for the confusion of the pious: Where did Cain get his wife?

These things are for me and my kinsmen in thought and life matters of no moment. The Scriptures give us so strong and steady a sense of the presence of God, so warm an assurance of his help and comfort, so clean-cut a revelation of his justice, his power, and his love that anything which interferes with this, its great purpose of showing us the face of the Almighty, is either absorbed or thrust aside. When I read the heart-lifting lines beginning:

> By the rivers of Babylon, there we sat down,
> Yea, we wept, when we remembered Zion,

I am prepared, when I come to the terrible words of imprecation at the end, to push them quietly aside, or, being taught by our present pain and grief, to understand while I cannot accept. Yet even in my rejection I am under the divine tuition.

I am more willing than ever to acknowledge the persistent rightness of the Scriptural judgment upon matters with which it deals. After reading all the Bible has to say about King David, I am convinced that the modern judgment of contemptuous condemnation is both uncharitable and psychologically unsound, and that the Scripture is quite right when it calls him a man after God's heart. And even if Sir Arthur Quiller-Couch declared (no doubt being acclaimed by a stirring round of modernistic applause) that Esau is a gentleman and Jacob is not, the fact still remains that the Bible is right in the plain assumption (not even underscored) that the great soul of these two is Jacob. All that would seem to prove that here, not for the first time nor the last, the gentleman proved unfit for great things while the rank outsider, with some unhandsome qualities but with unsuspected heights and depths in him, is all set to be God's man of destiny.

After what seemed for a while to be an irreconcilable conflict we are now sure that the priests as well as the prophets have their share of the divine will to impart. For those who are not too slow to learn the lesson that they are churchmen as well as preachers, the word of authority rings out not only from Isaiah and Amos and Hosea but from Ezekiel and Nehemiah, from that wonderful group of nameless lovers of the holy house on Mount Zion whose joys and sorrows and yearnings are alive even to this day in the moving rhythms of our Book of Psalms. All the sharp and even intense differences of point of view, yes, and of conviction, too, are quite incapable of breaking down our sense of obedient submission to this evident though various expression of God's inexhaustible truth.

When we come to the New Testament and begin to read the Gospel story we are at once reminded of evident instances of imperfect transmission. No doubt we shall hear repeated a famous phrase about the necessity of seeing Jesus above the heads of all his reporters. Nor shall we quarrel with that, but we shall acknowledge with gratitude the great merit of narrators at once so honest, so skilful, so humble, and at the same time such attentive observers and such good witnesses that they succeed to admiration in drawing for us the picture of One who towers not only above their heads but above the head of every reader for these many hundreds of years. No one can miss the air of high command, the unswerving intention, the warm and powerful goodness expressed in an astonishing and convincing series of stories about His mighty work, the dedication of self to life and to death in obedience to the will of God. Nor can we miss in all the rapturous and exhilarating confusions of the Easter story the majestic and overpowering fact of His rising from the dead. So follows the rest of the astoundingly rich and various matter in the remarkable volume in which we tread in the footsteps of our Lord's interpreters in holy speech and holy living, which has been, since the Christian Church became conscious of it as the New Testament, the fulfilment and conclusion of the story begun in the Old Testament, the story of the strange ways of God in the creation, preservation and redemption of us His children.

Without the Book we literally cannot move a step or speak a profitable word. With it we are armed with the first and obviously needful weapon for fighting the good fight of faith with an utterance worthy of our vocation. Without it we might well fear to speak with confidence about God lest unconsciously we should say foolish and unworthy things. With it we shall find ourselves enlightened by what is surely the perfect utterance, whether it be in the sublimity of "And God said, 'Let there be light': and there was light"—or in the teasing gentleness, flowing out into a boundless compassion, of the word of the Lord of Jonah, "Doest thou well to be angry for the gourd?" On the prophet's sour response, "I do well to be angry, even unto death," the voice of the Almighty replies, "Thou hast had pity on the gourd, for the which thou hast not laboured, neither madest it grow; which came up in a night, and perished in a night: And should not I spare Nineveh, that great city, wherein are more than six-score thousand persons that cannot discern between their right hand and their left hand; and also much cattle?" The man who takes to heart these two passages cannot be unready to speak of the majesty and the might and the goodness of God.

Again the question, "By what authority do you speak?" is answered, "By the authority of the church." We do not need to join the weaving procession of those who have sought out many inventions. What we proclaim is in every essential matter what Holy Church proclaims. What we say here has since the beginning of the Christian era been said in every clime, in every age, and by all Christian men. It is altogether a wholesome and heartening experience when we think of ourselves as members of a great society, a holy fraternity, inheritors together with our comrades of a great tradition in ideas and morals, who declare only what the great brotherhood has agreed to declare. What a magnificent meaning is given to the great cloud of witnesses when we think of our-selves in the exercise of our vocation as feeling the warmth of contact with all the great souls of the Christian Church from St. Paul and St. Peter and St. Stephen to David Livingstone and Williams of Nanking. How good to be assured that as we commend to all men the high ideas of Christian heroism and Christian service we can feel as it were the very touch at our shoulders of those who in life and in death gave to the standards we proclaim the exalted evidence of demonstrated fidelity, in scenes glorious and pathetic and infinitely uplifting.

When I say the church gives me the authority, I think of Polycarp, threatened first with the fury of wild beasts and then with fire, replying to the proconsul, "Why tarriest thou? Bring forth what thou wilt." I think of Tyndale in his cold prison asking that there be sent him out of his own goods a warm cap; "a warm coat, too," he adds, "for this I have is very thin." And then he asks for a lamp in the evening "for it is weari-some sitting alone in the dark." Most of all he begs to be permitted "to have the Hebrew Bible, Hebrew grammar and dictionary, that I may pass the time in that study." And all this, remember, in the very shadow of approaching death. I think of Father Jogues bringing back his maimed hands from his beloved France that he might hold forth in them once more the blessed gospel to the savages of America, not to suffer this time their cruel ingenuities of torture, but to meet the unpremeditated mercy of a quick death. I think of the eyes of Bishop Fisher opening on the day of his martyrdom to see the Lieutenant of the Tower standing by the bedside. Being told that this day he must die he inquired at what hour.

"At nine o'clock," was the answer. "And what time is it now?" said Fisher. "It is now about five." "Well, then, let me by your patience sleep an hour or two, for I have slept very little this night, not for any fear of death, but by reason of my great weakness and infirmity." And I think with perhaps the most profound emotion of all about a dimly-seen figure on its knees in a hut in darkest Africa; and I give thanks for that wonderfully good man who went to God in the very act of prayer.

Of such, my brethren, is the fellowship of the faithful in the Church. By these our companions, saints and apostles and martyrs, by their words and their deeds, by their holy lives and by their consistent proclamation of the truth are we upheld and empowered. All these live again before us when we are sensible of the authority of Holy Church. Concerning that which upheld them we need to say only that they relied in the hour of death upon that which had been ever their breath of life, even the solid substance of the Christian Creed, from "I believe in God the Father Almighty," to the crowning comfort of this: "And the life everlasting."

Midway of that Creed it is written "I believe in the Holy Ghost." And it is by the operation of the Holy Ghost that not only the last but the ultimate authority is given to the servants of God. Already the work of the spirit is implicit in the authority of the Bible and of the Church. It is the Spirit who takes the things of Christ and shows them to us. It is good Christian doctrine and especially good Protestant doctrine not only that the Scriptures are the work of men moved by the Holy Spirit but that the same Spirit interprets the sacred writings to the devout reader. Considering the many obvious misinterpretations of Scripture of the intellectual ungodly, I find less occasion than ever to quarrel with this ancient and honorable theory. Spiritual things *are* spiritually discerned and it is a lamentable experience to read a comment on some precious passage of Scripture by a person who has no right-loving feeling for its beauty or its truth. So in like manner it is the Spirit that gives to the Church all its Graces. Because of our poverty-stricken imagination we have often been at a stand before many of these brief stories in the Book of the Acts of the Apostles that tell of the imparting of the Holy Ghost to newly baptized believers in the Lord Jesus Christ. Surely that receiving of the Spirit, whatever it may have been beyond, was the receiving of power—the consciousness of having power given after such a fashion and to such a degree as to make the convert gloriously aware of his ability to do and to bear whatever God required of him. So, as we move in the world of our mind, in the company of the incomparable excellence of the Saints of the Church, we know that these are they upon whom the Spirit has been poured out in abundant measure. I for one take no offense at visible tongues of flame and aureoles. I myself have known some beloved heads that were so gilded and ringed about by our thankful hearts whenever our eyes beheld them.

One thing further I might dare to say as I draw near the end of this brief and imperfect answer to the query "By what authority?" This blessed and powerful gift of the Spirit is on occasion given to God's servants directly. So I believe it has been in every age and not only in those singularly bountiful times in which the word of Holy Scripture was coming into being. God's direct inspiration of his servants is surely not limited to any age or place. If I believe, as I certainly do, that Isaiah had authentic vision of the Presence when he wrote, "I saw the Lord, high and lifted up," can I dare to call it illusion or mere poetic feigning when Henry Vaughan writes, "I saw Eternity the other night," or when William Blake, after each of his strange deathbed songs, cries out, "Not mine, not mine." And so, dear brethren, it is with us in great moments. Out of the depths of heaven God's arm is stretched out and his finger touches us. To say this, is utterly remote from boasting. It is, on the contrary, a most humble acknowledgment of the tremendous fact that even as there came to the man of God in ancient days his "Thus saith the Lord," so that overpowering consciousness is sometimes upon us that in this which our lips are about to utter we are to speak the very words of the Almighty.

It is not a matter of worthiness, but rather of willingness. That is why it sometimes surprises us as it comes from a person of remarkable simplicity and goodness of heart like Brother Lawrence, who has no notion of doing or saying aught but what is merely right. It is not given to minds on their guard. It is given when we are most nearly free from selfish considerations, when we are utterly unconcerned about pleasing men, when we are really praying with all our hearts, "Lord speak to me that I may speak!"

For the end of all the utterance is in order that the living word may be communicated, that the gospel may be preached even to the ends of the earth, that the whole world may be evangelized. Every right man of God must detest as violently as Ezekiel did the very thought of being rated as a talented orator whose public speaking could always be depended upon to give pleasure to persons of taste. "Lo, thou art to them as a very lovely song of one that hath a pleasant voice and can play well on an instrument." With loathing and bitterness we reject the suggestion that we speak to tickle men's ears. No! We have one aim and one only, to call men to God.

And what invitation to sinful men to accept the everlasting mercy can be more majestic or more moving than that in which the Bible, the Church, and the Holy Spirit speak with one voice? "Thrice is he armed that hath his quarrel just." And as we summon men to take their stand in this just quarrel in God's name with the powers of darkness, how shiningly arrayed are we with this triple authority. So I read with peculiar joy that which is written in the last book of the Bible as it speaks both of the Church and of the Holy Ghost. Hear once more the blessed and familiar words:

> The Spirit and the bride say, Come.
> And let him that heareth say, Come.
> And let him that is athirst come.
> And whosoever will, let him take the
>   water of life freely.

The Church Speaks

REVEREND JOHN S. STAMM, D.D., LL.D.

*President of the Board of Bishops of the Evangelical Church,
Harrisburg, Pennsylvania*

BISHOP STAMM was born near Alida, Kansas; he began the Christian ministry in Missouri in 1899. He served missions of the Evangelical Church in Bloomington and Glasgow, Missouri, and in Manhattan, Illinois. From 1907 to 1912 he was pastor of First Evangelical Church, Downers Grove, Illinois, then spent the next seven years as pastor of First Evangelical Church, Oak Park, Illinois.

He was graduated from North Central College, Naperville, Illinois, and later, from the University of Chicago and The Evangelical Theological Seminary. Albright College conferred the LL.D. upon him in 1935.

In 1919, he was elected Professor of Systematic Theology in the Evangelical Theological Seminary and served until 1926, when he was elected Bishop of the Evangelical Church. From 1935 to 1941, he also served as President of the Evangelical School of Theology, Reading, Pennsylvania.

He is president of the Board of Bishops of the Evangelical Church, and a member of the Federal Council and the World Council of Churches. He is a frequent contributor to religious papers and is the author of *Evangelism and Christian Experience* and *Standards of Evangelism*. His sermons have an evangelical emphasis. This sermon shows what he believes the Church must stand for in the world and the message it must proclaim to those in and out of the Church. He pleads for spiritual leadership.

Sermon Thirteen

TEXT: *To the intent that now . . . might be made known through the church the manifold wisdom of God.*   EPHESIANS 3:10

NE OF THE MORE HOPEFUL ASPECTS OF THE PRESent time is an increasing sensitiveness to spiritual realities. Evidence of this is found in many areas of thought and activity. The recent emphases in education, science, philosophy, and social service reveal this fact. In both business and government there are many who are searching after the order of the spirit. In fact, many people are becoming urgent in their demand that the way of the spirit be more fully outlined and courageously followed.

Men in all walks of life are experiencing the pain of disillusionment. They are troubled by the insecurities of life and are seeking for sure foundations. While there is no marked turning toward the Church, there is a new recognition of the Church, and a new expectation that through the Church there will be made known the way of life. This presents to the Church a great opportunity and a great challenge.

Until very recently, what the Church said was often greatly discounted. There were those who boldly declared that the Church has no vital message for this day. When men wanted information and direction in the way of life, they went to the leaders in education, science, philosophy, social service, and, more recently, to political leaders and movements for guidance. Many who have sought in these areas have, however, been lost in their pursuits and disappointed in their quest. They have not found the way. The life of abundance which they saw in their vision has not become a reality. In their disappointment and losses, many are asking as did King Zedekiah long ago, "Is there any word from Jehovah?"

This growing sensitiveness to spiritual things brings to the Church a twofold challenge. First, the Church must re-think and reaffirm its faith. There are many in the Church who have a very limited conception of the spiritual ministry of the Church. The attitude of many church members does not indicate a very deep conviction that the Church has something to say that should be heard. There must be a requickening of the sense of mission before the Church can really meet the challenge of the present time. A half-hearted Church will never win a generation which is stirred to its depth. A Church which does not wholeheartedly believe in its message and ministry cannot win the world to the ways of the spirit. Second, the Church must act. Men are in the valley of decision. This issue must be met today. This is, indeed, the day of salvation. It is the day for action.

The Church must lead in defining the order of the spirit. Many people are today thinking of the postwar order of life. This is as it should be. Now is the time to think in terms of peace and those basic principles which must govern an order of peace. Already the stress and strain of the war is making clear thinking difficult. Unless we think now, we shall be greatly limited when the time comes to establish the order of peace. In this thought-activity the Church must take a leading part. The Church is the minister of the spirit. It is the task of the Church to think through the ways and the order of the spirit. There are technical questions which those trained in these areas must answer, but the Church is concerned that all these answers are definitely related to the order of the spirit. Either men will learn to walk in the spirit, or they will continue to walk in uncertainty, insecurity, fear, want, and loss.

The Church must also give all diligence to create the mind of the spirit.

More attention must be given to the "perfecting of the saints unto the work of ministering unto the building up of the body of Christ." The spirit of evangelism needs to be quickened. More people should be won to Christ and to the Church. More people who have been won to Christ must be won to the full acceptance of the redemptive purposes of God in Christ. Church membership is not the final goal. The Apostle Paul set forth the true objective when he said, "Till we all attain unto the unity of the faith, and the knowledge of the Son of God, unto a full grown man unto the measure of the stature of the fullness of Christ." There must be more spirtually minded church members. The rule of the spirit must become more evident in the Church.

The Church must enter into a fuller unity in terms of the spirit. There will always be differences in approach, in modes of procedures, in interpretations, but all these need to be subordinated to the order of the spirit. The world is not reaching out after a particular ecclesiastical form but after the power of redemption, the newness of life, and an order of the spirit. Unless this unity is experienced and expressed the Church cannot meet the issues of the present time and give the needed leadership.

The Church must speak in greater unity. To say that the Church speaks seems an almost unwarranted assumption. It often seems that the churches speak, and that their voices make it difficult, if not impossible, to hear the voice of the Church. That there is often a confusion of voices is painfully evident, yet in more recent times the voice of the Church is becoming more and more clear and commanding through increased unity. There are those things which all believers hold in common. These mark essentially the message and ministry of the Church.

Let us give heed to five great affirmations which the Church is today bringing to the attention of men:

1. The Church says to men that they must reckon with sin. There are many elements in the maladjustments of modern life. Some of these are primary, others are secondary. All need to be faced. There are political, economical, and social tensions which need to be released. There are attitudes that need to be corrected. There are social theories which need to be changed. To bring the world into an order of peace in righteousness is not a simple, but rather a very complex, task. It will take the very best thought and the fullest measure of co-operation. The road is long and hard, but we must have courage to walk in this way.

What the Church calls attention to is the fact that underlying all these disturbing elements there is sin, and unless sin is reckoned with there will be no recovery possible. The primary concern must be the removal of sin in its destructive workings. It is sin which causes divisions, sets men against each other in exploitation and war, and makes it impossible for them to live in peace and mutual service. Sin perverts the desires, enslaves the will, makes man selfish and self-centered, and makes impossible the order of the spirit. The Church, therefore, speaks with conviction regarding the fact of sin. A brotherly world cannot be built out of sinful men. An order of human welfare is impossible unless men reckon with sin. What the Church says is that sin must be reckoned with.

If we were dependent upon human resources, this emphasis might seem to be a pessimistic note, but we are not limited to man. Through the power of God sin can be removed, men can be renewed, and a new spirit become regnant. This is the message of Christianity. This fact is also vindicated in the history of the Christian movement. In Jesus Christ God has made His redemptive power triumphant. This is the distinctive contribution that the Church makes in terms of a better world order. It is the basic need in the establishment of the order of human welfare.

2. The Church says to men that it is possible to have unity in diversity. There is a power which makes men brotherly and there is an experience which creates fellowship. This fact has possibly never been more fully set forth than it is today. While in recent years divisions have increased in social and political relationships, unity has become more meaningful and expressive in the thought and experience of the Church. Churches in all lands are finding a new and increasingly satisfying fellowship in the World Council of the Churches. Through this Council, there is today a fellowship maintained even in warring nations. While other relationships have failed, the Church has increased in fellowship. This is what the Church is saying to men and women in all lands. Through the power of God men can become brotherly, and a fellowship can be established which remains unbroken when times of stress and strain come.

This fact has very great significance because there is a growing feeling that the new order of the spirit must be an order of the people, not merely an order of some nations. What is, however, disturbing many thoughtful people is the fact that there does not seem to be the necessary dynamic of motive to make men willing to walk in this way of human oneness. Some people are thinking in terms of forced obedience more than in an order of fellowship in and through which men will be made capable of wanting what they should want. Something more than organization is needed. There must be the renewal of life in terms of the oneness of humanity. This renewal is possible through the redemptive power of God in Jesus Christ.

This fact also has a very great challenge. The record of the Church has not always been a record of Christian unity. This should move the Church to true penitence and to a purposeful endeavor to enter more fully into unity. If the teaching and preaching of the Church is to persuade others of the possibility of unity in diversity, then there must be more unity in the Church itself. The Church has an unprecedented

92

opportunity today to serve as a minister of the spirit, but can only meet the challenge if it will reveal more fully the redemptive power of God in a vital fellowship.

3. The Church says there are some things which need to be remembered. The Church is the body of Christ and, as such, is the embodiment of his life and power. That which needs to be remembered primarily is the revelation of God in Jesus Christ. His coming to men in and through Christ should be remembered. Also the matchless teaching of Jesus, his gracious attitude, his enriching fellowship, his sacrificial self-giving on the cross, his triumphant resurrection, his enthronement with the Father, and his coming again must not be forgotten. These basic disclosures form the groundwork of the Church. In more recent years there has been a tendency to set forth the achievements of men as those things most needed to be remembered. The result is spiritual impoverishment. There cannot be an order of the spirit if we fail to remember the redemptive activity of God in Jesus Christ.

The Church also says that the stream of life that issued from Him who is the source of life needs to be remembered. There is a great company of noble souls who need to be remembered. Many have lived quiet, unassuming lives but they have lived dynamically. Many of us today have happy memories of some of these noble souls. We have forgotten many things about them and their environment, but their Christlike character lingers with us in blessing. The Church says we must remember these for in their lives we see what God can do in and through men who yield themselves to him in and through Jesus Christ. The Church has a great heritage in character. As long as it will produce such Christlike characters it will give to the world the greatest gift.

4. The Church also says that sacrifice is essential in the process of living. The history of the Christian Church is rich in sacrificial service. In most of these areas it is largely the expression of individual lives, sometimes lived in much isolation; it, however, applies to group life as well. Many have not thought of it in that way. Group life and activity are only too often interpreted in terms of gain, rather than in terms of sacrifice. Individual sacrifice is heralded as a noble expression of life, but group sacrifice is usually rejected. Here is what we need to make a very definite advance. During the time of war this fact is often enforced. It is not even then uniformly accepted. It is usually not accepted as a principle but rather as a necessity in an hour of emergency. It has never really been carried over into the area of peace. What the Church is saying is that sacrifice is a principle of life and it applies both to the individual and the group. It is called for not merely in times of stress and strain, but in the whole process of living

This principle is rooted in the nature of God and characterizes the revelation of God. It is also rooted in the course of history. The pages of history are replete with illustrations showing that without sacrifice there is no progress. It is also rooted in the deep urges which move men to a better life. The exigencies of the times are today enforcing this truth, but there is a great danger that many good people are thinking of sacrifice only in terms of winning the war. We must think of this in terms of that which will follow the war. The better life and the more satisfying order demand sacrifice. Unless men will be ready to sacrifice for peace as well as for war, they will not find the peace.

All this, of course, implies a changed attitude. It implies the great truth which Jesus so often set forth with emphasis—that true living comes not through being ministered to, but through giving one's self to service. Only as men give themselves to the enrichment of others will they find peace in righteousness. Only as this truth is accepted will men learn to live in a meaningful way. It is only as the motive of life is changed that the course of action will really be changed. When men learn the art of living for others they will find sacrifice not irksome but a means of service.

5. The Church says that the only order which is abiding is the order of the spirit. This is what Jesus meant when he said that men should change their minds, repent, and believe in the gospel. That is why he made the primary quest of life that of seeking the Kingdom of God and His righteousness. The only order which will ever bring redemption is the order of the Kingdom. This is true both in individual and group living. There is no other way in which men can enter into the secrets and enriching powers of the material world except through the relation of these to the order of the spirit.

This fact brings to the Church a challenge. In seeking after a pattern for a better world, it is becoming increasingly clear that there is no pattern which men have worked out which wholly satisfies. All the patterns ever designed and tried lack essential qualities. There are, of course, elements of strength in many of these, but all need to be reconstructed to bring hope and assurance to men. There is, however, a pattern given by God which is adequate for the needs of today and for every day. That pattern is the Kingdom of God. It is contained in the Word of God and expressed in the Living Word. It is God's idea of the ordering of human relationships both here and now, and in the future. It is the spiritual renewing of men, and therefore has social content; it applies to the ordering of things, therefore has economic meaning and significance; it relates to the fullness of life, therefore applies to all men; and it embodies the resource of God, therefore has adequacy and satisfying power. The order of the Kingdom implies the whole of man. It recognizes the order of things, but relates things to the spirit. Wherever men have dared

94

to accept this and order relationships in harmony with its demands, there has been human welfare.

There are some who will doubt this. Some who say that the Kingdom order is impossible. It will be the order in some future day, but not now. Let us not overlook the fact that it will be difficult to turn men's minds to the Kingdom of God. There will be many imperfections in the endeavor to work out the Kingdom principles. There will be much that will be discouraging. What we need to stress is the fact that the acceptance of the Kingdom of God as the order of human relationships must become the goal of all our striving. There will be limited understanding and imperfect responses, but if we dare to set this as the goal, there will be the coming of the Kingdom. In some areas it will be delayed because there is still lacking a spiritual response, but it will come.

In closing there is one other fact which should be stated. While the order of the Kingdom may seem to many as an impossible order, let us not fail to remind ourselves that it is the order designed in the infinite wisdom and goodness of God. It is the order which Jesus declared and urged men to enter. Is what God has designed impracticable? Is our wisdom greater than the wisdom of God? Men have been doubting God all too long. The result is confusion, suffering, loss, and death. God has, however, not left man alone. Through the Holy Spirit, God is working in the hearts and relationships of men. In this fact lies our assurance. Certainly we cannot build the Kingdom order, but we can receive it. We can yield ourselves to God and through His spirit be made citizens of the Kingdom. It is not through our might and power, but through His spirit that redemption is possible. God is able to establish His Kingdom. He will establish it if we will respond to His love and grace.

All this sums itself up in this word: Redemption is not an achievement of man. It is the work of God. It is, however, also the work of God and man working together. This fact needs to be stressed more and more. There are still so many areas of life where men try to order life without God. All such neglect of God brings disappointment and loss. In thinking of the future we need to make this fact very plain. God's order is the only order which will bring man peace in righteousness, but God's order cannot be established without God. We need God. If we choose Him, yield to Him, and are empowered by Him, we need not fear—He will bring in the Kingdom.

Sermon to the General Convention of the Protestant Episcopal Church

at Cleveland, Ohio, October, 1943

THE RIGHT REVEREND HENRY ST. GEORGE TUCKER, D.D., LL.D.

Presiding Bishop of the Protestant Episcopal Church in the United States

IN THESE TIMES of world upset Bishop Tucker administers the work of the National Council of the Protestant Episcopal Church and the Presidency of the Federal Council of Churches with poise, vision, and courage.

He became a deacon and priest of the Protestant Episcopal Church in 1899, and was sent as a missionary to Japan. Soon afterward he was placed in charge of Episcopal missions in Aomori Province. He was president of St. Paul's College, Tokyo, from 1902 to 1912, at which time he was made Bishop of the Diocese of Kyoto. In the last war he served on the American Red Cross Commission in Siberia as major in charge of civilian refugee work. Retiring from this post in 1923 he returned to the United States, became Bishop Coadjutor of the Diocese of Virginia in 1926 and Bishop of Virginia in 1927. He has been presiding Bishop of the Protestant Episcopal Church in the United States of America since 1938.

He was born in Warsaw, Virginia, in 1874, and is the son of Bishop Beverley Dandridge Tucker. His brother, also named Beverley Dandridge Tucker, is the Bishop of the Diocese of Ohio. The Tuckers of Virginia are known as a family of bishops. He studied at the University of Virginia and the Theological Seminary of Virginia. William and Mary College, Columbia University, Southwestern Theological Seminary, General Theological Seminary, and Hobart College have conferred the doctorate upon the Bishop.

He is the author of *Reconciliation through Christ, Providence and the Atonement,* and *The Episcopal Church in Japan.*

In this sermon he says that "the Christian conscience accepts this war as God's judgment upon sin," and discusses the price of victory, repentance, the hope of a new and better world, the meaning of redemption today, and the place of Christian men and women today.

Sermon Fourteen

TEXT: *The creation itself also shall be delivered from the bondage of corruption into the glorious liberty of the Children of God.*

ROMANS 8:21

HE CHRISTIAN CONSCIENCE ACCEPTS THIS WAR as God's judgment upon sin. Christian faith sees in it an opportunity to deliver the world from the bondage of corruption into the glorious liberty of the children of God.

To call war God's judgment upon sin does not mean that it is provoked by God. War is a reaping of that which man himself has sown. The consequences which follow man's misuse of the divine gift of freedom are used by God as a solemn warning to our conscience. They make us realize the evil of sin. They show us that sin leads on to more and worse sin, that its evil effects spread out into our social environment, and pass beyond our power to control or remedy them.

Judgment, however, does not express God's main concern in dealing with the sinner. When the coming of the Son of God was announced, direction was given that He should be called Jesus, "for He shall save His people from their sins." God does judge sin, but always He seeks to create through His judgments an opportunity for the redemption of the sinner. The Saviour found in the Cross, which humanly signified the ultimate judgment upon sin, the supreme opportunity for redeeming the sins of the whole world. In so far, therefore, as we interpret this war as God's judgment upon sin, we must also recognize it as an opportunity for redemption.

This does not mean that victory in war over the enemies of freedom will effect the deliverance of the world from the bondage of corruption into the glorious liberty of the children of God. The tragedy of war is a judgment not only upon the evil of those who were defeated, but is a warning to victors and vanquished alike of the terrible consequences of sin. "Those eighteen upon whom the tower in Siloam fell, think ye that they were sinners above all men that dwelt in Jerusalem? I tell you, Nay, but except ye repent, ye shall all likewise perish." We must not interpret victory as God's approbation of our own superior merit and, like the Pharisee of the parable, thank Him that we are not as other men are. As Christians, as those to whom God has committed the ministry of reconciliation, we must interpret the war as a reminder of our own faithlessness and inefficiency in fufilling this responsibility. If victory means that God has given us another and a greater opportunity to assist Him in carrying forward the work of redemption, the very fact that this opportunity came only through the evil and the tragedy of war points out to us the imperative need for repentance.

The repentance called for is something much more fundamental than a change of moral attitude, a resolve to turn away from evil and to devote our efforts to good ends. The prodigal, when he came to himself, said, "I will arise and go to my father." Repentance means a recognition of our own unworthiness and incapacity. It is the realization that our only hope of deliverance from the bondage of corruption lies in reconciliation with God. There is a real danger that the enthusiasm for high moral ideals engendered by the war may lead to a mistaken trust in our own ability to live up to them. Experience should have taught the fallacy of any such assumption. A wise bishop once remarked that the statement of a good intention is often made the vicarious atonement for its performance. As the difficulties of an enterprise, which from a distance were enthusiastically endorsed, become evident, as the effort and sacrifice involved in its accomplishment become immediate demands, the number of those who beg to be excused increases. Even where human effort is sustained and is for a while productive of good results, its accomplishments fail to stand the test of time. The Christian remedy for this failure is a return to God that we may first of all be delivered from the bondage of corruption by His redeeming power, and then that our efforts to attain to the liberty of the glory of the children of God may be guided and strengthened by His indwelling Spirit.

Let us apply these considerations to the fulfillment of our hope for a new and better world as the result of our war and postwar efforts. Negatively, the war represents resistance to an attempt to destroy freedom on the part of those who have lost faith in its value. Positively, it is an effort on our part to strengthen faith in the value of freedom by improving its quality and sharing its blessings with all the peoples of the world. The possessors of freedom must be missionary-minded, but their readiness to share their blessings with others will meet with a cold response unless they are demonstrating in their own lives the value of what they are eager to give. Like all of God's gifts freedom is held in trust. It is only as we are faithful in the fulfillment of our stewardship that we can retain unimpaired that which has been entrusted to us. The very fact that it required such an evil activity as war to awaken us to the danger that threatened freedom, to summon us to a united effort to improve and extend it, is a clear indication that the task that lies before us partakes of the nature of redemption, and therefore requires Divine aid.

Redemption is a figurative expression. Literally it means the paying of a ransom for the liberation of a prisoner, or the purchase price for the freedom of a slave. In general, therefore, it refers to the price that has to be paid in the way of effort or sacrifice in order to restore freedom to one who has lost it through some fault or misfortune. St. Paul describes it when he speaks of the creation being delivered from the bondage of corruption into the liberty of the glory of the children of God.

The Declaration of Independence asserts that all men are endowed with certain inalienable rights, one of which is liberty. Freedom, however, is not an endowment which can be bestowed once for all, and fully developed. It is a potentiality which has to be developed through a long process of training under guidance. The true meaning and purpose of this endowment is that by its means we can become like God in character and human society can be developed into the Kingdom of God. It is a charter not of our independence of God nor of our right to do as we please, but rather of our kinship with Him and of our dependence upon Him. In His service we find perfect freedom. The steps by which we reach this goal are not automatic. Each one must be taken of our own free choice. Much of our life is indeed determined, but at certain decisive points the responsibility for choice is laid upon us. Sufficient preparation and guidance are given us to enable us to know what we ought to do and to assure us of power to fulfill the same. Our own failure to solve the problem of how to guide freedom without destroying it demonstrates our need of Divine aid in its development.

In so far as our freedom is real, it may be misused. A wrong choice weakens our capacity for choosing aright. Its bad effect is not confined to ourselves. It exerts an evil influence upon the lives of others. In the course of time these evil influences combine to form sin-infected customs, traditions, and conventions, so that an individual born into a social group, instead of being prepared and guided to a right choice, both from within and without, is involved in a bias toward evil. This is the unhappy condition which St. Paul terms the bondage of corruption.

Redemption means primarily that God who gave us freedom does not abandon us when we use His gift to oppose His will and thus bring ruin upon ourselves. Because of His love for us He takes upon Himself the responsibility for repairing the damage done by our sin to Him, to our fellow men, and to ourselves. To these who have lost their freedom and forfeited any right to consideration, at great cost to Himself, He restores the opportunity and the capacity to choose freely. This assurance of redemption through our Lord Jesus Christ is the heart of the Christian Gospel. For it we offer grateful praise to God in the opening words of the Prayer of Consecration in the Holy Communion: "All glory be to thee, Almighty God, our heavenly Father, for that thou, of thy tender mercy, didst give thine only Son Jesus Christ to suffer death upon the Cross for our redemption; who made there (by his one oblation of himself once offered) a full, perfect, and sufficient sacrifice, oblation, and satisfaction, for the sins of the whole world."

The redemption thus described is not a magical process by means of which a change is effected in human lives at a distance. What Christ has done for us must be appropriated and made effective in the life of each individual before he can be delivered from the bondage of corruption. "By grace are ye saved through faith." Grace is a dynamic term. It is the power of God's love which had acquired redeeming efficacy through the sacrifice of the Cross. Faith is the condition upon which alone this power can be applied to the individual life. Christ the Saviour does not destroy our freedom by forcing His way into our lives. "Behold, I stand at the door, and knock; if any man hear my voice, and open the door, I will come in to him, and will sup with him." Christ can redeem only those who voluntarily, because of their faith in Him, admit Him into their lives.

The first step, therefore, in redemption is the bringing of men into vital and intimate relationship with God through Christ. In this effort the initiative is taken by God. God was in Christ reconciling the world unto Himself. Christ issues the invitation "Come unto me, all ye that labour and are heavy laden, and I will give you rest." He asks those who know by experience the benefits of His redeeming power to co-operate with Him in bringing this invitation to the attention of all who are still separated from God. He has committed unto us the ministry of reconciliation. "How shall they believe," asks St. Paul, "in Him of Whom they have not heard? How shall they hear without a preacher? And how shall they preach except they be sent?" To those who have accepted His gracious invitation to come unto Him, He says, Go, proclaim the good news to all nations.

Most thoughtful people agree that this war will have been fought in vain unless the victory which now seems assured is both regarded and used as an opportunity for bringing into being a new and better world. By a new and better world is meant one in which peace, freedom, justice, righteousness, and love will prevail. Plans for political, social, and economic reconstruction with a view to promoting and maintaining these ideals are being widely discussed. Earnest consideration of such plans is highly important. Our Lord has warned us of the folly of putting new wine into old bottles. But in our enthusiasm for the provision of new bottles, let us not forget the problem of producing the new wine. By new wine is meant a radical change in the characters and capacities of the people who are to live under the new world order. Our Lord, using a different metaphor, says categorically, "A good tree bringeth not forth corrupt fruit, neither doth a corrupt tree bring forth good fruit. . . . Of thorns men do not gather figs." To the ruler who came to discuss with Him plans for a better world order, He said bluntly, "Except a man be born again, he cannot see the Kingdom of God. . . . That which is born of the flesh is flesh; and that which is born of the spirit is spirit." St. Paul, speaking from experience, warns us that the blessings of peace, freedom, justice, and righteousness are fruits of the spirit and cannot be produced from the flesh—that is, from human nature unregenerated, unguided, and uninspired by the Spirit of God. Where the Spirit of the Lord is, there is liberty. Without that spirit, all we can hope for is the bondage of corruption.

It is obvious, therefore, that important as it is for Christian men and women to use their expert technical knowledge and their understanding of Christian moral principles in drawing up plans for a better world, the primary responsibility of the Church is to co-operate with God in producing the new and better men and women, without whom such plans are doomed to failure. Free institutions are workable only by those who have the inner freedom that is made possible by the indwelling of the Holy Spirit.

Our first obligation as a Church is to exercise intensely and widely the ministry of reconciliation committed unto us by Christ. He is the vine, we human beings are the branches. Apart from Him man can never hope to bring forth the fruit of righteousness. Cut off from Him, our capacity for freedom is blinded, weakened. We use our liberty for a cloak of maliciousness or for an occasion to the flesh, with the result that it degenerates into the bondage of corruption. As Christians we are the agents of reconciliation, bringing men to Christ and commending Him to them, by the witness of the change wrought by Him in our own lives.

Again Christ calls upon His Church to co-operate with Him in bringing His redeeming power to bear upon those who through our ministry have been reconciled, brought into true and intimate fellowship with Him. They have come to Him

> Just as they are, poor, wretched, blind.
> Sight, riches, healing of the mind,
> Yea, all they need in Him to find.

It is His purpose to rehabilitate them, to repair the ravages which sin has wrought in them and in their world. St. Paul says that the purpose of our ministry is to present every man perfect in Christ Jesus.

The evil results of sin, however, go beyond the lives of individuals. They infect the environment in which the individual's life is lived. This, also, needs to be redeemed. A large part of our missionary endeavor is necessarily directed toward the transformation of the social and physical surroundings in which our hoped-for converts will live. St. Paul had something like this in mind when he spoke of the hope that the creation also shall be delivered from the bondage of corruption into the liberty of the glory of the children of God. Environment plays a vital part in the development of the individual's character.

101

God was in Christ reconciling the world unto Himself. Does not this include bringing back the whole of our environment into accord with God's purpose? God looked upon the world that He had created and saw that it was good. The Christian religion does not teach that the world in which God has placed man is inherently evil. It does recognize, however, that because of man's sin, his environment, instead of being an asset, has become one of the chief hindrances of his moral and spiritual development. It also must be redeemed. We must help Christ to make true by His redeeming power St. Paul's assertion, "All things are yours, and ye are Christ's, and Christ is God's."

This war has focused our attention upon multitudes of people, both at home and abroad, who were previously outside the range of our consideration. We are being led to appreciate as never before the practical implications of the Christian belief that God has made of one blood all the nations of men for to dwell on the face of the whole earth. This general acknowledgment of the brotherhood of man does not arouse in us a sense of responsibility strong enough to impel us to make the effort and sacrifice required for its fulfillment. When, however, we look at these long-neglected brothers with a vision that has been illumined by the light of Divine love, we see stamped upon every brow the sign of the cross. This marks even the most degraded, unattractive, and apparently hopeless as a "purchased possession of Christ." He is one for whom Christ died, and whom He has marked as a selected subject for redemption. He is one of the other sheep not yet brought into the fold.

Do not the signs of the times constitute a clear call from Christ to His Church to reclaim these purchased possessions to help Him make effective in them the redemption which He guaranteed by His death? He offers to us the privilege of sharing in the sacrifice, which is always the price that must be paid for redemption. Is there any loyal follower of Christ, any one whose own redemption has been bought with a price, that will fail to respond to such a call? By answering it, we shall both show our gratitude to Christ and at the same time make an indispensable contribution to the cause for which we claim to be fighting. Those whom we help Christ deliver from the bondage of corruption will be duly qualified for citizenship in that free world for which we pray and strive.

The Voice of the Church in a World at War

THE MOST REVEREND GERALD P. O'HARA, D.D.
Roman Catholic Bishop of Savannah-Atlanta

IMMEDIATELY upon being installed as Bishop of Savannah, Bishop O'Hara set himself the task of becoming intimately acquainted with every community in Georgia. The South was regarded by many as the nation's number one economic problem. His Exccllency, having been Auxiliary Bishop of Philadelphia during the depression years, was keenly aware of the problems of the working man and he saw in the South the opportunity for spiritual leadership among the people of his Church.

Born in Scranton, Pennsylvania, in 1905, he received his elementary cducation in Philadelphia, then studied at St. Charles Seminary, Overbrook, in 1911, where his brilliant record led to his recommendation for advanced studies at The Pontifical Seminary in Rome. He was ordained to the priesthood by His Eminence Cardinal Pompili on April 3, 1920. In 1924, he returned to the United States and served for five years as secretary to His Eminence Dennis Cardinal Dougherty, Archbishop of Philadelphia. In 1929, he was consecrated Auxiliary Bishop and ap-pointed by Cardinal Dougherty as Vicar-General of the Archdiocese. He served in this important position until advanced to the See of Savannah in 1935.

As the Bishop of Savannah-Atlanta he found less than twenty-three thousand Catholics in a population of about three million in the state. His hard work and vision and courage have greatly strengthened his diocese and have led to the establishment of many new churches. Out of his mind and heart came the Catholic Conference of the South which has met the problems peculiar to the Southern dioceses with confidence and prudence.

The sermon that follows was delivered by Bishop O'Hara on the occasion of the Richmond Convention of The Catholic Conference of the South. In it he discusses the place of the Church in time of war and the need for following Christ faithfully if we would solve the perplexities of our world today. He demonstrates the clarity of his vision in his statement on the need for a mission of compassion after the war.

Sermon Fifteen

TEXT: *I am the Light of the World. He that followeth Me walketh not in darkness, but shall have the Light of Life.*   JOHN 8:12

CHRISTIAN ART HAS LOVED TO DEPICT THE SCENE of Our Lord stilling the tempest on the Sea of Galilee. The masters have vied with one another in drawing the striking contrast between the majestic calm of the Saviour of the world and the frank terror of His Apostles who were sure the end had come. "Lord, save us, we perish!" they cried to their Divine Master, who slept while the storm was raging. Our Lord rebuked them saying, "Why are ye affrighted, oh ye of little faith?" and, rising up, He commanded the winds and the sea, and there came a great calm. Who were those men who accompanied Our Lord on that perilous journey? They were Peter and Andrew, James and John, and the others of the twelve whom, not long before, He had called to be His Apostles and whom He was to send into the world to teach, bless, purify, and sanctify.

The choosing of these men is, in itself, a story of high dramatic significance. They were not selected at random. Indeed, as though to show the importance of the step—one is almost tempted to say, of the risk, that He was about to take—Our Lord prayed long with His Heavenly Father before He went in quest of His first Apostles, those men whom He was later to send forth into a world rotting with paganism, to carry His Word to the ends of the earth, even to the end of time. Humanly speaking, it would almost seem that Our Lord, in selecting those who were to be the first preachers of His Gospel, would have crossed over to the cultured Greeks and sought out the renowned philosophers of the day. Their fame and their learning would have seemed a sound basis on which Christianity could rise. Their brilliance might have added luster to their mission. Or again, considering the question from the standpoint of human standards, one might think that Our Lord would have gone even farther—across the seas to Rome to enlist the might and the prestige of Empire. But Our Lord, to confound mere human thinking, chose instead poor humble men to be His first ambassadors. "Passing by the Sea of Galilee, He saw Simon and Andrew his brother, casting nets into the sea. And Jesus said to them: 'Come after Me, and I will make you to become fishers of men.' . . . And going on from thence a little farther, He saw James the son of Zebedee and John his brother, who also were mending their nets in the ship. And forthwith He called them. And leaving their father Zebedee in the ship, they followed Him."

It is to this chosen band of Apostles that Our Lord will one day say, "Going, therefore, teach ye all nations—teaching them to observe all things whatsoever I have commanded you." What were the things that these humble men were commissioned to teach? No mere human philosophy was to be the burden of their message to the world. They were called to teach men to know, love, and serve God. They were to teach men how to live in peace and justice, honesty and charity. They were to proclaim the primacy of the things of God and to make known in clear and certain terms that this life on earth is but a passing phase of Man's existence, and that the years of mortal life are given to him in order that he may reach his eternal destiny—a place with God and the Angels and the Saints in Heaven. It was not an easy way of life that they were to announce as the price of Heaven's joy. They were to teach men the duty of self-sacrifice and self-denial as the price of God's friendship, and that happiness is to be obtained even in this world, not by rejecting but by accepting the Cross of Christ.

Remarkable indeed are the powers that Our Lord will bestow upon His Apostles and their successors, powers that otherwise belong essentially to God alone. "Receive the Holy Ghost," He will one day say to them, "whose sins you shall forgive, they are forgiven them." Our Saviour thus provided a means for healing the wounds of Society. Our Lord will call His apostolic group "the salt of the earth" and "the light of the world." He will give them a divine assurance that through their ministry He Himself will speak and act. "He that heareth you, heareth Me." At the Last Supper, He will address to them words of unparalleled beauty and tenderness as He tells them of His particular love for them and reminds them that charity must always be the distinguishing characteristic of their lives. "By this shall all men know that you are My Disciples, if you have love one for another." He does not hide from them the sufferings that they will be called upon to undergo for His sake. "The disciple is not greater than His Master," He tells them. "If they have persecuted Me, they will also persecute you. The world hateth you, but know ye that it hath hated Me before you." To them He will give that magnificent promise of His perennial assistance in the discharge of their apostolic ministry. "Behold, I am with you all days even to the consummation of the world."

We see, therefore, how the Son of God placed in the world men who in very truth would speak in His Name and whose mission would endure to the end of time, safeguarded by His Own special protection. The teaching office of the Church, therefore, is of Heaven and owes its origin to Jesus Christ. It is for this reason that we are able to explain the wondrous works that the teaching office of the Church has accomplished in the world from the dawn of Christianity and the sweet fruits of sanctity with which it has adorned the passing years. It is Jesus Christ Himself Who lives and acts and teaches through this sublime office. If the holy and noble enterprises expand and grow to be powerful instruments for good under the guidance of the teaching office of the Church, it is because Jesus Christ speaks and operates through those called upon to exercise this teaching function. History is the witness to the purifying and sanctifying effects not only of the immediate Apostles of Christ but of those who succeeded them. St. Paul preaches to the cultured Greeks and, ere long, Christian communities spring up in the Aegean Archipelago. St. Peter establishes the Church in Antioch and, later, in Rome where he died, a martyr on Vatican Hill, not many miles from the spot where his great co-laborer, the Apostle of the Gentiles, was beheaded. Asia Minor, the shores of North Africa, parts of Gaul, Italy, even far-off Spain are lit up with the torch of Truth carried by those brave men who were the first Christian teachers. Soon, we find St. Augustine converting England to the Christian faith. St. Patrick brings the Irish into the Christian fold. St. Boniface tames the fierce Teutons. St. Benedict begins his glorious apostolate, sending out from Monte Cassino saintly men who set up schools alongside their churches and gave an impetus to learning and culture that still endures. What words could adequately describe the profound effects in human society created by men like St. John Chrysostom, St. Gregory Nazianzen, St. Athanasius, and St. Augustine, Bishop of Hippo? Later on, St. Francis of Assisi fills the whole world with the fame of his sanctity and establishes an Order which, for six hundred years, has brought blessings on the Church. Who can praise enough the soldier, St. Ignatius Loyola, and his noble band of Christian champions? Even today, in the cruel, sinful world in which we live, there are countless numbers of saintly men and women leading heroic lives of virtue, sweetening the world in which they live because they listen to the Voice of the Church and abide by her teachings.

The tree is known by its fruits, as Our Lord Himself said, and it is a matter of history that, wherever the teachings of the Apostles and their successors were accepted and put into practice, peace and happiness reigned. They met with astonishing success. Armed with nothing but the Word of God and His Grace, they advanced from country to country, crossing mountains and seas and deserts in obedience to the divine command to "Teach all nations." Their work was truly revolutionary in the very best sense. They met cruelty and they tamed it into gentleness and charity. Sensuality gave place to decency. They found slaves and they turned them into free men. The frontiers of barbarism they pushed back ever farther and farther and, under the spell of their preaching, the black night of paganism gave way to the bright day of Christianity.

Everywhere, cruel tyrants—prototypes of the modern dictators—strove with might and main, with fire and sword and every form of torment, to bar their way. The prison cell could not stop them. Chained and handcuffed, even crucified like St. Andrew, they continued to preach Christ and Him Crucified, and to save souls to Christ. They surmounted every difficulty, undaunted by obstacles, unterrified by threats of torture, and, calm even in the face of death, they remained faithful to their God-given tasks so that, even as early as the year 100, God's Holy Word had been preached from Spain in the West to India in the East, and all through a large section of Modern Europe and the Northern Coast of Africa. In view of such success it is to be remembered that this gigantic task was performed by poor and humble men. Our Lord's Apostles were not conspicuous for learning or prestige. Certainly, they had no renown in the world nor did they have the wealth of empire or the force of arms to aid them. Surely their achievement was divine, for we can attribute it to no mere human influence.

Let us come now to our own day. Paganism has come back. It is no longer the dumb paganism of the decrepit age of the Roman Empire, but the clever paganism of diabolical genius. A cruel barbarity has prevailed. The slaves of the dictators can be counted by the millions. Chained and imprisoned and starving in concentration camps are God's ministers, and holy men and women who have chosen to follow conscience rather than bow down to tyranny. Darkness covers the face of the earth. But are we to be terrified by all this? Indeed not, nor are we to say, as some have said, that the Church has failed in her mission. The Church has not failed but, rather, men have failed her because they have rejected her voice and have refused to accept her teachings—those teachings expressed in a few words by Our Lord Himself when He said, "Thou shalt love the Lord, Thy God, with thy whole heart and with thy whole mind and with thy whole soul and with all thy strength, and thou shalt love thy neighbor as thyself." If we deplore the momentary triumph of darkness over light, of hatred over love, and of strength over meekness, it is because the Lord Jesus Christ and His Word have been rejected and mocked and scorned.

Our Lord tested the faith of His Apostles when He slept whilst the boat in which they were sailing was tossed about by the raging tempest. Our Lord is testing our faith today and He says to us, as once He said to His Apostles, "Why are ye affrighted, oh ye of little faith?" We venture to say also that our generation is being punished for the way it has forsaken God. Our Lord tells us that He is "the Way, the Truth, and the Life," and St. Paul makes plain that "there is no other foundation on which men should build except Christ Jesus."

But what have we been witnessing in our day? A growing spirit of irreligion that finds its roots in the abandonment of belief in the authority of God and His Church. Educators in high places have driven God from the schools. Statesmen have devised their theory of government in com plete disregard of Him Who said, "Render unto Caesar the things that are Caesar's, and unto God the things that are God's." Many of our men of science, departing from the procedure of authentic science, have proclaimed that there is no God. Schemes of social reform have been invented that are based on immoral premises. Little wonder if the evil tree has yielded evil fruits and that we, today, must taste their bitterness.

How is the tremendous and frightening monster of modern evil genius to be overcome? People talk of the "New Order" and of the "New World" that is being born. They are planning for a kind of civilization that will follow the present terrible conflict in which the entire world is engaged. The modern paganism, terrible though it appears to be, will be overcome by the same means by which its ancient prototype was overthrown. The world needs, as it never needed before, stouthearted, generous, self-sacrificing, apostolic men and women in every country who will not be afraid to put into practice in their own lives, and to preach to others by word and example, the pure teachings of Our Lord and Saviour, Jesus Christ. There can be no other way, no other solution. Change seems to be the order of the day, but Our Lord's plan for human living does not change. He said, "Heaven and earth will pass away but My Word will not pass away." The New Order and the New World, about which there is so much talk, will have sound and lasting value only if they are based on the eternal truths of God's Holy Law.

In the midst of the frantic search for a formula for the peace and security of the postwar world, let it not be forgotten that in this twentieth century the Voice of Christ, the Prince of Peace, rings out just as clearly as when He spoke to the multitude on the hillsides of Galilee. Our Lord still speaks to the world through those whom He has sent. Time does not change God's plan for the salvation of the world. It is the unhappy style today, so different from the Ages of Faith, to belittle the part that religion should play not only in the lives of individuals, but also in the lives of nations and in the great family of nations that makes up our contemporary world. "I am the Way, the Truth, and the Life," says Our Lord. And again, "He that followeth Me walketh not in darkness."

No one, be he king or peasant, president or plain citizen, capitalist or laborer, can claim exemption from the moral necessity of seeking the foundation of the New Order and the solution of all social and international problems, no matter what their nature, in the teachings of Our Lord and Saviour, Jesus Christ. There is no sense in talking about allowing each nation access to the raw materials of the world, so necessary for modern living, unless charity and justice, as taught by Our Lord, motivate the world's statesmen. There is no use in speaking of equal and proportionate opportunities for all nations and racial groups, large or small, unless the Charity of Christ be allowed to play its part in international relations. International conferences, meetings, councils, wheresoever held,

108

will labor in vain unless Christ, through His representatives, be present. "Unless the Lord build the city, they labor in vain who keep it."

No merely human plan will suffice for the peace and order of the postwar world. We have been surfeited with human schemes and plans. Never were there more schemes in the world, and yet never was there more widespread ignorance of the things of God. We have tried to have morale without morality, and religion without God, and humanitarianism without charity, and what has been the result? Nothing but class hatred within the nations and international hatred amongst them. "Thou shalt hate" has taken the place of the words "Thou shalt love."

Above all else, the postwar life of the world must be grounded on charity. The Old Testament and the New insist on every page on this fundamental virtue. "A new commandment I give unto you," said Our Lord, "that you love one another as I have loved you. . . . Thou shalt love thy neighbor as thyself." In the words of St. Paul, "There remain Faith, Hope, and Charity, but the greatest of these is Charity." And again, "If I speak with the tongues of men and of angels and have not charity, I am become as sounding brass or a tinkling cymbal. And if I should have prophecy, and should know all mysteries and all knowledge, and if I should have all faith so that I could remove mountains, and have not charity, I am nothing. Charity is patient, is kind; charity envieth not, dealeth not perversely, is not puffed up, is not ambitious, seeketh not her own, is not provoked to anger, yieldeth no evil, rejoiceth not in iniquity, but rejoiceth with the truth."

Man has tried in vain to live without God and the result has been disastrous. Why doesn't he try the opposite? In the midst of the tears that are now flowing and with the blood that is being shed on scores of battlefields, in the midst of mankind's anguish and heartbreak, it is to be hoped that we have learned our lesson and that, after the victory has been won, as certainly it must and will be won, there will be indeed a New Order, but based on the old truth that "We must first seek the Kingdom of God and His Justice," and that we must love the Lord God with our whole heart and mind and soul and with all our strength, and our neighbor as ourselves. Away with the hatred that has set race against race, class against class, nation against nation! We are all children of God. We are all the objects of His love. Why, therefore, should we not love one another as God has loved us? Why should we hate when it is so much easier to love? It is true that this life since Eden was never intended to be a Paradise. At the same time, it is true that it is not God's Will that there should be so much suffering and sadness and grief, and so many hearts that are breaking. It's a note of gladness that has sounded again and again, in the Old Testament and the New, a vibrant note of joy and peace and happiness. "My peace I give you," Our Lord tells us, and St. Paul says, "Rejoice in the Lord always. Again, I say, Rejoice." It is a happy and peaceful world that we wish to build when the war is over, and it will be such a world if the false prophets who led men astray in the past have no part in its rebuilding.

A task that awaits the Church after the war—one to which she has never been a stranger because it is part of her God-given mission to have pity on all those that suffer—is to assuage the great sorrow of mothers, wives and families who have lost loved ones in battle. Even now, as casualties are reported, it is to the Church that the bereaved look for that spiritual consolation that only a lively faith can give. God has ways of mending even broken hearts, and He exercises this merciful ministry through His Church. Everyone who visits a military hospital these days cannot but be deeply touched by the compassion and solicitude of the chaplains for the victims of war. Through the day, and even through the night, they go from bed to bed like ministering angels, like other Christs, indeed like Him who had compassion on the multitude, bringing cheer and spiritual comfort to the actual victims of war.

Out in civilian life, God's anointed ministers are doing everything in their power to bring courage and patience to relatives and friends of those who have been struck down in battle. By letter, by personal visits, by sermons, by administration of the sacraments, they are doing everything possible to lessen the grief of those who are left to mourn in this vale of tears. To them they hold out the bright hope that Christian faith can give, namely, that the separation wrought by death is only temporary and that those who weep will see again in a better life than this those whom the Angel of Death has taken from them. It is the precious duty of the Church to bid her children look up to Christ, even through a mist of tears, and to find in Him, and in Him alone, the only source of consolation.

There is a picture by Hoffman entitled, "Christ, the Consoler." It portrays a young man throwing himself, tired and exhausted, on the Bosom of Christ. That young man represents all of us today, tired, exhausted. Worn out by the cares and sorrows and the seething hatreds that we have experienced, we come to rest on the Bosom of Christ. He lets us throw our arms about Him as He, in turn, enfolds us. We have found that we cannot live without Our Lord. There is no peace, there is no true life apart from Him. God grant that all the world may harken to the Voice of Him Who said, two thousand years ago, and Who repeats it still today, "Come to Me all you who labor and are heavily burdened and I will refresh you."

four Sermons: on Denmark, God, and the War

REVEREND KAJ MUNK *

Late Pastor of the Lutheran Church, Vedersø, Denmark

WHEN PASTOR KAJ MUNK was murdered by his enemies, they thought he was silenced. But a martyr is never silenced. His death may stir the Danish Christians even more than his sermons.

Munk, whose baptismal name was Kaj Petersen, was born January 13, 1898, at Maribo, Lolland, Denmark. His father was a tanner by profession. He lost both parents while still a small boy, and when he was seven he was adopted by the Munks. As he grew up and proved alert and quick at learning, it became a tacit understanding that he was to use his gifts and talents as a clergyman.

Kaj Munk was a great poet and dramatist, but he was, nevertheless, always the preacher. His sermons reveal keenness and force, deep evangelical fervor, and a love of Denmark and its people. Other men became more careful in their speech, but the uncompromising spirit of Munk did not change. "We clergymen," he said, "exist to proclaim the Word and not to keep silent. To compromise with unrighteousness would have the most serious consequences for the country and its people."

When Denmark revolted in August, 1943, Munk's heart rejoiced. It was to a great extent the result of his preaching. He was arrested in the Fall of 1943, but at Christmas he was released to return to his wife and five children at Vedersø.

He was taken from his home again on January 4, 1944, by the Nazis, and the next day his body was found in a ditch by the roadside not far from Silkeborg. He had been shot through the head. His funeral was held at Vedersø with over four thousand people in attendance. (The foregoing adapted from the notes of J. M. Jensen.)

H. Skov Nielsen wrote of Munk, "The entire Scandinavian world was shocked and saddened at the news of the tragic death of the famous Danish patriot and author" who "had so fearlessly challenged . . . the brutal sway . . . of the Nazi power." Munk wrote with a "vigorous, challenging style" and freely used "modern colloquial terms."

There was an immediacy about his sermons that drove men to action. The four sermons are given in a composite as one, but roman numerals indicate the division points. The sermons came out of Denmark

* By permission of the Lutheran Publishing House, Blair, Nebraska, and John M. Jenson. Translated from the Danish by Mr. Jenson.

111

via the Underground and arrived unexpectedly after the manuscript for this book was complete. Therefore, another good Lutheran, Dr. Samuel Trexler, offered to withdraw his sermon to make room for Kaj Munk's message.

Munk reminds us in his sermons that John was ever on his way to be beheaded for his faith and that Jesus was ever on His way to the Cross. From the day the Nazis occupied Denmark, he too was on his way to a martyr's death.

Sermon Sixteen

TEXT: *John said unto Herod, "It is not lawful for thee to have thy brother's wife."* MARK 6:18

I. Christ and John the Baptist

"Truth cannot be pickled."

OHN WAS NOT A VERY CAUTIOUS MAN. HE BElieved in the truth.

King Herod was committing adultery. The Baptist called on him and told him to stop it.

He risked his life by doing so. And, more than that, he was in danger of provoking rebellion and civil war. It might even stir up the Romans, who could use this as a pretext to mix in the internal affairs of the country. This could have bloody consequences for the whole Jewish people.

Why, then, did not John keep silent? That would have been far more sensible and considerate.

Well, would it?

John was possessed of a burning faith—the faith that truth is to be preached.

There are people who believe that truth can be salted down. That it can be pickled, to be taken from the jar and used when convenient.

They are mistaken. Truth cannot be pickled. It is found only in living form, and it must be used the moment it appears. If not used it dies and decays, and it soon becomes destructive. The most dangerous of all lies is dead truth.

John the Baptist was a man of flesh and blood. But John was not merely a man of flesh and blood. He was also a man of spirit—of the Spirit of God, the Spirit of Truth. Therefore he had not the slightest faith in the idea that truth can exist hermetically sealed.

The day came when he was convinced that the time for action was at hand. He said to himself: Now the truth demands of me to be put into action. His heart beat fast. But within that jittery heart there was a great

112

peace. In his troubled heart there was a great calm. It gave him strength to utter the few but sufficient words: "It is not lawful for thee to have her."

"Peace be with you" is the greeting of the Church. We sing in one of our hymns of the peace that is "more than angel watch." And every Sunday we pastors stand before the altar and lift our hands upon the congregation (to make it as emphatic as possible) saying: "The Lord lift up His countenance upon thee and give thee peace." It is a great error to think that this "peace" means fare you well, live well, sleep well, and have a good time; God will see to it that you always have rubbers to wear in the slush. No, the peace of God means that the soul is at rest. Be it ever so jittery, it has found a place of rest in its relationship to the truth. Rest is a difficult word; for truth is ever on the march. Rest in this connection means, therefore, to march together with truth.

That is the peace which protected John when he appeared before Herod. It could not protect his body, but it gave him poise and dignity for all time.

The Bible speaks of John's time in such a way that his time becomes our time. Alas! The Bible is such a primitive book. It is quite out of place in diplomatic circles, and too uncouth for the propaganda ministry. But we have to take it as it is; there is nothing we can do about it. This event in the life of John the Baptist took place in ancient times and in a distant land. But it is also taking place in Denmark today.

Among us too there are good men who possess this burning faith in the truth to be proclaimed. They do not believe in truth as a stored substance. They cannot go about pretending, and look away from the truth. They are of flesh and blood, as was John; and they too know fear—fear of their own fate, fear of the tragedy that truth may bring down upon our people. But some day they will understand that cowardice must not make them tongue-tied; and that the tragedy which hypocrisy, silence, and lying bring upon a people will, in the course of time, be a thousand-fold more fateful.

Therefore the great peace fills their hearts, as it filled the heart of John, when they appear before the Herod of *our* native land and reproach him for his adultery.

For in our nation too there is a Herod who flirts with the idols—the spirit of compromise which for the sake of personal well-being permits itself unseemly conduct. Herod could marshal many excuses for his transgression. He was in love with this woman, and it is honorable for a man to be ruled by a great emotion. It gave him strength to perform his regal duties, and thus it was of benefit to the whole royal house as well as to the nation. In the final analysis it was only for the sake of the people that he compromised with lawlessness. The people were satisfied, and all was peaceful now. That was more than could be expected in such turbulent times when the enemy was in the land. Really, there was much to be thankful for.

And then this "ox" from the desert presented something so insignificant as the truth. He wanted to butt his head against the wall, and tumble the whole structure so painstakingly erected by Herod and so laboriously maintained.

It is worthy of note that the Baptist did not enter into any discussion with the slimy lizard. He simply said to him: "It is not lawful for thee to have her."

John wielded the ax of righteousness. Herod was but a tiny branch on the great tree of evil. But, great or small, judgment had been pronounced. The sprout* had to be cut off.

His Majesty, naturally, did not argue with John. He ordered handcuffs. Thus it has always been. Truth has the word at its command; error has sword and chains. And error continued to delude itself, even to the belief that it is the stronger of the two.

Now John was in prison. He had delivered his message. In the darkness of his dungeon he sensed the sword hanging over his head. But in his heart was the peace of God, the approval of a good conscience.

I readily admit that I do not understand why Jesus did not go to the friend of His youth in prison, and in some way try to help him. But who am I to criticize the Christ! There must have been something John had to fight through by himself. Can it be in the nature of truth that at times it makes a man very lonely?

But I am happy for what Jesus said to the people about the imprisoned and fallen prophet. Jesus defended His friend. He threw Himself into the breach for John with all His untried authority: "Though he be weak now, do not forget what he was and what he did in his strength." He was not a reed shaken in the wind. He did not straddle the issue. Go to the Rigsdag [the Danish legislative assembly] if you would see that sort of men.

And now Salome danced in the king's house. There was great merriment. It was a New Year's ball, and the entire palace had been transformed into "A Night in Hullabaloo."

Then, between dances, and to the accompaniment of orchestral strains, they brought in the Prophet's head on a platter.

Herod, Herod, are you so great an idiot as to think you serve the good powers of life with this evil game—that it can lead to anything but corrup-

---

* The Danish work used is "Kvistling," obviously a word-play referring to the Norwegian traitor Quisling.

114

tion of soul, and to ruin and damnation for yourself and your misguided people?

And you, my countrymen, who have been cast into prison because you found yourselves compelled by the voice of truth, I pray that you may be strong, and faithful to that inner conviction of having done the right. If there be those among you who are doubtful and uncertain, I absolve you from that sin on behalf of my Lord, as He forgave John. I assure you that He will judge you by your efforts in the cause of truth while some lied and others were silent. You have helped create the spirit out of which alone a sound future can grow. From the church let it be said to you: The Lord of truth has let His face shine upon you. May He grant you His peace! Amen.

II. The Christ Child and Stephen

"Let men stop being beasts. . . ."

E HAVE HEARD A NUMBER OF SERMONS ADVISING us how to obtain our share of Christmas joy: "If you are lonely and sorrowful, troubled with doubts and anxious thoughts, come, my friend, and kneel at the manger, and the manger Child will give you His peace and a share in the heavenly joy." To this we may briefly say that Jesus did not come to make us happy. God has not appointed Himself an entertainment committee. It may be true that to know Christ is to be truly happy. But if you want to know Christ in order to further your own well-being you are guilty of sacrilege.

Many nominal Christians place Santa Claus and the pastor on the same level. The vesper service is only a part of the sweets that belong to a good Christmas Eve. Among other pleasant things of the occasion we must have the sweet little story of the Infant Jesus, and afterwards two tea-spoonfuls of harmless Ingemann poetry to melodies that spark and sputter like spruce needles when ignited by the Christmas candles. And if there is a soul who sits in church with a heavy heart—well, then there is the pastor to help and comfort him.

What a fatal misunderstanding! It is not the pastor's business, primarily, to comfort people, nor is that the first aim of the gospel. The preacher and the gospel are here to make hell hot for folks. They can comfort one another, and they can comfort themselves. The preacher and the gospel are to bring people face to face with the realities of life; that is to make hell hot. Until that has happened they have no use for heaven.

That the church is ignored by so many, as something that doesn't concern them, is often because preachers speak of things that seem absolutely

115

useless to them. They feel as when someone tries to trick them into a bad deal. They live well inland, far from streams of any kind, and here we come breathlessly dragging cement with which to build bridges.

"Glory be to God in the highest, and on earth peace, good will toward men." That was the angels' song. What does it mean? Did the angels bring those gifts that night? No and yes. They did not deliver them magically finished. The world was not, all of a sudden, filled with godliness, peace, and good will.

It must be understood that the gifts were like weapons dropped by parachute. Fear of God, peace, and love of neighbor were brought by Christ to His disciples for use as weapons with which to conquer the world. And afterwards they were to teach the nations how to use them.

The Christ Child is the world's Saviour and Prince of Peace because He is the world's greatest war Lord. Jesus Himself took an interest in family life, and He attended parties; but He was, nevertheless, ever on His way to the cross. Let us sing Ingemann songs and eat goose and play with our children about the glittering Christmas tree; but we must never forget that the coming of Christ to earth means dauntless struggle against evil. And if we kneel by the manger in other than sentimental moods, we shall become aware that one hand of the little Child is open and kindly, the other clenched in blood.

The Christian's Christmas joy is in the privilege of being where the battle is fiercest, in proud consciousness of having been sent to the front. Jesus came as a gift to men that God's front might be established here on earth. He is Saviour of the world only to the extent that He conquers the world. Christianity is full of incredible things. The Trinity, the Virgin Birth, Baptism, and the Lord's Supper are only some of them. But most incredible of all is it that God has use for *me*. It is so incredible that it would be blasphemy had not God Himself said that He needs me. Such "nonsense" is life's profoundest wisdom.

To be a Christian means to belong to Christ, without being able to give reasons why. Not for fear of hell. Not to get a share in heaven. As parents are attached to their children, as man is drawn to woman, and as the most intimate friendship always has a mystic element, such is the Christian's relation to his Saviour. The Christmas gospel tells of the birth of One whose mystically radiant personality attracted a group of friends who endured through all vicissitudes, ever increasing from century to century, and whose high purpose is to make the whole world subject to Him—driven by His love and led by His power. True Christmas joy, no matter how much or how little of it you may comprehend, means that you have Christ, and that you go where He wants you to go.

Poor Christian world, how little of Christianity you have grasped at times! If Christianity brings no joy, it is musty. Without ever having

116

done the work of God it demands the benefits of God. How can you, my good man, expect God to give you joy when you never try to give your neighbor any?

Give God honor. Death and destruction to those who cause the world's wars! Let the work of peace prosper. Let men stop being beasts and go forward toward becoming men in God's image. Amen.

III. Christ and Denmark

"Jesus . . . who compels me."

IT IS NEW YEAR'S DAY—NOT FOR THE CHURCH BUT for the world. The church has its own New Year, the first Sunday in Advent. The first of January is no church holiday. It may well be called a holiday in a worldly sense. Our thoughts go from the church out to the world about us, to our native land. A new year comes to Denmark today. How has the old year been? What will the new year bring?

Many Christians will say: We thank God that we were kept out of the war the past year. Certainly, I, too, love my home, my house, my bodily well-being, my wife and children. I, too, would despair to see my home in ruin, and my children lying about maimed in the midst of dust and debris. Yet there are two things which I, God help me, would even less like to see: truth betrayed and my country without honor.

I cannot join in thanking God that we have been kept out of war. In the first place we have not been kept out of war. Our country has suffered occupation. What this may come to mean in terms of blood and fire, in bombing attacks and invasion, no one knows. And, secondly, you can't thank God that He helped you cheat in a horse trade. God demanded that we fight. We failed to obey His command. We failed to carry out our own decision. You must not mock God by thanking Him that the devil takes care of his own.

Do I exaggerate? No, he who fails God puts himself in the devil's hands. We are not heeding our call and destiny. Denmark is under the wrath of God. That's why we are so well off.

We have shirked our duty. We let others bleed for our guilt and for our cause. We have sold our souls to the evil spirit of compromise and have written the contract in the blood of others. That's how we come to be so lucky.

The pen burns my hand like a hot iron as I write these words. But I must speak out—because I am a Christian man, because I occupy a pulpit,

117

because the gospel for today mentions the name Jesus. He it is who compels me.

Where is our people's struggle for the faith we proclaim? Where is its contribution toward victory for the ideals we cherish?

Do not believe the politicians when they flatter you. True, there are many good and honorable men among them. Danish legislators are fully as good as those of other countries when it comes to clean hands. But they fail to see their task as one of leadership; they permit themselves to be led. Do not trust them. They have an ax to grind.

Do not trust the men of the Folk High Schools. Alas, where is the red faith and white wrath of the Folk High School in this black night! There are Folk High Schools from which come the sound of *Skræp,** and God be praised for them. But as a rule such schools have hard going.

Do not trust too much in the preachers. As a rule they are poorly paid. They are brought up as humanists. They have forgotten—or never learned —what Christianity is. They imbibed lo-o-o-ve with the bottle milk in the cradle. In a world of men they too often plead the cause of the effeminate. They "abstain from politics." They preach peace at any price for the uplift of the devil, who rejoices to see evil develop in peace. The Scriptures do not say: When your neighbor is smitten on one cheek it is your duty to hold him so that he may be smitten on the other cheek also. Do not trust the preachers until they wake up and remember that they are servants of the whole Gospel, and of the Prince of Peace who came not to bring peace but a sword.

And do not trust the majority, which likes to take things easy and therefore is easy to please. The great masses feel happy when their leaders praise them for self-discipline, matchless unity, and high culture. How much of the discipline is cowardice? Is the vaunted unity anything but inertia? And is their high culture other than fawning before him who kicks open the door to their dwelling? Do not trust the great neglected masses. I believe that the heart of the nation is strong, but it has become encased in fat. Our people are like spoiled children. When has there appeared among us a real will, with courage to demand something of us? Our greatest contemporary poet, whose books are best sellers, fills people with sunny tales of how well things always end in this wonderful world of ours. And one of our most popular lyric writers, one of the really great, nourished our people on such as this:

> Dingelinge lay,
> Dingeli and play,
> And dingelinge lay.

* Name of sword with which Prince Uffe defeated enemies from the South.

118

Have we, then, done nothing at all to meet our fate as men? Yes, we arranged some meetings for young people, to which a number of old people came, sang some national songs and then went home, feeling that they had done their full patriotic duty.

And now our nation has permitted itself to become so powerless that good men in high office can be forced out, and others in whom we have no faith at all take their places. Meanwhile our police force has grown to prodigious proportions, and our courts often seem to have forgotten the law to remember the laws.

There are so many who draw back, and so few that dare come forth. Those who scorn us can truly say that the free Danish people has, without one stroke of the sword, permitted itself to become enslaved. "Better a slave in the ashes than a hero in the cemetery."

On every festive occasion a speaker will open the evening's program with some vague phrase about the difficult conditions under which we live, and express the pious hope that we may soon regain our freedom and independence. After that they eat and drink and frolic most merrily. The youth of other lands—well, their bodies rot on the battlefield; but the souls of our young people rot in the dance halls.

We don't dare demand seriousness of them, for we are not ourselves prepared to become serious. We are steeped to our necks in materialism, and we haven't the slightest faith in the word of Christ that the soul is of greater importance than the body.

And the men who protest, men who really want to do something; they who know that our youth will become demoralized if they are forced into a passive state; and that the country is cheated of its future when men think only of the present; they who resist double dealing—what happens to them? Their own countrymen, at the behest of strangers, drag them to prison, though it flaunts our free constitution and outrages our people's sense of right and justice. So many of Denmark's best men and women have already been attacked, deported, exiled, that it may well be said we have civil war on our hands.

Henrik Ibsen wanted to teach the Norwegian people to be great in their thinking. Our poets and leaders have taught us only to prate and to beg. "Too bad about compulsory military training. . . . It is not right that young people are asked to abstain until they are married." We were Europe's most highly favored people, and yet we always pitied ourselves and bemoaned our very existence.

Great in their thinking! Did Ibsen succeed in teaching his people? Yes, behold his nation today. Their courage and power light the world. How the Danish Church has admired that of our brother nation for its erect bearing and clear thinking! The Finnish people and the Norwegian people are no greater than we—and yet how much greater!

What have we Danes to cling to? Our historic past? That is of no value unless it lives in us today. Our free constitution? That is of value only to a people highly resolved to respect it, and who demand that it be respected. Our king? He is no longer young, and illness and accident have been hard on him. Yet he is our rallying symbol, and he has our wholehearted devotion. But he is only one; and who are the men about him?

Our old nation needs a rejuvenating power, God's rejuvenating strength, that a new people may come forth, which is yet the old, worthy sons of the fathers. The gospel will have to teach the Danish nation to think as a great people; to choose honor rather than profit, freedom rather than a well paid guardianship; to believe in the victory of the spirit of sacrifice; to believe that life comes out of death, and that the future comes out of giving oneself; in short, faith in Christ. What would it profit a people if it gained all the advantages of the world but lost its soul?

The cross in our flag—it is long since we realized that it stands for something, and we have forgotten that now. And yet it is the cross that characterizes the flags of the North. We have come to church—the few of us who go to church, and we have heard about the cross, about Christ's example of suffering, and Christ's words about self-denial and struggle. We have thought that this was all to be taken in a spiritual sense, and that it did not pertain to our time. We thought we were Christians when we sat in church and sang Amen. But No! No! We are Christians only when we go out into the world and say No to the devil, renounce all his works and all his ways, and say Yes to the Holy Spirit.

Today, on the first day of the new year, we ask you here from the church, you men of the Danish government—if you truly desire to govern a Christian people—that you, in the year before us, act in the spirit of the power and love of Christ. We know that your task is titanic; but if you follow the Spirit of God, then He who is stronger than all the titans will give you fortitude, wisdom, and strength.

Our people are becoming more and more divided into rich and poor. You must persecute without mercy the wealth that comes of the war. You must tax those who take blood money and compel them to divide their profits with the tens of thousands who suffer from the high cost of living and the swindle of substitutes. You must erect a barricade about our youth, who are becoming more perverse and vulgar day by day. You must call to account parents who fail to guard their children against vermin and social disease, and against the vicious night life that threatens to ruin them for all time. You must be faithful to the God-given ideals of democracy; do not coerce conscience; do not use violence against religions other than those of violence; give every man access to honest

120

justice; shun as the plague any persecution of defenseless ones. And do not forget you are guardians of the crown jewels of a thousand-year-old realm. You are to guard them not only today but for a thousand years to come. The three largest and most precious of the jewels are honor, honor, honor. Guard these first, last, and always. If you cannot preserve them it were better that you did not exist.

The snow is melting, the fog is clearing away; and before us lies a land that will soon be green again. We love it, oh so much; for it is Denmark. We love it for the bravery of Rolfe, for the foresight of Thyra, for the Viking-Christianity of Absalom, for Margaret's nobility of soul, for the faithful work of Christian IV, for the faith and perseverance of South Jutland farmers, for our mother's toil-worn hands, for our loved one's midsummer night kiss. We love it for its open, cheerful capital, for Funen's unique beauty and for Jutland's English hue, for all its jabbering islets, and for the ocean that is our empire—from the River to the ends of the earth.

And we love our country when she prospers and laughs, and tells the world tales that are true; but we love her most when she lies prostrate in shame—because—because *we* failed. Oh, mother, forgive us!

Millenniums lie before us. Shall our children and their children think of this period—and of us—in such a way that we must blush in our graves?

No. Therefore we pray: Give us Christianity, give us courage and faith to rise out of despondency and fickleness to will only that which is right, no matter what the cost. Betrayal of ideals is alone enough to ruin land and people. May we have courage again to become loyal to that in which we believe—though the prisons be filled to the point of bursting. Those who have willingly let their necks be shaven in honor of the Philistines will have to pull the grinders in Gaza till their hair grows out again.

Lead us, thou cross in our flag, lead us into that Nordic struggle where shackled Norway and bleeding Finland fight against an idea which is directly opposed to all our ideas. Lead old Denmark forth to its new spirit. Not by the grace of others, or their promises, shall Dannebrog again become a free banner. For freedom only God can give; and He gives it only to those who accept its responsibilities. Lead us, cross in our flag, forward toward unity with other flags of the cross. With honor and liberty regained, the old Denmark in the young North—that vision looms before us this New Year's Day. We who have the vision will give ourselves to its realization. We promise we will. May God hear our vow and add His Amen!

IV. God and Caesar

"Christianity takes orders from nobody."

N THE GOSPEL OF ST. MATTHEW IT IS WRITTEN of Jesus:

Then went the Pharisees and took counsel how they might entangle him in his talk. And they sent out unto him their disciples, with the Herodians, saying, Master, we know that thou art true, and teachest the way of God in truth, neither carest thou for any man: for thou regardest not the person of men. Tell us therefore, What thinkest thou? Is it lawful to give tribute unto Caesar, or not? But Jesus perceived their wickedness, and said, Why tempt ye me, ye hypocrites? Shew me the tribute money. And they brought unto him a penny. And he saith unto them, Whose is this image and superscription? They say unto him, Caesar's. Then saith he unto them, Render therefore unto Caesar the things which are Caesar's; and unto God the things that are God's. When they had heard these words, they marvelled, and left him, and went their way.

We know now that the Herodians and Pharisees formed some kind of Coalition Government. The two parties had little in common, except their hatred of Christ. See how politely they approach Him—they are obviously men of culture! "Master, we know that thou art true, and teachest the way of God in truth, neither carest thou for any man: for thou regardest not the person of men." How finely they express themselves—we are almost moved to tears!

There is one peculiar thing about all men of such mettle. When they think they are lying, what they tell in fact is the pure and simple truth. And when they imagine they are telling the truth, one is safe in assuming that they are telling lies.

The Emperor may ask much of us: our money, our labor, our health, the best years of our youth, our lives.

But if he demanded that we should call black white, tyranny liberty, violence justice, we should answer: "It is written, Thou shalt have none other gods but me." And if he made the demand again, we should reply: "It is further written, Thou shalt not take the name of the Lord thy God in vain."

Let him come with his lions and his tigers, with his gallows and his stakes. That the blood of Christians is a seed, is a saying that existed as long ago as the days of the first Christian church. We conquer by our death. We must obey God before man.

Render unto Caesar those things which are Caesar's, and unto God those things that are God's. The Christian belongs to both these vast kingdoms. But if they clash, then he knows immediately to which is his greatest obligation.

Well, all this sounds very reasonable. But Christianity, we are told, *must* remain non-political. Who tells us this? Christianity takes orders from nobody. But, let's have it so. Let us say that Christianity *is* non-political. It's as true to say that Christianity is non-political as to say that it is political.

You can be a Conservative, or a Communist, or anything between the two, and at the same time be a Christian. Christianity is revealed by the *manner* in which one is a Conservative or a Communist. But it is nonsense to say that religion must keep its nose out of the affairs of this world.

Keep politics out of the church, we hear it said. We hear enough about politics on the wireless, and we read enough about it in the newspapers! Let us be free from it in God's House!

But in what manner are politics presented to us on the wireless and through the press? Perhaps in God's House we should hear about it in a different way from that to which we are accustomed outside. In God's House we expect to hear the things of this world judged in the light of God's Word.

Caesar, too, must be considered in church, and Caesar in relation to God.

There are those who would like us to believe that the Church is only a place of refuge for the soul. It is not the business, they say, of the Church to concern itself with things other than the saving of souls.

Well, that's a pretty sort of religion! If only little So-and-So can be kept out of harm's way while he's alive and find his seat in Heaven, what business of his are his neighbors of this world? Let it go to Hell! Such would certainly be a religion to the liking of Caesar! Upon such a religion he would be happy to bestow the favors of the State! For such teaching would never cross his path! Nor would it embarrass him in any way! The name of this religion is—Blasphemy!

But some people tell me the Church is a holy place. Divine service must be celebrated in an atmosphere of sublime calm. But what if such calm is obtained by subterfuge and by lies? Divine service which is afraid of the truth is the devil's service. For truth is neither calm, nor serene, nor dignified. Truth bites and scratches and strikes. Truth is of no importance to the cautious. All the cautious want is an armchair! What is the meaning of this absurd demand laid upon the Church, that it should be cautious? Was Christ cautious? Were the martyrs cautious? "Hush, hush, hush," is the watchword of the present day. Otherwise there may be serious consequences for the country and the nation! That may well be, but the way of apostasy and double dealing may be fraught with consequences even graver.

I prefer Jesus. "Hypocrites and whited sepulchres." That was what He called the political leaders of His country. "Remember me to that old fox," said He, referring to Herod, who fawned upon the Roman army of occupation in Palestine.

Things will not be better in Denmark until the Danish people have learned their lesson from the courage of Christ!

The Belgian Church and the Nazi Crisis

CARDINAL VAN ROEY,
Archbishop of Mechlin and Primate of Belgium

IN THIS SERMON, which came out of Belgium through the Underground, His Eminence, Joseph-Ernest, Cardinal Van Roey, Archbishop of Mechlin and Primate of Belgium, gives the position of the Church under the German occupation.

The Nazis have been defeated time after time by this strong, silent man, who has courageously led the Catholic Church in Belgium in a spiritual opposition to the enemy. Through his leadership the Church and the State still exist, even though the Belgian government has fallen.

Back in October of 1940, a few months after the capitulation of the Belgian Army, at a time when minds were still reeling under the influence of the blitz, Cardinal Van Roey issued a pastoral letter in which he outlined the duty of the citizen: "Nobody can forbid you to love your country. . . . Belgium is and will always be a nation and her children owe her allegiance and assistance." This letter was one of the keynotes which prompted the underground resistance of the Belgian people against the invader.

In many ways the Cardinal is the most powerful stabilizing influence in Belgium today. He protested against Sunday work enforced by the German decree of April 9, 1942, against the German seizure of the Church bells, and forbade the Clergy to celebrate Mass in the presence of groups of collaborationists in uniform or to give communion to them. When the Germans decided to deport workers for forced labor in Germany, the Cardinal, and the other Belgian Bishops, published a collective letter on October 25, 1942, condemning this new German exaction. Through such leadership Cardinal Van Roey has become the real "Pater Patriae."

This sermon was preached by the Cardinal in French in the face of Nazi spies, with the possible threat of prison over his head, during the occupation of Belgium.

125

Sermon Seventeen

Text: *Behold, I am with you all days, even to the consummation of the world.*   Matthew 28:20

IT IS OBVIOUS IN THIS HOUR OF PROFOUND MORAL crisis that the Church is exposed to grave, vital, and immediate peril. Is she to come forth victoriously from the cataclysm? The answer is that the Church can never fail; she has been given a divine promise that she will continue "even unto the consummation of the world. . . . The gates of hell shall not prevail against her." Such was the promise of our Lord to St. Peter. And this promise has been kept, as history shows, and will be kept to the end of time.

But it is important to understand that the promise is addressed to the Church as a whole. The Church will survive through the ages in spite of persecution and the disasters which befall mankind. The promise does not necessarily apply to any one country in particular; for instance, the divine promise does not contain the specific affirmation that the Catholic Church will always be maintained in Belgium, or in France, or in any other country whatsoever.

On this point people are often mistaken. To maintain the contrary would be to deny history. It is sufficient to enumerate the vicissitudes of the Church to understand at once that the promise of perpetuity was not made to the Church of any one country however Catholic or Christian.

Consider the early history of the Church. In Asia Minor, Palestine, and later in North Africa, Christianity flourished, for a time, magnificently. But the hour came when not a stone was left upon stone. Islam invaded North Africa and uprooted every remnant of ancient Christianity. And the same was the story of certain countries of the East. Persecution after persecution was unleashed upon the Church.

It is therefore clear that no Catholic country can look to the future with complete assurance. On the other hand, I believe it is true that many a nation can with good reason nourish the hope that it will survive precisely because it follows the teaching of the Catholic Church. It is difficult to conceive that Divine Providence will permit the destruction of the Catholic Church in European countries which for nineteen centuries have been the very heart of the Church. It is a great consolation to reflect upon the impossibility of any regime to persecute the Church to the point of annihilating her influence completely.

In another similar matter, I meet with confused thinking in many circles, particularly in the press. There are many—even among Catholics —who say, "After all, what does it matter to the Church what sort of government is imposed on our country after the war is over? The Church," so they say, "adapts herself to all forms of government." What are we to say of such an opinion?

Obviously we must make a distinction. The Catholic Church can adapt herself only to those forms of government which respect the liberty of the Church and the rights of conscience. But it is impossible for the Church to adapt herself to systems which deny this liberty or attempt to abrogate these rights. Moreover, the number of regimes to which the Church can adapt herself is relatively small. In the measure in which any system of government guarantees and conserves the rights of which we speak and allows the Church to fulfill her divine mission, to that extent she accepts it without opposition and adapts her work accordingly. That she cannot adapt herself to all forms of government whatsoever has been sufficiently shown by history. Has the Church, for example, adapted herself to Islamism? The answer is "No"—in fact, she was simply annihilated in all countries under Moslem rule. Can the Church then adapt itself to systems of persecution? NO!

It is nonsense then to pretend that the Church can adapt herself to *all* systems of government. The most that can be said is that the Church behaves like the human organism. A man can live in the icy regions of the North or in the torrid lands near the Equator, but there are conditions to which no man can adapt himself without being frozen or stifled to death. In the same way, man's organism can adapt itself to certain foods, but only within certain limits: he cannot eat poison!

The Church distinguishes three types of government: first, those that grant full liberty to the Church and respect the rights of conscience; second, those that merely tolerate the exercise of this liberty and of those rights; third, those that actively persecute the Church. While she naturally prefers the first type of regime, she is willing that Catholics collaborate with the second, but under no conditions can she ask her people to welcome a government of the persecuting type.

There is another opinion, even more extravagant than this. There are those who claim that a regime of the second type cannot do any harm to the Church. There are some indeed who insist that the clergy—bishops and priests—have sometimes acted beyond their rights and the limits of their spiritual mission. The Church—they say—has no other function than to guide the soul of man to its salvation. In other words, the clergy should be active only within the limits of the Church proper—the place for a priest is only at the altar, in the confessional, or in the pulpit, and even there he is restricted to the teaching of the faith.

The domain of the Church it is claimed is this: to teach faith, to administer the sacraments, to celebrate public worship. The rest is "political Catholicism." So that, if we have a government which limits the initia-

127

tive of the Episcopate and clergy, and restricts their influence, no great harm is done. This would be in full conformity with the words of our Lord, "Render therefore unto Caesar the things that are Caesar's, and unto God the things that are God's;" that is to say, give to the State what is due to the State, and to God what is due to God. Those whose duties lie in the sphere of religion are without any competence in the domain of the State.

What should we answer to that?

We see ourselves compelled to insist that we accept without reserve the words of our Lord. The Church has always held fast to this principle, but it is self-evident that this principle must be clearly understood.

In accordance with this maxim—the *total mission*—the Church claims for herself whatever belongs to God. This is revealed in the Gospel—in the whole of the Gospel. It is the truth contained in the Gospel—and all the truth contained in the Gospel; and the morality of the Gospel—and all the morality of the Gospel. To those who represent the Church our Lord entrusted the mission to teach both this truth and this morality. He confided this sacred trust to the Church and meant the Church to conserve and defend it against all those who attempt to diminish it. It is therefore not true that the functions of the Church are confined to the worship and the administration of the sacraments. She has a wider duty to perform: to teach the whole of Gospel truth and evangelical morality.

Moreover, the Church has the right to use, in the fulfillment of her mission, all natural means, that is, all the resources that have been put at the disposal of man by his Creator. Is there any reason why the Church should be barred from the resources of nature? The inventions of modern times should be at the disposal of all, both the Church and the State. Not only education, but also the press, should be available to Catholics, as to all others. And so, too, of the radio and the cinema, and all that education implies. All this the Church demands. There surely is no reason to call this "political Catholicism."

The Church must not only celebrate Holy Mass and administer the sacraments and preach the Word of God; she must share with the family the mission of intellectual and moral education. She has the right and duty of defending faith and morals against hostile propaganda. Catholics have the right to proclaim, teach, defend, and practice their religion in all its implications in regard to the individual, the family, the State, in public life, international life—and all this with all the means at the disposal of man.

When people speak of "political Catholicism," what do they mean? Are they referring to Catholic Action, or to Catholic education? Surely such activities belong to the authentic mission of the Church. In these spheres she will never renounce her right. The Church has the mission

128

to see that even in institutions of secular learning and profane science the environment is healthy and education truly Christian. That is the very *raison d'être* of the Catholic school. As to Catholic Action, what is that but the apostolate of the hierarchy extended to the faithful? That, too, is attacked under the name of political Catholicism. The Church claims the right to teach all the principles of faith and morals, the right of charity, and to spread apostolic doctrine. And she regards as a persecuting regime any government that takes this right from her.

Let us remember the example of our Saints. Saint Vincent de Paul lived in a time of terrible persecution, yet when his Congregation fearlessly entered the field of the temporal, like the divine Master, it was suspected by some of "political Catholicism." Or, take Saint John Bosco, who battled for the very existence of the poor in the streets of Turin. There he built houses for young workers, both to train them as Catholics and to teach them their trades. He did not hesitate to make use of the press, books, and pamphlets. Are we to say that he was engaged in "political Catholicism"?

In a word, to accuse the Church of "political Catholicism" is to attack her at the same time for fulfilling her function. The Church demands and will never give up her right to teach the principles of morality which concern not only the individual but also the life of society, the family, the State, the chiefs of States, kings, and powerful emperors. All are subject to the moral law in all their acts, even in the domains of national and international politics.

The Church will never renounce the right to proclaim what is just and what is unjust, to define and defend the obligations and the rights of individuals, families and states. To deny her this right is to limit a great part of the action of the Church. Let us consider—as proof of our assertion—the acts of the recent Popes. The Syllabus of Pius IX dealt with political questions; the Encyclical "Immortale Dei" of Leo XIII was on the constitution of states; Leo XIII and Pius XI handled economic and social questions in their "Rerum Novarum" and "Quadragesimo Anno." None of these problems is strictly religious, but no one can deny to the Pope the right to discuss and give directions in these matters. Pius XI published an Encyclical on marriage, "Casti Connubii," which is not properly a religious question; it concerns itself with the rights and duties of husbands and wives.

Pius XI also published an Encyclical on the Christian education of youth, a theme which is again not strictly speaking a religious one. He speaks of the rights and duties of the State and passes judgment on political and social doctrines which conflict with Christian ideals. This does not pertain strictly to faith or worship or the administration of the sacraments. And yet in all such problems the Church feels very much at home and intends to stay there. She judges the acts of man and the powers of this world not from a political point of view but weighs them in conformity with the principles of morality.

False opinions such as I have mentioned serve only to hide attacks against the liberty of the Church and the right of conscience. May Catholics therefore open their eyes! They must realize that there is a real peril, a peril which they must overcome with every means in their power. "Behold, I am with you all days, even to the consummation of the world."

God and the War

REVEREND JOHN MURRAY

Professor of Systematic Theology, Westminster Theological Seminary,
Presbyterian, Philadelphia, Pennsylvania

THE REVEREND JOHN MURRAY knows war at firsthand. Born at Bonar Bridge, Sutherland, Scotland, in 1898, he served in the British Army during World War I. A member of the famous Black Watch Regiment, he was wounded at Meteren, France, in July, 1918, and as a result he lost an eye. When the war was over he went back to Glasgow University, came to Princeton Seminary, then returned to Europe and spent a year studying at Edinburgh and in Germany. His postgraduate study in Edinburgh, 1928-1929, was made on a Gelston-Windthrop Fellowship in Systematic Theology, awarded by Princeton Seminary. On his return to the United States, he was called to the Seminary as an instructor in Systematic Theology. In 1930 he went to Westminster Theological Seminary where he is now Professor of Systematic Theology. He has been Joint-Editor of the Westminster Theological Journal since 1928.

Professor Murray was brought up in Scotland as a member of the Free Presbyterian Church and is one of the ablest representatives of historic Calvinism in this country. His approach to all theological problems is Biblical, as illustrated by this sermon. His articles are widely read and respected, especially in Presbyterian and Reformed circles. Although he would not lay claim to this, his knowledge of the Westminster Confession and the Westminster Assembly is undoubtedly as great as that of any one in this country.

This address was given before the Christian World Order Conference in Cincinnati and has been highly acclaimed. It was of this sermon that H. L. Mencken said, "I am, unhappily, a complete infidel, but nevertheless I see the force of the Fundamentalists' position, and I am delighted whenever it is stated clearly and logically." Mr. Murray asks quite frankly, "Does God have anything to do with this war?" His answer is provocative, honest, and deeply religious. His statement on justice and history deserves consideration.

TEXT: *When thy judgments are in the earth, the inhabitants of the world will learn righteousness.* ISAIAH 26:9

HE TOPIC ON WHICH I DWELL IS "GOD AND THE War." The question would very naturally and perhaps urgently arise, Does God have anything to do with this war? War is, to say the least, a ghastly evil. I did not say, war is wrong. The waging of war is often highly necessary and even dutiful. For a sovereign state or federation of sovereign states the waging of war is oftentimes the only resort that remains, to guard the paths of justice, to promote the interests of God-given liberty, and, paradoxical as it may seem, to conserve the blessing of true peace. The waging of war upon just and necessary occasion is no more wrong than is the execution of just judgment upon the violators of civil righteousness within a particular municipality or nation. But war is a ghastly evil in that it is always the consequence of sin.

As never before in the lifetime of the oldest of us, we are confronted with the barbarities and brutalities of which corrupt human nature is capable. We witness tyranny, oppression, cruelty, suffering, the destruction of precious life and property. As we think of all this there appears to be such foolishness and absurdity to it all, not to speak of the iniquity that lies behind the whole tragedy of turmoil and devastation. Can God have anything to do with such a spectacle of waste and destruction? Surely He is of purer eyes than to behold evil and He cannot look upon sin.

It is possible that our minds are not controlled by the thought of God's holiness. Perhaps our minds are controlled by an evolutionary philosophy, and we are incurable optimists. These ordeals are, we may be disposed to say, but the birthpangs of a better day. The evolutionary process proceeds through conflict and suffering, and the greater the struggle the greater hope we should entertain for the ultimate result. In the past we became too complacent toward things as they were, too complacent toward the obsolete or the obsolescent. It is necessary by the law of progress that the upheaval be all the more radical and even painful in order that we may shake off the scales or the chains that have clogged us in the past and step forward into the vistas and achievements of a new order.

But perhaps our minds *are controlled* by the thought of the holiness of God, and, if so, our answer to the question may be that it is more honoring to the one living and true God to say that this war is entirely of man's making and that God has nothing whatsoever to do with it. We perhaps think that it is beneath the dignity and majesty that are His to be in any way related to so wretched and despicable a thing as war with its entail of untold enmities and miseries.

Perhaps we might try to shield the integrity of God by supposing that the world has simply got out of hand. God is not able to cope with the perversity of human nature. He is doing the best He can with a bad situation and like our good selves He deserves our warm sympathy and support.

Or again, perhaps we entertain a more noble conception of the power of God and say that He has just left the world to go its own way. He has been pouring out the bowels of entreaty, He has been striving with men. But they have not been responsive to His pleadings and warnings. Men have proved themselves hardhearted, stiff-necked, and rebellious. In holy retribution He has withdrawn His hand and as a sad spectator leaves men to their own resources. He allows the world for a time to reel and stagger in the wisdom that is folly. And so He has no active providence in this war. His relation to it is one of bare permission.

All of these attempts to philosophize with respect to the rationale of the present conflict may be well-meaning. Indeed some distorted element of truth, twisted from its proper orientation, shifted from its proper context, inheres in each of these attempts. For if any system were entirely devoid of plausibility, devoid of any approximation to reality, it is not likely that it would have much appeal to any large proportion of men.

The question however recurs, are these the answers of truth? Are they the answers of God's wisdom as deposited in His Word? Are they the answers of the Christian revelation?

When the question is thus qualified the answer simply is that it will not do to say that God has nothing to do with this war. It will not do to say simply that God allows or permits this war. For the Scripture says, "Shall there be evil in a city, and the Lord hath not done it?" (Amos 3:6). "I am the Lord, and there is none else, there is no God beside me: I girded thee, though thou hast not known me: that they may know from the rising of the sun, and from the west, that there is none beside me. I am the Lord, and there is none else. I form the light, and create darkness; I make peace, and create evil; I the Lord do all these things" (Isaiah 45:5-7). "Surely as I have thought, so shall it come to pass; and as I have purposed, so shall it stand" (Isaiah 14:24). All things come to pass by God's ordination and in His Providence. We are faced with the inescapable truth that the whole of history in its broadest extent and minutest detail is the unrolling of the plan devised from eternity and accomplished by Him of whom and through whom and to whom are all things. If our thought is guided by the Christian revelation we are shut up to the recognition that it is no honor to God to say that He has nothing to do with this war, nor that He occupies with reference to it the position of offended but sad spectator. What then is the meaning of this war as that

133

meaning may be derived from the Biblical revelation? When we say *meaning* we are not presuming to claim that we in our puny finitude, and particularly we sinners in our sinful ignorance, are able to survey all the counsel of the Eternal as it is embodied in the events of history. God's way is in the sea and His path in the great waters. His footsteps are not known. Clouds and darkness are round about Him. "Canst thou by searching find out God? Canst thou find out the Almighty unto perfection?" (Job 11:7). How little a portion do we know in part, and God has not left us to wander in total darkness with respect to the mystery of His providence and the purpose of His will.

There are at least five propositions that may be elicited from the Scriptures with respect to the meaning of this war. If viewed from the standpoint of revelation they may be called reasons. If viewed from the standpoint of our responsibility they may be called lessons.

I. *This war is an evil consequent upon sin.* It is one of the logical issues of sin. "From whence come wars and fightings among you? Come they not hence, even of your lusts that war in your members?" (James 4:1). We cannot deal with the topic "God and the War" unless we first propound the topic "Man and the War." The sinful cause and occasion of war is the lust of the flesh, the lust of the eye, and the pride of life.

It is, no doubt, impossible for us to diagnose all the affections, motives, volitions, acts and purposes that have converged upon one another, that have interacted with one another, and that in unison bear the onus of responsibility for the gigantic catastrophe that has now befallen the world. We must recognize that a complex movement having its roots far back in history, a complex movement of sinful impulse, ambition, and action that only the all-seeing eye of God can fully view and diagnose, lies back of, and comes to fruition in, this present conflict.

While we are not able to survey that movement in all its factors and in their various interactions, nevertheless we cannot but recognize the broad features of that movement. It should be far from me, loyal as I trust I am to the cause being fought by the United States, Great Britain, China and other members of the United Nations, to disavow the responsibility that rests upon the nation of which I am a grateful citizen and upon the nation of which I am a grateful resident. But whatever of responsibility rests upon us for failures of the past and however much we must bow in shame and humility for the sins committed in our national capacities, we must not allow our judgment to be blinded to the stark specter that stalks before us in the crime and barbarity of the Axis nations. It surely must be said that Nazi Germany has been the main perpetrator of wrong in plunging the world into the holocaust that is now upon us. And why did Germany descend to such acts of iniquitous aggression? We cannot explain it on any other ground than that the moral fiber of the

German people had undergone some radical deterioration. There must have been an eclipse of those moral principles that guide just and humane treatment of fellow men. And when we say moral eclipse we must not dissociate that eclipse from its religious source and basis. This source we must find in departure from the one living and true God, and such departure, in a country like Germany at least, means departure from the gospel of our Lord and Saviour Jesus Christ.

We do not need any profound knowledge of history to be able to discover the source of this departure, and therefore the source of the moral and spiritual debacle witnessed in that religion of blood and race and soil embodied in the ideology of Nazi Germany. This source is found in the naturalistic and destructive criticism of our Christian faith that found a ready home and active sponsorship in German soil. This war is the logical issue of that religion of blood and soil embraced by German Nazism, and that religion is the logical outcome of that pseudo-Christianity that is based upon the denial of the divine authority and finality of Holy Scripture as the infallible Word of God. This diagnosis, I am making bold to say, is the root cause of the onslaught on decency, justice, liberty, mercy, and truth we have witnessed in the Nazi aggression.

But this indictment is a humiliating one for us. It is only too obvious that that same pseudo-Christianity and that same godless religion that is its child have found in our nations hospitable entertainment and sponsorship. It may not have produced in our nations the same notorious fruits that have been manifest in Nazi Germany. We should be thankful that some respect for truth and justice has survived among us. Yet the very same phenomenon is with us and prevalent among us. Let us painfully know that the virus that has produced in the Nazi regime those atrocities we severely condemn is a virus that we also have fostered and cultivated. It is the virus of a pseudo-Christianity that has denied the very foundations upon which the Christian faith rests.

The roots of these crimes reside in our fallen nature. For that corruption there is but one cure—the gospel of the grace of God. In this pseudo-Christianity we have the denial of that which is our only salvation from the corruption that issues in just such barbarous acts of tyranny, oppression and destruction as have confronted us in the avalanche of Nazi power. "The earth also was corrupt before God, and the earth was filled with violence" (Genesis 6:11). This is "Man and the War."

II. *This war is divine retribution for sin.* We may think lightly of sin, we may be indifferent to it. But God cannot. Sin is the contradiction of His glory, the contradiction of that law that is the reflex of His holy nature. And so "the wrath of God is revealed from heaven against all ungodliness and unrighteousness of men, who hold the truth in unrighteousness" (Romans 1.18).

135

It is, of course, true that God does not execute all His wrath in this world. But it is a settled datum of history, as recorded in the Scripture and abundantly corroborated by subsequent history, that when iniquity abounds the Lord rises up out of His place to punish the inhabitants of the world for their iniquity. He did this in the case of the Old World by destroying men from off the face of the ground. He did this in the case of Sodom and Gomorrah by destroying them with fire and brimstone. The divine philosophy of history forces us to the conclusion that in this present conflict we must discern the rod of the divine anger and the staff of the divine indignation.

We rightly regard with the utmost disapprobation the unspeakable iniquities committed by the Axis nations. We think of treachery and deceit, treachery that baffles our ability adequately to depict its true character—and our minds immediately travel to Pearl Harbor. We think of tyranny and ruthless persecution—Nazi oppression of Jews and Christians in Germany and in the conquered states of Europe is the very acme of this iniquity. And if we are looking for the most classic example of the inexpressibly mean and contemptible we find it in the actions of Mussolini and of the Fascist regime in Italy. We can say that these are incarnations of blatant wickedness.

There often surges up in our minds the question: Why, if God is the God of justice, if by Him actions are weighed, does He not forthwith destroy such perpetrators of iniquity from off the face of the earth? We are disposed to reiterate the plaint and question of the prophet, "Righteous art thou, O Lord, when I plead with thee: yet let me talk with thee of thy judgments: Wherefore doth the way of the wicked prosper? Wherefore are all they happy that deal very treacherously? Thou hast planted them, yea, they have taken root: they grow, yea, they bring forth fruit: thou art near in their mouth, and far from their reins" (Jeremiah 12:1, 2). Or perhaps we reiterate the questions of the Psalmist when we, like him, observe the prosperity of the wicked: "How doth God know? And is there knowledge in the Most High?" (Psalm 73:11).

If our minds are imbued with the principles of the divine government as set forth in the Scriptures and as exemplified in history, we cannot escape the application to Germany, Italy and Japan of the word of God through Isaiah the prophet, "O Assyrian, the rod of mine anger, and the staff in their hand is mine indignation. I will send him against an hypocritical nation, and against the people of my wrath will I give him a charge, to take the spoil, and to take the prey, and to tread them down like the mire of the streets" (Isaiah 10:5, 6).

Assyria was not more righteous than Israel, and Assyria did not set out on its campaign of conquest and destruction with the motive and intention of executing the dictates of divine retribution upon Israel. Oh no!

For Isaiah continues, "Howbeit he meaneth not so, neither doth his heart think so; but it is in his heart to destroy and cut off nations not a few" (Verse 7). Assyria's purpose did not coincide with God's purpose, and neither does the purpose of the Axis nations with which we are now at war. Nevertheless, their campaign, as the campaign of Assyria, fulfills in the grand strategy of God's plan the purpose of holy retribution and judgment. We cannot diagnose the meaning of the crisis that is upon us nor derive the appropriate lessons from it unless we see in large letters the writing of divine displeasure upon *us* for *our* sins.

It is true that in due time the divine judgment will be executed also upon the instruments of this judgment upon us. Again, as in the case of Assyria, "Wherefore it shall come to pass, that when the Lord hath performed his whole work upon Mount Zion and on Jerusalem, I will punish the fruit of the stout heart of the king of Assyria, and the glory of his high looks" (Isaiah 10:12). "Therefore shall the Lord, the Lord of hosts, send among his fat ones leanness; and under his glory he shall kindle a burning like the burning of a fire" (Verse 16). But the greater iniquity of the instrument of judgment, and the greater judgment that will in due time be executed upon that instrument, must not blind us to the iniquity that is the ground for the divine anger against us. God is punishing us for our iniquity, and let us in submissiveness and humility bear the rod and Him who has appointed it. When we stagger let us know that we stagger under the staff of God's righteous indignation.

III. *This war is the divine call to repentance.* "When thy judgments are in the earth, the inhabitants of the world will learn righteousness" (Isaiah 26:9).

Naturally we all long for the date when the bells of a victorious armistice or peace will begin to toll. We naturally think of days approximating those of the past. We think in terms of economic stability and comfort, and we perhaps pray for the early cessation of hostilities. But surely we have learned that there is something more important and precious than peace. Why have we gone to war? Is it not because we have deemed something more precious than peace? We must read the text again—"the inhabitants of the world will learn righteousness." That is the lesson of "God and the War" that bears upon us with more practical moment than anything else. It is the lesson that we have been loath to learn, the lesson of individual and national repentance. I don't think I am unduly pessimistic if I say that the signs have not been pointing in the direction of penitence and humility. We have had much humiliation, but have we put on humility as a garment? Have we acquainted ourselves with the alarming prevalence of sexual immorality and of marital infidelity? Have we followed the history of the divorce courts, the facility with which divorce may be secured, and the frequency with which divorce is sought and granted? Have we witnessed the appalling increase in profanity, a tendency given impetus, deplorable to relate, by the example of some who occupy positions of high public trust? Have we taken cognizance of the lamentable increase in desecration of the Sabbath? Have we not rather heard or read the proclamation from the highest seat of government of a seven-day week, when God has said, "Six days shalt thou labour, and do all thy work: but the seventh day is the Sabbath of the Lord thy God" (Exodus 20:9, 10)? Have we not heard, in the terms of a pernicious antithesis, that this war is to be won in the workshop and not in the church? Can we fail to discern that the economic and educational systems of this country are very largely devised and conducted in systematic disregard of the authority and will of God? Our defiance has surely reached Babel proportions when we think that in the interests of defending our civil and religious liberties we can dispense with the laws which God has ordained. For the laws of God are the only basis and guarantee of true liberty and true worship.

Our minds are ready in these times to be blinded by a certain kind of panic. We quite properly desire and set our minds upon the preservation of our national liberties and integrity and, in order to that end, upon the defeat of those enemies that are arrayed against us. But in preoccupation with that end we are too prone to that panic that blinds our vision of the kingdom of God and His righteousness. I would not set up a false antithesis. But we should remember that no temporal catastrophe can be as bad as the strengthening of the bands of godlessness. I am not saying that it is necessary for us to undergo ultimate defeat in order to learn righteousness. May God forbid that this should be the case. But it would be better for us to suffer the humiliation of defeat, if thereby we should learn righteousness, than to be crowned with sweeping military victory if thereby we are to be confirmed in the ways of ungodliness. "Seek ye first the kingdom of God, and His righteousness" (Matthew 6:33). "The kingdom of God is not meat and drink; but righteousness, and peace, and joy in the Holy Ghost" (Romans 14:17). Let us ever remember the sovereign prerogatives of God's kingdom, and even in the pursuance of a life-and-death military conflict let us learn to think even then in terms of the kingdom of Him who is "the King eternal, immortal, invisible, the only God" (I Timothy 1:17). "If my people, which are called by my name, shall humble themselves, and pray, and seek my face, and turn from their wicked ways; then will I hear from heaven, and will forgive their sin, and will heal their land" (II Chronicles 7:14).

IV. *The perfecting of Christ's body, the church, is being promoted by this war.* The whole of history is the unfolding of God's purpose. But we must also remember that all authority in heaven and in earth has been committed unto Christ. He is Head over all things, and He is Head over all things to His body, the church. It is with respect to Him that the Lord says, "Yet have I set my king upon my holy hill of Zion." "Ask of me, and I will give thee the nations for thine inheritance, and the uttermost parts of the earth for thy possession" (Psalm 2:6, 8). He is Head over all things and is ordering all affairs in the interest of promoting the welfare of His bride, the apple of His eye. "All things work together for good to them that love God, to them who are the called according to his purpose" (Romans 8:28).

We quite properly view with dismay and even horror the way in which true and faithful believers are downtrodden and persecuted in many parts of the world. We cannot but view with the keenest alarm the way in which the enemies of the gospel have been successful in frustrating the efforts of the true church to propagate the gospel, and the jeopardy into which the cause of evangelization throughout the world has been cast. We should cry from the depths of distress and real solicitude, "Lord, how long shall the wicked, how long shall the wicked triumph?" (Psalm 94:3). And we should with grief reiterate the complaint of the Psalmist, "O God, the heathen are come into thine inheritance; thy holy temple have they defiled; they have laid Jerusalem on heaps" (Psalm 79:1). The false optimism of indifference to, or escape from, the realities of current history should have no place in our outlook. The extinction of the true church is inherent in the philosophy of Nazi Germany and pagan Japan. Here we have a religious philosophy at work that is the antithesis of the Christian faith.

But as we confront the grim realities of the present situation we must not forget the reality of the situation that is more ultimate, the situation created by the transcendent kingship of our Lord and Saviour Jesus Christ as the King and Head of the church. Through all the upheavals, sufferings, tribulations, persecutions, and even executions of God's people, there runs an invincible purpose that cannot fail of execution, the completion of the whole body of Christ. In line with the word of the apostle, "I would ye should understand, brethren, that the things which happened . . . have fallen out rather unto the furtherance of the gospel" (Philippians 1:12). These sufferings fill up that which is behind the afflictions of Christ to the end of furthering the great purpose that Christ had in view in coming into the world, and of bringing that purpose to its consummation in the glorification of a countless multitude whom no man can number out of every nation and kindred and people and tongue. It cannot fail to be true, "These are they which came out of great tribulation, and have washed their robes, and made them white in the blood of the Lamb" (Revelations 7:14).

Let not our certitude and peace be disturbed. Christ sits as King and He must reign until all His enemies shall have been made His footstool.

He will not leave off until He will bring forth the headstone of this living temple with shoutings, crying, grace, grace unto it. "The hands of Zerubbabel have laid the foundation of this house; his hands shall also finish it" (Zechariah 4:9).

V. *The war vindicates God's sovereignty.* It is an inexpressible comfort in these days of upheaval and turmoil to know that all events, great and small, are embraced in God's sovereign providence. He has not resigned the reins of government. Present history is not moving toward chaos. It is moving in the grand drama of God's plan and purpose to the accomplishment of His holy designs and to the vindication of His glory.

Before the avalanche of totalitarian human government many professing Christians are capitulating and many have also enlisted in the unholy crusade of taking "counsel together, against the Lord, and against his anointed, saying, Let us break their bands asunder, and cast away their cords from us" (Psalm 2:2, 3). With respect to the true church of God they have said, "Come, and let us cut them off from being a nation; that the name of Israel may be no more in remembrance" (Psalm 83:4). We must be reminded in such a situation that in this universe there is only one totalitarian government, and that men must assume in it the place of humble submission and obedience. "The Lord reigneth; let the people tremble: he sitteth between the cherubims; let the earth be moved. The Lord is great in Zion; and he is high above all the people" (Psalm 99:1, 2). "Be still, and know that I am God: I will be exalted among the nations, I will be exalted in the earth" (Psalm 46:10). All history is under God's governance and is moving toward His tribunal where every infraction upon truth and deviation from justice will receive its final adjustment and adjudication. "He cometh to judge the earth: with righteousness shall he judge the world, and the people with equity" (Psalm 98:9). It is here that the believer finds solace, for it is the secret place of the Most High and the shadow of the Almighty. Through all the disquieting events of our history there runs the sovereign and holy purpose of the Lord God omnipotent. And even though clouds and darkness are round about Him, justice and judgment are the habitation of His throne. He fulfills His righteous purpose through the unrighteous wills of wicked men.

We must assert, and take refuge in, the absolute sovereignty of the eternal God, the absolute sovereignty of Him who is the God and Father of our Lord Jesus Christ, and with equal universality the mediatorial sovereignty of the Lord Jesus Christ, the God-man, the incarnate Son, the Saviour-King, the King of kings, and Lord of lords. In the words of Isaiah (2:10, 11), let us say to ourselves, "Enter into the rock, and hide thee in the dust, for fear of the Lord, and for the glory of his majesty. The lofty looks of man shall be humbled, and the haughtiness of men shall be bowed down, and the Lord alone shall be exalted in that day."

140

Civilian Standards in Wartime

REVEREND DAVID DE SOLA POOL, PH.D.*

Rabbi, Spanish and Portuguese Synagogue, Shearith Israel,
New York

DR. POOL is the leader of the famous Spanish and Portuguese Synagogue, Shearith Israel, which was founded in 1655, when New York was a village and the western boundary of what is now the United States was east of the Delaware River. This great synagogue has had a distinguished history, and Dr. Pool has shown himself to be a capable leader of the Orthodox faith, a scholarly preacher, and a good pastor. He is active in interfaith work and has the respect of Catholics and Protestants.

He was born in London, England, in 1885, and was educated in the universities of Europe, being graduated with honors from the University of London in 1903. Later he studied at the universities of Berlin and Heidelberg, receiving his Ph.D., summa cum laude, from Heidelberg, and at the Rabbinerseminar, Berlin. Since 1907 he has been minister of the Spanish and Portuguese Synagogue. He is a representative of Jewish Army and Navy chaplains to the Chief of Chaplains.

In 1917, he was one of three Jewish representatives appointed to serve on Herbert Hoover's food conservation staff; in 1919, he was one of three American representatives on the Zionist Commission to Palestine; and from 1938 to 1940, he was president of the Synagogue Council of America.

Dr. Pool has written numerous prayer books, pamphlets, and reviews, and is the author of *The Kaddish, Hebrew Learning among the Puritans of New England,* and *Capital Punishment in Jewish Literature.*

This is a sermon for the people in time of war. Dr. Pool looks at the evil in the world and at the history of man, and sees in each generation struggle and pain enough to break man unless God helps him to find redemption. In times of resurgent evil and violence, we need to keep before our eyes the eternal God-given standards of right and wrong. Religion has comfort and strength for man now, and the power to help him refashion the world and build a nobler generation. Dr. Pool shows how man can know and realize God on earth.

* Sermons by members of the Advisory Committee were contributed at the special request of the editor and are included on his responsibility.

Sermon Nineteen

TEXT: *O Generation, see ye the word of the Lord.* JEREMIAH 2:31

HEN ONE LOOKS AT THE WORLD OF TODAY AND sees the evil which grips our entire generation, and when one looks back upon the history of man and sees the struggle and the pain in each generation, one almost accepts the initial pessimism of Ecclesiastes in the Bible, that "that which is crooked cannot be made straight"; "that which hath been is that which shall be, and that which hath been done is that which shall be done, and there is no new thing under the sun" (1:9,15). One is tempted to believe that fallible and foolish mankind will be guilty of the same faults and the same evils in each generation. One wonders at the challenging optimism of the rest of the Bible which, while recognizing man's fallibility and weakness, nevertheless lays stress on his possibilities of high moral achievement in the quest of perfection. Looking on God's universe and then on little man, the Psalmist cries out to God, "When I behold Thy heavens, the work of Thy fingers, the moon and the stars which Thou hast established, what is man that Thou art mindful of him, the son of man that Thou givest thought to him?" The Psalmist is no pessimist. He does not despair of man, and he answers his own question with the superb affirmation, "Thou hast made him but little lower than the angels, and hast crowned him with glory and majesty" (Psalm 8:3,4). Everything on earth is placed in man's power, the Psalmist says; man is the architect of his own destiny. He can build this world into a paradise or make of it a hell. For in all nature, man alone has conscious mind. Man alone has moral will. Man alone is not driven solely by sheer instinct and blind fate. Man alone can mold this world of plastic circumstance into whatsoever form he will. It is entirely the result of our own doing whether our generation is on the whole better or worse than the generations of the past. Our generation is what we make it.

In the light of this, let us attempt realistically to answer the question whether we have made our generation better or worse than past generations.

The dominating fact about human life today is that we are at war. Because we are at war, we on the home front are necessarily paying a penalty in deterioration of standards.

Not that any generation has been perfect. In every generation there have been manifold injustices and evils in human society. But in comparison with our world of today, a world that was not at war was a good world to live in. When we were at peace, we were normally sensitive to great evil and suffering, and eager to heal it. Our sympathies were not

142

jaded and hardened by endlessly repeated stories of wasted human bodies in the streets of great cities of Europe. If the newspapers printed the story of a single family found starved to death in our city, it was a sensation which stirred our philanthropies and our civic conscience to take action so that such pitiful and needless suffering should be impossible in the future.

In days of peace, before blockbusters and incendiaries were deliberately dropped on fair cities, leaving them as flaming infernos with thousands upon thousands of dead, a single accidental fire claiming ten or a dozen victims was felt to be a major disaster.

A generation at war is in constant danger of its civilians becoming desensitized to the sacredness of human life. In happier generations of peace, when blood and destruction were not so much in use and dreadful objects not so familiar, a single murder could be a sensation featured by the newspapers for days and even weeks on end. The lynching of a single Negro could send a shudder of horror and shame through us. Our little children and very babies were not likely to be dressed up in uniform, shooting off toy machine guns, and playing war, war, war.

But there is another aspect from which we can look on the character of a world at war. Who can close his eyes to the idealism which war calls forth? On the home front it often produces a more considered and a more serious way of living. It awakens a vast outpouring of generosity to refugees and other sufferers from the war. It summons up endless warm-hearted personal service for our uniformed men. Who can measure the unselfish service for our country, and the unstinted self-sacrifice and heroism which war evokes even unto death itself? It has produced the UNRRA (United Nations Relief and Rehabilitation Administration) through which forty-four nations are planning to stanch the wounds of the unhappy, devastated peoples of Europe, feed their hungry, and rebuild the broken lives of tens of millions of human beings.

Can we strike a balance between the good and the evil of a generation at war? On the one side are these stirring qualities; but on the other we see the hardening of our sympathies, the growth of juvenile delinquency everywhere, the self-indulgence from the prosperity which seems to have come with the war boom, the necessary concentration on war, the dislocation of normal living and of our normal interests, the world scene of destruction piled on destruction, the ravaging of lands, the razing to earth of cities, the shattering of homes, the uprooting of men by the tens of millions, the scattering of families, the starving of whole peoples, the spread of typhus, malaria and other ordinarily controllable diseases, and the utter poverty and helplessness of untold millions of civilian victims on every war front. We must indeed bend the head and shamefacedly avow that we have made our generation one that shames the moral achievements of so much of our past.

What then can we do about it? Shall we despair? Does war force on us a necessary and enduring lowering of moral standards? Is ours to be a lost generation, a generation doomed? Or is it in our power "to grasp this sorry scheme of things entire . . . and then remold it nearer to the heart's desire"?

Repeatedly the Bible tells us that though not all generations are the same in quality, even the worst of them is given another chance to retrieve itself. In the symbolic story of the beginning of mankind, under the idyllic conditions of the Garden of Eden, man failed. But he was given an opportunity to retrieve himself and conquer life through his own efforts. In the generation of the flood mankind again corrupted itself, "and the Lord saw that the wickedness of man was great on the earth." But God did not entirely blot out mankind. He gave man another chance to work out his own salvation. The cities of Sodom and Gomorrah, the very symbols of infamous corruption, could have been saved had there been but fifty, forty, thirty, yes, even ten good men in their generation. The people that under the very shadow of Mt. Sinai fell into the worship of the golden calf were not blotted out, despite their corruption. They were given another chance to realize their potential glories. In a moment of despair the Psalmist looked out on his generation and exclaimed, "the pious cease, the faithful fail from among the children of men." But he never doubted that God would yet save the good of his generation, and he said, "Thou wilt preserve us from this generation for ever" (Psalm 12:2,8). The piercing moral gaze of the prophets revealed the evil of their generations. But those same prophets always held before the eyes of their people the possibilities, yea, the promise, that they could and they would overcome their corruptions. Righteousness will rule, they declared; men will yet guide their lives by justice, by mercy, and by love; they will beat their swords into plowshares and their spears into pruning-hooks, and "none shall hurt, none destroy in all God's holy mountain, for the earth shall be full of the knowledge of the Lord as the waters cover the sea" (Isaiah 11:9).

That is the unfading vision of unfailing hope which the Bible always holds before us. There is hope of our latter end, and it is within our own power to realize that hope. We can save ourselves and our generation. We do not have to see ourselves destroyed body and soul.

In times of resurgent evil and violence there is all the greater need to keep steadfastly before our eyes the eternal God-given standards of right and wrong, of good and evil. To a troubled generation such as ours religion says, O pitiful, suffering men, your only hope of coming through your trial and agony unbroken, if not unscathed, is to hold fast to the

144

moral and spiritual standards of your religion. If you would not be brutalized by a world at war, hearken the more steadfastly and the more earnestly to your religion's teachings of the sacredness of life, the wonder and the beauty of life, the divine possibilities of life. Even when at war do not allow your standards to be compromised and dragged down to the mire by war's degradation of man. Turn away from its cruelties and abominations and strive for the glories that may be yours. Make your own the discipline which war imposes on the home front as well as in camp and in the field. In a world debauched by unscrupulous propaganda hold yourself and your generation fast to religion's eternal standards of truth. In a warring world which breeds epidemics of intolerance and destruction, cling to your religious teachings of justice and right. In a world given over to pitiless war, do not yield up the ideal standards of mercy that you have learned from your God. Give yourselves generously, selflessly, to service of your fellow men, so that you will be fulfilling religion's primary law of conduct, "Thou shalt love thy neighbor as thyself" (Leviticus 19:18). In a generation given over to hatreds of other nations and races, hold fast, unyieldingly, to your religious ideals of love of God and love of neighbor. Stand firm in a morally reeling world. For in a generation of moral catastrophe it is religion and religion alone which preserves uncompromised meaning for the words right and wrong, good and evil, virtue and wickedness. In such a generation it is in the homes of religion that God still can find sanctuary on earth.

So speaks religion to a world at war. In words of comfort and strength it says to us that out of the divine powers which are in the spirit of man we refashion this tottering world of ours and build a nobler generation.

All over the world the wisest of our statesmen, economists, professors, and experts of various kinds, are working on plans for what they significantly call, not the peace, but the postwar world. They are trying to insure that the generation to follow shall be better and happier than ours. They are planning to give man another opportunity of achieving his destiny of happiness, security, justice, brotherhood, freedom, peace, and glory. But the realization of their blueprints of that new society and the final success of all their planning cannot be looked for solely from political alliances or federations or from a planned co-operative world economy. Ultimately it can come about only through a change in the soul of man. A political or economic system will rise no higher than the soul of the men on whom it is built. It cannot assure us liberty, justice and a warless world unless religion strengthens and inspires the soul of glory. But the realization of their blueprints of that new society and the man. Therefore, let us treasure as God's supreme gift to man religion's firm faith that spiritually man is little lower than the angels. We are not compelled to failure. We can build out of the ruins a generation that shall serve and love man, and that shall know and realize God on earth.

145

Some Salvage from the Wreck of World War

Reverend Frank Halliday Ferris, Ph.D.
Pastor, Fairmount Presbyterian Church, Cleveland, Ohio

Frank Halliday Ferris stays close to the work of his own church, "doing his own knitting." Year by year his preaching and pastoral work attract new members to this strong church and give help and comfort to all who are touched by his ministry.

He was born in Brooklyn and was educated at Amherst, Columbia University, Union Theological Seminary, and Drew University, where he received his Ph.D. in 1931. He was ordained to the Congregational ministry in 1917, but transferred to the Presbyterian ministry in 1920, and has been in his present pastorate since 1931.

From 1917 to 1919, he was a chaplain in the United States Navy, serving at first on board the U.S.S. *Mercy,* and then on the U.S.S. *Texas.* Therefore, his understanding of the problems of war, as indicated in this sermon, has come from firsthand experience. His point of view is positive, analytical, and full of Christian hope that men may take religion now and after the war, not as an opiate, but as a commitment of life to God. The salvage from the wreck of war must reach the souls of men.

Dr. Ferris' sermons are scholarly and have a spiritual quality needed today. His discussion of President Harding's statement after the last war, of the World Court and the League of Nations, and of the world after this war, will make readers stop and think. Dr. Ferris' use of literature and history as an integral part of his sermons is an excellent example of the force and effectiveness of well-chosen references. He preached this sermon on September 12, 1943, in his own church.

Sermon Twenty

Scripture: Hebrews 12

THE SEA LANES OF THE WORLD ARE STREWN WITH sunken ships. Back in 1940, *Life* magazine published a double page of pictures of the proud liners that had gone down, carrying with them costly cargoes and the more precious lives of men. Hundreds of tankers and freighters lie deep beneath the waves. But the burial places of many of these ships have been marked. After the war, divers will examine them. Some will be raised, others will have their cargoes and machinery removed. It is slow, difficult work, this work of salvage, but what patience and persistence can accomplish, the righting of the *Normandie* and the reclamation of the ships sunk at Pearl Harbor show.

The battlefields of the world are strewn with abandoned equipment. The course of Rommel's retreat across North Africa was marked with litter and debris, which the salvage corps of the British Army has collected and classified. At Stalingrad is a mountainous heap of wrecked German tanks, guns and planes, so huge that hard-bitten Admiral Standley, our ambassador to Moscow, after seeing it declared he would never again be skeptical of Russian claims. After the war, the metal in these machines can be salvaged, Isaiah's prophecy be fulfilled, "They shall beat their swords into plowshares"; farmers in the Ukraine will perhaps work their fertile fields with plows and tractors made of steel once put to sterner use.

The military hospitals of the world are full of broken men—men with eyes gone, faces gone, limbs gone, men with gaping wounds. But the use of sulfa drugs and blood plasma is saving the lives of thousands who in previous wars would have died. The skill of surgeons plus training in occupational therapy will enable many victims of war's cruelty to live useful lives again.

But it is not of the salvage of sunken ships, of battered war machines, of the broken bodies of men I wish to speak, but of other salvage from the wreck of war. Whenever we let our minds dwell on the destruction of life, of the world's wealth, of our fondest hopes, our hearts grow sick. What I want to point out is that though the waste is appalling, all is not lost.

I

For one thing, we have not lost our sense of values. We are more realistic than we were in the last war. So far as America is concerned, the war is being waged without hullabaloo, without hysteria, without hurrahs, and—to a surprisingly large extent—without vindictiveness and hate. We realize we are engaged in a grim and detestable business and that we'll not be happy till it's over. We did not will the war; it was forced upon us. Nevertheless our consciences are troubled about killing. The consciences of the young men in our armed forces are troubled as they learn the art of destroying their fellow men. In their Sunday School days they learned the ten commandments, one of which is, "Thou shalt not kill." They were indoctrinated with Jesus' teaching on the sacredness of human life. They remember how he said, "It is not the will of your Father that one of these little ones should perish"; "Not a sparrow falleth to the ground without your Father; ye are of more value than many sparrows." It is not easy for them to disregard the teachings of religion in which they were reared, nor to reconcile them with the task to which their nation has called them. President Conant of Harvard tells of a soldier who told him he had decided not to take communion for the duration of the war. When asked why, he said it did not seem right to him to share in the Lord's Supper as long as his business was killing. It may seem quixotic, but to that decision he had come. One of our Fairmount boys wrote me just before being shipped overseas: "The Army is adept at psychology. Step by step for nine months they have transformed us from peaceloving citizens into killers. I have gone along with it, but I do not feel right about it, so I think about it as little as I can." Another of our young men, pilot of a navy bomber, sat in my study and asked, "What shall I do if I am ordered to bomb a civilian objective?" I gave him no answer. Deeply troubled, he had come to his minister for help and his minister gave him no help. His conscience was uneasy and so was mine.

For, God help us, we are all in the business of killing. Everyone who pays his income tax or buys a war bond or fabricates weapons or makes the machine tools with which weapons are made is in it, just as much as the young men to whom we have given the dangerous and disagreeable assignments: the bombardier who has learned the split second in which to release the bomb, the infantryman who has been taught to use the bayonet, the commando who has been instructed in the gentle art of sneaking up behind a sentry and strangling him with a piece of wire. We are all in it and our consciences are uneasy. We are not feeling cocky, we are feeling sober and penitent. I am glad our consciences are uneasy. As long as our consciences are uneasy, there is hope for us. We shall be in earnest to see to it that the boy babies on our cradle roll are not called upon to do violence to their best instincts twenty years from now.

II

This leads to the next item: our deep concern about the postwar world. President Harding, standing on a dock in Hoboken as caskets containing the bodies of men slain in France were taken from the hold of a ship, said solemnly, "It must never happen again." It has happened again, and we repeat his words with heightened resolve. For we know now that any major war anywhere on the planet will engulf us. How far away from us war seemed in 1914, when the Austrian archduke was assassinated at Sarajevo! What did we have to do with the immemorial vendettas of the Balkans? But step by step we were drawn in. How remote war seemed from us when on September 1, 1939, Germany invaded Poland! We were sure we could keep out this time. But history repeated itself.

Step by step we were drawn in. We were in months before Pearl Harbor. It was our preoccupation in the Atlantic which emboldened Japan to strike.

When this war ends, we shall be war-weary, we shall experience the same revulsion we felt in 1919, the same temptation to draw back into our shell, to say, "How do the boundaries and rivalries of Europe and Asia concern us? We want no part in it." I shall feel that temptation. So will you. We must not succumb to it. Had we given our support to the World Court and the League of Nations, the course of history might have been different. This time we must stay with the task until some form of world organization supersedes the present world anarchy. As Mr. Churchill told us in his speech at Harvard recently, world power such as America holds today carries with it world responsibility which we cannot evade.

Long before Mr. Willkie wrote his travelogue, the missionary-minded people in the churches realized that this is "One World." The God they worshiped is not the God of Americans only, he is the God and Father of mankind. They did not believe Christ died for some favored group or race. They quoted Paul: "Christ died for all; wherefore henceforth we know no man after the flesh." The world is learning the hard way what missionary-minded Christians have known all along: one world, one family of mankind.

Still we find our marching orders on the last page of the first Gospel: "All authority is given unto me in heaven and on earth. Go ye therefore and make disciples of all the nations. . . : and lo, I am with you always even unto the end of the world." We Christians do not draw our inspiration to spend and be spent for a redeemed earth from anything in the human scene. We draw it from him who said and says, "In the world you have tribulation: but be of good cheer, I have overcome the world." Men with those words ringing in their ears can dare anything, bear anything, if only they can help answer the prayer of Jesus "that they may all be one," and help bring a lost world back to God.

III

A third item: we have not lost our belief in progress. When I was in college I read Professor J. B. Bury's *The Idea of Progress,* one of the most exhilarating, emancipating books I ever read. He points out that the idea of progress is of modern origin. The ancients had no such conception. The noblest of the ancient philosophies is the Stoic. The Stoic conception of history is of cycles of existence, ever returning upon themselves, like a man lost in the woods who, vainly imagining he is coming out somewhere, finds himself at last back where he started. Declares one Stoic, "He who has lived to be forty years of age has seen everything that has ever been and everything that will ever be." That is typical of ancient thought. The cycle theory of history has been revived in our day by the German, Oswald Spengler, in his influential book, *The Decline of the West*.

You would suppose that on the basis of our experience we should accept the cycle theory: in the business realm we have seen boom followed by panic, panic followed by boom; in the political realm, war followed by peace, peace followed by war, peace conceived not as the world's normal state but as the interval between wars—the interval between the last two not a true peace but a twenty-one year armistice, which means literally, "a standing-at-arms," waiting for the next war. Yet, curiously, we still cling doggedly to our faith in progress.

The idea of progress, I repeat, is a recent one. It is part of the bequest of the Victorians to us. In our day the Victorians are the butt of ridicule—a stuffy, stodgy lot compared with us bright moderns. In point of fact, the Victorian age is, next to the Elizabethan, the great creative age of English history, just as it is, next to the Elizabethan, the great creative age of English literature. What poets has the English-speaking world today to put beside Tennyson and Browning; what essayists comparable to Ruskin, Carlyle, Matthew Arnold; what novelists equal to Dickens, Thackeray, George Eliot?

Especially have the Victorians been reproached for their "romantic optimism." True, they did not know what rough going lay ahead. True, the newly discovered principle of evolution seemed to assure them that life moves in an upward direction—from amoeba to man. Not true, that they rested complacently in the belief that the world would roll on to glory by the resident forces which produce evolution, while they sat with folded hands and were rolled along with it. Darwin did not so believe. He did not even wait for a knowledge of evolution to evolve, but worked like a termite to collect and collate his facts. No, the Victorians' optimism was born of a faith that this is the kind of universe in which intelligent effort brings desirable results. "Strive and thrive" was their motto. So believing, so striving, they built the modern world of scientific knowledge and industrial skills and freer governments and more enlightened religion than man had known before.

Tennyson in "In Memoriam," the greatest poem of the nineteenth century, the greatest poem on immortality ever written, fights his way through the intellectual doubts and difficulties of his time to a faith

> That nothing walks with aimless feet;
> That not one life shall be destroyed,
> Or cast as rubbish to the void,
> When God hath made the pile complete.

150

Browning in "Paracelsus" declares that "Progress is the law of life"—no ancient ever said that—and in "A Death in the Desert" speaks of

> . . . progress, man's distinctive mark alone,
> Not God's, and not the beasts': God is, they are;
> Man partly is, and wholly hopes to be.

This belief in progress the Victorians passed on to us and we have not discarded it. When our fathers pushed the frontier westward from the Appalachians to the Mississippi valley, from the Mississippi to the great plains, on across the Rockies to the Pacific shore; when they planted fields, built churches, schools, cities, founded libraries, laboratories, museums, orchestras, they were saying to themselves and to the world: "America has a boundless future. Humanity has a boundless future." It was this faith which strengthened their hands and steeled their wills.

Says Aldous Huxley, English man of letters, who after going up and down this country for years on lecture tours has decided to settle here, "The thing that impresses me most about this country is its hopefulness. It is this which distinguishes it from Europe, where there is hopeless depression and fear."

This hopeful attitude toward the future, this belief that there is such a thing as progress and that men can do something about it, need not supinely accept things as they are, is the faith which our fathers bequeathed to us. I am glad that the disheartening experiences of the past quarter century have not robbed us of it, for there is still much progress to be made.

IV

But surely the experience through which our generation has passed has made us see that progress is not enough, human effort is not enough, that unless One stoops down and wrestles with us in the conflict our striving is in vain, that without God we are lost. True, the war has underscored the old, old problem of religion: If God is good and in control, why does he allow such tragedies to be? But also true, the war has brought a deepening interest in personal religion, much more marked than in the last war. Chaplains report that soldiers and sailors are eager to read religious literature, and the various churches are endeavoring to supply it. Men are thinking about religion in general, and about their own relation with God.

I am not greatly impressed by the story of the soldier who carried in his tunic pocket a Bible which stopped a bullet. When he examined it, he found the bullet had penetrated just to the verse in the ninety-first Psalm which reads, "A thousand shall fall at thy side and ten thousand

151

at thy right hand, but it shall not come nigh thee." That story with variants is told in every war, and it partakes more of the nature of magic and superstition than of religion. The skeptic cannot help wondering whether a deck of cards would not have stopped the bullet as effectually as a Bible; or why, if it be deemed miraculous intervention, God did not likewise intervene to save the choice young men who have been killed?

I do *not* disparage the religious experience which has come to men in dire peril: the soldiers in foxholes where, we are told, "there are no atheists"; the castaways on rubber rafts who "thought they heard the angels sing"; the airmen on hazardous missions who declare that "God is my co-pilot." There may be more reality in a cry to God out of the depths, even from a man who rarely thinks of God when life is safe and easy, than in the routine pieties of some who say their prayers regularly but without a deep sense of need. The Psalter is full of such cries *de profundis*. The one hundred and seventh Psalm describes the tempest-tossed mariners who when they "are at their wits' end . . . cry unto the Lord in their trouble and he bringeth them out of their distresses." The forty-sixth Psalm declares flatly: "God is our refuge and strength, a very present help in trouble." Sometimes he rescues us from our trouble, sometimes he gives us inner reinforcement with which to bear it, with which, if need be, to meet death with fortitude and composure; in either case he is "a very present help in trouble."

> When other helpers fail and comforts flee,
> Help of the helpless, O abide with me.

Age after age men have prayed that prayer and found it answered. Man's extremity has ever been God's opportunity. A religion that is no good in trouble is no good. It is when he is in trouble that a man is most keenly aware that his own resources, his wit, his cleverness, his strong arm are not enough. I do not question the sincerity or the validity of the religious experience which comes to men in dire peril; though, of course, the test is, will it carry over when the danger is past? Will it issue in permanent Christian convictions and a disciplined Christian life?

The religion in which I am *most* interested is not religion as a refuge, a life preserver, an opiate, a last desperate recourse, but religion as communion and commitment. Since last I stood in this pulpit, the panorama of war has unfolded on an unexampled scale. On the steppes of Russia vast masses of men have hurled themselves upon each other in mortal combat. Destruction has rained on western Europe from the skies. From the Aleutians to the Mediterranean the mighty drama has moved swiftly toward its denouement. We here at home feel utterly impotent in face of the world cataclysm. What can we do?

152

My brethren, we can keep the torch aglow until the dark night is past and morning comes again. We can remember that Emerson's words are everlastingly true, "The soul of progress is the progress of the soul." Paul in his second letter to the Corinthians speaks in high terms of the churches of Macedonia, what they gave and what they did; "but first," he says, "they gave their own selves to the Lord." This brings us back from the far-spread panorama to the place where religion for us begins: to the church at the six corners which God has entrusted to our care, to lives not partly but wholly committed unto him.

I said to you on the Sunday after the war began four years ago that I should not keep harping on it (I have no wisdom to offer those charged with the fearful responsibility of waging it); that I should assume that after having it brought to you by newspaper and radio all week, you would want and need something else when you come here; that I should endeavor to say nothing during the heat and passion of the conflict which would keep me from devoting what remains of my life to the cause of world peace and world brotherhood when the war is done; that I should keep my sermons as cheerful as I could, dwelling much on the eternal truths of the Gospel of Jesus which have survived a thousand wars and will survive until war shall be no more. I renew that pledge today. I promise you my sermons this year will not play around the fringes. They will deal with the redeeming love of God as revealed in Christ Jesus our Lord, with His power to save to the uttermost them that come to God through Him. The first business of the church is to call men to God, and I shall be about my Father's business.

And you—pray this year as you have never prayed before. Pray that God will stretch forth His hand to save this strife-torn world, for His is the only hand that can save it. Pray that God will use you to bind up the world's wounds, to comfort and heal and bless the stricken and forlorn, to help lift the world back to Him.

So shall the salvage of the war become the salvation of our souls.

PRAYER: *Eternal Father, strong to save, we thank thee that this is thy world, that from the beginning it has been carried on a heart that is infinite in its compassion; that because thou dost carry it, sin and strife will some day cease and love will reign. For thou art love; we build our faith on that. Of thee and through thee and unto thee are all things to whom be the glory forever.*

Now unto him who is able to guard us from stumbling, and to present us before the presence of his glory with exceeding joy, to the only God our Saviour, be glory and majesty, dominion and power, now and evermore. Amen.

God and the Farmer

Reverend Murray L. Wagner
Pastor, Pleasant Valley Church of the Brethren,
Weyers Cave, Virginia

Murray Wagner's church is in the country which he loves. Preaching there, he feels, is his life work. Born in 1905, in Glen Rock, Pennsylvania, he went to high school for a while, then left school to work in a factory.

He felt the call to preach, studied at Blue Ridge and Elizabethtown Colleges and Crozer Seminary. On week ends and during summer vacations he preached and carried on pastoral work in mountain sections of Maryland and Virginia. He had always had a love for the out-of-doors, and these interludes gave him an opportunity to understand rural life—living and thinking and preaching for farmers. Each summer since then he has devoted much time to work in camps with young people.

On September 3, 1939—the day World War II was officially declared—he was installed as pastor of Pleasant Valley Church of the Brethren, Weyers Cave, Virginia. This church, situated in the heart of the Shenandoah Valley, is one of the finest of this denomination. It is also the rural church at its best, in its most challenging aspect. Murray Wagner has become a farmer-preacher. He has his family, his garden, his church. He works with farmers and their wives in local projects and he is a devoted friend of every child in his congregation.

In this sermon he shows his love for the farm and the farmer, a knowledge of his problems and a desire to help to meet his needs. He believes the farmer can best solve his problems with the guidance of the Heavenly Father, who is the Good Shepherd of His sheep.

Sermon Twenty-one

Text: *As the mountains are round about Jerusalem, so the Lord is round about His people.* Psalm 125:2

THE BIBLE IS A BOOK OF RURAL LIFE. ITS STORY begins in a garden, and ends with a vision of a city whose features are those of the countryside—"a river of life, bright as crystal, proceeding out of the throne of God, and of the Lamb, in the midst of the street thereof." The lawgivers of this Book were men who followed the flocks; its prophets were, for the most part, men with the desert sand in their beards and the smell of the sod in their homespun clothing. And when the Saviour came He was presented as a child of a peasant couple, born in a stable. The countryside was good to Him, but when He came to the city His spirit was burdened by the sin and the artificiality He found there. It was "just outside the city wall" that He died, and it was on a cross which had been carried to the spot by a Cyrenean farmer. A country garden was the scene of His triumphant resurrection and the story insists that it was from a country hilltop that He took His departure from His disciples.

The Old Testament has a keen interest in fertile valleys but its people sought the high places. The mountains promised security and strength. Quite early men came to think of their god as one who dwelt in the high places. The God-fearing found the mountains suggestive of their deity.

We who dwell in this fruitful valley, hemmed in by mountains on every hand, feel a close kinship to those men and women of old in finding our God, like theirs, so vividly suggested by the hills. Our house of worship, like that so dear to the Psalmist, "stands by hills surrounded," and our daily lives are enriched by the fact that even as "the mountains are round about Jerusalem, so the Lord is round about His people." In His presence and in sight of His hills we feel faith and courage rising within us to meet the daily task.

Consider that the God of the devout farmer is as *real* as the hills. Here, where life is more simple, we see rather clearly that every need of physical man is met by Mother Nature. Food, clothing, shelter, fuel, oils, medicines, and metals—to mention but a few of the more obvious of our needs—all have their origin in the ground. We come to see that "our civilization is based upon nine inches of topsoil, and when that's gone our culture is gone." Facing that stern reality we ask for a God as real as the hills.

It is good to know that we can find just such a God and that our own experience leads us to know, firsthand, that

> Raise the stone and there thou shalt find Me;
> Cleave the wood, and there I am.

We are not asking for theological discussions as to the discovery of God, and we have not concerned ourselves overmuch with such matters. We want God to be so real and so vivid to us that no argument will be necessary. One Whom we will adore but Who needs no adornment is brought to us as we live by the side of these mountains. We are not inclined to plant daisies on the sides of Horseheads Mountain, nor do we feel we could enhance the beauty of nature by painting the pine trees. Our adornment would not increase our adoration, nor yet would theological fineries increase our appreciation of God.

Because He is just as natural and more real than the mountains, we have no inclination to doubt Him nor occasion to defend Him. How would one proceed to *prove* the existence of Hawk's Bill? All we need to do is open our eyes and point to that peak. Or how shall we *defend* Massanutten Peak? That mass of storm-carved limestone needs no defending. We stand silent before it; we take a deep breath and look at its topmost pinnacle, then walk away, "strangely warmed"—stronger and straighter and more courageous, for we have heard a voice saying, "As the mountains stand round about thee, so the Lord is round about His people."

Furthermore, this God, Who is so very real to us, is silent in His power. For unnumbered centuries the storms have broken over Massanutten, but always the last thunderclap rolls up the Valley and leaves the Peak unmoved, cleaner for the engagement.

So theological controversies, storms of doubt and of criticism, leave the true God unscathed, silently victorious. As against the Peak, so the storms beat out their very existence against Him, and His only reply is as the silence of the mountain itself. And that power inspires us in the same direction:

> I need not shout my faith. Thrice eloquent
> Are quiet trees and the green listening sod;
> Hushed are the stars, whose power is never spent;
> The hills are mute, yet how they speak of God!

Again, the God Who is round about His people is an *intimate* God. Even though "no man hath seen God at any time" we know that "He is not far from each one of us, for in Him we live and move and have our being." The mountains round about remind us that their Creator is even nearer than are they.

Paul wrote, "they that wait upon the altar have their portion with the altar," and even so, they who labor in these hills and in their shadow have their portion with them.

Several years ago I met an elderly man working in a cabbage patch on the slope of a steep, rocky hill in Maryland. I had been accustomed to fertile fields and gently rolling land and was curious about the possible crops on such soil as that which the old gentleman was working. I said:

"Tell me, what *can* you raise in these hills?"

His answer came like a rifle shot:

"Men!"

Stalwart and courageous are the men who come from the daily life and struggle with Mother Earth. Their sharing at the altar has been a sharing with God in an intimate fellowship. We inherently regard this intimacy as being just as natural as anything can be, and we express this relationship in many ways, one of which is in the employment of the phrase, *"Mother* Nature."

The awareness of the presence of God as an intimate companion brings us, through the simplicity and fullness of the mountains and other evidences of His handiwork, to a place of resolution and repentance. "It is the goodness of God that leadeth men to repentance," and we behold that moving goodness on every side. Tilling the soil at the foot of these peaks and between those worn mountain fingers, pointing ever upward, simply must make the farmer aware that even so "the Lord stands round about His people."

This goodness of God's leads men more powerfully than can any concept of His wrath.

Finally, the hills remind us of the *Eternal* God.

It is a natural desire of ours to want to be worthy of immortality. We long for permanence. We are made for eternity, and we see that sooner or later our search is doomed to failure if we fall short of finding Him Who made "the eternal hills."

Yet those very hills, which the writer of Genesis calls "eternal," may fail us! We know the mountains are not eternal. Very, very slowly do they waste away, but their imperceptible change is continuous nonetheless. On these very hills, within the sight of each of us as we now sit here, we may find the fossils of marine life which flourished when the sea covered this spot. And those mountains, slowly pushing their way out of the sea, carried with them this sea-borne life whose fossils remind us over and over again that:

"Change and decay in all around I see"; and from the innermost recesses of our souls comes the yearning cry, "Oh! Thou Who changest not, abide with me!"

In our desire for the eternal we can understand, in part, the spirit of the Psalmist. We picture him in distress; he has been everywhere in his search for deliverance. He looks in every direction, but no help is evident. He paces about, and then looks to the mountains close at hand, hoping that some sign of an approaching friend may be seen, but there is none. "I look unto the hills. From whence shall my help come?" No refuge; no salvation from the mountains for the oppressed. And then, ah! "My help cometh from Jehovah Who made heaven and earth!"

We, as that one long ago, come to find security and permanence not in hills but in their Creator. For He is able to "take up the islands as a very little thing," and for Him the centuries pass as the hours. He is permanent. Our God is not hurried in His plans. His design is not frustrated by a few men nor by a few nations nor yet by a dozen generations on as many planets. God can wait—He can outwait the hills. While scorching heat and splitting frosts combine with drought and flood to disintegrate the mountains and carry them into the sea, the Lord "stands round about His people."

In God's waiting for mankind to return unto Him He places a special blessing upon One Who reveals the Father unto us. Jesus was especially intimate with His Father and with His Creation. The sower, the lilies, the harvest fields, and even the sparrow did not escape His attention. He brought the Creator and His Creation together in the soul of man. Those who would follow Him will find themselves ushered into the Presence Divine whenever they look unto the hills.

It is this same Jesus, Whom we have properly come to call "Lord," Who shows in His life the very thing that our souls have sought. In His magnificent life we see so clearly that power and assurance that we have sought in nature. The mountains were but His shadow, and their attributes were simply to bring us closer to the Christ in Whom we find personified all of the answers to our searching. He is always reminding us that God is very real; that He is intimate with each of us and that He is the Eternal. All who would find eternity; all who would have permanence in life must know that "in Him is the life."

Jesus not only *told* men about it; He revealed unto all mankind that even more truly than of the mountains, can it be said of the Father that "As the mountains are round about Jerusalem so the Lord is round about His people."

Where Is He?

REVEREND MURRAY ALEXANDER CAYLEY
Minister, First Presbyterian Church, Rochester, New York

THE REVEREND MURRAY ALEXANDER CAYLEY, widely known as a teacher and lecturer, has been minister of the First Presbyterian Church since February, 1940.

The Canadian-born clergyman is a graduate of the University of Toronto and Columbia University. He studied religion at Victoria Seminary, Toronto, and Union Theological Seminary, New York. After serving in the Royal Air Force in World War I, Mr. Cayley was ordained by the United Church of Canada and occupied a home mission charge in Saskatchewan for one year.

For nine years before his present pastorate, he served at Greystone Presbyterian Church of Elizabeth, New Jersey. Before that, he was assistant pastor of North Avenue Presbyterian Church of New Rochelle, director of Religious Education of Mount Washington Presbyterian Church, New York, and for three years he was a teacher of public speaking at Drew University and assistant in that department at Union Seminary.

Along with other duties, Mr. Cayley serves on the staff of the Rochester Institute of Technology, where he has classes in psychology, economics, and philosophy. He also works a great deal with young people, spending much time in summer conferences.

He is the author of two books, *Are We Spiritually Dead?* and *Drama and Pageantry,* and he has contributed poems to various magazines and devotional booklets.

Sermon Twenty-two

TEXT: *Where is He?* MATTHEW 2:2

HE WISE MEN ASKED THIS A LONG TIME AGO. IT IS a very pointed question. Where in Heaven's name is He today?

O where is He for whom the wisest seek?
Not men whose wisdom is but shrewdness
Coldly drawn in lines which point to human arrogance—

But men who know the emptiness of life
Without the gentle trust in manger humbleness.
The soft warm clasp of baby fingers brings
To this wise man
The wisdom of a soul upon its knees before its king.

O where is He for whom the shattered world still seeks?
He came so long ago—
The stars His beacon lights—
The angels sang His lullaby—
The Kingdom of our God of Love, His theme.
He came.
He lived in three short years
A life so rapturously full of kindliness,
Of hope, of gentle helpfulness to all
Who longed for life at its full best!

He died
A vicious death
When men in savage fury vented out
Their screaming trust in self—
With cheap defiance of a far-off God.

He came again—
I know not how—
I only know
That in some quiet moments I have found Him here.
One day I walked a shaded path
Beside a gossiping stream.
The trees were gold and russet.
Autumn sunshine filled each gap
The falling leaves had made.
The crisp and quiet air
Had fragile shelves of drifted smoke—
Ambrosial—from many little fires by tidy lawns.
A chattering squirrel—a pheasant flushed—
A far-off bell—the springy turf
All soothed with mystic medicine
The tattered nerves of life.
I found Him there.

I found Him too
When once in simple trust,

I put prudential carefulness aside
And gambled on a life in His own cause.
I little recked the urgency it meant
That I should trust Him, then,
Down each dim hallway of tomorrow's life.
Such unknown quantities were lurking there!

And I had pride!
O I was proud of my own strength.
Did I not know a lot of things?
I knew that power, comfort, profit
Were the goals which satisfied one side of me.
I want them still—
But they must wait—
While His hand guides me,
Where, I scarcely know.
And then,
Because I felt so sure that I was right.
I found it easy to assume a righteous pose.
I looked on life with crafty eyes
And loved to fling my taunts and arrows
At my fellow man
Because he walked his wilful way.
I found it easy then to judge, condemn, upbraid;
And all the while my righteous little soul
Fed on the very chaff I sermonized upon.

But now—His day is here again!
And where is He?

Let go our towering boast in self.
Let go our easy damning of our neighbors' strife.
O let us seek His manger majesty
In every common walk of human life.

'Tis Christmas now—
And we would have it nestle in our homes
Around the fireside bright
A sacred light—
A presence—
Else the day will come and go
And emptiness of heart and soul
Will be our boon.

So—let us look
At what we've done to crown our King.

We buy—we sell—
We give—and take
And all too oft we do it
With a jaundiced eye.
And why?
Perchance because there's little now
That's sacred in the enterprise.
My soul revolts
When from some trash-strewn entryway
A speaker blares in tinny notes
The carols we have learned to love.
So—we pass by with callous ear,
And lose the sheen of tenderness
These hymns once stirred within our hearts.
The bargain counter's hiding now
Beneath each lovely green fir bough.

A window holds a lovely crèche
And in we go to buy and thresh
'Mid churning crowds and think it fine
That business flatters things Divine!

And that's not all we've done
To Christmas Day and Him.
Our printing presses grind anon
An endless stream of manufactured wishes
We have not the wit to voice.
With tailored dogs and sailing ships
With bulging Santas, candles, bells
We celebrate our Saviour's birth.
We wildly dash through address books
And then blue-pencil Cousin Sue
Unless she wrote last Christmas too.

It's scarcely to be wondered at
When all is said and all is through
That now instead of angels' songs
A whistling bomb comes down the blue.

It's Christmas now—and where is He,
The Master, Babe of Bethlehem?
Not in those scenes I fear.
But you can find Him—still—this year.

In quiet homes where 'round a tree—
No matter if it's large or small—
Sometimes there'll be no tree at all—
A little group, in happiness is found.
You'll find Him there.
I felt His presence as I rang a bell
And took the handclasp of the folk
Who came and pulled me in.
"Here's where we sing the carols," someone said.
And one imp whispered, "That's for Ma,
Don't you dare tell!"
I felt Him near, when, by a bed of pain,
I heard these words
"Look what they sent! It touched me so
To know they thought of me."
And then
The 'phone bell rang and someone asked
"Can we have one with us who'll be
Away from home on Christmas Day?"

And then—one day—
I found Him once again.
I read the story of a little lad.
(It crushed my very heart in two).
His Christmas Day was coming too,
But screaming shells had made
A shambles of the place he once called home.
Yet there he trudged, and in his arms
A smaller waif was tightly clutched.
Then presently a man was passing by,
And as he stumbled through the rubble and debris
He briefly paused and said,
"That's quite a heavy load for one so small.
You'd better let me carry him."
But this reply came from the other:
"O he's not heavy, he's my brother."
I found Him *there.*

Resurrection

THE RIGHT REVEREND MONSIGNOR FULTON J. SHEEN, D.D.
Associate Professor of Philosophy, The Catholic University of America, Washington, D. C.

MONSIGNOR SHEEN'S is one of the important living voices of our day. His forceful and convincing preaching makes every listener eager to catch each word. To hear him is to realize that here is a man who believes what he says and who has thought out his message calmly and prayerfully.

He was ordained in Peoria, Illinois, in 1919, then did graduate work at the Catholic University of America, the University of Louvain, Belgium, and Angelico University, Rome. Step by step he has risen from very modest places in the Church to be one of the most honored Catholic preachers. He taught at St. Edmund's College, Ware, and the Westminster (London) Diocesan Seminary in 1925-26; in 1926, the University of Louvain, recognizing his genius, awarded him the Cardinal Mercier prize for International Philosophy, the first time this honor was ever given an American.

Before the war, he was called to preach in Europe nearly every summer from 1925 to 1939, speaking in London at Westminster Cathedral and St. Patrick's Church, Soho Square; at the University of Cambridge Summer School, at Glasgow; in Rome, and elsewhere on the continent. In 1934, he was named a Papal Chamberlain of the late Pontiff, Pope Pius XI, with the title of Very Reverend Monsignor, and the following year, Pius XI made him a Domestic Prelate with the title of Right Reverend Monsignor.

During most of the year, he is busy teaching Philosophy at The Catholic University of America, but is in such demand as a speaker, that he gives more than one hundred sermons and addresses each year, speaking in almost every major city in the United States to secular and religious groups who throng to hear him. For years he has been the regular Lenten preacher at St. Patrick's Cathedral, New York, and is the special Advent preacher at the Church of the Blessed Sacrament, New York, where his Advent messages are enthusiastically received.

He has written some twenty books on philosophy, religion,

morals, and socio-economic questions, including *Freedom under God, Whence Come Wars,* and *Philosophies at War.*

"Resurrection" was his Easter sermon on Sunday, April 9, 1944. In it he discusses the Easter message in its relation to men in a world at war, and pleads for a Christian world and brotherhood. It is included through the cooperation of the National Council of Catholic Men, sponsors of the Catholic Hour.

Sermon Twenty=three

TEXT: *I am the resurrection and the life.* JOHN 11:25

HE WORLD IS ONE VAST GOLGOTHA AND WE CELEbrate an Easter. What a Paradox! How justify a Christ rising in the glow of the morning and Christians dying in the blackness of the night.

If Christ has won a victory, why do we fear defeat? If Christ has conquered evil, why do we still have to defeat it?

If Christ is Peace, why is there war?

The answer to the paradox is this: Christ by His Cross and resurrection has overcome sin and death and evil *in principle,* but we have not overcome them *in fact* until we appropriate His merits by right living and obedience to His Holy Will.

He overcame sin and evil in principle, for the very worst thing that sin can do is not to steal, or wage war, or persecute, or murder. The worst thing sin can do is to kill God, for that is sin in its essence. Sin is essentially anti-God. The Crucifixion is therefore the final act of sin.

When sin did that, by nailing Him to a cross, it exhausted itself; it was sin's utmost, its dying gasp. It could do no more if it lived a million years.

But though sin had done all that it could, the Son of God had not done all that He could; for by the Power of God He could rise from the tomb where sin interred Him and evil governments stood guard. The Resurrection, therefore, was sin's defeat. From now on sin could bomb cities, persecute religion, and torture women, but it could never do anything so wicked again. Having been defeated in its mightiest deed, it could never be victorious again, for the Devil's worst was conquered by God's best. Sin had been overcome in principle; and in the truest sense the Saviour standing by an empty tomb could say, "I have overcome the world."

But though Our Lord overcame sin in principle, sin is not overcome in *fact;* and it is not overcome in fact, because we are free. A scientist may discover an infallible cure for disease. The disease in that case has been overcome in principle. But since patients are free not to accept the remedy, the disease may every now and then win a momentary victory.

In like manner, the Victory over sin and death may be rejected at any particular moment of history. The same divine love which permitted men to reject Christ on Calvary, still permits them to spurn His conquest over sin—for God is not a dictator. Man is still free even in the face of God. The Good News of Redemption may be eternally broadcast from the Empty tomb, but we are all free not to tune in on its saving grace. No man is forced to live a resurrected life. Man's evil is still his own. He can still win his passing victories over Divine Love, until the final gathering-in when Christ shall come with His Cross to judge the living and the dead.

Divine Love is doomed to passing defeat, because men are free.

He went to the Cross because there is so much sin in the world that sinlessness cannot exist in it. He suffered not because He was vicious, but because He was virtuous, and we were not; not because He had sinned, but because He had not, and we had. Hence, Divine Love entered history as suffering love—and necessarily so, for the Cross is the inevitable consequence of sin's rebellions against goodness. For how else shall the Divine Goodness be shown in history except by a momentary powerlessness in the face of the perverse wills He came to redeem?

The Risen Christ walks through secular history holding in His scarred hands the promise of victory, the pledge of peace, and the seal of happiness, but so long as men are free they will always have the power to say "Nay" to that love. Human freedom is capable of rejecting victory at any moment by confronting the sacrificial love of Christ with its own sinfulness and sin. Given these two elements—the freedom to rebel on the part of man and perfect love on the part of God—and you have historical tragedy; you have your Easter celebrated in a terrible and awful war, a cross above the altar in a Resurrection Mass, and the scars of a Christ beside an empty tomb. Sin was overcome in principle, but not in fact, for the love that seeketh not its own can always be recrucified by the love that seeks its own.

Hence, with a frightening realism, Our Lord never taught that His Resurrection would banish evil from history, except to those who profit by it. Therefore, He sent His apostles out as sheep among wolves, warning that cockle would be planted among the wheat, that foolish virgins would mingle with the wise, that the sea would be filled with good and bad fish, that as the world persecuted Him so it would persecute them, that as it hated Him so it would hate them, that they must be prepared to be led before Magistrates and Kings, to be accused falsely, and to be put to death, until the coming of the Christ in power and glory. The world must be the battlefield of the City of God and the City of Man, the city of love and the city of hate, until the trumpet blows and Christ shall reign in Mercy to the saved and in justice to the lost, for sin then will have been defeated in principle *and* in fact: "I am the resurrection and the life."

Turn now to the world at this moment. There is darkness over the earth; Christ has been recrucified; Evil has its hour. Are you who believe in the Risen Christ surprised? Of course not. We know that no world which rejects the sovereign love of God, which disrupts family life, propagates evil, fosters irreligion, can live short of war. But the modern pagans are surprised. Things did not turn out as they planned. They thought science, progress, and education would banish sin and evil. Now they are downcast because they find thistles where they planted figs. Things simply did not act as they expected. They cannot understand how paganism in thought should end in barbarism of action, how the outlawing of God should end in the tyrannization of man. And they are destined for still greater disillusionments. They are strangers in the houses they planned for homes. They are utterly repudiated and pessimistic. They made a Godless world, now they must live in a loveless one.

Share not this pessimism. Evil is now in the ascendancy; but its victory is transitory; the powers which rule are already dethroned in principle. The Captain of the Wars, the Risen Christ, could be summoned by the free will of man to smite evil and bring peace, but He will come only when man begins to be disillusioned not about his politics and economics, but disillusioned about himself, for self-disillusionment is the beginning of repentance.

Despair not! Hear ye Him: "I have overcome the world." Say with Paul: "Who then shall separate us from the love of Christ? Shall tribulation? or distress? or famine? or nakedness? . . . or the sword? As it is written: For thy sake we are put to death all the day long. We are accounted as sheep for the slaughter. But in all these things we overcome because of him that hath loved us. For I am sure that neither death, nor life, nor angels, nor principalities, nor powers, nor things present, nor things to come, nor might, nor height, nor depth, nor any other creature shall be able to separate us from the love of God, which is in Christ Jesus our Lord" (Romans 8:35-39) .

Despair not! Ours is the tragic beauty—not that of a Fair Lady safe from combat, nor even of a Widow mourning over a Spouse so full of promise, but rather the Lady in a Fortress in the midst of an assault, holding the fortress, preventing a break.

Despair not! Ours is a religion of catastrophe. We were born in the midst of the worst world-shattering catastrophe of the ages—the defeat of Our Leader and Our King. But we shall never forget that it was the very moment He said He was the Son of the Living God that He foretold He would be crucified; and that while describing the terrible catastrophe of the destruction of a city, He said: "Lift up your heads, your redemption is at hand" (Luke 21:28).

Despair not! The Stone which the builders rejected will be made the head of the corner. There are treasures even in darkness! The Christian law of progress is the reverse of the law of the world. The world makes progress when all goes well; the Church makes progress even when all goes ill and it seems that no human power can stop it. The world is ripe for renewal. Out of the catacombs it will come again to give Europe new souls and new hearts! But this regeneration must begin with you and me, as individuals, in which we will repeat a great moment of history.

Centuries ago, Robert Bruce, the great leader of Scotland, willed to go on a pilgrimage to the Holy Land. Before his departure he was stricken ill. He called his friend, Lord Douglas, and said to him: "When I am dead, I want you to take out my heart, put it in a small casket and take it with you to the land that was sanctified by the feet of the Saviour." Accordingly when Bruce died, Lord Douglas took out his heart and put it in a small golden casket and took it with him to the Holy Land. Arriving there he was engaged in battle by the Moors who were putting his own soldiers to rout. Turning to them and holding up the heart of Robert Bruce he said to them: "Where the heart of Robert Bruce was wont to go, there go ye." Then throwing the heart of Bruce in among the enemy, his followers, anxious to recover that which they loved, went in amongst the enemy and won the day. And may we of the Western World so love, not the heart of Bruce, but the Heart of Christ, that we may throw it in among the enemy to bear witness that He is the Redeemer of them as well as of us; and then, loving that Heart, may we go in amongst them to reconquer it and win the day for a Christian world wherein we are our brothers' keepers. For in the eyes of God this war is already over, and God knows who has won! And, please God, victory may be ours!

PRAYER: *O Lord Jesus Christ, Who in Thy mercy hearest the prayers of sinners, pour forth, we beseech Thee, all grace and blessing upon our country and its citizens. We pray in particular for the President— for our Congress—for all our soldiers—for all who defend us in ships, whether on the seas or in the skies—for all who are suffering the hardships of War. We pray for all who are in peril or in danger. Bring us all after the troubles of this life into the haven of peace, and reunite us all together forever, O dear Lord, in Thy glorious heavenly kingdom.*

NIHIL OBSTAT: Arthur J. Scanlan, S.T.D., *Censor Librorum*

IMPRIMATUR: ✠ Francis J. Spellman, D.D., *Archbishop, New York*

168

Why Weepest Thou?

REVEREND HAROLD COOKE PHILLIPS, D.D.
Pastor, First Baptist Church, Cleveland, Ohio

HAROLD COOKE PHILLIPS is one of the outstanding Baptist ministers of the Middle West. He is a forceful, thoughtful, and deeply spiritual preacher. Born in Westmoreland, Jamaica, British West Indies, in 1892, he came to the United States in 1912 and studied at Denison University, Columbia University, and Union Theological Seminary. He received the honorary degree of D.D. from Wesleyan University.

In 1922, Dr. Phillips was ordained a Baptist minister and served First Church, Mt. Vernon, New York, from 1922 until 1928, when he was called to First Church in Cleveland, Ohio. He has contributed numerous articles on relig-ious subjects to various publications, and is the author of *Life That is Life Indeed, Seeing the Invisible,* and *Sails and Anchors.*

"Easter Sunday is a strange combination of the human and the divine," Dr. Phillips says. He discusses the immortal scene in the cemetery where Mary Magdalene stands, weeping for Jesus. He reminds us of the three great enemies of man, shows that Christ brought deliverance, and asks quite disturbingly if even now we recognize the full significance of Jesus' life and teaching, crucifixion, death, and resurrection. He feels that much of the tragedy among men is due to the fact that we do not know salvation.

Sermon Twenty-four

TEXT: *Woman, why weepest thou?* JOHN 20:15

EASTER SUNDAY IS A STRANGE COMBINATION OF the human and the divine. For what is more human than death, and what is more divine than the faith that in Christ Jesus God has conquered death and brought life and immortality to light? Death of course is a reality which we cannot evade nor belittle. Human bravado never seems quite so out of place as in the presence of death. Not long since, Mr. Irvin Cobb died. Of his type he was, I suppose, our best-known and loved humorist. I heard him once long ago and liked him. He was no doubt a man of very fine qualities. His humor was always clean and wholesome. But Irvin Cobb tried, unfortunately, to make fun of death, and failed miserably. His wisecracks about it, given such wide publicity in our papers, were nothing more than silly bravado and cheap exhibitionism. That is one area where humor goes sour and backfires. To profane the dignity of death is to profane the dignity of life. For life and death are inseparable. They are both of a piece. Let us turn our minds today, then, to an incident in the twentieth chapter of the Gospel of John, which reveals at once the human and divine aspect of this Easter Day.

The scene is laid in a cemetery. Mary Magdalene stands there, by the tomb of Jesus, weeping. Jesus comes to her and asks, "Woman, why weepest thou?" She replies, "Sir, if thou have borne him hence, tell me where thou hast laid him. . . ." She does not recognize Jesus. She thinks He is the gardener. He reveals His identity and commissions her to tell the disciples that He is risen from the dead. As we know, there are two types of Resurrection stories in the New Testament. There is one that stresses the nonmaterial, yet none the less objective, reality of the Resurrection. This type predominates in the New Testament. There is another type, however, such as we are considering now, which emphasizes the reanimation of a physical body. I am glad that there are these two types, for some of us find one more convincing and reassuring than the other. Remember, however, that the primary matter on Easter Sunday is not the manner of the Resurrection—whether Jesus appeared in His physical body or in a nonmaterial, spiritual form—but the indisputable fact of the Resurrection. Let us then take this question which Jesus addressed to Mary Magdalene and think about it today.

It seems on the face of it a strange question. If you or I were to see a woman in tears, standing by a newly-made grave, we should probably not ask her why she was weeping. We should know. We should know that someone very dear to her had gone away and that her tears were the natural expression of her grief-stricken heart. And yet, even though the question seemed unnecessary, we are very glad that it was asked, because the first observation we want to make about this text is that the glory of the Christian religion lies in the fact that it is not afraid to get to the bottom of the deepest tragedies of life. It probes to the root of sorrow: "Why weepest thou?" The Christian religion does not turn aside from tragedy. It does not squint at it or cast at it an evasive look. It does not glance at it momentarily and then start talking about something else. It faces tragedy squarely, fearlessly and thoroughly. "Woman, you are in trouble. Something is wrong. You are weeping. Why are you weeping? Let us get down to the bottom of this matter." We should thank God

170

that the religion we profess is not afraid to face the worst. Indeed, how could our religion do less? Its symbol is a cross. It started in starkest tragedy. It began in the darkness of human sin, suffering, and death. It started because it won an initial victory over such tragedies. On Good Friday hearts were heavy, spirits weighted down with sorrow, and eyes dimmed with tears. From that, Christianity emerged victorious. It has faced the worst; it knows the worst; it has triumphed over the worst. Christianity is not afraid of tears.

How fortunate that this should be so! A religion that could not face the worst would have no message for this world. For has the world ever harbored more grief-stricken lives, more broken hopes and hearts and homes, more shattered plans, more just plain tragedy and grief, suffering and tears, than now? It is beyond imagination to conceive. If it were possible for any one human being to comprehend the weight of the world's woe, he would go mad. Fortunately no one can comprehend the suffering of the human family today. Only God can. And only God, or one who speaks for Him and can make available the resources of the Eternal God, is equipped to face up to such a world. Only Easter can answer Good Friday. Nothing else can. "Woman, why weepest thou?"

In the second place let us ask, why was she weeping? When asked, "Why weepest thou?" she replied, "Sir, if thou have borne him hence, tell me where thou hast laid him. . . ." She had lost something beautiful. Something lovely had gone out of her life. Jesus had done much for Mary Magdalene. He had brought her relief from a serious malady. He had brought her life. He meant much to her. He meant more to her per-chance than all else—and now he was gone! How do we feel when some-thing lovely goes out of our life? Perhaps there was some ideal that once meant much to us: the vision of purity, the sense of honor, or integrity. But we have compromised these values away. Do we feel the touch of remorse? Or perchance we had a rich and meaningful friendship, and, like Judas, either through ignorance or wilful evil, we have betrayed it. And the light has gone. Do we miss it? Perchance we had a fine and potentially meaningful spiritual capacity. We were once very sensitive to the appeal of beauty; we never failed to admire goodness. Our con-science was such that, like a delicate instrument, it registered the ap-proach of what was jarring or discordant. But maybe now, through neglect or disuse or self-indulgence, this lovely meaningful capacity has gone—atrophied, or died. Do we miss it—miss it enough perhaps to weep? Would we be willing to go to the sepulcher where it lies buried and pray for its resurrection and return?

Speaking more generally, let us ask, why do people weep? What are the sources of human tears, of human sorrow, of the tragedy that stalks the earth today? May we not say that they derive from three sources—

sin, suffering, and separation? These are not necessarily exclusive. Sin and suffering, for example, are often closely allied. Sin invariably brings suffering, though not all suffering is the result of sin. And separation, by which we mean death, that, too, is sometimes due to sin, as are hundreds of thousands of deaths in this war-torn world. Shall we not on this Easter morning have the honesty to admit that the main source of human grief today is human sin? We may speak and write quite learnedly about the causes of war—economic, social, political—but when you come right down to it, this hideous war which haunts us day and night with its sinister shadow is due primarily to human sin. The plain truth is that this is a moral universe, and that immoral principles or practices simply do not work in a moral universe. We are but kicking against the goad. Some moderns are inclined to belittle sin, to make light of it. Anyone who in the presence of this world makes light of sin needs to have his mind examined. For sin is no more of a joke than is death. We can laugh off the one no more than the other.

Here, then, are the three great enemies of man—sin, suffering, and separation; these bring tears to our eyes. It is heartening to realize that these are the very enemies that Christianity boldly confronts. It faces the worst that befalls us and offers deliverance. Matthew's Gospel boldly declares, "The people that sat in darkness have seen a great light." And the darkness that enfolds human life, whether it has its source in the mind, the heart, or the conscience, is somehow related to these great realities—sin, suffering, and separation. These are the three enemies that Christianity singles out and from which Christianity offers man deliverance. Sin—"Thou shalt call his name Jesus: for he shall save his people from their sin." Suffering—"Our light affliction, which is but for a moment, worketh for us a far more exceeding and eternal weight of glory." "All things work together for good to them that love God." Separation— "I am the resurrection and the life . . . whosoever liveth and believeth in me shall never die." Christianity assures us that through God's grace we can conquer sin, suffering can be made our servant, not our master, and death not a tomb that enfolds us but a door to eternal life.

Let us observe in the third place that Mary, in her distress, did not recognize her deliverer. She mistook Him for the gardener. It is instructive to recall how many times Jesus is reported to have appeared to His disciples or His friends without being recognized by them. We have at least three instances of this. On the road to Emmaus, we read that "their eyes were holden, that they should not know him." Another incident occurred on the seashore. At the suggestion of Simon Peter, the disciples, after the Crucifixion, had gone back to fishing. Jesus appeared to them, a solitary figure on the beach. We read, "The disciples knew not that it was Jesus." And in the incident today, the same fact occurs. Mary Magdalene is standing by the grave of Jesus, weeping. Jesus appears to her and asks, "Why weepest thou?" She does not recognize Him. She mistakes Him for the gardener. The answer to her question was before her, but she did not recognize it; the solution of the problem was at hand, but she was not aware of it; the power which could have assuaged her grief and turned her sorrow and her tears into joy, and death into life, was by her side, talking with her—but she did not know it. She thought He was a gardener.

This fact is more than just an interesting occurrence. It is one of the sobering truths of our religion. The truth is that the significance of Jesus' life and teaching was not recognized by His generation. "Had they known it," said St. Paul, "they would not have crucified the Lord of Glory." "O Jerusalem," said Jesus, "if thou hadst known, even thou, . . . the things which belong unto thy peace! but now they are hid from thine eyes." Do we recognize even yet the full significance of Jesus' life and teaching? Might we be still regarding Him as though He were only a gardener? Can it be that much of the continuing tragedy, suffering, and woe of the world is due to the fact that we do not recognize the source of our salvation?

Why did not Mary recognize Him? Was it perchance because she had a wrong conception of reality? "They have taken away my Lord," she said, "and I know not where they have laid him." She was identifying her Lord with a dead body! Imagine that! She came looking for Him in one form, while He appeared in an entirely different guise. She was thinking of Christ in terms of death and so did not recognize Him, since He appeared in terms of life. Her salvation from sin and suffering and death was therefore before her though she knew it not. Many of us may lose our faith or our sense of religious reality just that way. Here is a young person brought up in a Christian home and church. He goes away to college, where his horizons become extended. New facts, scientific or historic, come moving across the frontier of his mind. He looks for the Christ of his less mature years and cannot find Him. Like Mary, he exclaims: "They have taken away my Lord and I know not where they have laid him." Yet he has not really lost the Christ. He has perhaps lost an immature conception of Christ. And all the while the Christ may be standing by, not in a dead idea but in some new, more vital and challenging truth. Indeed, this has been true of the history of the church itself. The Christian church began in a primitive simplicity. But, as Christian faith spread through the Roman empire and the Greek world, a more elaborate type of organization became inevitable. No doubt there were some souls who said, "They have taken away my Lord." Not so! Christ was not taken away but risen in a new form suited to a new situation.

That form, too, was to become obsolete. There came the Protestant

Reformation, which swept away many of the dogmas which were not only dead but decayed. And again devout souls, viewing the work of Martin Luther, said in substance, "They have taken away my Lord, and I know not where they have laid him." Not so! Christ simply appeared in a new form, more relevant to the vital needs of the world. And this was not the last word. For once again living truth was to harden into lifeless dogma. Someone remarked, "They practice fastidiousness at Oxford, and call it righteousness." So came the evangelistic revivals headed by the Wesleys and Whitfield. And once again Christ appeared in a new form more relevant to human need. Mary's grief, then, was due ultimately to the fact that she failed to recognize reality in its most pertinent, vital form. In thinking of her Lord, she was so preoccupied with thoughts of a dead body that she failed to see Him alive—she thought this pulsing being was a gardener.

One wonders this Easter Day whether that may not be precisely the trouble with our world today. What after all is the ultimate source of the world's tragedy? Does it not spring out of the terrific tensions of our modern life? And whence do these tensions come—tensions between races, classes, nations that have brought hell to the earth? They spring, do they not, from our blind loyalty to dead ideas, our preoccupation with outworn concepts which keep us from seeing reality in its most vital, relevant guise? In the field of race relations we cling to race superiority. That is where we think reality is. On the contrary, as we believe, there are advanced and backward races, but there is no scientific evidence for the belief that there are superior and inferior races. That concept is born in human prejudice, and nurtured by human pride. That idea is a dead one. And blind loyalty to it keeps us from seeing reality today. In the field of industrial relations we cling to the idea of unrestricted freedom. We believe in free enterprise with all our heart and soul. We are opposed to regimentation in any of its forms. But the kind of free enterprise that leads either capital or labor to further its selfish ends by endangering the public welfare is not reality. It is a dead concept. In the field of international relations we cling to national sovereignty. We believe in national sovereignty, but the kind of national sovereignty that makes a nation think it can do anything it wishes, any time it wishes, in any way it wishes, regardless, we do not accept. That is no longer reality. That is a dead concept.

"Why weepest thou?" Because Mary Magdelene was identifying reality with a dead body and so could not recognize it as it really was. Just that too has laid on our hearts this burden of war with its incredible woe. Let us bury the idea of race superiority, for it is dead. Then will it rise from the grave in a new form—interracial fellowship. That is reality. Let us bury the idea of selfishness and greed and undisciplined freedom

174

in industry, for it is dead. Then it will rise from the grave in a new form—co-operation for the common good. Let us bury the idea of national sovereignty, for it is dead. Then shall it rise from the grave in the form of international co-operation, collective good will. These new ideas which are struggling to be born may seem to us as unimpressive as did the risen Christ to Mary. She thought he was the gardener. So may we. Yet only in these new concepts can we find life. As long as we cling to the old ones, this world of ours will continue to be a place of darkness and death and winter's gloom. Spring will not come to us until we turn our minds to the new truth. For is it not in these new ideas that the risen Christ appears? Where does one find Christ today? Not with those who preach the gospel of racial arrogance, but with those brave souls who are pioneering on the road of interracial fellowship. Not with those whose controlling idea is selfishness and greed, but with the socially sensitive who try to practice the Golden Rule in industry. Not with those who sponsor the doctrine of national bigotry and arrogance, but with those who are building bridges of international co-operation and peace. It is along these paths the living, risen Christ walks today in life's garden. But he is not the gardener! He is the Lord and Giver of life. Some day, please God, like Mary, our eyes too will be opened and, like her, we shall say, "Master!"

for This We Fight

THE VERY REVEREND ERIC MONTIZAMBERT
Dean of the St. Matthew's Cathedral, Protestant Episcopal, Laramie, Wyoming

DEAN MONTIZAMBERT, one of the leaders of the Episcopal Church in Wyoming, is active in church affairs throughout the State. He is also dean of the Wyoming Missionary College, president of the Church Council, chairman of the Board of Examining Chaplains, and student pastor for the University of Wyoming.

He speaks at various Episcopal summer schools and is known as a conductor of retreats. He has written two books, *Faith Triumphant* (1921) and *The Thought of St. Paul in the Light of the Modern* *World* (1941).

This sermon was preached to the annual convention of the Episcopal Diocese of Western Nebraska, by invitation of the diocese. In it he asks the old question, "What think ye of Christ?" and discusses the temptation to forego the central principles of the Gospel in times of security. He believes that "This is a different strife from any we have ever known. Not sword against sword, not tank against tank, not men against men; but ideas against ideas, and a Faith against a Faith!" He presents a faith for today.

Sermon Twenty-five

TEXT: *What think ye of Christ?* MATTHEW 22:42

NCE, AT A CRUCIAL POINT IN HIS MINISTRY, OUR Lord pressed the disciples for an answer to this question. They had known Him long. They had listened to words "such as never man spake." They had seen the full glory of His life. Yet, when confronted by this hour of decision, only one caught the meaning of His query and saw the vision of the Divine Life in its eternal significance for mankind.

True, that was but an episode in history. The terrible testing of Good Friday was yet to come with its utter shattering of every man's faith; and still undreamed of, was the triumph of Easter Day by which men were lifted out of the shadow of death and the crusade for earth's redemption was begun. Now these men knew the final answer to the great question of Jesus! Now began the most heroic adventure ever wrought into the fabric of history! That day the flaming revolutionary power of the Gospel of this Christ was flung against the terrible might of the Roman totalitarianism and, ere long, as time is measured, the brazen Eagles of the Caesars were prostrate before the Cross of the everlasting King.

2. The very wonder of that picture compels us to set it against the black screen of this present. The scroll of history has unrolled to reveal the meaning of our yesterdays in the horrid blasphemy against God and man in which we are engulfed. Someone has described us as "comrades of chaos." So, indeed, we are. Who can coin a more apt description of the state into which our own history has brought us? *Our own history!* Yes, the record of the thought and action of that great segment of mankind to whom this Gospel has been revealed, and by whom so often betrayed. There is no past. The thing called "history" is far more than an exciting account of things done and done with. It is a mirror of the inner reality of human life. It drives beneath the surface of this present. It tells the modern man why and what he is. We may forget what we call "the past," but we cannot shake it off even if we would because—like our ancestors— it is part of what we are. There is no past. All that in this present we are is the issue of all that we have been—its loves and its hates, its good and its evil, its triumphs and its betrayals! The answer to the questions which surge up into our minds as we look upon this horror is not to be found in an episode nor in a single man drenched with evil though he be. This is a world calamity. It must have a world explanation—and a world expiation. We can no more be rid of our essential responsibility for it than St. Peter, in the midst of the joy of the Resurrection, could crush out of memory that terrible moment when the eyes of Jesus had caught him in his act of denial. He had no alibi. Nor, though "blood, and sweat, and tears, and terror" be our lot in expiation of our failure to fulfill the command of Christ to win mankind for Him, can we forget. What is our alibi for this long, continued smuggery of self-contentment and racial superiority which has led us to starve the missionary, and so to withhold the redeeming Gospel from God's children over the seas? To be sure, we have had our "missionary programs," our pitiful driblets of spare pennies into mite boxes; but, in the face of Calvary and His bitter cry of dereliction, dare we say that we have gone "all out" in obedience to His Will?

In times of security and ease men and nations have succumbed to the temptation to forego the central principles of this Gospel, and to ignore the universal mission to which it commits them. In hours of stress and terror there has always been a rallying to its banner, a resurgence of penitence, a desperate hope that in it might be found the secret of needed strength, the inspiration, and the power that a blatant secularism is impotent to produce. But one who has long given himself to the idolatries of the worship of material things—of wealth, and "bigness," of exaggerated nationalisms, of American or Germanic or British supermanism—does not easily rediscover the deep realities of the spiritual world. The God Who has been kept at a distance seems strange to all who have not tried to know Him, and even the action of prayer becomes difficult indeed. This spiritual isolationism, this habit of separating God from the normal behaviors of existence, has borne evil fruit. It has led us into a false sense of values. It has caused us to describe progress in the terms of the grinding machinery of World's Fairs, as it has blinded us to the truth that all human advancement issues from man's discovery of the meaning of the spiritual realm, revealed through the life and the message of the redeeming Christ. Work is a glorious thing; but he who can work yet cannot pray is defeated from the start.

At this hour, with the strife still heavy upon us, we may think of all that Christian faith and life can be . . . personified in the persons of such saints as Kagawa and Niemoller. Though we are unable to suppress the horrible memory of Pearl Harbor, Hongkong, and Corregidor, where all the horror of a pagan ethic stood revealed, neither can we forget the pure sublimity in heroism of those men and women who, with their nations against us and our cause, have faced imprisonment and torture for their Christ and ours. The power and the glory of Christ has never been more vividly exhibited than in the lives of these Japanese and German believers who stand alone against the mad paganism of man's enemies. Yet who among us has the audacity to condemn a pagan people for putting into action the faith of a pagan life? For more than a hundred years our choice has been between Kagawa and the other, and we chose the other. That has been our answer to the imperious question burning in our ears this day as never before, "What think ye of Christ?" But all that is over. The lesson of our betrayal of Him has been learned. We have set our teeth for the struggle that will not let us go until the victory is ours.

3. This is a strife different from any we have ever known. Not sword against sword, not tank against tank, not men against men; but ideas against ideas, and a Faith against a Faith! Columnists incessantly tell us that "this is a war of machines," that "the nations with the most and the best machines will win." That is either a black lie, or a stupid illiteracy. Which does not matter, for, either way, it is but the resurgence of that false philosophy of living which plunged us into this valley of destruction—that man lives "by things," "by bread alone," by "the idols of his hands," rather than by the spirit within him. The machines are but the

178

instruments of struggle. It is the men who count. Not the men themselves but the ideas, the faiths that drive them to the achievement of their end. Never is it "things" that matter. Always it is ideas. Always it is faiths. Always it is that which possesses the minds and the hearts of men with the spirit of invincibility, and impels them to the goal that is the dearest hope in time and in eternity.

Adolph Schickelgruber knows that. This mad genius, this tenacious prophet of an evil religion, spent, and yet spends himself, in breeding into the youth of that sad land a mighty faith in the gods of his invention. The gods are false, but the faith is real enough: a terrible, relentless, exultant force of evil that cannot be thwarted until it is met by the resistless power of a people wholly dedicated to the "Lord of lords and the King of kings." It is only as we believe enough that we shall be enabled to win enough. For, though it be true that the tools are so essential that they must be vomited from our arsenals in incredible volume, this war—thrust upon us by "the sins, negligences, and ignorances" of the past—is neither struggle of machines nor conflict of economic rivals nor craving for land expansion. Those are secondary things which appear only when men and nations have been trapped in the moral bogs of false and fatal concepts of God and man. This is an infinitely deeper and more far-reaching thing. We, the people of the earth, are engulfed in the mighty Apocalyptic conflict between the monstrous forces of the father of all evil and the powers of Truth and Holiness and God. Yet we dare not rest upon even such a point as that. No disciple of Christ dare think of this as "a holy war." No war is holy. No war, as such, can have upon it the benediction of the Lord of Love. The truth to be realized, if the end is to be gained, is that we and our allies have been caught in a maelstrom of evils—in part, at least, the issue of our negligence—and left no choice but to choose the lesser one. We shall drink this bitter draught of expiation, and pray that its purging may cleanse and transform us with a new vision of God's Will for a different and a better world.

4. "What think ye of Christ?" The question is not rhetorical. It is vital. By each of us it must be answered, and answered in its relation to the world that shall be when the strife of arms is ended. Churchill once said that, with the weight of the war upon him, he could think only of the present. But God forbid that we should be so bound—we whose mightiest task is the creation of a new kind of civilization in which these dreadful things cannot happen to the sons of our sons. Is it not incredible that anyone should tolerate the thought that our loved ones are being sent out to suffer, perhaps to die, for the type of life which has spewed this thing upon us? We have boasted, loose-tongued, about "a high standard of living"; but, all the while, we have had a lowering standard

of life—a world order which, ignoring the dominant ideals of Christ as the supreme principle of human government, has exhibited the full measure of its futility in the sorrow that is ours. We do not fight for that. The freedom that must issue from our struggle is freedom from that which made the struggle possible. We must not battle stupidly for "old things." We must spend ourselves in the fight for true things, however great the sacrifice or frightening the thought of change.

Thus the battle that is upon us now is the beginning of the crusade—like unto that which possessed the disciples on the day of Pentecost—to bring into control of all the wide sweep of life, its business, its industry, its politics, its government, the ultimate principles that inhere in the Gospel of our Lord. No more can we look calmly upon the palace set against the background of the slum! No longer can we tolerate "the family of nations" breeding hatred and war in separate rivalries, and dare to face the shattering implications of the question beating relentlessly upon our consciences—*Is this what you think of Christ?* Clearly, if mankind is to be rescued from the bitter fruits of its ancient folly, the Church to which Christ has given His program of Redemption must gird her loins and go "all out" for the re-creation of the whole fabric of the world. When the last war concluded with the parody of human decency at Versailles, and the desertion by our nation of the cause it had espoused, no single voice of leadership broke through the darkness of that night. This time Christians throughout the world look confidently toward the powerful and fearless leadership of believing men who, like William Temple in England, give utterance in every land to the spirit by which they are possessed. The churches may not sit at the peace tables, but within them there is power enough to control for good the programs of the aftermath.

5. Sometimes thoughts like these are challenged by men who think, mistakenly, that democracy is a strangely self-contained philosophy of life with the seeds of survival within itself. This is not so. This freedom, this democracy, this "way of life"—what is it but the fruit of the Incarnate life of Him who died on Golgotha to make the whole world one? As to that, history has but one thing to say. It is that whether we be Jews or Gentiles, atheists or believers, our entire heritage of liberty is the child of the Gospel of Christ. Separate from this Faith it can be no more than a political expedient subject to the winds of chance. Apart from this Faith, the grand phrases of its constitutions are but the wishful thinking of armchair idealists. For Democracy is Christianity in social action: the revealed Will of God projected into the relationships of human government and there sustained by the active faith of them that believe. True, you may not hold to this Faith. You may not share its worship nor prac-

tice its fellowship nor believe its Creeds. Yet you are inextricably entangled with the gifts of its labors, and for you there is no escape from its rewards. Your debt to it is so long-lasting and so deep that you cannot repay it in this life, nor yet exist even for a day without some vivid reminder that Calvary was for you. "And Jesus turned and looked upon Peter."

What of us, a handful of people on the fringe of a prairie state? No, members, living segments of a mighty supernational Communion whose believing fellowship spans the earth: companions in a universal brotherhood which still upholds the Cross despite the swastika and the rising sun. Kagawa in Tokyo, Niemoller in Berlin—millions of other unnamed heroes in every possessed, yet unbeaten land. These, our spiritual allies, these our brothers in deeper things than blood, will rise to meet us in the struggle of the aftermath! May our penitence, our courage, and our faith make us worthy to stand with them on that day. They have answered. How shall we answer, "What think ye of Christ?"

If the foundations Be Destroyed

Reverend Teunis E. Gouwens, D.D.
Pastor, Second Presbyterian Church, U. S., Louisville, Kentucky

The Preaching of Teunis E. Gouwens, who has been minister of Second Presbyterian Church, Louisville, for twenty-three years, is well represented by this sermon.

Dr. Gouwens was born in South Holland, Illinois, in 1886. He studied at Hope College, Princeton Theological Seminary, New Brunswick Theological Seminary, and Union Theological Seminary. In 1912 he received his B.D. from Rutgers College, and in 1924, his D.D. from Centre College, Kentucky.

Dr. Gouwens was ordained as a minister in the Reformed Church in America in 1913 and became associate pastor, then pastor, of Fort Washington Reformed Church, New York City. In 1915 he was called to Mountain Lakes Community Church, New Jersey, where he remained until 1921, when he became pastor of Second Presbyterian Church, U. S., in Louisville.

From 1916 to 1921, Dr. Gouwens was a member of the Commissions on Social Service and International Relationships of the Federal Council of Churches, and later he was vice-president of the Louisville Council of Churches. He is on the Board of Directors of Louisville Presbyterian Theological Seminary, where he taught Homilectics during 1940 and 1941. Dr. Gouwens was an exchange preacher in England in the summer of 1938. He is the author of *Why I Believe, Can We Repeat the Creed?, The Far Horizons of Scripture, Keep Your Faith,* and other books.

𝔖𝔢𝔯𝔪𝔬𝔫 𝔗𝔴𝔢𝔫𝔱𝔶-𝔰𝔦𝔵

Text: *If the foundations be destroyed, what can the righteous do?*
Psalm 11:3

THE ANSWER, OBVIOUSLY, IS THAT NOTHING CAN be done. Scripture lays strong emphasis on the importance of foundations. A superstructure without a firm base cannot stand in time of storm. On Sable Island, off Nova Scotia, a lighthouse, a hundred feet in height, was erected. Winds, icebergs, and shifting sands made the vicinity so dangerous that it was known as the "graveyard of the Atlantic." In order to make navigation safe, engineering skill had done its best to make the lighthouse permanent. But they had only sand on which to build, and soon the waves threatened to undo all that their labor had accomplished. The lighthouse was taken down and set on another location, but it still rests on sand, and will yield at last to the encroachments of the sea. If the foundations are not reliable, what can the builders do?

The purpose of the Psalmist's question, of course, is to arouse in the righteous a vigilance which shall guard against the collapse of the pillars by which human life is supported. Let those who know the basic requirements of the soul and of society see to it that they are met. In order that life may be sound, that its values may be preserved and increased, and that a better world may be built, it is of the first importance for good people to pay attention to their foundations.

Many things are essential, but we shall limit our discussion to only a few. For one thing, consider the proper regard for the value and dignity of the human soul as a foundation for life. One of the chief errors of men consists in their acceptance of that which is secondary, and setting it in the place of that which is primary. Let us not despise the physical forces of the universe and its material gifts. These make a valuable contribution to our lives. But, at the same time, let us not be unmindful of the stupendous fact that we are souls having bodies rather than bodies having souls. Everyone who thinks is persuaded in his own mind that the distinctive, the permanent, the most valuable features of human life are not the acquisitions which accrue to man from without, but the qualities of spirit which are cultivated within. No possession is so precious that he who seeks it is entitled, in his quest, to defy the laws of decency. However important and necessary certain things or attainments may seem, they must yield to the rules which God has decreed for good living.

There are young people in our day who are offering the terrible emergency of the world as an excuse for parting with something sacred in their lives. What is thus lightly and foolishly squandered can never be regained. I do not want our young people, in the confusion of our time, to surrender any precious quality or conviction whose loss they will always regret. When a man, in the secret chambers of his heart, begins to compromise with evil, when he starts to barter his soul for worldly pleasure, possession, or promotion, he is on the verge of utter collapse. If that deal goes through, there is nothing left. If I could catch the ear of the world, and especially of the young people, long enough to sound just one note of warning, I would shout, "Watch your soul!" Every person must guard his own battlements and fight for his own integrity. There can be no substitute for this engagement, nor can anybody else meet it for us. The problem of character is paramount, and no man can evade it.

Character has been called "a diamond that scratches every other stone." It constitutes the richest contribution that any man can make to his home and his country. It is the grandest endowment which any father can bestow upon his children. It is not required of us that we achieve what the world calls success, or that we sun ourselves in what our pleasure seekers name happiness. It is not necessary to be the owner of much property or the master of much learning. But it is demanded of a man that he have integrity. To be able to stand firm when enticements call to soft indulgence, to adhere to convictions of the truth when doubt makes its subtle suggestions, to retain faith when afflictions multiply, to remain steadfast in spite of ridicule, and to insist on the right in the face of persecution—these are the characteristics of genuine manhood. If a man has a good spirit, no amount of adversity can defeat him; but if corruption and weakness are in his heart, no amount of good fortune can bring triumph to his life.

In these days of intense physical activity, we do well to bear in mind the merits of culture. When every effort is put forth to train hands for the performance of certain tasks, we are in peril of neglecting those exercises which develop the soul. When truth is distorted and hate is engendered, we need to be careful lest we lead the rising generation into a cheap view of life. It has been wisely said, "What is morally wrong cannot be politically right!" And it may be added that what is morally wrong cannot be right in the home, the school, the factory, the office, or the individual heart. For what is morally wrong defies the all-embracing commandments of God and violates the integrity of the human spirit.

In the turmoil of our time, when values are confused and many things are being destroyed, we do well to recognize the exceeding importance of a right spirit. One of the foundations which all worthy and satisfying life requires is sound character. If by passion or neglect we permit our souls to be undermined and weakened, we sustain a loss for which no gain in other spheres can atone. Character is fundamental. But if the foundations be destroyed, what then?

The second foundation necessary for building life is the law of mutuality. You may call it the Golden Rule or the principle of unselfishness or the rendering of helpful ministry. Joseph Parker, speaking of various ways in which Christ comes to us, imagines a man standing idle in the market place. "While I was enjoying myself and taking my ease," this man says, "it suddenly came to me that idleness was crime, that neglected responsibilities become aggravated guilt, and that I was bound to be a brother and a helper to every man to whom I could minister!" He added that, in that moment of rebirth, he was taught that "piety without beneficence is either sentiment or hypocrisy."

He who, by his own rules and for his own gain, without regard for the welfare of others or respect for the laws by which good men have agreed to live, wins a little eminence or accumulates a little property, may catch the eye of the world for a day or a year, but suddenly the Lord says, "This night, thy soul," and then whose shall those things be? But he who, though frail and not very clever, honestly seeks to know the will of the Lord and humbly tries to obey it, rendering his bit of service cheerfully, helping where he can, and suffering without complaint, lays up for himself treasure in heaven and is rich before God.

John Howard, an English philanthropist of the eighteenth century, a man of whom it was said that he "lived the life of an apostle and died the death of a martyr," devoted his wealth and his time to the correction of abuse in jails and houses of reform, to the care of the sick and outcast, to the erection of hospitals for the reception of the poor who had infectious diseases, and to the visiting and encouragement of the forgotten and afflicted. At last he fell victim to the fever he had fought, but he left a record of glorious service, and he knew the joy of the Lord. "Inasmuch as ye have done it unto . . . these, ye have done it unto me." There is an unshakable foundation which, even in the last judgment, will stand.

An English essayist once said, "A curse on optimism if it means content with a system which keeps any mortal of us out of his sunshine." God has so ordered this world that he who helps others enriches his own soul. Unselfish ministry is of the very essence of the kingdom of heaven. Life is made worthwhile not by a few bold ventures and outstanding achievements, but by an accumulation of smiles, kind words, gracious remembrances, and benevolent acts. "All things whatsoever ye would that men should do to you, do ye even so to them; for this is the law and the prophets." This is one of the foundations on which God ordained that our common life should be built.

Once more, consider the recognition of God as an indispensable foundation for a good life. There may be temporary setbacks in spiritual progress, but there is no final defeat for the kingdom of heaven. Man is naturally religious because he was created in the image of God. The soul was made for communion with its Maker, and only by abnormal conduct and violation of its character can it degenerate. There is a saying among certain African tribes that in earlier times heaven was nearer earth than it is today, and that in those blessed eras, God himself imparted wisdom directly to man. There was a closeness of approach and a harmony of relationship which the more secular interest of busier times cannot appreciate. "Why!" said a Kaffir, when the Gospel was preached in his hearing, "we had this word long ago, for when a man was dying he would say, 'I am going home.'" And one of our own American Indians, when a missionary had been laboring to prove that God exists, turned to his friend and asked, "Does he think we don't know that?"

From the beginning it was the will of our Father in heaven that human life should maintain its contact with him. Man was meant to live with

185

God, not without him. When, therefore, he neglects the Almighty, he despises his chief support and prepares for a sure fall. On the other hand, if he maintains his relationship with his Maker, nothing can undo him. Jesus Christ is not going to be defeated by anyone who attacks his Church and persecutes his followers. If he is conquered anywhere, it will be in the hearts of those who have lost their faith in him.

The things which oppose Christianity sooner or later reveal their weakness. It is becoming increasingly apparent that there is no hope in them. What a day this is for the Church! The road is wide open for a mighty spiritual crusade, a gospel campaign up and down the land and throughout the world. This is the enterprise for which Christ went to the Cross; and by the grace of God, it will issue in the salvation of mankind. We have been timid and silent too long. The time is here for Christians to speak and to let loose the floods of God's redeeming love upon a lost world. When the Church can convince the world, by her passion for God, that she knows what she is talking about when she preaches salvation through Christ, a new day will dawn.

When Scripture calls for a decision or an action, it impresses the reader with a sense of urgency. Now is the acceptable time. It is not suggested that man by his resistance can stop what God proposes to do. As John Donne has it, "Our God is not out of breath, because he hath blown one tempest." But the warning is clear that today you and I can so harden our hearts against the promptings of the Spirit that the progress of the Almighty leaves us behind in unending desolation.

Ultimately this world rests on God, and those who refuse to acknowledge that fact and adjust their lives to it will perish. If the sense of the Divine Presence is removed from the life of our day, we may as well write "Ichabod" over our achievements and drop our enterprises as hopeless. It is impossible to build a better world with a pagan design. Unless God has the directing hand in it, we exert ourselves in vain.

The terrible scenes of the French Revolution have been described frequently. The irregularities of those awful times were accompanied by, and often the result of, infidelity and atheism. Corruption was so flagrant that it amazed even the unbelief which approved it. It is said that matters went so low that a harlot was worshiped "on the polluted altars of Notre Dame." But then, we are told, "God awoke once more," and with a thunderclap smote the leaders and prostrated the people. As one of the heroes of that dismal day of carnage and blasphemy was being carried to the guillotine, an old man approached the cart in which he was being taken, and said, "Yes, Robespierre, there is a God!" The world has always returned to a point at which it found that out.

When Ajax left for Troy, he said to his father, "With the help of the gods, even a nobody might win a victory; but I hope to gain that honor even without their aid." This was his boast, and the result was that Athena made him mad and drove him to suicide. The lesson, even in that ancient story, is plain: life can find no alternative to God.

We have been urged by mankind's supreme Teacher to seek first the Kingdom of God, and we have been assured that those who observe this rule will not lack the things needful for life. No one is asked to seek first the Kingdom of God in order that he may possess these lesser gifts. Such a motive was not intended, and such a sequence was not in the Master's mind. We are not suggesting that a man should become religious in order that he may become rich, nor that a person should unite with a church to secure an easy charity. We believe we interpret the mind of Jesus truly when we say that those who trust in Divine Providence, and sincerely try to obey the will of God, will find that the needs of their lives are met.

Our age has been remarkable for the size of its constructions, the scope of its enterprises, and the amount of its fortunes. Consider the traffic of the world's business, the roar of its factories, and the zeal for its goods; and then remember that the benefits represented in all this quest and undertaking are referred to by Jesus as merely things which shall be added to those whose main purpose is right. If all the wealth, the raiment, the food, the splendor, and the comfort that engage us are only an adjunct, how marvelous, how unspeakably majestic, must be that chief pursuit to which they are only incidental! If all that men achieve on earth by eagerness and labor is only a byproduct of that sacred devotion which, in the sight of God, is paramount, how compelling and comprehensive an employment is involved in following Christ!

Someone points out two Scriptural statements which speak volumes of truth concerning our human life. They are: "We have no continuing city . . ." and "We have an altar." That describes our condition, indicates our high destiny, and reveals the source of our inspiration. The altar is permanent; it speaks of an everlasting order—in its presence we are enlightened regarding our way and strengthened for our journey.

The cultivation of your own character, a life of unselfish service, and a recognition of the redeeming God whom Christ reveals, these are three foundations of life that must not be destroyed. These elements and all others that are necessary for the enrichment of our souls and the rebuilding of our world are included in this definite word of the apostle, "Other foundation can no man lay than that is laid, which is Jesus Christ."

History Does Not Repeat Itself

REVEREND JOSEPH R. SIZOO, D.D.*

Minister, St. Nicholas Collegiate Church (Reformed), New York

BEFORE HE CAME to this strategic pulpit adjoining Rockefeller Center, Dr. Sizoo was for twelve years minister of the New York Avenue Presbyterian Church in Washington, D. C.

He was born in the Netherlands and, except for his years in Washington, his whole life has been spent in serving the Dutch Reformed Church. He was graduated from Hope College and the New Brunswick Theological Seminary. In 1942 he was president of the General Synod of the Reformed Church in America.

The Collegiate Church of St. Nicholas is the oldest Protestant congregation in New York City which has had a continuous ministry. It was organized as "the Church in the Fort," now the Battery, in 1628. President Theodore Roosevelt attended the Church as a young man, and his pew is marked by a memorial tablet. The Collegiate Churches are part of the old Dutch Reformed Church.

Dr. Sizoo is president of the Greater New York Federation of Churches, vice-president of the Protestant Council, and chaplain of the Twelfth Regiment, New York Guard. He is the author of several significant books: *Make Life Worth Living, Not Alone,* and *On Guard* —a little book of daily readings for men in the services. During the past year, he has visited many Army camps and Navy bases for the purpose of speaking both to the chaplains and the men. In this message he gives a different interpretation of history and shows that there were three distinct times when history did not repeat itself.

Sermon Twenty-seven

TEXT: *But now we see not yet all things put under Him—but we see Jesus.* HEBREWS 2:8, 9

ANY PEOPLE ARE FALLING INTO THE DANGEROUS mood of skepticism. They lack utter confidence in any hopeful future for mankind. They have developed the convenient and comfortable habit of doubting every aspiration and hope for man. I need not add that such a frame of mind is fatal, for no improvement is possible while it prevails. This skepticism does not turn upon a

---

* Sermons by members of the Advisory Committee were contributed at the special request of the editor and are included on his responsibility.

concern for immediate events, but rather on things that are in the future. We are not losing confidence in the outcome of the war. We are quite sure that we shall win it; sometimes I feel we are too confident. But we are losing confidence in the peace which will follow the war. We are determined to hold together while the crisis is on, but we are not sure that it will last beyond the crisis.

This skepticism about the future is expressing itself in a vague philosophy which is becoming current. It is the attitude which affirms that the life of mankind runs in cycles. What has happened once will happen again. The past is eternally present with us, and tomorrow will be as yesterday. If you know what has taken place in the past you will know what will take place in the future. One era is much like every other era which has preceded it. Civilization walks an eternal treadmill. There is neither end nor goal in history. The life of mankind is like a chariot race on the stage: the horses are running furiously but getting nowhere. Just as a day begins with morning and runs into evening, only in turn to begin another day, so is the life of mankind. We keep running around in circles.

Some time ago an eminent educator, a distinguished and brilliant president of a great university, addressing the students at an autumn convocation, had for his subject, "History Always Repeats Itself." What has been, will be—what is, has been. We are forever repeating the past. If you know what happened yesterday, you will know what will happen tomorrow. The world is a gigantic squirrel cage, and the life of mankind runs in cycles. Some years ago a traveling circus came to a community in Brooklyn. One afternoon a lion broke loose from its cage. As soon as the escape had been discovered, the hunt was on, and all evening and all night the keepers traveled throughout the community trying to find the lion. At dawn they located it and, strangely enough, the lion had wandered to the water front where there was an old, abandoned house with a fence about it. There was the lion, walking back and forth before the fence, continuing the treadmill into which it had been born in a circus cage. There are many who find in it a parable of what is always happening in the world. Each generation keeps walking back and forth with a reasonable contentment in the prison cage of fate. What has happened always continues to happen. Poverty will always prevail, disease will always be rampant, wars will always ravage, and the four horsemen of the Apocalypse will always ride.

One often comes upon this same fatal attitude in people. They are quite conscious of their failings and willingly confess that life is not as it should be for them. They may envy the saint and applaud evidences of nobility and virtue. They are quick to express regrets and acknowledge their own blunders and imperfections. But these foibles and inconsistencies have persisted so long that they have become part and parcel of their very being. They conclude that they can't help themselves and blithely accept the status quo. They just shrug their shoulders in the face of these shortcomings and say that one might as well stop breathing as to cease doing wrong. They have come to believe that they can't do anything about it; after all, they were born that way. The only thing they can do is to keep on repeating the blunders of yesterday. What has been, will be. History always repeats itself.

Now there is nothing heroic about that kind of double talk. To live with that philosophy reduces life to gloomy frustration. It drips with defeatism, justifies incompetence, and rationalizes indifference and inconsistency. Whenever they yield to temptation or surrender to some compromise, they shout the word, *kismet*. They just conclude that you can't make things different in this world and that we live our lives in the groove of the past. People like that propose to let the world run its course. They make no effort to change it. They have lost all faith in the recoverability of mankind and no longer believe in conversion or the second birth. They are content to let things happen rather than make them happen. They permit themselves to be carried downstream by any current. It is an easygoing attitude. It lifts no crosses, it exacts no hardships, it does not compel sacrifice or struggle. It takes the sting out of failure and the bitterness out of defeat. What has been, will be. There is in the world eternal change, but no improvement; there is evidence of motion, but not direction. It is a sign of decadence and not hope. It comes from people who are jaded and fed up, who have lost the high dreams and adventures of youth. To maintain that history always repeats itself is the voice of despair.

Now the Christian philosophy is a thousand miles removed from that attitude. It stands at the opposite pole and has nothing in common with such cowering despair. Christianity is infinitely more heroic. It kindles the fires of faith and faces the stars. It affirms that Pilate never speaks the last word. It is founded upon the assurance of the New Testament, "In this world ye shall have tribulation, but be of good cheer, I have overcome the world." Jesus of Nazareth gave men a braver outlook when He urged upon them the assurance, "Greater is He that is in you than he that is in the world." History does not repeat itself; it is coming out somewhere. Mankind is marching to its predestined goal. The Gospel proclaims liberty to the captive, setting free those who are bound, opening doors to those who are in prison, proclaiming the acceptable year of the Lord. Civilization is not a circle, but a spiral. It is not an everlasting on and on; it can also be an up and up.

It is true, of course, that history has a place in our planning and thinking. History is all that we know of every thought, every feeling and every accomplishment of man. It is the collection of the human affairs of yesterday. Only as we know history shall we live with perspective and poise. If we knew history better today, we would not be so disturbed. One must know what has been, in order to determine what ought to be. A knowledge of the past helps one to determine the course of the future. The purpose of history is to point out the flaws, lift warnings, and flash red lights upon things that won't work. It makes man grimly aware of the things that in the long run can only fail and fade. But the purpose of history is not to repeat itself but to improve the world and life and mankind. We are not here to duplicate the past, but to change it. God did not bring us into being to let things happen, but to make them happen.

As a matter of fact, that is the supreme business of the Christian. He is commanded to leave the low evaluations of yesterday and climb to a dome more vast. We are here to break the squirrel trap, not to keep it going. The Christian refuses to accept any status quo. He believes with Lincoln that nothing is ever settled until it is settled right. The Christian has learned to heed the assurance of the Gospel, "All power is given unto me in heaven and on earth." He stands upon the sure foundation, "I can do all things through Christ who strengtheneth me." The Christian does not live by frustration, but by faith; not in disillusionment, but in hope. He is not here to repeat history, but to change it.

We are on solid ground, believe me, when we make that claim, for it is not an idle boast. There have been three times in the past when God has come into the world to break the chain of events. Upon three different occasions God ended something in this world and broke the treadmill of existence. The first was at the Cross. There He broke the treadmill of guilt. All through the unbroken eons of time man has been haunted by the inescapable fact of sin and guilt. With the dawn of man there came the dawn of conscience. He became aware of forces at work in the world which were estranging man from his fellow men and from God. Something seems to take possession of man, wear his clothes, use his name, and drive him where he does not want to go. All through life he walks with the haunting sense of guilt. He is conscious that there is a great gulf fixed between him and His Maker. The ageless, poignant cry of man in every century and country has been, "I, wretched man that I am, who shall deliver me from the body of this death?" Tennyson has spoken for all mankind in his lines:

> O for a man to arise in me
> That the man I am may cease to be.

All his efforts and all his sacrifices seemed to be in vain. Every attempt to throw off this burden of sin proved futile. The more he sought to build a bridge across this gulf of despair, the deeper and wider the gulf became. Generation after generation carried the dreadful sense of guilt and man seemed to be walking the eternal treadmill of evil. Then one day Christ climbed His Calvary. Something happened on that Cross which has forever lifted the burden from the heart of man. He who knew no sin became sin for us. He gave His life as a ransom for many. By his stripes are we healed, and His blood can make the foulest clean. It has been shouted across the centuries, "It is a faithful saying, worthy of all acceptation that Christ Jesus came into the world to save sinners." Man does not know the full meaning or mystery of the Cross. Who can fathom the unfathomable mystery of redeeming grace? But we do know that God broke the chain of history—man need not go on sinning. History does not repeat itself. His grace saves to the end of the end. On the Cross God broke the treadmill of sin.

The second was at the tomb, where He broke the treadmill of the fear of death. Always since the beginning of time man has faced the appalling fact of death. Coming out of nowhere into somewhere, man began the long, winding journey called life. But always, sooner or later, that journey ended at the caravansary of death. There was no halting at the tavern of the Lotus Eater, and death was no respecter of persons. The haunting cry, "If a man die, shall he live again?" has followed generation after generation. Death was so inexorable and final. To be sure, here and there some rare soul caught the vision of something beyond; but at best it was only a hope, for no one had come back to tell us that there was a better country. Then one day the Son of God walked out of the sepulchral gloom of the garden of the Arimathean. Angels in shimmering white announced, "He is not here, but He is risen. He goeth before you into Galilee." Across the lonely reaches of time, like the bells of Angelus, there rang the assurance, "I am the Resurrection and the life; He that believeth in me, though he were dead, yet shall he live again." Once and forever the word *finis* was written across that haunting fear. History was no longer to repeat itself. "As in Adam all die, so in Christ shall all be made alive." That assurance changed everything for man. Standing upon the broken shores of time, thinking of those who have gone before, we know we shall meet them again. God has broken the cruel treadmill of the fear of death. History did not repeat itself.

The third was at Pentecost, where He broke the treadmill of disunity. Always through the long ages has man been hopelessly divided. Nothing could be found to bring about a unity among men. The world seemed to be a place where men fell apart into groups, races, nations, always at war with one another. There were irreconcilable estrangements of race and color and nationalism, and each group seemed determined to seek some advantage at the expense of the other. To be sure, there were occasional attempts at unity through political technique. There were attempts to create a unity through fear or hate or prejudice. But these did not solve the problem; they only deepened it. Then came Pentecost, when in the Upper Room the Holy Ghost came upon a company of twelve. People of every color and nation and race were transformed by the preaching of the Gospel and found in that Gospel a new kind of comradeship which swept across the frontiers of life and time. At long last a unifying force had come into this world to bind the nations into a new kind of brotherhood, the brotherhood of the twice-born, released from fear and sin. The treadmill of disunity was broken. History did not repeat itself, but history was changed.

Men and women, the external assurance of that Gospel of Christ is that life does not go round in circles. God has put within the reach of man forces which can change him and change the world. He has made available infinite resources of power that can open any prison door of disillusionment and sin. Greed and force are not the inevitable and final forces of history. To be sure, wickedness dies hard in this world; the struggle for truth is still on, and goodness is still fiercely contested, but He who broke the treadmill of sin, death, and divisiveness is at work in the world making all things new. Believe me, the hope of mankind is in the hands of those who keep the fires of that faith burning in their souls.

What a light that lifts upon our day-by-day lives! This intolerance, greed, hate, and lust can be crushed. They are never the final force of mankind. However poor and shoddy our lives may be, the Christian Gospel guarantees we can be made over to a diviner design. The things that have been are not necessarily inevitable or final. Life that is cabined and confined may break from its prison house and come to a new and more glorious freedom. In 1880, a Chinese boy, a homeless waif, was wandering across the wharves and docks of Shanghai. An American vessel was loading cargo at the dock. He determined to smuggle himself on board, and hid in a drain into which food and rubbish were swept. There he hid and fought with rats for the scraps that were swept into it. But the battle with the vermin was too great, and he had to come out of his hiding. It was the custom that those who had stowed away were tossed overboard without ceremony when discovered. But the captain of this ship, Charles Jones, kept the boy with him until he docked at Wilmington, North Carolina, where he turned the boy over to the minister of his Church, who befriended him and gave him the name of Charlie, after the captain who had saved him, and provided for him a shelter and a home. The boy went to school and later graduated from Trinity College, now Duke University. Then he entered a theological seminary from which he graduated, and was ordained. Then he returned to China and married a Christian girl and set up a home out of which there came six children. One daughter became the wife of the Minister of Finance; another daughter became the wife of Sun Yat-sen, founder of the Chinese Republic; and the third daughter became the wife of Chiang Kai-shek, the gallant leader of the Chinese Republic. One son became the founder of the Bank of China, another son became the Collector of Customs of Chinese ports, and the third son became the manager of the export-import business of China. So the Soong dynasty was founded. That homeless waif playing on the wharves and docks of Shanghai seemed to have no chance. He was just walking the treadmill of an unbroken and eternal poverty. But history did not repeat itself. The treadmill was broken. The God who makes all things new laid His hands upon him and made him the founder of a new order for the Asiatic world. That is the glory and the romance of the Christian Gospel.

So it is in the world of today and of tomorrow. Civilization is not a circle, not a dead-end street, but a spiral; a long pilgrimage to God. Time is coming out somewhere, and man is marching to his predestined goal. One day through travail and toil and tears there will come the new heaven and the new earth. The kingdoms of this world shall one day become the kingdoms of our God and His Christ and "He whose right it is to rule, shall reign supreme and reign alone." History is coming out somewhere.

You Can't Escape History

Reverend L. Wendell Fifield, D.D.
Minister, Plymouth Church of the Pilgrims, Brooklyn, New York

Dr. Fifield was born in Benton Harbor, Michigan, in 1891. His early life, as the son of a Congregational minister, was spent in Chicago and Kansas City. In 1913 he was graduated from Oberlin College and in 1916 received his B.D. from Chicago Theological Seminary. For two years he was professor of Biblical Literature and Public Speaking at Yankton College, South Dakota, before he assumed his first major pastorate at First Congregational Church, Sioux Falls, South Dakota.

At the conclusion of a successful ten-year period at Sioux Falls, he was called to the pulpit of Plymouth Congregational Church, Seattle, where his Sunday morning services were broadcast to the Pacific northwest. He also conducted a weekly radio book review program, "It's a Case of Books."

Dr. Fifield's career as a religious and civic leader in Seattle is epitomized by the signal honor conferred upon him as "The First Citizen of Seattle for 1940," by a secret committee of Seattle leaders.

He began his pastorate at Plymouth Church of the Pilgrims, Brooklyn, on October 1, 1941. This is the church made famous by Henry Ward Beecher.

In this sermon, given on November 14, 1943, he traces some of the facts and ideas of history which affected and were affected by the forces of justice and faith.

Sermon Twenty-eight

Text: *Seek ye first His Kingdom and His righteousness and all these things shall be added unto you.* Matthew 6:33

HIS IS THE STATEMENT OF JESUS CHRIST CONcerning the lesson of history and of human experience.

In his annual message to Congress on December 1, 1862, Abraham Lincoln wrote these words: "Fellow citizens, we cannot escape history. The fiery trial through which we pass will light us down in honor or dishonor to the latest generation. We shall nobly

195

save or meanly lose the last, best hope of earth." Those words are just as applicable today as they were to 1862. In them Abraham Lincoln set forth the consideration that there are certain inevitable principles in human history, certain changeless factors in the course of human experience—factors which are never altered and never pass away.

In his most recent book, *Between Tears and Laughter*, Lin Yutang, when he speaks as a philosopher and not a partisan, discusses the lessons of human history. He says that the Hindu theory of Karma is applicable. It is a theory of moral action in human life. Lin Yutang states it in these words: "We are responsible for our moral thoughts and actions. These thoughts and actions have a causal relationship with the past and the future. We cannot escape from them." You see he is saying exactly the same thing that Lincoln said. He goes on to quote Buddha who said, "All that we are is the result of what we have thought. It is founded on our thoughts. It is made up of our thoughts." Lin Yutang concludes his interpretation of what he means by Karma, saying that the lesson of the past bears out the fact that there is only one adequate interpretation of human history, and that is the spiritual interpretation of history.

Immanuel Kant, the great German philosopher of some centuries ago spoke of the "categorical imperative." In that phrase he says exactly the same thing: There are certain considerations absolutely essential to the life of the world. Affirm them, and there is progress; neglect them, and there is destruction. Some things are inescapable in human history.

Often as I think of the advice which Kant gave to his people I think how different the world would be had Germany followed the suggestion of Kant, the moralist, rather than the suggestion of Hegel, the mathematician; if centuries ago that nation had dedicated itself to idealism rather than to materialism. But the philosophy of Hegel became the dominant philosophy of Germany. And when one says that and indicates that choice on the part of Germany, he but illustrates the truth of our theme, "You cannot escape History." There are certain courses of action which produce certain inevitable results. When those courses of action are set into being, nothing can stay the results which flow from them. You can't flaunt the moral laws of the ages in the life of the nations. You can't flaunt God's will and God's purpose in the life of the world and expect to have a world of peace, prosperity, and growth.

"You cannot escape History." The story of the tragic fall of all the races and of the empires of the past brings attestation to the truth of the simple statement of Lincoln.

This morning, then, as the thoughts of Armistice Day are still in our minds and hearts, this question is uppermost: "How can we so conduct ourselves that when the next Armistice Day comes the world will do a better job than it did with the last one?" With these thoughts in our minds, we turn to consider some of the inevitable trends of history, their meaning for today and for the time of peacemaking which lies somewhere ahead.

The first thing that we learn about the nations of the world and their relationships, as we thoughtfully and honestly study history, is this: no unholy alliance can survive. This was even true of an alliance which men called holy but which in the sight of God was unholy. The so-called historical "Holy Alliance" had the name but not the meaning. Soon it broke beneath the impact of the relentless trends of human history.

What do we mean by an unholy alliance, the kind that cannot survive? History tells us that several kinds have no chance. Here are some of them:

Any alliance based upon the power of the strong over the weak cannot survive. Time after time there have been strong nations. They have banded together to enforce their wishes upon the weak nations and, sooner or later, such a set-up has brought war. And those alliances once so strong crumbled into dust. The Roman Empire is a case in point.

Again, history teaches us that any alliance is an unholy alliance, and so lacks the capacity to survive, which is based upon the principle of the promotion of national self-interest at the expense of others. One nation draws a number of other nations into its orbit in order that it may secure what it wishes. Such a process never escapes history. Jealousy, bickering, misunderstanding, treachery, and collapse have always been the fruit of that kind of unholy alliance.

Another unholy alliance is one based primarily upon economic considerations, an alliance where nations band themselves together in order that they may secure and protect THINGS and nothing more. If, out of this war, there comes an organization to build international cartels, to develop the material interest of four or five primary nations of the earth AND NOTHING MORE, the indisputable record of history reveals that that kind of solution for the problems of mankind will fail.

Another unholy alliance is one based upon the idea that freedom should exist in the world, but that it should be the kind of freedom that some one nation thinks constitutes genuine freedom. That sort cannot endure. It has been tried before—the idea of having a democratic world following the pattern of the nation initiating the idea of the democratic world.

Remember the golden days of Greece? They were not golden at all, unless the gold which comes to the sky to herald the sunset was the golden age of Greece. Those were the days when already the rumblings of the collapse of the Greek Empire could be heard. You remember from your student days the name of Pericles? He had a great dream for the future of the world. It was to be free. The democracy of the Athenian hills was to be the democracy of the entire world, but there was one catch to it. In Sparta and in Phoenicia, there was to be the kind of freedom that Athens thought should be. Everyone was to be free, but he was to be told the nature of his freedom, and the extent to which he could practice it. The consequences of such a spirit of democracy were that the Greek Empire fell. We need to remember that lesson of the past in these times. There is going to be a tremendous temptation when this war is over for our country to say to the other nations of the world, "You must all have democracy but THIS is the kind you must have."

Again, as we study the history of the past, we find that no grouping of the nations has survived when this grouping has depended upon superior military strength. We have an illustration of it now. At the beginning of this war the military strength of our opponents was far superior to the military strength of those who now oppose them—armies the like of which the world had never known. Yet, military strength didn't save these nations. There is something else in the world in addition to armies, and finally that something else asserted itself, "not too little nor too late." That experience has repeated itself time after time in human history. When a nation or a group of nations depends upon power alone to assert its will, that power to assert itself will hasten the fall of any nation or group of nations. In the midst of the building of military power, defeat is beginning to loom across the horizon. Were the nations not so busy with the fashioning of the weapons of war, they could look up and see the handwriting of destruction on the wall.

The second inescapable fact of history is this: no nation can successfully live unto itself. It could not even be done back in the days when transportation was very slow compared with what it is today. We are living in an interrelated world. We always have and always will. What happens anywhere affects life everywhere. That is one of the irrevocable, fundamental lessons of human history. Years ago, President Monroe thought it would be for the well-being of this country if we adopted the "Monroe Doctrine." So it was framed and adopted. Most folks thought that it meant that we could live unto ourselves in North and South America, and pay no attention to the rest of the world. But one thing they failed to realize. The effective protection of South America depended upon the capacity to keep any nations who might have designs upon South America away from her shores. We were not in a position to do that. And why? We didn't have the fleet. It was the British fleet which stood as a barrier between other nations and South America. So our ability to support the Monroe Doctrine depended upon the British fleet and, in turn, upon the stability of Great Britain. Anything, therefore, that menaced Great Britain menaced the safety and peace of this continent.

This is why Germany has for many decades now been a potential enemy of the United States. Germany has for many years been the rival of Great Britain. This traditional rivalry between Germany and Great Britain menaced Great Britain and so threatened the Monroe Doctrine. Therefore, Germany's policy concerned us. That is the kind of world we are living in—everything is tied up with everything else.

This interdependence is clear to us now because of the rapidity of transportation, but it has always been thus. It is the way God made this world and intended it to be. All countries are related. If there are problem conditions in one country in the whole wide world, there are problem conditions everywhere in the world. This, then, is one of the inescapable facts of human history. The only way to make a great nation safe is to have a world of decency and of safety. There is no national security apart from world security. We learned that in the First World War, and yet already some are beginning to forget.

There is a third lesson that comes to us from the inescapable record of human history. Selfishness and greed inevitably bring destruction in the international sphere. This is a lesson of history. It is one of the facts you cannot escape in the unfolding panorama of human experience. Why was it that last Thursday we celebrated Armistice Day and nothing more? Why did we have to say that the period between the two wars was just an armistice and nothing more? Why was it that when men cried, "Peace," there was actually no peace in the world? It is because the period from the First World War to the Second was a period of selfishness and of greed in international history.

I have not time to go into the details this morning nor would I if I could—the story of a Britain financing the rise of Hitler to power; the story of a France refusing to make minute concessions in order that democracy, when democracy was having its chance in Germany, might live; the story of Abyssinia and Manchuria; the story of the withdrawal of the United States from the League of Nations, and the embarkation of our country upon a course which we called "nationalism" ("Let us look after ourselves and let the rest of the world go by." But the rest of the world didn't go by, and now into your home and mine the rest of that world comes to take our sons); the story of scrap iron shipped to Japan, and all the rest of it. Surely, if one can read history at all he must realize the truth of the statement that selfishness and greed in this world inevitably bring trouble. Here, then, is one of those lessons in history that Lincoln tells us we cannot escape. There is no lasting peace in life based upon selfishness and greed. There is none, even if we dress up the peace and call it economic necessity or national opportunism. It just is not there. When Christ talked about "losing your life to find it," he said things that most of the diplomats of the world, from the dawn of history until now, have said were the utterances of a fool, but history believes

Him and writes irrevocably upon the record of time and of human experience the fact that He spoke the truth.

May we then, summarize these lessons that come to us from the history of the past? Selfishness, greed, nationalism, power politics, sinful alliances—all are linked in a structure that brings destruction. In them there is no peace. But the converse is also true. Unselfishness, spirituality, altruistic alliances, will create a structure that will bring progress. Then there is peace. THAT is what Jesus meant when he said, "Seek ye first the Kingdom of God and His righteousness and all these other things shall be added unto you."

With the thought, then, of this text confirmed by the experience of the past, may we turn toward the future. This war is going to be over sometime, possibly sooner than most of us think. And the problem of what is going to happen then will be upon us.

Did you read the story of the man who fell from the roof of a house? Someone asked him if it hurt him and he replied, "No, the fall didn't hurt; it was the stopping that nearly killed me." That is what is going to happen in the world at the end of this war. All the tendencies developed during the years of suffering and terror will be let loose. Many restraints will be lifted from lives. For example, as soon as this war is over, there is going to be a tremendous effort to end the "lend-lease" program. Some people have said, "As long as we are in danger I can adjust myself to heavy taxes, but when it is over I am going to be against them." God help us if this proves true! Millions have been sent to destroy and millions more must be sent to rebuild if this world is going to have a chance for peace. Many people are just waiting for the war to end so that they can fill up their gasoline tanks, forgetting that tractors and trucks must carry food and materials to almost every spot in this world except the United States of America in order to rebuild this world. We must not forget another lesson of history—that if large numbers of people are permitted to suffer while others sit back in complacency and relative ease, the seeds of destruction once more are sown. The only chance for peace is that we will remember in the period of cessation that we can't escape history and be true to the message that history teaches.

Here are three primary propositions before the American people at the present time relative to the postwar world. I merely cite them. The plan by Ely Culbertson illustrates the mathematical plan for the future of the world. It carries the technique of the bridge table into world affairs. The author forgets that there is a human element involved. His rules do not even make perfect bridge players. People have to play cards. So nature must rebuild. No mathematical formula will suffice. Those who believe it will have failed to read the lesson of human history.

Then there is the idea of power politics. Walter Lippmann in his book,

U. S. Foreign Policy, is the primary exponent of this idea. Put the four leading nations, Great Britain, Russia, China, and the United States together on the basis of their own interests. Make them so strong that no other nation can attack them. I think if Lincoln were to speak today he would say, "Before peace is based on another attempt to build power politics, reread history. God has written there some truths that need to be known."

Over against those two, there is a third, the proposition of the religious forces of the United States. Recently there was presented a statement of the Protestant, Catholic, and Jewish faiths setting forth the seven basic principles for peace. I cannot discuss these this morning. But I believe as earnestly as I stand here that they represent genuine effort to capture the lesson of history and apply it to the future:

1. The moral law must govern the world.
2. The rights of the individual must be assured.
3. The rights of the oppressed white and colored peoples must be protected.
4. The rights of minorities must be secured.
5. International instruments to maintain peace with justice must be organized.
6. International economic cooperation must be developed.
7. A just social order within each state must be achieved.

There is the best thinking that you can find at present in the religious world. It is an interpretation of Jesus' statement when he said, "Seek ye first the Kingdom of God and His righteousness." There is not a selfish idea in it. All propositions recognize the fundamental truths of God about the life of the world. They do not represent final wisdom. The thinking of no man is adequate to the times in which we live. But they indicate a program which seeks to recognize the fact that we cannot escape history, that the way to co-operate with history is to "seek first the kingdom of God and His righteousness," and to make it always and eternally our prayer in these dark days as we move toward what may be a better day:

> Lord God of hosts, be with us yet,
> Lest we forget, lest we forget!

War and Resurrection

Reverend Eugene Carson Blake, D.D.
Pastor, Pasadena Presbyterian Church, Pasadena, California

Dr. Blake is one of the younger ministers of force and power. He was born in St. Louis, Missouri, in 1906, attended Princeton University, then studied for two years at New College, Edinburgh, Scotland. He entered Princeton Theological Seminary in 1932, and received the D.D. from Occidental College in 1941.

He was a teacher at Forman Christian College, Lahore, India, in 1928 and 1929, and became assistant pastor of the Collegiate Church of St. Nicholas, New York, in 1932, where he remained until 1935. Then he went to Albany as pastor of First Presbyterian Church. In 1940 he was called to the Pasadena Presbyterian Church.

From 1938 to 1940, Dr. Blake was visiting lecturer on religion at Williams College. He is a trustee of Occidental College, a member of the Board of Monte Vista Grove Homes, a member of the Board of Christian Education of the Presbyterian Church in the United States of America, and pastor of radio station KPPC. His religious views have been influenced by Professor Theodore Meyer Green, by the late Hugh R. MacIntosh, and by Reinhold Niebuhr. He is in favor of Church union to strengthen the Protestant churches.

"War and Resurrection" combines a discussion of Easter, Life, Death and Immortality in a manner to strengthen faith in these days, when our sons and husbands and brothers and friends are on the battlefields of the world. He offers a dynamic faith for our day.

Sermon Twenty-nine

Text: *Therefore my beloved brethren, be ye stedfast, unmovable, always abounding in the work of the Lord, forasmuch as ye know that your labor is not in vain in the Lord.*   I Corinthians 15:58

WHAT HAS WAR TO DO WITH RESURRECTION? "Keep war outside the cloister of the church," some would say. "Do not blast the beauty of Easter morn with the horrid scream of shells of death. Let not soldiers' tramping feet trespass into that garden where the stone is rolled away. Let us hear the

202

songs of Easter in the breathless wonder of the long ago when early to the tomb the women went to hear the marvel spoken: 'He is not dead but risen.' Let us be transported back with John and Peter to run to peer within the empty tomb and see once more the hollow cerements. For one morning let us forget the heartbreak and the cruelty of war and lose ourselves in Easter song and poetic memory." So we all might wish and yet we dare not try escape this total war which intrudes itself into all our life this Easter. I speak therefore on "War and Resurrection."

A ranking Army officer was heard not long ago to say: "The only trouble with the young soldiers of our new army is that nobody has taught them how to die." By which I take it he meant that these young men, though coming out of Christian home and church, lack faith in God enough to be able to face the prospect and the likely possibility of early death without thinking of it as anything less than final catastrophe.

And my guess is that this religious uncertainty does not confine itself to those in uniform. For it is a full generation now that it has been our fashion not to think of death. Even within the church all our emphasis has been on this world, on our duties in life now. We have not wanted to sing the last stanzas of many of our hymns. How many times do you suppose it has been announced: "Let us sing 'My Faith Looks Up To Thee,' *the first three stanzas only,*" so omitting:

> When ends life's transient dream
> When death's cold, sullen stream
> Shall o'er me roll,
> Blest Saviour, then, in love,
> Fear and distrust remove;
> O bear me safe above,
> A ransomed soul!

For that last stanza didn't harmonize with the modern mood. We were out of the habit of remembering that human life is short, that death is always near.

Although in our time religion has often been charged with being an escape from the harsh realities of life, it is interesting to note that it has been not religion merely but the whole modern mood, the total cultural pattern of our thought that has been an attempted escape, a sugar-coated camouflage to cover from our consciousness the truth that life is always closely pressed by death. And it is only now when a war is here, threatening a world-wide holocaust of casualties that the modern mood begins to face previously unwelcomed facts. Now men are asking themselves the questions which before they put off asking until they were older: "Is death really the end? Can one believe in resurrection?"

But though it is war that turns our thoughts to religion, let us not make the mistake of thinking that war really increases the relevance of religion. For war does not radically change the human situation. Apart from war, we live in a hard and cruel world—we manage easily to forget it in peace and prosperity. Apart from war, young men die, some of them, and old people all the time. But we manage to forget it easily in youth and health. Apart from war, there are sad young widows and orphaned children; there are heartbreaks and tragedies all about us. But most of us manage to forget these things when they do not touch us.

The sole effect of war is to foreshorten life, not greatly to change it. By war's drama are highlighted death and other evils. These things are no more true now than at any time, but war does not let us put off, as we were wont, deciding what our faith will be. War cuts the issues clear. The agnosticism that gentler times have fostered is now revealed for what it has always been—a foolish putting off until tomorrow of a choice we need to make today.

War makes the young and strong understand that it was not so smart to joke about old people's interest in religion. War makes us see (if we did not before) that the old tend to be religious not because of approaching senile foolishness but because of age's wisdom which forces every man to consider the questions which modern culture had decided to forget, as long, at least, as the road of life stretched out beyond the immediately approaching hill.

War merely makes pertinent to the most obtuse the Christian faith of Easter—a pertinence which should have been apparent to any really thoughtful person at any time. For leaving out agnosticism, which the foreshortening of war reveals to be quite foolish and unsatisfactory, there are really only two ways to look at life and death, and they present a sharp and simple contrast that we must choose between. One is materialism, whether crude or subtle; the other is Christianity (which, of course, also may be either crude or finely wrought).

Materialism, stripped of nonessential variations, is the faith that, despite all experiences to the contrary, human life is only, even at its highest, some sort of stuff, a material substance. Ideas, ideals, spirit, bravery, cowardice, and God are all but froth on the foam of meaningless matter. Life doesn't mean anything, finally, because meaning is after all but a peculiar arrangement of electrons. What is, is. What ends, ends. There could be no resurrection, no immortality! Death is tragedy in the single sense that men after all like to live. But really nothing is better than anything else, nor worse. For only senseless time is eternal and space is infinite and matter is indestructible, though its forms of organization are always changing, usually to masses more and more inert. However you disguise it, that is the faith of many men today. And it is a *faith,* for it cannot be proved. It is a conviction that some have made their own.

204

But there is little comfort in the faith of materialism when life seems to mean something or at least seems that it ought to mean something. It is a hard faith to hold when you are young and strong and facing death and separation from those whom you love. And the result of such faith in human life is at the best a hard stoicism: "I'll take what comes, well— because I must. I'll not whine." And it can be beautiful as in the poem of W. E. Henley:

> O gather me the rose, the rose,
>   While yet in flower we find it,
> For summer smiles but summer goes,
>   And winter waits behind it.
>
> So were it well to love, my love,
>   And cheat of any laughter,
> The fate beneath us and above,
>   The dark before and after.

At best it can be brave and beautiful, this materialism, but at its common worst it can be a selfish pleasure-snatching at the fruits and flowers that oh, so quickly, rot and fade—it can be reckless squeezing of life's juice and scent.

On the other hand is Christianity. It, too, is a simple faith when you strip it of any distorting over-draperies. There is a God who has made the world and man. And although man is involved in and bound to and confused with the apparently material substance of the universe, it is right to hold with Percy Dearmer that "Man is not a body possessing a soul, but a soul possessing a body."

Again whatever appearance to the contrary, this Christian faith holds that God is good and God is strong, that He is a Father who ever cares for all His children. Love abides—it lasts beyond all earthly changes.

> The grave itself is but a covered bridge
> Leading from light to light through a brief darkness.

It is Christianity to believe that we may trust God and His love beyond our bounds of vision; that Jesus Christ is both the pattern-perfect man and the revelation of the love of God; that death did not hold Him and will not hold us nor those we love.

I say this, too, in its essentials, is a simple faith. To me it is easier to believe than its alternative. And it is further clear that, when truly held, it has its characteristic results in human life. At best it bestows the gifts of courage, kindness, unselfishness, and love to those gripped by it. It produces soldiers like Stonewall Jackson, about whom I have been reading this week, who fought without fear for a cause he believed was right, and when he met his death in the wilderness of Spottsylvania, he was at peace with God and confident in his Saviour. His cause, his wife, and baby girl were all entrusted to the eternal Father whom he loved and served.

At its best, this faith has produced mothers who bravely sent their loved sons off to fight or die for good and justice as they saw it; it has produced men and women of all occupations and in all ages who forgot themselves in devoted service to God and man, regardless of the power of evil and regardless of their own comfort.

And, even at its least, this faith helps all who even faintly grasp it to be comforted in tragedy and hopeful in disaster.

So Paul when he had outlined to the Corinthians this Christian faith in winged words, concluded: "Therefore,"—therefore—because we believe in this God and His everlasting love for us, "therefore," because we believe in this Jesus Christ who was not held of death but rose triumphant, and 'thanks be to God' giveth us the same victory, "therefore," because of this faith—"Therefore, my beloved brethren, be ye stedfast, unmovable, always abounding in the work of the Lord, forasmuch as ye know that your labor is not in vain in the Lord." That is the Christian Easter faith and life.

Here then are the two faiths. One: all is vanity. The other: nothing is in vain. One: death is the end, a tragedy. The other: death is a new beginning, a triumph. One of these is true. But how can one choose between them? How does Christian conviction come? How can we stop wavering between these two incompatible views of life and death?

The answer to these questions lies in this: For either of these faiths to become strong in a man there is required the same procedure—an *act* of faith.

The materialist says to himself, I will live my life on the basis of here and now. I'll get what joy I can, and I'll hope for happy fortune. I will forget God and high duty and immortality. I will live as if they were proved illusions. The result of such a step of faith is an increasing conviction through the years that there is no God, no hope, no meaning to life; and its end result is the tragedy of death, whether soon in war or late in age.

The act of Christian faith is exactly similar. I'll devote myself to the highest and bravest and best that I even dimly apprehend. I'll give myself to God, to Jesus Christ, to love all men, to the high duties and simple joys of friendly companionship along a pilgrim way of life. And the result of such a step is the abiding and strengthening conviction that God is no illusion, that Christ is all in all, that death is but an incident, hardly an interruption in a life bravely and beautifully lived.

Yes, it is before each of us to make our choice of faith. At best both

206

can be heroic; I do not deny it; at best both can be beautiful, but oh, the difference in their beauty! Here is the one:

> I am not resigned to the shutting away of loving hearts in the
>   hard ground.
> So it is, and so it will be, for so it has been, time out of mind;
> Into the darkness they go, the wise and the lovely.
> Crowned
> With lilies and laurel they go; but I am not resigned.
>
> Down, down, down, into the darkness of the grave
> Gently they go, the beautiful, the tender, the kind;
> Quietly they go, the intelligent, the witty, the brave.
> I know. But I do not approve. And I am not resigned.

Or will you choose this other faith? For it is yours to choose if you will.

> No! let me taste the whole of it, fare like my peers
> The heroes of old,
> Bear the brunt, in a minute pay glad life's arrears
> Of pain, darkness and cold.
> For sudden the worst turns the best to the brave,
> The black minute's at end,
> And the elements rage, the fiend voices that rave
> Shall dwindle, shall blend,
> Shall change; shall become first a peace out of pain,
> Then a light, then thy breast,
> O thou soul of my soul! I shall clasp thee again,
> And with God be the rest!

PRAYER: *O God, in whom we live and move and have our being, give us faith to live wisely and bravely in this present life and that further grace to see thee behind its shadows and to trust thy love beyond our sight. Through Jesus Christ our Lord. Amen.*

The Mirror of Immortality

REVEREND EDWIN MCNEILL POTEAT, D. D.

President of Colgate-Rochester Divinity School (Baptist), Rochester, New York, and a Minister of the Baptist Church

IMMORTALITY haunts the minds of men today more than it has at any time in the last twenty-five years. The war—and death on a grand scale—make it the most arresting subject of our time. "If a man die, will he live again?"

Dr. Edwin McNeill Poteat, for six and one-half years pastor of Euclid Avenue Baptist Church, Cleveland, Ohio, and now President of Colgate-Rochester Divinity School, theological seminary of the Northern Baptist Convention, approaches the problem fearlessly. He arrives at certain conclusions which answer many questions and goes on to show how to find further answers in the Bible, in the Church, in life, and in one's own heart and mind.

From 1917 on, for thirteen years, he was a missionary in China. Part of the time he taught Ethics and Philosophy at the University of Shanghai. He traveled around the world, observing the churches and people, and has written a number of books, including, *Four Freedoms and God, Centurian* (a book length poem), and a trilogy of Lenten books, *These Shared His Passion, These Shared His Cross,* and *These Shared His Power.* Duke University, Wake Forest College, and Hillsdale College have honored him with the D.D. in recognition of his preaching, church work, and leadership.

He believes that "preaching in the next twenty-five years will depend largely upon the kind of training men get for the kind of world we need tomorrow, and that education must largely be remade after the war." In this sermon he takes Paul's famous statement on immortality, in the Moffat translation, and brings hope and vision to all who will accept it. His direction of this great seminary should give the churches of his denomination ministers of exceptional training for the years immediately ahead. His positive faith will help many in this time of war.

Sermon Thirty

TEXT: *Baffling reflections in a mirror (Moffat's Translation).*
I CORINTHIANS 13:12

IFE IS THE MIRROR OF IMMORTALITY. WE DO NOT see eternity face to face, as through an open window. Such glimpses as we are permitted are the reflections returned to us when we look into the mirror of life. Life is the mirror of immortality.

There are two ways of thinking about life beyond the grave. One may approach it, so to speak, from the outside. This is an interest in a question of fact. Is there such an experience awaiting us? And so we puzzle about it endlessly. Recently in a Cleveland paper this approach was presented in a poem entitled "Sure":

> Father of the bare boughs, and the leaves that die,
> Father of the beaten grass, where dead flowers lie,
> Father of the pale fields where the snow has lain,
> Are you always very sure
> Spring will come again?
>
> Father of the gray world, sick for spring's return,
> Father of the dank damp, where the willows yearn,
> Father of the cold wind and the haunting rain,
> Are you sure that after March,
> April comes again?
>
> Father of the bare heart and the dreams that yearn,
> Father of the gray soul and the thoughts that burn,
> Father of the beaten hopes and the haunting pain,
> Are you sure that after death
> Life comes again?

The other way of thinking about immortality might be called an approach from the inside. Assuming the fact, what is it like? This is interest in a quality of being. When John the Exile saw the eternal city in a vision, he went into raptures as he contemplated it. "He carried me away in a trance to a great, high mountain, and showed me Jerusalem, the holy city, coming down out of heaven from God, in all the glory of God. It shone with radiance like that of some very precious stone, like jasper, clear as crystal" (Revelation 21:10-11).

"The principal street of the city was pure gold, as transparent as glass. I saw no temple in it, for the Lord God Almighty and the Lamb are its

209

temple. The city does not need the sun nor the moon to shine in it, for the glory of God lighted it, and the Lamb is its light. The heathen will walk by its light. The kings of the earth will bring their splendor to it. Its gates will never be shut by day—for there will be no night there and they will bring the splendor and the wealth of the heathen into it. Nothing unclean will ever enter it, nor anyone who indulges in abominable practices and falsehoods, but only those who are written in the Lamb's book of life" (Revelation 21:22-27).

These two approaches to this perennially interesting matter are suggested by Paul in his famous chapter on Love. Is it not striking that in a lyric on love he should exhibit a wistfulness for the larger fulfillments of eternity? He speaks of seeing face to face, knowing even also as we are known, and observes that this experience is to be deferred until some later stage, but "Now," says he, "we see baffling reflections in a mirror." We cannot stand face to face with immortality and return its stare as we return the scrutiny of the stars. If we could we might be as certain of immortality as we are of those spinning vortices of light. But in a strange way, this is not possible, for mortal life itself seems to stand between us and a clear view of immortal life; a barrier to clear sight and thinking. In this discerning figure of Paul's, however, life may be a mirror. If we hold LIFE up before our eyes, we may be able to see in the reflections that return our gaze, intimations of immortality. These reflections may be distorted because life is so often so; our vision may be defective or our focus inaccurate. But even if we saw the reflections perfectly, they would *prove* nothing. We prove things with microscopes and telescopes, not by hand mirrors. But such reflections will provide us inferences that may prove important.

I propose therefore to look at immortality today with the aid of a mirror. I am assuming the fact of eternal life. Of course there are some who will want to argue that point; but for the moment I shall decline their offer of debate. And I shall say, in defense, if necessary, that since one day in the year is allowed for the celebration of peace when there is little peace in the world; and another is allocated to the celebration of liberty when there is a diminishing return on our 1776 investment; we ought to be permitted a day for the celebration of immortality, even if some *do* deny it.

Hold up the mirror of life and look into it. What do we see? Paul has stated it accurately—"baffling reflections." There seems to be an endless confusion of opposites: beauty and ugliness, joy and sorrow, harmony and discord, bitterness and ecstasy. And amid it all, and perhaps the most confused of all, is a strange figure we call Man. What is man that we are mindful of him? Never mind what he looks like. Observe that he appears primarily engaged in making himself at home amidst the confusion, and does so with extraordinary success. And to aid him, he possesses certain tools or instruments which we call the senses: touch, sight, smell, hearing, taste. He touches a thorn and recoils from its sharp point; he touches satin and strokes its softness. He looks at the dazzle of the sun and blinks defensively; and watches the diffusing light of the dawn and sings. He smells the fetor of death and retches, or breathes the fragrance of a flower and smiles. He hears the crash of thunder and hides, the harmony of soft music and is still. He tastes gall and winces, or sips slowly the sweetness of nectar. And by the wise and diligent use of these amazing tools, he fashions the house of his earthly life.

There we are offered our first intimation. Pondering these reflected images, we conclude that man's effort to make himself at home in his universe is no accident. He would be less than human if he felt no such urge. And, therefore, if life is to continue beyond what we call the barrier of death, man will still seek to make himself at home in whatever new environment is provided. He will, we assume, certainly not have duller or fewer tools for this task. To think of man's senses being merged into one great capacity is like thinking of all the highways being merged into one flat surface. In such case we would be as lost as if we had no road. Nor will we have more tools. At least it is quite impossible to imagine what further avenues of sense are available. What we *do* assume is that in a larger environment, such tools as we now possess to aid our adjustment will be infinitely refined and strengthened.

What would this mean? Shall we know our loved ones who have passed out of the reach of our senses? Well, how do we know them now? We can recognize a form at two hundred yards now. Why not be able to recognize at infinite distances then? We hear a familiar voice, nearby or coming from remote distances by electrical impulses. Why not hear from infinite distances then? We feel a hand's touch, tender and full of meaning here. Why not a clasp infinitely tender, infinitely understanding there?

And shall we enjoy what we know? Shall we feel more at home? Why can we not assume that harmonies that are beyond the reach of mortal ears will flood immortal listeners; and even that discord, through the waves of deathless air, will be transmuted into harmony? Who knows but so dull a sound as a footstep here may become as clear and satisfying as a major triad there!

Hold up the mirror of life and look into it again. What do you see now? Action, motion, change; all under a fascinating sort of order that continues without interruption, never hurried, never delayed. And once again, in the midst of this precision, stumbles the form of Man. How does he behave? Never mind his success or failure. Observe that he seems able to do things, independent of the order of the world. He has a mind and a will of his own, sometimes wise, sometimes stupid; sometimes gentle, sometimes savage. He can upset and restore balances; he can create and he can despoil.

And in doing these things he is making use of a tool he calls his brain. He tries to think what is good for him; then he seeks for devices to help him achieve the good; and finally makes up excuses or reasons for his failures or successes. Thus, he says to himself, he fulfills his destiny, he justifies his living.

This allows us our second inference. Pondering these reflections, we assume that if life is to continue in a brighter, ampler way, it will not be defrauded of the powers of mind and will. To suffer such a denial would be the very death of the soul. So, as in the other case, we infer, rather, that these two capacities will be infinitely enlarged and fortified. What would this mean?

That our capacity to know will be bound by none of the limits that now keep our wisdom partial and contingent. "Then shall I know even as also I am known." Also that our wish to do the right and true thing will be undisturbed by the circumstances that distress our mortal existence. "Beloved, now are we the sons of God, but it doth not yet appear what we shall be. But we know that when He shall appear, we shall be (do?) like Him; for we shall see Him as He is (does?)." Think of the rapture of unlimited knowledge, and unhindered impulse to know and do the wise and true thing! It is more entrancing a prospect than hearing a footfall as a musical note!

Life, we have been saying, is the mirror of immortality. We see, by looking at life, reflections of immortality in which our instruments for adjustment are infinitely refined; and our capacities for knowing and doing the true and the good are infinitely strengthened. This is a delightful prospect, and it would be encouraging if we could let the matter rest there. But, unless we are perversely blind, we cannot stop at such a point. For, in spite of ourselves, we see other reflections dancing before our eyes. Besides tools for adjustment to life, we see tools that have been neglected or abused. The love of truth, the listening to the multitudinous voices of God, the impulse to worship and to do the bidding of the Spirit—what has happened to these tools? They have not merely been cast aside. By a relentless law in an orderly universe, these discarded tools have become the instruments of evil. Indifference to God's voice becomes eagerness to attend to the voice of selfishness; contempt for love and gentleness becomes greed and cruelty and hate; neglect of truth becomes obsession with a lie. Is not the agony of Europe at this hour a testimony to the operation of this law? And who are we in America to shut our eyes in refusal to see its inevitable workings among us? Indeed, so clear and threatening are these reflections that some will say: If life *is* the mirror of immortality, then I hope death will be the end of me. It were madness to prolong the intolerable agony of life even for an hour after death!

We must pick up the mirror again, this time not to look at *life*, but to look at *our lives*. It is easy to look at *life*, idealized and remote. But when I look at my life, I find I am confronted inescapably by a question. DO I DESERVE IMMORTALITY? Would not a continuance of *me* make the very idea of immortality odious to *you?* If I neglect the things of the spirit when the world so desperately needs them; if I am intolerant and bigoted and suspicious when the world starves for understanding and compassion, dare I hope for my continuance, with my capacities sharpened and empowered? Would not such a condition convert our hopes of heaven into a dread of hell? Look at your mirror and see whether its image is touched with glory or shadowed by despair.

This stops us dead in our tracks. We are forced to look at life under the aspect of eternity. The child's quaint Sunday School question: "What sort of Sunday School would this School be if all the scholars were just like me?" grows into a mature and challenging question: "What sort of life were immortality if it reflected all there is of me?" That *is* a serious question. And it drives us forward to seek a standard by which we can measure our deserts. Nor is this hard to find. No matter how perverse and ill-deserving *man* is, Jesus deserved immortality. No doubt has ever been seriously cast on that fact. It would appear obvious then, that the way we can deserve immortality is to bring our capacities under His control. How else, in fact, can we count ourselves worthy? Is this not what John meant when he wrote: "In Him was life, and that life was the light of men"? To choose any other way to deserve eternity is to come under the condemnation of a companion verse: "This is the final condemnation, that men preferred darkness to light."

We return finally to our opening word: Life is the mirror of immortality; but we discover that it needs—in the light of what has been said—some amendment. Our first look into the mirror disclosed an idealized humanity; our second caused us to ask whether we deserved immortality; and our third suggestion grew out of the discovery that there was One altogether lovely who, by any and every standard, deserved immortality. It would then seem more true to say that Jesus Christ is the Mirror of Immortality. Since this is so, our last look must be into the face of Him whose triumph we celebrate today. We exchange the mirror of our lives for the mirror of His face.

This is what those who loved Him in earlier days knew. When Paul wrote the second time to the fellowship in Corinth, a city corrupted by greed and the worship of lust, notorious for its dark and depraved and daring wickedness, he said: "For God who commanded the light to shine out of darkness hath shined in our hearts to give the light of the knowledge of the glory of God in the face of Jesus Christ." And as we, in a world that is in some respects not dissimilar to that ancient metropolis, look into that face, what do we see there? What is reflected back in splendor into our faces? Faith in God's power to grant us eternity; Hope in our ultimate achievement of it; and Love for Him who makes it possible for us to deserve it. And the greatest of these is love.

If in a world filled with hate we need the testimony of love, where do we find it today? In the gay throngs that crowd our streets, or in the flowers that brighten our homes and decorate our sanctuaries? No. To those men and women of faith, hope, and love there is only one necessary witness. It is the ever-recurrent, ever-encouraging, ever-triumphant fact:

HE IS RISEN FROM THE DEAD

214

It Matters What We Think

REVEREND RUSSELL HENRY STAFFORD, D.D., S.T.D., LL.D.
Minister of the Old South Church in Boston

IN THIS SERMON Dr. Stafford shows clearly that the intellectual nihilists and pessimists are defeated before they begin, while the man with whom faith and thinking go hand in hand is on the road to the right interpretation of life and God.

He was born in Wauwatosa, Wisconsin, in 1890. He studied at the University of California, the University of Minnesota and New York University, and took his B.D. at Drew Theological Seminary. He has had a distinguished career and has been honored with the doctorate by Chicago Theological Seminary, Oglethorpe University, and Columbia University.

He was the assistant pastor of Central Congregational Church, Brooklyn, in 1912-15. He was ordained as a Congregational Minister in 1914 and was, in turn, pastor of the Open Door Congregational Church, Minneapolis, First Congregational Church, Minneapolis, and the Pilgrim Congregational Church, St. Louis. He has been Minister of the Old South Church in Boston since 1927.

He served as a First Lieutenant (Chaplain) in the Army in 1918, and was a member of O.R.C., 1919-24. He is a trustee of Drury College, Anatolia College, Piedmont College, and Emerson College; a fellow of the American Academy of Arts and Sciences; a member of the Society of Mayflower Descendants; a member of the Society of Colonial Wars and of the S.A.R.; and a member of the Society of the War of 1812.

He is the author of *Finding God, Christian Humanism, Religion Meets the Modern Mind,* and *A Religion for Democracy.*

Sermon Thirty-one

TEXT: *Understandest thou what thou readest?* ACTS 8:30

HE WORLD MISSION OF THE CHRISTIAN CHURCH began to come out of theory into fact at that very spot on the road from Jerusalem to Gaza where Philip encountered the Queen of Ethiopia's finance minister and, by explaining a perplexing oracle of Isaiah to him, won his personal commitment for Jesus Christ. And this first non-Jewish convert was a black-skinned

215

African. If it had no other significance, that episode would still stand out forever in the annals of the Church as the first concrete demonstration and the perpetual symbol of international and inter-racial brotherhood realized through consecration to Our Lord.

But a further significance is not hard to find. The African official had been conning, perhaps in little more than desultory curiosity, an ancient writing alleged to be sacred, which had come into his hands during his visit at the Judean capital. It may not have seemed important to him at first whether he understood it or not. But when it had been explained to him, in terms that touched his heart and quickened his mind and threw a searchlight into his conscience, it became the most important truth he had ever found in his life. And he continued on his way a changed man, with a glow in his breast and an aim for his life which, we may suppose, grew stronger instead of fainter as the years followed on. The Ethiopian eunuch was one man who had discovered that it does matter what we think.

I judge there is nothing very farfetched in treating this episode as an allegory. For it is certain that we all spend our time in conning the book of life itself, scanning our chapter of experiences for their meaning—idly, it may be, at the outset, but with mounting seriousness as it is borne in on us that the page we are reading is an enigma, and in some of its lines, at least, dreadfully somber.

There are people, to be sure, who claim that they never think; that it is not worth while to think, for nobody knows, anyway, what it is all about; that all we can do is to live from day to day and make the best of life as it happens, and refuse to addle our brains with vain endeavors to interpret what as a whole probably has no meaning to reward such probings. But people who make that claim have without realizing it already thought their way through to a conclusion—a conclusion completely negative; usually a snap judgment entered upon without cognizance of all available facts, and always denied in practice by every positive position they take and every definite action they perform in everyday life. Agnostics in profession, they have to desert their profession every time they take a hand at living. There are no really thoughtless people, except the congenitally subnormal. And people who profess to abjure thinking because they judge that life is too difficult a conundrum must needs be ever at war with themselves. For it is impossible to live consistently by the principle of despair and cynicism which they proclaim.

The only way a man can live is by expressing some idea in practice. All conduct at the human level springs from, or is in some way modified by, an idea. Conscious action is a translation of mind into matter. Action being by its nature positive, the negative idea that no action is worth doing because nothing means anything, or really gets anywhere, is obviously suitable only to hamper us in whatever we are prompted to undertake, in spite of our world-denying slant. To continue to live is in itself an acknowledgement of a vital conviction, more organic than any doubt of life's value. That being so, and since we accept life for the time being, at least for whatever we can get out of it, it is clear that we shall get more out of it, and it is probable that we shall discover more hopeful perspectives in it, if we work our way through to some set of affirmative ideas about living which will match the urgency of our life-loving feelings.

Beside the intellectual nihilists who never quite get away with their attempt to reduce life to dust and ashes in their thinking, there is another group which makes light of thought's importance out of sheer lazy good nature, it would seem. These are the people whom we often hear saying, "After all, it doesn't matter what we think, provided we live by the Golden Rule," or ". . . provided we keep decent and are fair to other people." And one must admit that sometimes these are truly decent souls, who do live by the Golden Rule, and make pleasant and trustworthy neighbors. But why do they live by the Golden Rule? Why do they keep decent and behave fairly to others? Are we for one moment to suppose that principles like these rest on no foundation in mind, but spring into a man's heart out of the blue, like lightning?

Moral ideals with enough grip in them to master a man's way of living represent an enormous amount of subsurface thinking. And when this thinking is brought to the light it will be found to contain the essence of faith, in a genuinely religious spirit. He who believes in being good believes in goodness as somehow substantial—and that is God. He believes also in his own power and obligation to be good—and that is duty plus freedom. And he believes that in the outcome only goodness will yield satisfactory results in individual living; that must be immortality, since it does not recognizably happen so here with any degree of uniformity. But if a man has come to the conclusion, no matter by what method, that he must believe in God, duty, and immortality, there is no getting around it that he must have done a heap of thinking on his way to that conclusion, whether he realizes it or not.

To be sure, there are connections in which it is true that it does not much matter what we think. But to cover those exceptions I should prefer to put it this way, that it does not much matter what we think we think. Most of us have a lot of notions floating about in our heads which seem to have drifted out of the everywhere or the nowhere into the here without any legitimate line of approach. These things that we merely think we think are likely to sneak into our heads when we are off our guard from three directions: our prejudices, or ready-made notions, taken over without alteration from environment; our argumentative positions, assumed at first from sheer love of the off-side, then clung to out of pride and obstinacy; and the overbeliefs of theological detail embroidered upon basic religious truths, which include most of the dogmas that divide the sects. All these things that we only think we think really do make little difference one way or the other, so long as we do not take them too seriously.

But it is important that we should see the difference between them and what we really think; that we should either give up what we think we think, or at most hold to it in a humorous and tentative fashion; that we should find out exactly what we really do think about life, and true it up to the best teaching we can find that we may think straight and be able to live accordingly. That old abused word, "orthodoxy," carries many overtones by which I set no store at all. But the word itself is good Greek, and means "straight thinking." I do set immense store by straight thinking. For I am sure that we shall never lead straight lives until we think straight about the great issues of our living.

Let me illustrate the importance of straight thinking in the right direction by a simple analogy. Suppose I hold my hands together in such a position that from the base of the palms the fingers of one hand point up and the fingers of the other point down, at only a slight angle. The distance then between the two sets of fingertips will be so small as to be negligible. I can make them meet each other by a barely perceptible turn of the wrist. But suppose, now, that while I hold my hands at that slight angle, you project both lines on and on into space. Before long they will be as far apart as some point above the earth and some point below the earth. In just that way, when people leave the right line for the wrong line of thought, at the outset the difference seems hardly measurable, and doubtless those on both lines mean equally well. But follow out that deflection from the right line long enough, and the two groups will be as far apart as up is from down, or heaven from hell. And so will be their respective types of behavior. For we always act on what we really think. Right people become wrong people when they keep on thinking in the wrong direction.

Where then does the right direction lie? And how shall we think straight?

It can be demonstrated that the morally right is in the long run alone socially constructive. And it requires no demonstration that the constructive runs true to the cosmic lines of energy. I have already suggested that mere belief, such as all men and women of good will hold, in the Golden Rule, in decency and fair dealing, as a sufficient principle for human conduct, actually implies an affirmative answer already endorsed to the three most searching queries man can address to his surroundings and destiny: Is there a God?—that is, has the universe such a constitution as to be regardful of personality and its standards and values? Are our wills free, so that we can choose the spirit and tone of our living, even though our temperament and circumstances be given us without our choice? Shall we live beyond this day on earth—is our life real in itself—instead of being a flame that goes out with the guttering candle of the body?

Now I am not saying that nobody practices the Golden Rule unless he consciously believes in God, freedom, and immortality. That would be false in fact and unjust in temper. I have known vociferous atheists who were better men than some churchgoers. But the point is that they did not live like atheists. They lived better than they thought they knew, but not better than they really did know in the unscrutinized depths of their minds. For the good life takes God, duty, and immortality for granted. And such nominal atheists could have lived still better if they had seen their own thoughts clearly and stopped pretending not to believe in what they did believe in, and been consciously occupied in carrying their real ideas out toward practical conclusions. For we always do more efficiently what we do deliberately.

On the other hand, a man who really means his atheism, who thinks and thinks about not believing in anything but the present moment and his own advantage, will come in time to mean business by it. Then he will perforce give up the Golden Rule and become a human wolf. For he will have embraced an affirmative judgment, suitable for action, yet affirming what should be denied—therefore he will be led to wrong action. If we care about our characters and our fellow men, or even about their esteem to feed the flame of our vanity, it is to the last degree dangerous to dally with positive judgments repudiating life's supreme values and asserting the sole prerogative of self-interest—lest shortly we begin to act on them and, in a true sense more terrible than any eschatological nightmare, go to hell here and now.

That is what is the matter with the world at this moment. The war is the result of wrong thinking. It is not Hitler and Tojo and Mussolini who have captained all the wrong thinking, either. They could not have got anywhere without a world-setting favorable to their criminal vagaries. For many generations now, ever since the rise of the national state and modern industrialism, the Western world, ex-Christendom, has deserted the altars of the God of love and righteousness in all but form, and followed its political and economic leaders in

219

brutal worship of the Main Chance wherever it could be found, no matter at whose expense. For two or three generations, moreover, our schools have been in the main poisoned with false philosophy derived from the natural sciences by illicit and extravagant inference far beyond their ascertained findings. So successive contingents of youth have been sent out into life under the delusion that only a machine-model interpretation of the universe and their own nature deserved the respect of their intellects, and there was no room for God or freedom or immortality save in old wives' tales.

The pathos of it is that the tide turned some time since. Philosophers of science are no longer dogmatizing against the age-old beliefs which are the prime motors of constructive human action. Many of them are groping their way back toward faith that goes beyond the senses to affirm the reality of the spiritual informing the material and molding it to transcendental ends. But public opinion lags regularly about a quarter-century behind the academy. And the world is in hell today because without belief in God, or freedom and duty its correlate, or immortality, the men who have climbed into the saddle have not been able to see beyond things, and their own passion to have more and more things to enjoy.

That is why a just and durable peace cannot come out of this war, and will not come after this war by mere negotiation and the devising of further international machinery. We need that machinery, to be sure; but no machine can ever be built which men maddened by wrong thinking will not break into bits, unless there comes a revival of religion. When I speak of a revival, however, I would not be taken to intend emotional exhortations and a sawdust trail to a more or less fake mourners' bench. I mean the real thing. I mean a return in penitence deeper than tears from our foolish ways of denying the great and asserting the little, to straight thinking about God, the Personal Meaning in and through all things, the Love that holds the stars to their courses, whom we find in our hearts; the duty our consciences can dodge, to be sure, but must acknowledge even in evasion; the eternal life, beyond as well as within time and space, for which we need no sage to tell us that we were born, since every impulse of our being is freighted with that message. Then and only then, when the mental climate of mankind has been transformed by restored adherence to the cardinal truths of existence, can we hope that the world which wrongminded men have turned into a hell will mirror at last the abiding tranquillity of heaven.

Such a revival of religion is our direct concern in so far as it affects us personally. So we arrive at our second question: How shall we think straight?

It is not altogether an individual process. There remains the age-old tradition of Christian wisdom, of tested expertness in fundamental truth and in living based upon it, made available through the testimony of the Church. The Church has erred and sinned, as have all men. Yet stands its witness sure and unequivocal in Catholic and Protestant branches alike to God, to man's freedom and his potential dignity, and to the deathlessness of all God's children—the whole family of man. And to interpret these truths within the frame of ordinary human appreciation, the Church points beyond its faulty self to its glorious Lord, Jesus Christ, in whom dwelt all the fullness of the Godhead bodily, or, to use a contemporaneous metaphor, who is our index figure as to God's character and what man is called to become.

But this teaching we must be willing to receive, bending our pride of intellect in docility before expert advice here as we do in every other region of knowledge in which we are learners, not masters. Then, having received this teaching, we must live on the assumption that it is true. We must sternly conform our activities of mind and body, our vagrant ideas and our wayward impulses, under the discipline of high doctrine. We must take that doctrine at its face value as a rule of thought and conduct. When we think no thoughts and do no deeds save such as proceed from prior recognition of the truth about our being and the Supreme Being, seeing Him and ourselves in Christ's likeness, then the global revival of religion will have begun at that point of the globe which we occupy.

You and I spend our days in conning the book of life, as the Queen of Ethiopia's finance minister conned the book of Isaiah, to see what it means. "Understandest thou what thou readest?" It does matter what we think. For if our interpretation of life be wrong, then our living will be empty and self-doomed to frustration. Human life can never get away from being thought in action. We have one greater than Philip to construe the difficult text of living to our minds. We will heed his rendering of the word, for he himself is the Word to our understanding. So shall we find a happiness greater than pleasure, and a hope brighter than success, and a security unshaken though the earth should tremble and fall from its pillars into the boundless void.

Gaining Emotional Poise

Reverend James Gordon Gilkey, D.D., LL.D.
Pastor, South Congregational Church, Springfield, Massachusetts

MEN AND WOMEN find comfort and help in the sermons of Dr. James Gordon Gilkey. He combines religion, psychology, and personal living into messages which assist those who are emotionally upset.

In 1916 he was ordained as a Presbyterian minister and served as assistant pastor of Bryn Mawr (Pennsylvania) Church in 1916 and 1917. Since that time he has been minister of South Congregational Church, Springfield, Massachusetts. This Church has a membership of nearly eighteen hundred people and has one of the largest Sunday morning congregations in New England. Dr. Gilkey was one of the first ministers to preach on the radio, broadcasting his morning service regularly as far back as 1923.

Since 1927 he has published thirteen books dealing with problems in religious thought and everyday living. Among them are *Solving Life's Everyday Problems* (which has been transcribed into Braille for the use of blind readers), *How to Be Your Best,* and *God Will Help You.*

"Gaining Emotional Poise" was preached November 14, 1943, to present the secret of inner quiet through contact with the "Divine Power."

Sermon Thirty-two

TEXT: *Is not easily provoked.* I CORINTHIANS 13:5

AS ALL OF YOU UNDOUBTEDLY REALIZE, THAT phrase was originally written in Greek. In its original form it contained only two words. The second word—here translated "is provoked"—came from a verb that had several shades of meaning. Used in a literal sense it meant "to sharpen," as, for example, to sharpen a knife. But the verb also had a figurative meaning, one applied to people. Used in this figurative sense it meant to rouse a person, stir him up, incite him to intense feeling. Such a person was, the Greeks said, "sharpened." From this Greek verb, used in this figurative sense, came a Greek noun which is the source of our English noun "paroxysm." A paroxysm is the state of violent feeling attained by an individual who has been "sharpened." With all these facts before you, the picture hidden in this familiar phrase "is not easily provoked" begins to be clear. Frankly it is not the picture of a person who has been mildly annoyed: rather it is the picture of a person who has been completely upset emotionally, who is on the verge of a paroxysm. When three centuries ago the King James Translation of the Bible was made, the translators studied this Greek phrase and finally put it into English as "is not easily provoked." Evidently the word "provoked" had stronger connotations then than it has now. Today we would probably translate the phrase "is not easily upset," or "is not easily thrown into a turmoil." Then the true meaning comes clear.

Here and there in the world we find individuals to whom this phrase actually applies. They are not easily upset, not easily thrown into a turmoil. Whatever happens they maintain their mental and emotional poise. Such a man was living here in western Massachusetts two centuries ago. His name was Jonathan Edwards, and the story of his extraordinary self-control ought to be more widely known. Jonathan Edwards was born in the little village of East Windsor, Connecticut, in 1703. His father was minister of the Congregational Church there for no less than sixty-four years. Jonathan entered Yale at the age of thirteen, and graduated at seventeen. Then he spent two years studying theology, was ordained, worked for a year in a Church in New York, and then returned to Yale as a tutor. In 1727, when he was only twenty-four years of age, he was invited to become the junior minister at the Congregational Church in Northampton, Massachusetts. The senior minister there was his maternal grandfather. Young Edwards went to Northampton, and when his grandfather died two years later found himself in sole charge of the Church. That was in 1729, when he was only twenty-six years old.

Five years later Jonathan Edwards stepped suddenly into fame. He began preaching a series of sermons based on his conviction that God has the right to do anything He wants to with human beings. They are His creatures: therefore He can give them any treatment He chooses. He can even sentence some of them to torment in hell, and no criticism can be made of His action in doing so. He has the right to do anything He wants to with the men whom He has made. The titles of some of young Edwards' sermons were, to say the least, startling. One sermon was called "The Justice of God in the Damnation of Sinners," another "Wicked Men Useful Only in Their Destruction," still another "The Eternity of Hell's Torments." The most famous sermon in the series was entitled "Sinners in the Hands of an Angry God." The effect of these sermons on the people of Northampton was astonishing. Men, women, and children flocked to Church, presently an unprecedented revival started, and soon the revival spread in all directions. Jonathan Edwards, still in the thirties, suddenly found himself one of the most famous and influential ministers of his time. Then, in 1744, everything went wrong.

By that time the intense emotions roused by the revival had subsided, and in Northampton a period of religious apathy ensued. Between 1744 and 1748 not one person in the town applied for admission to Edwards' Church. This unexpected cessation of local interest gave Edwards' critics their chance, and they began suggesting that the Church locate a new minister. The agitation spread, much personal bitterness was roused, and in 1750 the Church actually voted to dismiss its once-famous minister. Jonathan Edwards hoped the other preachers in the area would stand by him, but when an Ecclesiastical Council was called to review the Church's action, five of the nine ministers present voted to sustain the dismissal. Thus poor Edwards found himself out of a job. He was then forty-seven years of age, and he had a wife and ten children to support. The subsequent struggles of the Edwards family to maintain itself financially were pitiful. Mrs. Edwards and her daughters set to work making embroideries and painting fans, and then sent them to Boston to be sold there. Meantime all the Edwardses, Jonathan included, continued living in Northampton. They remained there (and it must have been decidedly unpleasant to do so) because they had literally nowhere else to go. How, in that trying situation, Jonathan Edwards maintained his serenity of spirit and his kindness of heart is a mystery. But that was the very thing he did.

Before long the Northampton Church found it was not easy to locate, in the New England of that day, a new and satisfactory minister. Then the Church did an almost unbelievable thing. It asked Jonathan Edwards for help. Would he be kind enough to serve occasionally as a supply-preacher? Most ministers would have refused such a request, refused it indignantly. Imagine trying to preach in a pulpit from which one had just been ousted! But Jonathan Edwards controlled his feelings, told the Church he would help, and actually resumed preaching in his former pulpit. Then the following year he met another situation quite as trying. The only new pastorate offered him was the one in the tiny Congregational Church in Stockbridge. Part of the work there consisted in preaching once a week to the Housatonic Indians. Once Jonathan Edwards had been the most popular and influential preacher in all New England; now he was invited to talk to a few ignorant savages! But again he controlled his feelings, moved to Stockbridge, and in the summer of 1751 began a seven-year pastorate there. Now comes the climax of the long, strange story. In spite of the uninspiring surroundings at Stockbridge, in spite of the disappointments and frustrations of preceding years, in spite of the disturbing emotions which must repeatedly have surged within him, Jonathan Edwards wrote in Stockbridge the four theological treatises which stamp him as the most original religious thinker America has yet produced. You want a description of this amazing man? Listen.

> He that of such a height hath built his mind
> And reared the dwellings of his soul so strong
> That neither fear nor hope can shake the frame
> Of his resolved powers, nor all the wind
> Of vanity or malice pierce to wrong
> His settled peace or to disturb the same—
> What a fair seat hath he, from which he may
> The boundless wastes and wiles of Man survey!

Or Jonathan Edwards might be described even more briefly, in a four-word phrase of long ago: "Is not easily provoked."

Now suppose this sermon is verging on a problem which greatly concerns you. Suppose you *are* easily upset, easily thrown into a turmoil. Suppose you would like to have some such self-mastery as Jonathan Edwards had. Can you gain mental and emotional poise? If you can, how can you gain it?

I ought to say frankly that your difficulties may be produced by factors with which a minister is not competent to deal. Thus your emotional instability may be rooted in physical weaknesses which only a doctor can locate and correct, or in mental tangles which only a psychiatrist can unearth and eradicate. Or your present difficulties may be traceable to external situations which, at the moment, put impossible demands on you. Thus you may be forced to work under cruelly exhausting conditions, or you may be facing at home strains and tensions which are inevitably fatal to your peace of mind. If these are your handicaps, a minister who is preaching a relatively simple and general sermon can bring you little help. But if your situation is less complex and more manageable, I think I can aid you. I can aid you by reminding you of three rules for gaining emotional poise which have grown out of long and bitter human experience.

The first is this: Get the right mental picture of your own life. What is the right mental picture? Most of us think of ourselves as standing wearily and helplessly at the center of a circle bristling with duties. From every side tasks and burdens, problems and annoyances and responsibilities, rush in upon us. At every moment we have a dozen different things to do, a dozen different problems to solve, a dozen different strains to endure. The cruel pressure never relaxes: always we are overdriven, overburdened, overtired. A common mental picture—and it is totally false.

No one of us, however crowded his life, has such an existence. What is the true picture of your life? There is an hour-glass standing on your desk. An extremely thin tube connects the bowl at the top with the bowl at the bottom. That tube is so thin that only one grain of sand can pass through it at a time. So the grains slip down in single file, always in single file. That is the true picture of your life, even on a super-busy day. The crowded hours come to you one moment at a time, always one moment at a time. That is the only way in which they can come. The day may bring many tasks, many problems, many strains, but invariably they come in single file. They never make a mass attack. I, for example, may have a hundred different things to do before tonight, but those hundred things will come to me one by one. At the present moment I have only one responsibility—to finish this sentence. The coming moment will bring me my next responsibility—to complete my next sentence. Because my day thus comes to me moment by moment, because its many tasks are invariably arranged in single file, I can stop thinking about my future responsibilities. I can ban from my mind the sense of strain which is automatically created if I picture all my tasks as arriving simultaneously. Thus I can make my way through the day in perfect quietness—living one moment at a time, doing one thing at a time, facing one problem at a time. You want to gain emotional poise? Remember the hourglass, the grains of sand dropping one by one. There is the true picture of your life.

The second rule for gaining mental and emotional poise is this: Scale down the demands you are making on other people. What are those demands? One is the demand for notice, attention, evidences of interest. Little children make this demand openly and unblushingly; we older people make it in secret ways. But all of us make it, make it continually. We make it because we cannot endure being ignored. We also demand from other people commendation and praise, particularly after we finish a difficult piece of work. Of course we do not make the demand openly and noisily; we make it silently and maybe unconsciously. Have you never caught yourself, after you have completed an exacting piece of work, waiting to hear what other people will say about it? That is your silent and unconscious demand for commendation and praise. Surely *someone* noticed how skillful you are! Surely *someone* will have a few kind words to say! And obviously we all demand expressions of gratitude from the individuals we help. How soon will their letters of thanks arrive? Surely they will not accept so much from us and show no appreciation in return! These are the demands which all of us, old as well as young, continually make on our associates. Are the demands met? Do we actually get attention, commendation, expressions of gratitude? Usually we do not. This is not cynicism on my part: it is the actual and painful record of experience. When we do not receive all we think we deserve (and in many instances *do* deserve), what happens? Promptly we are upset, upset mentally and emotionally. We say bitterly that people are cold and unfriendly, that we are foolish to put so much effort into our work, that hereafter we shall stop doing so much for others until they begin doing a little for us. Do you know how to avoid this inner turmoil? The way is simple. Scale down the demands you are making on other people. Expect less—less attention, less commendation, less appreciation. Years ago I read an essay with the quaint title, "Fishing for fish not in the pond." To learn what fish are not there to be caught, and then to stop trying to catch the absent fish—to do this is to save one's self much fruit-less effort and many bitter heartaches.

The final rule I mention may seem vague and relatively unimportant. You may wonder why I mention it at all. But if you had a minister's opportunity to watch individuals reach middle life, and then move toward old age, you would realize how important this final rule is. Here is the final rule: At any cost in effort keep your world from growing small. A contemporary novelist draws this brief but unforgettable picture of one of her characters: "Edith was a little country, bounded on north and south and east and west by Edith." As we grow old many of us, perhaps most of us, repeat Edith's blunder. We let our world grow smaller and smaller, and finally a day comes when we find ourselves living in a miserably restricted area surrounded only by our own feelings and our own interests. Strangely enough, many of the individuals to whom this happens do not realize it is happening. They tell themselves they are getting on in years, that their strength is not what it used to be, that they should cut down the number of their responsibilities. So, mistaking inertia and self-interest for wisdom, they "retrench." How they retrench! They drop most of their earlier activities, resign from most of the positions they once held, even stop writing letters to their friends. Then they repeat to themselves the dreary proverb about the old dog and the new tricks, and on the assumption they belong to the canine species stubbornly refuse to try to acquire any new skills. Thus gradually and without realizing it they become like Edith—wholly self-centered. Then what happens? They are mentally and emotionally upset, upset most of the time. Why? Because they are thinking continually about themselves. Because they are living solely for themselves. Because they are expecting other people to identify their little country with the universe, and because other people persistently refuse to do so. You want to escape mental and emotional turmoil in your later years? At any cost in effort keep your world from growing small.

> The world stands out on either side
> No wider than the heart is wide,

Above the world is stretched the sky
No higher than the soul is high.
The heart can push the sea and land
Further apart on either hand,
The soul can split the sky in two
And let the face of God shine through.
But East and West will pinch the heart
That cannot keep them pushed apart,
And he whose soul is flat—the sky
Will cave in on him by and by.

Suppose you start making these efforts. Can you get help from God? You can. You can get it by doing the things you have been doing here in Church during the past hour. Here in Church you have withdrawn from the noise and tension of daily life. You have made yourself inwardly quiet, you have joined in acts of worship and prayer, you have focused your thought on one of life's deeper issues. As you have done those things God's help has come to you. It has come as a new serenity, flowing into your heart from the Divine Silence at the center of things. It has come as a new insight, invading your mind from the Divine Wisdom at the core of life. It has come as a new strength, rising within you as you made your own contact with the Divine Power permeating the universe. You wonder whether you can face the busy week ahead, manage all the work it will bring, still keep inwardly serene? Listen. "Strained by the drive of modern life, most of us are haunted by the realization that there is, that there must be, a better way of living. It is a way of unhurried serenity, unfailing power. Here and there we see individuals who have actually found this better way and are actually following it. They are not people of dallying idleness or mooning meditation: rather they are individuals who carry their full share of the common burden. But they do it without chafing under the load. We are strained and tense: they are poised and at rest. How do they win this victory? By making their way to the Deep Center of life. By entering the Hidden Silence behind and beneath all sound. By finding God, drawing from Him strength and wisdom and quietness. Their victory is within our reach. The peace of God can guard our minds too."

New Year Summons

RABBI ISRAEL GOLDSTEIN, D.H.L.
Rabbi, Congregation B'nai Jeshurun, New York

DR. ISRAEL GOLDSTEIN is the heart and soul of Judaism and Zionism in America. He lives and breathes it, works for it and talks it. Recently he said, "I haven't time to bother with incidental things. Men and women are dying while we waste time." For twenty-five years he has been the Rabbi of Congregation B'nai Jeshurun, New York's second oldest Jewish Congregation, now in its 118th year. He recently flew to England to assist in plans to aid Jewish refugees in the warring nations.

He is the very active president of the Zionist Organization of America; president of the Synagogue Council of America; co-chairman of the Interim Committee of American Jewish Conference; and president of the Jewish Conciliation Board of America. He is also chairman of the Jewish Section of the Interfaith Committee for Aid to the Democracies. The British War Relief Society has established, in his honor, the Dr. Israel Goldstein Children's Nursing Home in England. He is a member of the Board of Trustees of the National Conference of Christians and Jews; of the Army and Navy Committee of the Jewish Welfare Board; of the Governing Council of the World Zionist Organization; of the Council of the Jewish Agency for Palestine; of the American Zionist Emergency Council; of the National Council of Joint Distribution Committee; of the Boy Scouts Jewish Advisory Committee, and of the Girl Scouts Jewish Advisory Committee.

He is the author of *A Century of Judaism in New York* and *Toward a Solution*.

His sermon, given at Rosh Hashonah, in 1943, touches the core of certain aspects of the Jewish problems today, problems that Jews face in Europe, America, and Palestine. He is the champion of the downtrodden and fights with all that is in him for human betterment.

Sermon Thirty-three

TEXT: *Blessed are they who understand the sound of the trumpet; they shall walk in the light of Thy countenance.* PSALM 89:16

ITH MONOTONOUS REPETITIVENESS THE SOUNDS of the Shofar [ram's horn] peal forth, as a new year punctuates the Jewish calendar. With undisciplined staccato its shrill notes rend the air. A crude instrument, producing a crude sound, the ram's horn has stubbornly resisted the improvements of modernity. We would not have it otherwise. A resourceful bandleader might out-shofar the Shofar and orchestrate its weird sounds. An ingenious composer might build a symphony in E minor around the *Tekiah-Shevarim-Teruah*. It might entertain and even impress us in the concert hall, but it would only annoy us in the Synagogue. We want the ram's horn without art or artifice. We want it to produce its natural sounds, just as our fathers heard them. It is the call of the ages, as unpolished as victory or disaster, raw and penetrating, shrill and stirring, unmelodious but compelling.

It would be a study in Jewish folklore to trace the different interpretations which have been read into the Shofar. Its three main functions adumbrate the message of this day as we enter the New Year. These functions were: to sound the alarum of war, to call the people to penitence, and to lift the hopes of the people to a better future.

War's alarum is in its fifth year for many of the nations, past its second year for Russia, and almost past its second year for us of the United States. Eleven million American boys have responded to the trumpet call, and the end is not yet. There is not a family in this congregation which has not at least one human life invested in this war, not to speak of the investments of substance, time, and energy. I have seen many of your sons and brothers in my visits to training bases across the country and back, and have corresponded with many more. Your most precious investments punctuate the map of the world. You know now what global war means, you whose sons sail on the seven seas and occupy outposts in Panama and Natal, in Casablanca and Salerno, in Iceland and Alaska, in Belfast and Hawaii, in Guadalcanal and India. Your boys are maturing under the impact of the great responsibilities they are carrying.

The war, still remote from most of us a year ago, has come right into our homes and hearts. Each of us who has a relative in the armed forces will be praying today and tomorrow with special devoutness. Mothers and fathers will be thinking the same trembling thoughts and yet withholding these troubling thoughts one from the other—hopes shadowed by misgivings, fears dissolved in prayers. This is what all of us are going through on this day of contemplation.

The best remedy for worry is work. Let us keep so busy with our own civilian war tasks that we shall have no leisure for anything else. There are war bonds to buy and to help in selling. There are the Red Cross and USO to serve, not only in the hospitality services where the supply of volunteers exceeds the demands but also in the daily routine of sewing and knitting, of securing and sending packages; there is the salvage program to assist; there is a variety of civilian defense services for men and women to render. For most of you I know these suggestions are superfluous because you are already busily engaged. Yet I also know that there are still some men and women who have not geared up their lives to the war effort, who pursue the even tenor of their ways and their idle amusements, as if nothing had happened, merely taking advantage of the fact that they are living in a metropolis where they can hide behind the anonymity of the crowd. I wish I had my own FBI to smoke them out and shame them into action. If there are any such in this Congregation I hope they have enough conscience to be prodded on this day of self-examination.

Fortunately for all of us, and especially for those of us who have kin on the war front, the greater portion of the war is behind us. The beginning of the end is in sight, though not so near as some of us wish or think it to be. Luckily for us, Russia is bearing the brunt of the ordeal. It is something to think about when we think about Russia. True, Russia is fighting for her own life and had no choice but to fight. Yet the fact remains that five million Russian dead and wounded have made it possible for us so far to win our victories at a relatively small cost in human life. Let us not forget our debt to Russia when the time of reckoning comes.

And let us not forget or permit others to forget our Jewish contribution to the war effort.

Three hundred and fifty thousand Jewish boys are serving in the American forces and are more than adequately represented in the lists of heroes. Probably twice as many are fighting in the magnificent Russian armies where Jewish names galore have been singled out for special praise, and probably another hundred thousand in England and the Dominions. In little Palestine, where there is no conscription but only enlistment, thirty thousand Jewish men (ten per cent of the Jewish manpower in contrast to two per cent of the Arab manpower) have enlisted in the British forces. Wherever around the world Jews are free to join the forces of the United Nations they have eagerly thrown themselves into the combat. And even where they were not free, witness their participation with the guerrillas of Yugoslavia, and their gallant although hopeless stand in the ghetto of Warsaw. And there have been not a few episodes of special gratification that have brought rejoicing to the hearts of Jews everywhere, such as the fact that Captain Klein of New Jersey was the first American soldier to set foot on the North African soil in the invasion which began the end of the beginning; and the story of Sergeant Cohen of London, now known as the "King of Lampedosa," to whom that island surrendered as a prelude to the invasion of the continent of Europe. The alarum of war has found our people eager to respond.

The Shofar is also a call to penitence. Again, I am thinking in larger terms than the Jewish people or the Jewish religion. The whole world is called to penitence for having permitted this war to come to pass. It is a man-made catastrophe, not like the earthquake or the flood which we call an act of God. Just as surely as some personal loathsome disease is the inevitable aftermath of an individual's abuse of his body, the disease of war is the inevitable aftermath of collective man's abuse of social relations, internationally and intranationally.

I am not one of those who believe that the Treaty of Versailles was responsible for this war, although I share the view that it had many faults. The cause of the war in my opinion was twofold. The first cause was the abstention of the United States from the League of Nations. Of all the nations in the League, ours, as the largest nation, relatively unencumbered by empire commitments or private understandings with smaller nations in the European complex, was in the best possible position to exert its moral and economic influence for the safeguarding of the peace of Europe. The second cause, ancillary to the first, was the confusion, timidity, and hypocrisy, which together spell appeasement, of England and France who ran the European show without regard to Russia—half fearing Hitler and half encouraging him, hoping he would turn his martian face eastward and lay the ghost of communism, so that the Cliveden set in England and the 400 "Bank of France families" in France might be able to sleep at night. Hitler could have been stopped half a dozen times between 1933 and 1938. Japan could have been stopped in 1931. Italy could have been stopped in 1936. One doesn't know whether it was more confusion than timidity, or more timidity than villainy. It was a compounded felony.

And, as always happens, the Jewish problem is a reliable barometer. Where was the conscience of Europe when Hitler proclaimed war against the Jewish people in 1933? The statesmen in the chancelleries of England and France preferred not to see and not to hear. It was Germany's internal affair, said the meticulous lawyers. Hitler must not be crossed, said the timid politicians. He has a great mission to immunize Europe against Bolshevism and must not be disturbed, said the reactionaries. So the Jew was left to his fate. Only an Isaiah could muster the language fit to excoriate the misleaders of our generation: "Thy leaders are misleaders who have corrupted the highways. . . . Woe unto those that draw iniquity with cords of vanity."

So let no one wring his hands against God's injustice. Let us rather indict our own human stupidity, cowardice, and venality.

The Rosh Hashonah Shofar calls the nations to penitence. "United States, repent of your isolationism and join the international forces for safeguarding the peace of the world after this war. England and France, repent of your stupidity, cowardice, and hypocrisy and learn the lesson at last that just as in the long run honesty pays in private business, so also honor pays in conducting the business of international relations."

There is reason to believe that this call is not going unheeded—that the Congress of the United States will not repeat the mistakes of 1919, and that England will not soon forget the bitter lessons of the past decade.

The Shofar also proclaims the message of hope. Every world-shaking war releases new hope for humanity's future. The very grimness of the tragedy creates its own antidote in the form of hope. Otherwise it would be impossible to go on. Men would refuse to go to war, and their parents, wives, and children would refuse to let them go, if they did not feel hopeful that the outcome would justify their sacrifices.

Unfortunately wartime illusions too often give way to peacetime disillusionments. That is what happened after the last war. In the wake of the disillusionment, a great wave of pacifism swept over the world. Books like *The Great Illusion, Sergeant Grischa,* and *All Quiet on the Western Front,* became best-sellers. Cynicism about war became the vogue in college halls and on lecture platforms. It had its effect on American policy, aiding and abetting the forces of isolationism and influencing neutrality legislation. All this is exactly what the warmongers of Europe and Asia wanted. It played right into the hands of Hitler, Mussolini, and the war party in Japan. They prepared for war feverishly, while England, France, and the United States were indolently basking in their fool's paradise. The mistake proved almost fatal. Hitler was a mere hair's breadth removed from victory in September, 1940, when a few hundred British lads policing the skies over their native England were all that stood in the way of the Nazi invasion of the British Isles.

This was the price we paid for excessive disillusionment when the hopes of the last war turned to bitter disappointment.

What justifies the belief that the hopes of this war will not similarly turn to bitter disappointment? It is important to consider this question because already the notes of disillusionment are being heard. Already there are forewarnings that this war will have been fought in vain. China is disgruntled with the meagerness of the help she is receiving from England and the United States. Russia is suspicious of the ultimate inten-

233

tions of her allies. Liberals are disappointed with the premium we are putting on the Darlans, Badoglios, and Francos. Negroes are vehemently resentful of being subjected to treatment here at home which is in direct contradiction to our profound war aims abroad. Jews have a deep grievance as the forgotten ally in this war, whose contribution to the struggle is nameless, whose unparalleled tragedy at the hands of mass murderers is barely noticed, and whose just claims to Palestine are shunted.

Yet in spite of all this, one is justified in taking a hopeful view of the kind of world which will emerge from this war, provided it is recognized that good and evil are relative terms. Those of you who are inclined to become moody and cynical about the future are invited to do one thing—just contemplate what kind of world would face us if Hitler were to be master of the world. Just imagine what the Norwegians or the Czechs or the Poles would say if you offered them an alternative between the present yoke and the opportunity to revert to the condition of independence despite its flaws and imperfections in the 1920's. Merely the fact that the world will not be a Hitler-ridden world is already cause for rejoicing. That does not mean that we must be satisfied with the status quo ante bellum. On the contrary, intelligent, forward-looking men must seize the opportunity of a world-in-the-making—to try to remake it, to abolish its age-old evils, and to fashion it after a high and noble pattern. The conclusion of every war presents so many revolutionary opportunities, and it would be a pity to leave them unused. All that I am saying is that even at the very worst, even if the postwar world is not drastically different from the prewar world, it is no mean salvation to have been saved from living in Hitler's "New Order."

I believe, moreover, that our postwar world will be better than our prewar world for the following reason: We still remember the last war, the last peace, and why the last peace failed. Because the failure took place in our time, we can learn our lesson from our experience. Human nature is so constituted that we learn more readily from firsthand experience than from secondhand experience. Franklin D. Roosevelt is already demonstrating that he is benefiting by the mistakes of Woodrow Wilson in dealing with the American Congress. The American Congress is already demonstrating that it is benefiting by the mistakes of the Congress at the end of the last war. Churchill is benefiting by the mistakes of Lloyd George. The man in the street is more sober, more circumspect, and more world-minded than he was in the last war. The boys in the Army and the Navy are better informed, more critical, more aware of world problems than their forebears of a generation ago. There is infinitely more discussion going on about the postwar world and postwar problems than we heard during the last war. Literally hundreds of groups are engaged in these studies. Newspapers and magazines are filled with their pronouncements. The air is agog with postwar formulations.

Religious bodies have never before given such close attention to the bases of a durable peace. The best minds in the Church and Synagogue organizations are at grips with the thorny problems of a durable peace. A joint declaration of peace aims has been issued by the three great religious bodies in American life, the Federal Council of Churches, the National Catholic Welfare Conference, and the Synagogue Council of America. It is the first joint declaration of its kind, and it will be a milestone in the history of interfaith relations.

All in all, therefore, is there not reason to believe that we of this generation are approaching the problems of the postwar world with greater discernment than did the generation of 1918, and with more sober realism, born of experience? It is not fantasy but realism to look forward to the possibility of a century of peace, which will be a century of unprecedented material and spiritual progress. Mr. Churchill, when he was here recently, took occasion to speak of basic English as an international language. There is, I believe, reason to look forward to a basic international morality, which will undergird the pattern of a durable peace. That will be religion's ultimate triumph.

Therefore, the Shofar's call to hope is not a call "crying in the wilderness." It finds an echo in the minds and hearts of men seasoned by trial, but not defeated.

Thus, the Shofar sounds the alarum of war, the call to penitence, and the summons to hope.

If the world hears aright the sounds of the Shofar, the year 5704 may mark not only the beginning of the end, but the end—the end of the dynasty of wickedness, the end of enslavement for peoples and of terror for individuals, the end of the dark age that for a time threatened to last a thousand years, the end of bottomless tragedy for the Jew.

If the world hears and heeds, the Psalmist's word will yet be fulfilled, "Blessed are they who understand the sound of the trumpet; they shall walk in the light of Thy countenance."

Where Now Is Thy God?

RABBI LOUIS L. MANN, PH.D.
Rabbi, Chicago Sinai Congregation, Chicago, Illinois

ONE OF THE distinguished Rabbis of America, Dr. Louis L. Mann is widely known for his interest in education, social problems, and social reform. Since 1923 he has served the Chicago Sinai Congregation.

Dr. Mann is noted for his lectures on comparative ethics at Yale from 1920 to 1923; he has been professorial lecturer in the Department of Oriental Languages at the University of Chicago since 1924; he was lecturer on the "Evolution of the Soul" for the W. F. Ayres Foundation in 1931. He holds a number of important positions as a member of the executive board of the National Institute for the Prevention of Crime, a member of the Commission of Religious Education of the Central Conference of American Rabbis, as president of the Big Brothers Association of Chicago; as a Conference member of the Church Peace Union (founded by Andrew Carnegie); and as a member of the Illinois Society for the Protection of Medical Research. He is one of the founders of the Hillel Foundation of the National Conference of Christians and Jews.

On several occasions Dr. Mann's ability has been publicly recognized. He was decorated with the title "Officer of the French Academy," was appointed member of the White House Conference on Children by President Hoover, and was made an administrative member of the War Labor Board Department of Textiles by President Roosevelt.

Sermon Thirty-four

TEXT: *My tears have been my meat day and night while they continually say, "Where now is thy God?"* PSALM 42:3

 DOUBT WHETHER JEWS HAVE EVER FACED A ROSH Hashonah with hearts more contrite and spirits more humble. Everything that Judaism stands for—justice, love, brotherhood, the sacredness of human personality, the inviolability of the human spirit, democracy and freedom—has been and is being ruthlessly challenged. 'Tis not the first time that it has been thus. It is,

236

however, the first time that persecution, expulsion, and crucifixion have become well-nigh universal.

Some of my friends, knowing that Rosh Hashonah is based upon the idea of Providence, with *Yom Haddin,* the reign of justice, and *Yom Hazzikkaron,* historic continuity, as its corollaries, have said plainly, "I pity you having to preach this year. Haven't the events of the last years shaken your faith? How can one believe in a good God, with so much evil? In a just God, with so much injustice? In a merciful God, with so much misery? In a loving God, with so much hatred? Why doesn't something happen to Hitler? If God loves man why is there so much human misery, social chaos, and political upheaval? Since Germany is clearly in the wrong, why should she conquer a dozen or more countries with a population of 150,000,000 and add to herself 600,000 square miles of territory? Why should millions be haunted, hounded, and harried, forced from one country to another until the thought of death seems sweet? Why should the innocent be robbed, pillaged, plundered, and dispossessed? Are not the events we are experiencing enough to make a scoffer's delight, an atheist's paradise, and a skeptic's holiday? People are asking the questions, 'What on earth is God doing?' 'What in heaven is man thinking?' "

The Psalmist must have experienced such cosmic agony when he cried, "My tears have been my meat day and night while they continually say, 'Where now is thy God?' "

We are in need of clear thinking. The higher one's concept of God the more difficult it is to explain evil. Polytheism explained good and evil by holding various deities responsible, the deities themselves differing in moral quality. Hinduism approached the problem in terms of the conflict between reality and illusion. Zoroastrianism pictures life in terms of the struggle between the forces of light and darkness. Platonism pointed to the conflict between spirit and matter. Early Christianity viewed the problem of evil as a struggle between God and Satan. Judaism insisted that God is the Creator of good *and* evil. As a matter of fact, unless both exist, neither can exist. Nothing can exist unless its opposite exists also. If there could be no Hitler there could be no Abraham; if there could be no Nero there could be no Isaiah; if there could be no Caesar Borgia there could be no Florence Nightingale; if there could be no Torquemada there could be no Lincoln. Either man has a measure of freedom, or humanity must be envisaged as a cosmic Punch and Judy show in which man is not a child of God, but a puppet of Providence. Evil has always existed. The only difference in our day is one of quantity, not of quality. Philosophically speaking, therefore, the problem has not changed.

Man can choose, and because he can choose he *must* choose, and the character of his choice establishes his moral stature. If there were no freedom of choice there would be no responsibility; if there were no responsibility there would be no accountability; if there were no accountability there would be neither praise nor blame; if there were neither praise nor blame there would be neither good nor bad; if there were neither good nor bad, the most or least that one could say about anything would be, that it is. That is fatalism—insisting what will be *will* be. Fatalism suffers from two fallacies. Philosophically speaking, to be a fatalist one must prove that man is an automaton without reason, and then *use* his reason to prove that he has no reason. Psychologically speaking, fatalism must prove that all actions are motivated *a tergo* from the accumulated events of the past, thereby outlawing the power of ideals to beckon man on to the future. Judaism's attitude may be stated in the form of a paradox. If man is fated at all, he is fated to be free. He is fated to choose. If he chooses not to choose, he has chosen—to leave it to chance. If he doesn't choose the higher, he has already chosen something less than the higher. Either man has choice, or God is responsible for every crime, disaster, and murder. Fatalism makes God the cosmic scapegoat for all ills. We Jews know more intimately than others what it means to be a scapegoat, the object of the wrath and anger of people not mature enough to assume responsibility for their own deeds and misdeeds. Mankind is using a shabby device in making God the scapegoat for human failures. The planets are still moving in their orbits in silent majesty. No catastrophic meteors have ripped open the earth. Man, man alone, has transformed the garden of earth into a wilderness of desolation. If any one should say he can no longer believe in man, I might understand though not sympathize with him. But why should anyone cast the blame on God?

Let us think clearly. Conditions as they exist are the result of our choice, either individually or collectively. The individual is responsible for the group and the group is responsible for the individual. There can be no escape. We must realize that we are intermeshed in unescapable mutuality. The invention of a new cotton machine in the United States may close the factories of England, and affect 320,000,000 people in India. Life is not a game of solitaire. In a baseball game, if the shortstop makes an error, the whole team may lose. In a football game, if a linesman is off side, the entire team is penalized. If the garbage in one neighborhood is not collected, the whole community may be the victim of disease. If my finger is infected, I cannot laugh at it and treat it lightly. As there is a bloodstream biological, so is there a bloodstream sociological. Man cannot live by himself alone. There are social inevitabilities. Society *is* organic. Man *is* his brother's keeper.

Let us oversimplify the problem for just a moment. Suppose a physician diagnosed a case correctly and prescribed the proper remedy. But the

238

patient threw the prescription in the wastebasket and the cure was not effective. Would you say that medical colleges ought to be closed and that medicine had failed? Suppose a father begged his adolescent son not to drive the machine recklessly and a few hours later the son, after emerging from a tavern with some of his friends, put his foot on the accelerator at the rate of ninety miles per hour—and then a crash! Would you lose faith in fathers? Because human speech is so inadequate, because our minds are so limited, because our knowledge is but a drop in the ocean of our ignorance, figuratively, poetically, and anthropomorphically, we speak of God as "Father."

"There are natural laws in a spiritual world," said Drummond. The universe is law-abiding. We cannot break the law of gravitation with impunity. In like manner we cannot break the moral law without having the moral law break us. The Rabbis of the Talmud poetically pictured God as saying to Israel, "Either you stand on Sinai or else Sinai will stand on you." The moral law will sustain or crush.

Rosh Hashonah is known in Jewish tradition as *Yom Haddin*—a day of justice. This justice is not only moral but also cosmic. It is intermeshed in the warp and woof of the universe. "As ye sow, that also shall ye reap," is as true today as when it was first written. If you "sow the wind you will reap a whirlwind" has been exemplified a thousand times. As one would not think of sowing wheat in order to reap strawberries, so in like manner, one should not expect to sow greed, suspicion, murder, injustice, exploitation, and war and reap generosity confidence, love, tranquillity, and peace.

People in all walks of life today are asking the question, "What's happened to religion? Has it become antiquated? Is it being eliminated? Has it become annihilated?" The simple truth is that in our day and in our generation we have witnessed neither the elimination nor the annihilation but, on the contrary, the vindication and the verification of religion. If the war with its cataclysmic chaos and heart-rending calamity had not come to pass, then would we have witnessed the eclipse of religion whose fundamental concept is that of justice echoed in the *Yom Haddin* of Rosh Hashonah, exemplifying the simple yet far-reaching concept "As ye sow, that also shall ye reap."

God is revealed in nature. Not only does creation imply a Creator, but there are only two alternatives. Either the world created itself and is due to chance, accident, and fortuity, as materialists from Empedocles in ancient Greece to Ernst Haeckel in modern Germany claimed, or it is the result of Mind, Purpose, and Design. Bachya, the mediaeval Jewish philosopher, refuted the accident theory of the universe by asking whether a bottle of ink accidentally spilt would write the Twenty-third Psalm or the Book of Job. If footprints in the desert reveal the presence of man, how deny the existence of God when "the heavens declare his glory and the firmament showeth forth his handiwork"?

God is revealed not only in the physical but also in the moral order. It is now almost twenty-seven hundred years since Amos taught that God is justice. Justice cannot be attained through ruthlessness, intimidation, and violence. Almost as many years ago, Hosea taught that God is love. Where there is love, there is God. Where there is God, there is love. When men give themselves over to hatred they are exiling God from their hearts, or better, they are exiling their hearts from God. It is more than twenty-six hundred years since Isaiah taught that men "should beat their swords into plowshares." Where war is, God is not; where God is, war is not. "The work of righteousness is peace and the effect thereof is quietness and security." The prophet Micah added to these concepts the idea of mercy. The Rabbis of the Talmud often designated God by the word *Rachmanah*, the merciful one, and added that the unmerciful man is an atheist since his actions deny, defy, and belie his faith in a merciful God. We have heard that dictators make war. That is true but it is only a half-truth. The question remains, "What makes dictators?" Herein have we sinned the sin of omission most flagrantly. Scan the pages of history and see how each "peace treaty," so called, was an act of war treachery, conceived in hate, born in malice, and desecrated by revenge. As long as there is no peaceful way of changing the status quo required by shifting populations, markets, and raw materials, so long will force remain the supreme arbiter of the world. As long as every attempt to establish some international tribunal, whether the Hague, the League of Nations, the World Court, or the Kellogg Pact, is selfishly aborted, the alternative to international order, international chaos, will prostrate the world and claim its victims by the millions. As long as the force of faith is brutally transformed into faith in force, as long as the free spirit of man is ruthlessly regimented for purposes of national conquests, as long as the supreme object of man's devotion is the state and not God, as long as we sow the wind, so long will we reap the whirlwind, the ancient faith revealing its somber verification and its tragic vindication, due not to the abdication of God but to the willful and wanton neglect of man.

Fascism has denied God in deed, advocating the supremacy of the state, the rule of might, the method of ruthlessness, the suppression of freedom, the indoctrination of hate, the exploitation of the rights of labor, and the deliberate substitution of propaganda for truth. Communism has denied God in creed, insisting upon the economic determination of history, the worship of the machine, faith in the class struggle, the utter avowal of crass materialism, and belief in violence as the way out. Hitler has insisted that "the state can do no wrong." Stalin has said that "man was made for the state." Mussolini boasts that "beyond the state there is

240

nothing." The message of religion in general and of Judaism in particular, as it has reverberated down the ages, is that beyond the state lies humanity and beyond humanity lies Divinity. Men *will* worship, if not God, then something else. Both Fascism and Communism, after deposing God, have enthroned the state as the supreme object of man's devotion. When the state is God and the first Commandment reads "Thou shalt have no other gods before me; I am a jealous God," we find that the deification of the state leads not only to the desecration of God but also to the degradation of man. When the state is God, force becomes *the* cardinal virtue. The supreme tragedy in the world today is that those who do not believe in force must yet use force or be destroyed by force.

The universal bankruptcy that in all likelihood will follow this greatest of all catastrophes that has ever visited our globe will not disprove the claims of religion but, on the contrary, verify them. Our sages of old said that the Bible and the sword came to the earth together, bearing an inscription, "By choosing one you thereby reject the other." They were not naïve; they simply diagramed and epitomized the fundamental truth which centuries earlier had been formulated by the genius of the prophet: "Not by physical strength and not by brutal or mechanical force, but by the spirit of God shall man prevail."

It has now become clear why dictators persecute Jews. Jews stand for everything that dictators defy. The dictators stand for everything that the Jews deny. If you should think that this statement is a bit overdrawn, read Rauschning's *The Revolution of Nihilism,* in which it is made clear that Fascism is destructionism, the destruction of all values—justice, love, mercy, morality, decency, righteousness and God. It is the destruction of everything except force. It is destruction for destruction's sake. That alone will explain why in the early days Hitler used Capital to destroy Labor and then used Labor to destroy Capital. That also will explain the fiction of a pure race, the "Aryan," and then the attempt to gather into the crusade the Czechs, the Japs, and, for a time, the Slavs. That alone will explain the ancient orgy of burning great books and closing the universities thereby prostituting the greatness of a once cultured country. That will explain the utilization of anti-Semitism as a spearhead to destroy every form of liberalism and co-operation looking to the ultimate brotherhood of man. That will throw light on the false identification of Judaism and Communism, making each of two unpopular philosophies of life doubly unpopular by linking them together. That will explain the hypocrisy of Hitler in shamelessly aligning himself with Russia for a time and then, without rhyme or reason, going forth to crush her. The differences between Judaism and Christianity pale into insignificance when compared to the colossal challenge that now confronts them both. Now, they will stand or fall together.

241

The Judeo-Christian civilization finds itself in a head-on collision with the ideology of Paganism. All who today are indifferent to religion, whether they know it or not, are indirectly on the side of totalitarianism. Only in a world in which religion is blotted out, in which atheism is rampant, can totalitarianism succeed. In all forms of totalitarianism— whether it be Fascism, Nazism, or Sovietism—in which God is dethroned, the people become Godless, not only theologically but morally as well. "The fool saith in his heart there is no God. They have all done abominably." These verses from the Psalms follow one another, although many critics felt the text needed revision. The Psalmist was wiser than his critics. As surely as night follows the day, atheism leads to nihilism. When there is no government *of* the world, there will be no government *in* the world. Atheism is not merely academic, it is extremely practical. I said before that men *will* worship, if not God, then the state. In like manner it is equally true that men *will* sacrifice, if not for ideals then for idols, if not for souls then for sovereignty. Man *is* a worshiping being. Man *is* a sacrificing being. The supreme question today is "What will men sacrifice for? What will men worship?"

So long as God and morality are exiled from international relations; so long as there is no peaceful way of changing the status quo; so long as each peace treaty is an act of war treachery; so long as the motivation of man is "each for himself and the devil take the hindmost"; so long as nations demand absolute sovereignty which, as John Dewey pointed out, is merely another name for international anarchy; so long as double standards of ethics prevail, one within the nation and another between nations; so long as we proclaim a moratorium on the Ten Commandments by worshiping a false God, the state, by taking the name of God in vain, by killing through the arbitrament of war, by stealing through the ruthlessness of conquest, by bearing false witness through the technique of propaganda, by coveting as a basis of national ambition— so long will man, spiritually exiled, morally isolated, and mentally estranged, ask "Where now is thy God?"—not because God has forsaken man, but because man has forsaken God.

> Were half the power that fills the earth with terror,
>   Were half the wealth bestowed on camps and courts,
> Given to redeem the human mind from error
>   There were no need for arsenals and forts.

At a time when rapid transportation and communication have conquered famine, at a time when the "death-fighters" and the "microbe hunters" have decimated disease, at a time when the machine has lifted the burden from the shoulders of man and beast, at a time when mass production has created an economics of plenty, eliminated the economics of scarcity, at a time when the human voice has transcended national boundaries and encircled the earth, at a time when the standards of living, even of the humblest, in some ways have surpassed those of kings in the Middle Ages, at a time when the utopias of the past have lost their glamour because of these realities of the present, at a time when heaven on earth was so near—we have now, in reality, created hell on earth. We have used the inventions and discoveries that should have made for the abundant life, to kill, to maim, and to mutilate; we have permitted greed to cause aggressive wars; we have allowed multitudes in an age of plenty to suffer from dire want; we have permitted the masses to be exploited in order to keep the classes exalted; we have caused insecurity to drive people to sell their birthright of liberty for a phantom mess of pottage, security; we have unwittingly helped dictators to thrive because of the fears that have consumed the multitudes; we have permitted hatred to spread like an invisible poisonous gas laying low its victims in every country; we have stood idly by while propaganda, once used to free people, has been used as a fifth column to enslave them; we have been inactive while the termites of wishful thinking, apathy, indifference, smug complacency, and sleek self-satisfaction have corrupted and corroded the souls of men; we have sanctioned selfishness until it was accepted as the first law of life; we have witnessed morals scoffed at, religion ridiculed, and the values that have been so laboriously evolved throughout the painful centuries sink into insignificance. Then we presume to ask, "Where *now* is God?"

> Injustice like a dark volcano grows,
> Unknown beneath the citadels of power.
> Until the boiling cauldron overflows
> With furious energy, and giants cower
> Before the fiery elemental might
> Of that volcanic vengeance. No escape
> Is there for men and nations who will slight
> God's law of justice. Oh, grievous rape
> Of Freedom on a hundred fun'ral pyres
> Shall be avenged: The awful hour draws nigh.
> Come, Freedom's lovers, let your agonies
> Become the bonds of brotherhood, defy
> The priests of Baal—Race, Class, and Creed—and stand,
> Ye dauntless spirits, God-inspired to build
> From out the wreckage, with repentant hand,
> That beauteous world which God's own love hath willed.

God is not mocked. "As ye sow, that also shall ye reap." The Ten Commandments are not violated; they are simply illustrated. If one could break moral laws with impunity, if one *could* play fast and loose with ethical principles, if one *could* neglect the voice of experience

243

and the declarations of religious genius, if one *could* substitute hate for love, if one *could* introduce the fifth column of treachery for the imperative mandate of loyalty, if one *could* substitute treason for truth, regimentation for freedom, exploitation for co-operation, and still enjoy peace, prosperity, and good will—*then* would I cease to believe in a God of righteousness, and this *Yom Haddin* would have no significance whatsoever.

"Religion or ruin" is the way Mumford sums up the challenge of our day. Unless we dedicate ourselves to a standard of ethical values, unless the code of moral laws becomes our categorical imperative, unless a God-consciousness distills into our souls a sense of human brotherhood, unless a vision of a new and better day gives us a sense of dedication to the true, the good, and the beautiful, unless a spirit of consecration to the ideal really takes possession of us, unless we pray, not that God may be on our side but that we may be on the side of God, unless we realize that "righteousness exalteth a nation" no less than the individual —chaos will reign supreme. This is what God meant to our fathers. This is what God means to us. "Why sayest thou, O Israel, my way is hid from the Lord, my judgment is passed over? Hast thou not heard that the everlasting God fainteth not, neither groweth weary?" God is near to us only when we are near God.

When the architect of the future will seek the weaknesses of the old order before attempting the plan of the future, he will find amid the debris of our world the immortal truth: "The stone which the builders rejected must become the chief cornerstone. . . . Unless the Lord build the house they that build it labor in vain."

That Neighbor of Mine Again

Reverend Albert Edward Day, D.D.

Pastor, First Methodist Church, Pasadena, California

DR. ALBERT EDWARD DAY has had a distinguished career in the Methodist ministry. Ordained a minister of the Methodist Episcopal Church in 1904, he spent thirty-three years in pastorates in Ohio, Pennsylvania, and Maryland. In 1937 he was called to the pastorate of the First Methodist Church in Pasadena and has been serving there ever since.

During the last war, Dr. Day was chaplain of the 117th Field Signal Battalion, A.E.F. He has been active in many fields and has served on groups dealing with foreign missions, social service, and international co-operation and peace. He is now a special ex-aminer for the National War Laboi Board and active in the Federal Council of Churches. He is a frequent guest lecturer at colleges and universities throughout the country. Among the many books he has published are *Jesus and Human Personality, The Evangel of a New World,* and *The Faith We Live.*

In this sermon Dr. Day discusses the old concept of a neighbor, then goes on to interpret the word in terms of races, nationalities, and world relationships. (For a different interpretation of the Good Samaritan, see Bishop McConnell's sermon "Human Neighborliness and Eternal Life.")

Sermon Thirty-five

TEXT: *Which of these three think you was neighbor to him that fell among thieves?*   LUKE 10:37

HO IS NEIGHBOR TO ANYBODY? THE MAN WHO lives beside him? If that were the case we should all have many neighbors and ourselves be neighbors to many people. For we now live side by side in towns and cities. But the urbanization of life, instead of giving us neighbors, has taken them away from us. We have more people *around* us by far than our fathers had, but we have fewer people *near* us. We townspeople live and die closer together than the pioneers did. But in a real sense we live and die farther

245

away from each other. To live in an apartment is often to live apart. City blocks are often what the name may signify, blocks to intimate human relationship. Babies are born and old men die within five hundred feet of us and we do not know it unless we assiduously read the birth and death columns.

THE NEIGHBORLINESS OF YESTERDAY

We are not so obviously dependent on each other as we once were, and our apparent independence seems to make for indifference. Once a birth was a neighborhood event. The neighbors were there. They had to be or the event would not come off properly. Funerals were no less a communal event. The neighbors moved in and took charge of the dead and the living both. They cooked the meals, notified friends and relatives, dug the grave, wove the wreaths, sang at the service, tenderly carried the departed to his burial, lifted the whole burden of bereavement. The sickness that came saw the same communal spirit at work. Neighbors took turns sitting up at nights with the afflicted. If it was plowing time, neighbors' plows turned the soil; if harvest time, neighbors' toil cut and husked the corn, or mowed and stacked and threshed the wheat. If winter drew near, neighbors' saws felled the trees, neighbors' axes split them into firewood, neighbors' horses hauled the wood to the shed where willing hands carefully piled it away. When bars were raised, or apple butter was made, or extra covers were needed to give warm sleep in bitter weather, or butchering was to be done to provide the family's meat, the neighbors all turned out to help. And such fun amid the heavy toil! Such mingling of sweat and laughter!

MEMORIES OF AULD LANG SYNE

The era of neighborliness was drawing to a close when I came on the scene. I am glad I arrived when I did. Because I did, I shall have to leave this earthly scene before are solved many problems whose solution I should like very much to aid as well as witness. But at least I have had some joys which later comers have missed. When anyone speaks of genuine community happiness, memory flies at once to days when the young minister was invited to be a part of the camaraderie of shared work and rapture in threshing or butchering or wood chopping. Football is a fascinating game, especially when it achieves the expertness required of contestants in Pasadena's annual New Year's fiesta. Pity him who, with bated breath, never followed the tide of battle back and forth across the gridiron. But I would still give my ticket to the Rose Bowl any year to be able to travel back to rural scenes, to smell the frosty woods, hear the sound of the saw as it made its way through

246

the oak log, or listen to the ring of the axe and the crack of the riven wood, or know the keenness of hunger that awaited the distant call of the farm bell as it summoned us to steaming plates piled high with unrationed food—to the democracy which claimed us as we worked and ate and talked together.

THE PASSING OF NEIGHBORLINESS

That is all gone. Neighbors have nothing to do with birth now. People do not even have birthplaces any more. They are born in a blank room in a blank hospital very antiseptically and very efficiently and almost painlessly, while the father paces up and down tiled corridors without benefit of clergy or neighbors. That has its advantages. But something still is lacking.

Now, when death pays its unwelcome call, the Director takes charge. He does it efficiently and graciously. There are no worries and no mistakes. Every one of us who has passed by the valley of the shadow remembers him with gratitude. But still there is something missing.

Now we all do our own work or hire it done. What we eat and wear and live in comes by purchase. It brings no neighbors on the scene—only the bill collector or the monthly statement.

We are so organized and so independent of spontaneous and voluntary help, and therefore so socially isolated, that all the richness has dropped out of the word, neighbor. In fact, we seldom use it except to designate someone whose address happens to be on the same street as our own. Probably nothing less than an earthquake or an air raid will ever bring any of the old meanings back into the word for us. We have friends, and fellow townsmen, and fellow clubmen, and fellow churchmen, but not *neighbors*. To our children, who have grown up in these later days, "neighbor" suggests someone in physical proximity, nothing more.

JESUS' CONCEPTION OF NEIGHBOR

If Jesus were living He would probably not use this word at all. It has become so devitalized, so empty, so inconsequential. What He meant was not that thin, attenuated, unexciting, uninteresting relationship which now passes for the old reality. He was thinking of the life-making bond and action of more primitive days, when other men's need was the recognized problem and the glad responsibility of all within reach. That was the world in which he lived. In spite of Rome, in spite of Jerusalem, life in Capernaum and in Nazareth was primitive and interdependent. Unless one had true neighbors one was in a sorry plight. Jesus knew what a real neighbor was. He himself was one. He had often been blessed by the neighboring of others. But even in His

247

day some people were inclined to set narrow limits on neighboring. The Jew and the Samaritan, the Roman and the Greek, were not likely to offer to, or expect from, each other any real neighborliness.

For that reason Jesus told a beautiful story:

"A certain man went down from Jerusalem to Jericho, and fell among thieves, which stripped him of his raiment, and wounded him, and departed, leaving him half dead.

"And by chance there came down a certain priest that way; and when he saw him, he passed by on the other side.

"And likewise a Levite, when he was at the place, came and looked on him, and passed by on the other side.

"But a certain Samaritan, as he journeyed, came where he was; and when he saw him, he had compassion on him.

"And went to him, and bound up his wounds, pouring in oil and wine, and set him on his own beast, and brought him to an inn, and took care of him.

"And on the morrow when he departed, he took out two pence, and gave them to the host, and said unto him, Take care of him: and whatever thou spendest more, when I come again, I will repay thee.

"Which now of these three, thinkest thou, was neighbor unto him that fell among the thieves?"

The meaning of that story is crystal clear: to take neighborliness at its best and extend it to everybody who needs you and whom you can reach by your kindness. The man who fell among thieves was a Jew. Other Jews, physical and racial neighbors, came along the road, but never lifted a hand to help. They were either afraid or too busy. But the Samaritan, not a neighbor geographically or racially but a man of an alien and a despised race, took whatever risk and expense and time were involved, to lift the wounded Jew out of the dust and transport him to safety and life again. *Neighborliness isn't a thing of race or creed or convenience. It is a response to human need within reach, whatever the response may cost.*

THE WORLD WITHIN OUR REACH

The whole world is within our reach now. Neighbor, in the sense in which Jesus meant it, has global range. You can feed a starving child in Greece or rescue an African from his ignorance, or get Christ and the Indian who needs the Great Physician together with less difficulty than that Samaritan encountered in lifting that unconscious Jew to the saddle and carrying him to safety in the distant inn. The teeming millions flung across the wide-open spaces, or crowded into cities, or hiding away in jungles, or dwelling in lonely islands are within an arm's length of our kindness and love. If we turn away from bruised humanity in the Sudan or the Sahara or the Solomons, it will be as heartless as the conduct of those Jews in the parable who saw their wounded countryman lying in the road, deliberately turned away, and passed by on the other side. The millions of sick, suffering, broken, wounded, sinful, ignorant, dying people in the world are actually as near to us as that.

The fact is not going to be abrogated by the wisecrack of the Connecticut Congresswoman who in her maiden speech in the House, dismissed certain aspects of our world responsibility by coining a smart-alec word, "globaloney." I do not wonder that the *Saturday Review* said of that utterance: "It is a disservice to the nation, a curious and unforgivable insult to Americans who happen to be fighting a global war and who will have to fight and die again in other global wars unless the world is able to make a global peace."

Nothing global is "globaloney," whether it be global commerce, global education, or global religion. Nor will anyone, whose outlook on world problems is summed up in such a contemptuous word, be likely to make much of a contribution to the better world we must have, if we are to have a world and not a jungle or a wilderness. This is a global life we live now and *must* live. If we remain provincial in our thinking and planning, in our sympathies and strategies, we perish. If we want peace here, we must have peaceful minds in Europe and Asia. If we want to enjoy our own bread, we must see that men and women and children in the streets of Rotterdam and Poland and Athens and Warsaw have bread, or their quest for it will ultimately snatch our own bread from our fingers.

RECENT HISTORY A COMMENTARY

When Hitler and Mussolini began to tell their dreams, we dismissed them from our concerns. But their dreams have become our nightmare. When underprivileged nations began to cry for more generous daily rations for their underfed millions, we thought it no business of our own. Now we are all going to be rationed. Every table in the land, except those of hoarders and black marketeers, will become a problem and a disappointment. When other peoples began to want decent shoes and clothes, we shrugged our shoulders and pointed with pride to our own, and archly called ourselves the best-dressed people on earth. But because we did not play neighbor to them, we are going to find our own wardrobes scantier. When the Nazis began to scoff at the Sermon on the Mount, and miseducate their youth in the ethics of the buccaneer and the brigand, and preach a new social frenzy in the place of religion, we

249

regarded it as a curious but remote phenomenon. But because they spurned Christ, other millions are having to forget what Jesus said and under grim necessity engage in what a Navy commander recently, with devastating honesty, called "the devil's art of bayoneting, bombing, and killing."

WE ARE ALL NEIGHBORS

Nothing that occurs anywhere is distant from us now. Everybody is a neighbor of ours. If "neighbor" means only proximity, every nation lives next door to us. What happens in streets and schools and clubs and parlors and parliaments anywhere is happening not to somebody else, but to us. We cannot say of any tragedy, "It's their funeral." It is ours, too. We dare not ignore the needs of bodies or minds or souls anywhere. A couple of Army majors on a mission that took them to many camps throughout the country found that most of the men assigned to do their driving drove with a true soldier's disregard of life and limb. When they arrived at a camp in the Middle West, a Negro corporal who was appointed to drive them about in a jeep proceeded at the conservative speed of thirty miles, carefully rounding the turns, stopping at the ditches, avoiding bumps. They felt impelled to compliment his unusual vigilance. The corporal's simple reply was, "Well, sirs, Ah look at it in this way. Ah'm in this here jeep, too." The world is one "jeep" and we are all in it. Whether we *drive* as Clare Luce wants us to, or *ride in the back seat* as the isolationists would like to have us do, we are all in the same car. We all shall either smash up, or we shall arrive safely together.

BECOMING TRUE NEIGHBORS

Not only do we need to awaken to the fact that revolutionary changes in communication and transportation and the momentous interrelatedness of our time make every man as much a neighbor to every other man as was that Samaritan to the Jew who lay wounded and helpless in the road, we must also realize the consequent imperative, to change the neighborliness of mere proximity into a neighborliness of loving concern. We must carry into the new extensity of the word the old and rich intensity of meaning. We *must* feed the hungry, clothe the naked, minister to health, illuminate minds, transform souls, create a humane and Christian world, or we shall have a world forever plagued, tortured, blasted by evil.

Does it matter whether the Japanese people are Christians? "Oh, no," we said. "They have Shinto, glorious Shinto, that touches every phase of their life and binds them together in a brotherhood of life and

250

death. Why bother them with Christianity?" Ask yourself that question now. Are you satisfied that they have Shinto? If they had Christ and his pity and love, and Christ's pity and love had them, there would have been no Pearl Harbor. They would not now be slaughtering our boys in the jungles of the Southern Pacific. At the mid-week service we were told about a man who had just come back from Guadalcanal, who, reciting his harrowing experiences there, said, "The Japs are not human." *They are human. But they are Shintoed humans.* If we had expended the money and the energy to take them Christ and show them the Christian way of living that we are now expending to stab and shoot and bomb and destroy them, the history of Japanese-American relations would be vastly different from the bloody tale unfolding itself before our shocked eyes.

Does it matter whether the Germans have an interpretation of religion that makes it not something to do on Sunday in the church—a mere subject of speculative theology, a private affair between a man and his God, a ticket to heaven—but a consecration that brings their voting, their buying and selling, their statecraft, their social and political ideals under the domain of love and goodness? Germany did not have fair treatment after the last World War. In our anger over her present crimes, we must not abate the solemn judgment we formed in less strenuous days nor forget the humble and sincere confessions once made of our international folly. Only as we keep that judgment in mind and maintain our attitude of repentance, shall we be fitted after this war to construct a peace whose foundations, laid in justice, give a promise of endurance. Germany did not receive redemptive treatment from the victor nations. But even a Germany much worse mistreated than it was would not have followed the leadership of the Folly of Berchtesgaden, if its millions of people had been enthralled by the Man of Calvary.

Does it matter whether the colored races have Christ and Christ has them? Well, if that cannot be, not only is the day of white domination done, a day whose passing we need not moan, but the day of white man's doom is not far distant. They outnumber us so badly that unless they so out-Christian us that they will treat us better than we have treated them, we shall be vastly fewer than we are today.

The hope of the future depends upon whether we shall be neighbors to the world; whether we, who at this moment have economic and political power and at least a knowledge of the moral power and spiritual resources of Christ, really play neighbor to all men on the face of the earth. Sharing with them, we shall save ourselves and our future. Serving them, we shall serve our children and our children's children. Enriching their heritage, we shall preserve our own.

We are going to have a Christian world or we are doomed to burn up our wealth in gunpowder, build ships whose destiny is the bottom of the sea, rear boys to be blown to pieces after days and nights of torture, deprive our girls of husbands and homes and the right to be loved. We have no other choice. It is neighborliness or nothing.

Our value as neighbors will be determined by the acuteness and catholicity of our insight into the truth of Christ, and by the reality and depth of the life of Christ within us. Recognizing the menace of a Japan which has nothing better than Shinto, or of a Germany infected with Nazi ideology, we must also recognize that it is as Christians, and only in so far as we are truly Christians, that our neighborliness will mean salvation for humanity. Much as we love America, we are not called to Americanize the world. There are *some* elements of our life that are not worth sharing with all mankind.

The Christianization of the world is our task, and humanity's hope. It must begin with us. But it must not end there. As far and as fast as the grace of our Lord Jesus Christ becomes our grateful experience, as true neighbors we must share Him with men and women and children everywhere.

The World Vision of Catholicity

RIGHT REVEREND MONSIGNOR THOMAS J. McDONNELL, LL.D.
National Director of The Society for the Propagation of the Faith

As NATIONAL DIRECTOR of The Society for the Propagation of the Faith in the United States and Secretary of the Supreme General Council of this Society in Vatican City, the Right Reverend Monsignor Thomas J. McDonnell represents in the United States the voice of the Catholic Church in all that concerns her foreign mission program. For more than twenty years Monsignor McDonnell, a native-born New Yorker, has been associated with this oldest and largest mission aid organization. In 1923 he was named Diocesan Director of The Society for the Propagation of the Faith in New York and in 1936 was appointed its National Director. In 1941 notice of his nomination as International Secretary of the Supreme General Council in Vatican City was received.

In his vast task of co-ordinating spiritual and material aid for the thousands of missionaries laboring in every part of the world, Monsignor McDonnell is assisted by Catholic leaders throughout the United States with one hundred and fifteen local directors in charge of the Society's interests in the dioceses of the country.

This sermon was delivered on the "Church of the Air" program over Columbia's network on October 17, 1943, as a preparatory address for the universal observance of Mission Sunday on October 24th. The reader will discover in Monsignor McDonnell's sermon a combination of deep feeling, clear thinking, and universal knowledge of the mission problems of the Catholic Church, particularly at the present time when America constitutes the sole hope for manpower and monetary aid in the interest of the missions.

Sermon Thirty-six

TEXT: *And He gave Him power, and glory and a Kingdom; and all peoples, tribes and tongues shall serve Him. His power is an everlasting power that shall not be taken away; and His Kingdom that shall not be destroyed.* DANIEL 7:14

IN ORDER TO HAVE A MORE COMPREHENSIVE understanding of the world vision of the Church founded by Christ, let me transport you in spirit to the hill of Golgotha upon which, in the year 33 A.D., three dark crosses were silhouetted against the bleak sky of that first Good Friday. Upon the center gibbet hung the lacerated body of the God-man, Second Person of that Blessed Trinity who created, redeemed and sanctified the human race. The eyes of that divine Face rested not upon the jeering crowd gathered to gloat over His apparent downfall; rather they envisioned the people of the world, from the moment of Adam's creation down to the end of time. They viewed the past, they scanned the future, but always they saw all men—men of every generation, of every clime—men of every color and of every race. There was an all-embracing comprehensiveness in that vision, just as truly as there was a complete out-pouring of the Precious Blood for the salvation of all mankind. God's love equaled in infinity His power, His justice and His mercy. It was His will that His love be shared by all men at all times.

There can be no doubt that there were certain parts of the dying Saviour's vision which shone with sunlit brilliance; there were darkened sections obscured by defection, schism, and heresy. There was the heartening sight of the first Pentecost in which He viewed His chosen few as they left the "upper room," over which His Mother presided, to go into the radiance of a crowded Jerusalem. "Devout men of every nation" were among those baptized on that first Whitsunday, as the clarion call to Christianity was sounded for the first time to an assembled world. The thirst—the unquenchable thirst of Christ for the love of all men—received its initial assuagement as Peter, His first Vicar, brought three thousand followers to the divine Victim on Calvary's Cross—three thousand among the men of all nations.

But the vision from Golgotha's heights knew no limitations of time or space. It was as infinite in its conception as the power and love of the Victim on the central cross. Thus, while His tortured Ears listened to the future shouts of the Roman populace, who would glory in the sufferings of the martyrs, those dying Eyes rejoiced in the growth of the mustard seed of faith planted by the great sowers, Peter, Paul, Thomas, Mark, Bartholomew. They witnessed the charity and zeal of the lay men and women who contributed, from the pittance of their meager earnings, or from the largess of their princely wealth, the offerings for the furtherance of Christ's doctrine of love to all men. Before the eyes of the Victim, God's only Begotten Son, was unfolded a union between prelates, priests and people which made possible Christianity's greatness, unfettered by the limitations of nationalism. There were no selected few for whom Christ was willing to die. His Blood was shed for the salvation of all men, regardless of color, race or creed. Thus within His vision He viewed Europe, once barbarous and uncouth, transformed into a mighty powerhouse of action from which the lessons of Calvary would be taught to the entire world.

Then came a darkening of the vision of the Victim on the cross. The followers of the prophet, Mohammed, having laid waste the mighty structure of Catholicity in Arabia and northern Africa, sought new outlets in Europe. But, as the Moslems were pushed back by united Catholic action, new forces of evil threatened Christianity. Perfidy within the very ranks brought heresy and destruction to thousands of once-faithful followers of Christ. However, the darkness of the Saviour's vision was dispelled by the brilliance of another sight. New gateways to hitherto unknown, or unreachable territories, were opened by the journeys of the fearless Columbus, and those who followed in his wake. While zealous leaders of Christianity struggled against the forces of insubordination and heresy in Europe, and the America's were being won to Christ by Father Marquette and Fra Junipero Serra, valiant missionaries, like the tireless Francis Xavier, brought knowledge of the crucified Saviour to the Far East.

There were many flashes of steel to be seen by Christ on the Cross, as He viewed these new conquests made in His Name in the Orient. The axe, the sword, fell in almost rhythmic regularity, as persecution after persecution raged in China, Japan, Indo China, India, and the South Seas. Around the foot of the Cross spread an ever-widening circle of blood, joyously shed by white and dark-skinned martyrs to mingle with the precious outpouring of the Redeemer. Certainly the thirst for souls was beginning to be slaked as all nations felt the pulsations of divine grace.

Then flashed another vision before the eyes of the dying Saviour. The bright new land—our own America—came into sharpened focus. From the tiny beginnings, upon the dot-like islands of the Caribbean, the boundaries of Christianity spread from ocean to ocean, from pole to pole. While the weary steps of valiant men and women carried the standard of Christ from the eastern seaboard districts, across almost unending mountain peaks until they gained the westernmost borders, the unstinting support of European generosity made possible a young, virile American Catholicity. What an inspiring history of prayer and sacrifice, of conquests and victories in souls won for Christ, stood revealed to the gaze of the Reedeemer on the Cross as He viewed America's growth and progress!

But now to the Ears of the Victim on the Cross comes a new, a more intense and discordant note. The drone of the world-encircling bees of destruction is heard as these mechanized wasps launch projectiles which spell ruin and suffering for the peoples of all lands. The echo of the bugle call to war—global, devastating war—reaches Calvary's mount, and the Head of Calvary's Victim slumps lower upon the Shoulders which have tried so hard to lighten mankind's burden during nineteen long centuries. Once more the cry, "Father—forgive them—for they know not what they do,"—is forced from almost lifeless Lips. Once more He gives His mother to the world, even as He places under her maternal care the children of all mankind. "Mother—behold thy son," He whispers, "not only thy Son—hanging here on the cross but all the sons of your great human family. The sons who man the planes, the ships, the tanks and guns of this twentieth-century conflict. The sons who tread the jungle trails, the sand dunes, the scorched plains. I willed not that they should become the holocausts of war but that they become My brothers, in the Fatherhood of God."

Then from the foot of that cross seemed to come the murmur "Thy will be done." Through this agony of suffering will emerge a realization of the true brotherhood of man, that realization for which You, our Redeemer, have waited for nineteen long centuries. Thus while the way has been long, while there still remain dark vistas within the range of the Saviour's vision, the brilliance of the future already begins to dispel the gloom of the present.

Amid the horrors of modern warfare, our Catholic people, perhaps because of the very global nature of the present conflict, are for the first time understanding fully the lesson of Calvary's cross, upon which Christ died that all men—men of yesterday, today and tomorrow—men of all colors and nationalities—might live. Operating in the far-flung theaters of war, the heroic men and women in the armed forces of our country are seeing for the first time, and telling us at home of the dark-skinned Polynesians, the Hindus, the Africans, the Orientals assembling by their side to approach the Divine Banquet of Christ's love. Within the bombed interiors of mission hospitals in the Far East they find Catholic Sisters nursing American troops back to health. Storming the heights of a contested hill they find missionaries refusing to seek shelter when helpless natives cannot be evacuated. The love of Christ for all men is becoming a reality, it is being understood today as it was never understood before.

With that realization has come a conviction. There remains but one nation able to accept the challenge of the Saviour's thirst for souls. Bleeding Europe is powerless for generations to come to answer that challenge. The strength of her manhood, the glory of her womanhood, have been sacrificed upon the altars of destructive force. It is true then that the eyes of the Victim of Calvary are turned hopefully, longingly to our own land. From our country must come the twentieth-century Paul, Boniface, Patrick, Xavier. It is from our United States that the modern Mary, Martha, Catherine, Ursula must emerge to bring the ministrations of Christ's sweet charity to all peoples. It is within this nation that the modern Timothy, Titus, Aquila will be found to provide the support necessary to complete Christ's quest for souls.

And it is encouraging in this regard to know that, while we view the longing of the Crucified Saviour's Heart, we feel within ourselves the power to satisfy it. Here, within this nation we know we have the gallant youth willing and eager to answer the call "Follow me—follow me to the ends of the earth to win all men to My knowledge and love." Here within this land we have the generosity and the understanding which makes support of that youth and its noble mission part of our treasured prerogatives. Here, within the boundaries of this great country, stands organized The Society for the Propagation of the Faith which is as universal in its scope and aid as the Saviour's love for mankind. Here, too, is the opportunity for all America to take an active part in Christ's search for souls, since Mission Sunday, October 24th, is the day upon which prelates, priests and people are united in the common bond of action for the missions.

As National Director of The Society for the Propagation of the Faith in the United States, I feel justified in repeating to our Saviour on Calvary the pledge of our Catholic people that His death has not been in vain. I know too that I may pledge to our beloved Pope Pius XII the assurance of the prayers and the charity of Americans which will make possible the restoration of Christ crucified as King of the world. Our people alone now have the privilege of furnishing the keys which open the doors of charity through which will flow the redeeming Blood to all peoples, whether at home, in the foreign field or within the Near East. Today, then, America takes her place among the truly apostolic nations of the world, as her clergy and laity universally prepare to observe Mission Sunday under the auspices of The Society for the Propagation of the Faith.

NIHIL OBSTAT: Arthur J. Scanlan, S.T.D., *Censor Librorum*

IMPRIMATUR: ✠ Francis J. Spellman, D.D., *Archbishop, New York*

America Reborn

THE MOST REVEREND FRANCIS J. SPELLMAN, D.D.
Roman Catholic Archbishop of New York

ARCHBISHOP SPELLMAN is the worthy successor of Cardinal Hayes in the important archdiocese of New York. His Excellency delivered this unusual address at the Holy Name Religious and Patriotic Rally at the Polo Grounds, New York City, October, 3, 1943, where seventy-five thousand people gathered to worship and pay their devotion to God and country, under the leadership of the Archbishop. Eleven Bishops, fifty Monsignori, seven hundred priests, including the Franciscans, the Dominicans, the Jesuits, the Carmelites, the Augustinians, and other preaching and monastic orders, seven hundred and fifty choristers, and three thousand altar boys participated.

The Archbiship's address was half in prose, half in blank verse. He read the sermon with deep feeling, ease, and grace, and the poetical section with pleasing rhythm.

His Excellency was born in Whitman, Massachusetts, May 4, 1889. He took his A.B. at Fordham University, and his S.T.D. in Rome in 1916. He was ordained in the Basilica of St. John Lateran in Rome, May 14, 1916, and celebrated his first Mass at the Tomb of St. Peter, in the Basilica of St. Peter, Vatican City, May 15, 1916. After serving on the editorial staff of the *Boston Pilot* and as Assistant Chancellor of the Archdiocese of Boston, he was Attaché to the Secretary of State's Office at the Vatican, 1925-32.

In September, 1932, he was consecrated as Titular Bishop of Sila by His Eminence Eugenio Cardinal Pacelli, and was Auxiliary Bishop of Boston from 1932 to 1939. Pope Pius XII appointed him as Archbishop of New York on April 15, 1939, and he was installed in St. Patrick's Cathedral on May 23. The motto he chose then was *Sequere Deum* (Follow God). On December 11 of the same year he was appointed Military Vicar for the Armed Forces of the United States. Fordham University, Notre Dame, Manhattan College, Jefferson Medical College, Duquesne University, and Columbia University have conferred the honorary doctorate upon the Archbishop.

He is the author of *The Word of God, In the Footsteps of the Master, The Road to Victory, Action this Day* (1943), and *The Risen Soldier* (1944). On Sunday, March 26, 1944, he participated in the unveiling ceremony of the oil painting of Our Lady of Fatima, which marked the inauguration of a crusade by Catholic clergy to intensify devotion to the Virgin Mary through the Rosary. He recently toured the battle fronts.

Sermon Thirty-seven

ASK YOU TO CONTINUE TO PRAY FOR OUR beloved country that she may be in the forefront of nations that under God stand for liberty and justice for all men, especially the persecuted, the oppressed, and the minorities. Every country and every race has contributed to the building of America; and America, grateful, has given of her heart, her head, and hands, has given of her body and her soul to help all men, to help all nations both small and great.

I beg you to pray for our President, for all our duly elected and appointed officers of government, that they may be guided aright in these perilous times, that they may be strong in the courageous doing of their superhuman tasks.

I ask you to pray—I need not ask you—for our boys in the armed services, the millions of them from all parts of the Nation, the hundreds of thousands of them from our city and State, the 126,584 from this archdiocese of New York. Particularly will you pray for those soldiers, sailors, and marines who are on foreign duty in the battle areas. From moment to moment they are facing death, bravely accepting dangers for America and for us. You will pray for the wounded in hospitals, who have so gallantly performed noble service for our country's life, our country's ideals, our country's future. Nor need I ask you to remember and to pray for all our honored dead, whose crosses dot the hillsides and vales around the world, 572 of them from our archdiocese.

I ask you to pray for our Holy Father, Pope Pius XII, as he with sorrowful heart looks with appeal to his children in all the world; not that he be spared to life, for death to him in his agony of suffering would be a mercy, and a martyr's death for him would be the traditional following of the way of many who have sat in Peter's chair. Not for him therefore do I plead, but for his cause, the cause of Christ, the cause of right, the cause of civilization. I beg for prayers that Rome, the city of the soul, eternal Rome, be spared destruction; and above all that Rome be not destroyed by us by baiting us.* And from our soul's deep depths we plead again for our beloved land.

* Since this sermon was delivered, Rome has been liberated, the Eternal City has been spared from destruction.

Lord, lift this mighty host that is America;
Reconsecrate us in devotion to Thee.
Too oft have we forgot our heritage of faith—
The mess of pottage to our eyes was dear,
The gold within our coffers deadened us;
We, who by nature are between the earth and sky,
Earthward have sunk, and drunk of miraged visions.

But now, reborn,
We lift again to Thee our nation's soul.
Behold, we are Thy wheat,
Nurtured beneath the sunshine of the plains;
We are Thy grapes from vineyards in the sun,
And timber from Thy forests;
Ours are the iron sinews torn from earth's deep breast,
And oil from her rich arteries.

O God, we build anew and dedicate again to Thee
The host and temple of America—
Many we are, in space wide worlds apart,
But we are one today,
Made one by this, our common will:
That righteousness again shall walk among the sons of men.
Now, welded of our pain,
We would again be what our forebears were,
Men who did worship Thee,
And mindful of Thy Fatherhood,
Could reach to brothers o'er the sea a brother's hand.
In every man we found Thy image then,
And, finding, wrote our nation's creed,
A pledge that made us the Samaritan
To the oppressed and lowly of the earth.
In those far days, our soul was young and clear,
We opened arms to all who suffered wrong;
We bowed not, in our youth, however strong the foe.
For we were strong in loyalty to Thee,
And strong in faith that all men should be free
And worship Thee in liberty, as conscience should direct.

And now,
Amidst the ruins of a world that strove
To prosper and to live apart from what was bought
On Calvary by Christ, Thy Son—
Now we come back by that well-trodden way
That prodigals of every age have walked,
Back to our higher destiny—to Thee,
Our Father and our God,
And, kneeling in the valley of our grief,
Rededicate (both we who here must work

And those, our sons and brothers overseas,
Who still perhaps must die),
Rededicate ourselves to the great task that still remains,
That on the altar of our common victory,
Not to a god of war,
But to the Lord of Peace,
We give ourselves anew within the wounds
Of Him in Whom all men are one—
For all may yet redeem their faulty past,
Held in these wounded Hands of Christ, our
    Great High Priest.

We are a single host of grateful love for Thee,
A single will for universal peace for men,
A single soul of righteousness to come!
Lord, lift this mighty host that is America,
Reconsecrate us now in Thy Son's Holy Name.
Amen.

The Two Cities

Most Reverend and Right Honorable
Cyril Forster Garbett, D.D.
Archbishop of York and Primate of England

"CYRIL EBOR" is the official signature (following the ancient Latin usage) of Cyril Forster Garbett, D.D., Archbishop of York and Primate of England. From his student days, when he was president of the famous Oxford Union, to the years of his three Bishoprics in Southwark (London), Winchester, and York, he has been a fearless and direct speaker and preacher gifted with deep insight and inspired by profound social consciousness. His half-dozen books reflect those qualities as does this sermon. His earlier years in the Anglican Communion were spent in rural areas; his later ones in urban centers. He used the opportunities of both to become acquainted with the chief concerns of common folk, and their interests have never been out of his thoughts. He is famous for his pastoral visitations on foot.

In 1938, the Archbishop took a leading part in the World Missionary Conference in Madras, India, and is still vice-chairman of the International Missionary Council. After repeated urgings, he found it possible late in 1943 to visit Russia where he re-established Anglican contacts with the Russian Orthodox Church. A visit to America, which included his appearance in the pulpit of the Cathedral of St. John the Divine in New York on Sunday, April 23, 1944, was in response to a joint invitation from the Protestant Episcopal Church and the Federal Council of Churches.

His concern for a greater Christian unity has long been known and his services to the ecumenical movement are of great importance because of their quality and likewise because of the influence which he wields in the British Isles. Like his late colleague, Archbishop Temple of Canterbury—whom he succeeded in York—he stands for the very best in the modern interpretation of the Gospel of Christ.

This sermon demonstrates the Archbishop's grasp of world affairs, his appreciation of history and its significance. His discussion of St. Augustine and *The City of God* brings a lesson from yesterday into the life of today.

HENRY SMITH LEIPER

Sermon Thirty-eight

TEXT: *And there was given unto him dominion and glory and a kingdom that all the peoples, nations and languages should serve him: his dominion is an everlasting dominion, which shall not pass away and his kingdom that which shall not be destroyed.* DANIEL 7:14

OUR HUNDRED YEARS AFTER THE COMING OF Our Lord the whole civilized world was then tottering to its ruin. Over the Roman Empire there swept a storm which laid city after city to the ground. The Goths and the Huns had broken down the barriers which had defended the Roman State from the barbarians, who swept on with relentless force, leaving in their path burning cities and slaughtered citizens. Roman envoys were sent to a city which was besieged; when they reached it they found it silent and empty, save for the bodies of the slain. And then the end of all things seemed to be reached when Rome itself was captured: though it had lost most of its ancient grandeur and many of its most famous buildings were already in ruin, it was still a great and sacred name, and the news of its fall caused a cry of horror through the civilized world. The last days indeed seemed to many to be close at hand. The news of the catastrophe reached St. Augustine who was living in a North African city. To encourage his fellow Christians he set himself to write one of the most famous books the world has ever known. It was called the *City of God;* perhaps we should call it *The State of God.* In it he describes two cities, two civilizations. They were built by two loves, the earthly built up by the love of self to the contempt of God, the heavenly built up by the love of God to the contempt of self. All through history you can discern these two cities, mingling with one another from the beginning of the human race. It was the first of these cities, built by the love of self to the contempt of God that was collapsing, but the other, the city of God, of which all Christians are citizens will abide for ever. St. Augustine's message can be summed up briefly—it was a call to his contemporaries not to be dismayed at the fall of the old heathen civilization built on violence and fraud, for the City of God still stands firm as on a rock.

We live in an age of tremendous change. The human race is once again on the march. It has left behind its old camping grounds. It is moving on, no one yet quite certain as to the destination it will reach. We see the collapse of the long-cherished traditions and customs. Change is almost incredibly rapid and sudden. There have been more changes in the last hundred years than in all the previous nineteen hundred. There have not only been changes in outward customs, due to new and startling inventions, there have been not only the fall of time-honored institutions and policies, but there have been revolutionary changes in thought. Our outlook is strangely different from that of our forefathers. We are passing rapidly into a new age, as different from the nineteenth century as the eighteenth and nineteenth centuries were from the Middle Ages.

Amidst all these changes there has been one of special importance to the social life of mankind, the development of the nationalist and totalitarian State. We have been steadily raising the walls of the earthly city. In the Middle Ages it was accepted that above all kings and all nations there was the sovereignty of God and His universal law which had to be obeyed by all. In the Holy Roman Empire and in the medieval Papacy an attempt was made to give some expression to this ideal. It failed through practical and moral difficulties, and each State claimed to be its own lawmaker free of all external control. And with modern technique the State claimed to mold and master its citizens in the interest of those who governed it. Through universal education, skillful propaganda through the press, the wireless, and the cinema, the State gained control of the minds and souls of its subjects. In some countries it became the Great Leviathan dominating and absorbing the lives of its citizens. The individual had no longer a life or rights of his own, he became a mere cog in the great machine of the State. It became a rival to God, claiming that religion itself should be an instrument of its ambitions and subservient to its aims. We, indeed, in our day can see what St. Augustine could not see, that the powerful State has its good side. It calls forth self-sacrifice and devotion from its citizens. It provides them with opportunities which otherwise would not be theirs. But when it claims to have no other laws but those which serve its own interests, no other ideals but those of power, and when it recognizes no limits to the demands it makes upon its citizens, then it is in rebellion against God and an inevitable menace to the peace of mankind, for it recognizes no rights save its own and none in nations weaker than itself.

But the walls of another city are also seen rising. The Church has never lost altogether the vision of an international order in which nations and individuals alike recognize the supremacy of God as the Father of all. And from various directions there has come the vision of a new order which, while leaving room for national independence and self-development, will for certain purposes transcend them. Before the war many international organizations had come into existence, some of them for intellectual and business purposes, others for social and political co-operation. We were learning that nations to some extent were dependent upon others. The wireless and the aeroplane have brought all nations nearer to one another. The war has taught us in stern tones that we must help to bear one another's burdens. And with these secular movements, this seeking for international co-operation, there has come closer co-operation between the Churches and especially those engaged in the work of extending the Kingdom of Christ overseas. There is growing in the minds of all men of good will the vision of some international order within which all the nations will find a place to develop in security their special gifts and to make their own special contribution to the building up of the human race.

What then are the special characteristics which the Christian hopes to see in the city of God on earth?

First it will have peace. St. Augustine living in wild days wrote: "The good of peace is the greatest wish of the world, and the most welcome when it comes." I need not dwell on this. We are today all longing for a true peace. We know too well the ruins and horrors of war. We know how God's heart must grieve over the hatreds and cruelties which have been unloosed. I remember walking through the streets of Southampton one Sunday morning, when the houses were still burning and the streets full of smoke after a raid which had brought wholesale destruction, a man called out to me, "What does One above think of all this?" And I answered, "He hates it even more than we do." We know that while there is war there can be no fellowship. We look for a city in which the nations and races rest secure from the violence and barbarity of war.

But peace is not the highest virtue, justice is more important than peace. Btween the two evils of injustice and war, injustice is the greater wrong. There can be no permanent peace unless it is built on the foundations of justice. The word justice is really the Latin and imperfect translation of a far wider term—righteousness. This is the most distinctive characteristic of the City of God. It is ruled not by violence; and the relationship of its citizens is not decided by their wealth or position, but by their righteousness. This is the great contrast between the earthly State, in which injustice and oppression are found, and the heavenly city in which the whole order is governed by righteousness.

And because there is righteousness there is also freedom. In the totalitarian State there is no freedom, men are degraded into robots manipulated by the State. In the Christian city there is freedom. This follows naturally from the whole Christian idea of man. Man is a child of God, he is created by God so that he may love, serve, and obey Him. He cannot do this unless he has freedom. Without freedom he cannot develop the gifts bestowed on him by God, he has not the liberty to serve God. In the Christian State every individual irrespective of class or wealth will have the freedom to serve God. He will not be hindered by political or economic barriers, the State instead of enslaving him will give him the opportunities of making the best use of any natural talents he has. And the righteousness of the State will come from its obedience to God Who is above and over all.

But this city of God will never be found perfect on earth. In its perfection it is only in the spiritual places. Its foundations, its walls, and its gates of precious stone are in the unseen world. It is not, however, only an invisible city to be seen only in the future. Earthly kingdoms and states must be made after the heavenly pattern of which we are from time to time given some vision. Though in the heavenly places it exists in perfection, yet it overflows its boundaries into the earthly places. Here and even now on earth there are signs and features of the Kingdom. There are men and women who carry within them the city of God as with faith, hope, and love they go through life, cheered and inspired by the presence of the Lord of the City.

> And there's another country, I've heard of long ago
> Most dear to them that love her, most great to them that know.
> We may not count her armies, we may not see her king
> Her fullness is a faithful heart, her pride is suffering,
> And soul by soul and silently her shining bounds increase
> And her ways are ways of gentleness and all her paths are peace.

And where in societies, communities, and nations there are found peace, righteousness, and freedom, there can be seen shining through legislation and administration the outlines of the City of God. Partly here and partly in the future, partly in the world and partly in the spiritual world, partly visible but largely unseen, the City of God exists and will exist forever.

The realization even partly of the City of God on earth will largely depend on Christian faith and witness. It will not be built without great effort, and only by hard toil and sacrifice will its foundations on earth be laid. The Christian Church seems a weak and impotent body to accomplish this great task. We are in a minority in almost every land. But a resolute minority has an influence out of all proportion to its numbers. And a great idea is more powerful than vast armies. A philosopher of our time (A. N. Whitehead) says that a great idea in the background of dim consciousness is like a phantom ocean beating upon the shores of human life in successive waves of specialization. A whole succession of such waves are as dreams slowly doing their work of sapping the base of some cliff of habit: but the seventh wave is a revolution "And the nations echo round." We have more than an idea, even than a great idea, we have a vision, a vision given by God Himself of a universal kingdom of peace, justice, and freedom in which all peoples, nations, languages serve the Living God Who reigns over an "everlasting dominion which shall not pass away and a kingdom which shall not be destroyed."

266

The Valley

Reverend Lynn Harold Hough, D.D.
Dean of Drew Theological Seminary, Madison, New Jersey

Lynn Harold Hough is a distinguished Methodist Minister and teacher. As Dean and professor of Homiletics and the Christian Criticism of Life at Drew Theological Seminary, Madison, New Jersey, he influences the future career of every man who attends the Seminary.

Beginning his pastorates in 1898 in a small church in New Jersey, he rose through his preaching ability to be the pastor of churches in Brooklyn and Baltimore. Then from 1914 to 1919 he was professor of Historic Theology at Garrett Biblical Institute, Evanston, Illinois, and in 1919 he became president of Northwestern University.

In the following year he was called to be pastor of Central Methodist Church, Detroit, where his preaching attracted wide attention. In 1928 he was called to the American Presbyterian Church in Montreal. In 1930 he took the chair of Homiletics at Drew and has been Dean since 1934. In the last thirty-eight years he has written thirty-eight books, including *In the Valley of Decision, The Significance of the Protestant Reformation, The Civilized Mind, The Christian Criticism of Life,* and *Patterns of the Mind.*

He gave the Cole Lectures at Vanderbilt University (1919), the Merrick Lectures at Ohio Wesleyan University (1923), the Fernley Lecture, Lincoln, England (1925), the Fred J. Cato Lecture, General Conference of the Methodist Church in Australasia, Brisbane, Australia (1941), and half a dozen other famous courses.

In 1918 he was sent to England by the Lindgren Foundation of Northwestern University to interpret the moral and spiritual aims of the First World War. At the invitation of the British Ministry of Information, he spent eleven weeks in England during the summer of 1942 preaching to the congregation of The City Temple, London, and making addresses in army camps and to the general public.

This sermon was preached Thanksgiving Day, November 25, 1943, in St. Bartholomew's Church, New York. He discusses the military necessities of the hour, the tragic seriousness of not knowing which of our homes will be affected before the end of the war comes, the quality of the moral issues at stake in the war, the Christian philosophy of war and peace and the spiritual valley of decision facing all of us. He shows how nations justify their existence.

Sermon Thirty-nine

TEXT: *Multitudes in the valley of decision!* JOEL 3:14

N EVERY SORT OF CIRCUMSTANCE, IN THE MOST amazing and fascinating fashion, there is some sentence from the Holy Scriptures—sometimes a sentence from the Old Testament, sometimes a sentence from the New—which seems to gather up the very meaning of the experience and to express it in imperishable speech. On this Thanksgiving Day, if one tries to find a sentence for this hour, surely the sentence is the one I have just read: "Multitudes in the valley of decision."

In the first place, of course, there is the valley of military decision. That has entered upon a certain change in recent months. When I was in England in 1942, bad word was coming from almost every front. One had the opportunity of sensing the rare and magnificent courage of a great people in a bitter, difficult hour. But recent months have often reminded one of a sentence in one of the letters of Horace Walpole in the eighteenth century when, full of enthusiasm for the victories on many fronts, he said that it really seemed that every morning in London one had served with one's breakfast a new victory.

If that is a somewhat heightened expression of what has been going on in recent months, it is at least a heightened expression of something which has been going on. The strain has not been relieved; the sense of tragic necessity is still upon us. There is not a moment's right of lassitude, of complacency or assurance. And yet, when that has been said, it is true that we know, and the people in the enemy countries know, that there is one inevitable end, and that is their defeat and the victory of the democracies of the world.

In many regions all about the world, young people from our own land have gone to places, many of which they did not know about until military necessity brought them to these places. The war has been a kind of tremendous university in the study of geography—the far North, the far South, under the Southern Cross, in North Africa, in Italy, all about the Mediterranean. This nation, as one among the Allied Nations, has girded

268

itself and has put into the great enterprise every ounce of its power, every ounce of its fighting energy, all the qualities of organization which belong to this country as particular characteristics.

So on this Thanksgiving, with a certain soberness, with a touch of awe, because we do not know what homes will be struck before the end comes, we do not know what bright youth shall be snuffed out in the name of the great enterprise, so with a certain sad and solemn awe and yet with a certain profound faith we can be grateful to God that this military valley of decision quite clearly is to be the valley of the sort of decision which will make the life of everyday men and women all over the world more just, more full of genuine opportunity, with a certain freedom from the things which tear out of life its very joy and hope. We have not yet received from God the gift of victory but we can see it in His hand, and for that we can be very grateful.

There is not only the valley of military decision; there is the valley of intellectual decision. The importance of that is so great that perhaps we have failed to understand just how great it is. Military victory is the crushing of the foe. The intellectual valley of decision means the working out of an interpretation of life which gives us a cause for which to fight and gives us something very definite to do when the victory is won.

One wonders, looking back over the years which have passed since, say, 1914, how thoroughly we have learned the intellectual lessons of these difficult, tragic, bewildering years. Will it be true, the moment victory is won, that once more sentimental people will begin to talk as if there is no such thing as a genuine evil which must be put down and a genuine good which must be enthroned? Will it be true again that generous and sentimental people become so busy being tender to the conquered foes that they will not be able to be just to their broken friends?

Of course, one is not pleading for a view of life which shall have any element of cruelty in it. One is not pleading for a view of life which makes us unwilling to allow nations which have gone wrong to learn the lesson and to go right; but one is saying that in all our thinking as a nation between, say, 1914 and 1939, we were assuming that there is no such thing as genuine evil in the world; and while dark and sinister forces with triumphant skill and organization were preparing to hurl their fury upon the world, we were busy thinking kindly thoughts and assuring each other that all would be well.

Dean Inge used to say that there is such a thing as a convention of lambs passing a unanimous resolution to the effect that they will not attack the lions. That is fairly caustic even for Dean Inge; but does it not get to the root of the matter? Is it not true that the possession of good will on the part of a particular people and a particular group of people never means that that good will, just by the gentle beauty of its own gracious quality, will be triumphant in the world when it is confronted by recalcitrant evil? Is it not true that we betray ourselves if in a kind of sophisticated misreading of ethical signs we become so busy thinking of things that can be improved in the democracies that we blur the distinction between the democracies and the totalitarian states—and especially if we work out a theory of life which makes it impossible for us to believe that God does anything in the world unless he is using human instruments of impeccable perfection; of course, that would mean that God never does anything in the world at all.

I confess—and this is a triumph of understatement—that I have been very much annoyed by the people who seem to have no sense of the very quality of the moral issues at stake in the world. There is such a thing as goodness to which one can be loyal. There is such a thing as a powerful person who makes evil his good, and it is perfectly possible for a powerful nation to make evil its good. The moral limitations of the democracies, however grievous they are to us and however much we rightly remember them in Lent and at other times, one hopes, are not for a moment to be compared to the central poison of the disintegrating evil which we have been fighting in this war.

Of course, anybody who reads the Old Testament and the New, discovers at once that God does not wait for perfect people. I am very much interested in the people who have been greatly excited every time they thought we might claim too much of the help of God in this war. As a matter of fact, God has used some extraordinarily imperfect people, who had a central drive toward goodness, to accomplish His purposes in the world. If we take the revelation according to the Old Testament and the New with seriousness, God does not have the moral scruples some of us have.

Jesus says to Peter, "Thou art a rock." Peter is anything but a rock; he is a living example of vacillation. But he becomes a rock because His Master believes in him.

David is a very vivid, hot-blooded, amazing person, and a good many of the episodes of his career do not give us any great ethical comfort. But he had a way of facing the moral situation when he had done wrong, and he had a way of caring at the center of his life for the things that are good. So David becomes the Messianic King at the very center of the Messianic tradition.

No, the truth of the matter is that we could not get along in this difficult world if God were not willing to reach through the entanglement of moral confusion and much evil in our lives, and find some spot of moral splendor; and having found it, if He did not say, "This, if you will have it so, by my grace is to become you—not the worst thing you have done, but the best thing you may be is the standard by which I judge you."

270

The tradition is absolutely unbroken. God has made His power in the world imperial through using partly good, partly earnest, partly noble men, to realize the highest thing they dreamed in their rarest moods.

We have learned, then, that we must take moral values seriously, and that that means always that the good will of the world must be kept obviously stronger, more commanding, more effective, than the ill will of the world, always ready to use that mighty power for the overthrow of evil. Of course, if we do come to that position and hold it, we will avoid many a war, because the good will of the world is always strong enough, if it is adequately ready to meet the military situation, to make the ill will of the world hesitate about breaking the peace.

It is a simple argument: whenever you have goodness without real and objective force, you have inefficient tenderness; and whenever you have force without goodness, you have ugly tyranny. But whenever you have goodness united with powerful force, that force held under the high command of ethical demand, then there is some hope for a good world. I hope that, in this intellectual valley of decision which we are experiencing, some of these things will become so clear that we will not have to debate about them.

I hope, for instance, that there will not emerge again the type of person who does not feel that he is good enough to represent the Divine justice in war by being a soldier—of course, somebody better than he could do that; but at the same time, with breath-taking inconsistency, he tells us that he is one of those who will represent the impeccable beauty of the Divine love by refusing to participate in any military struggle, incidentally being perfectly willing to represent God at the point where he so interprets God as to relieve himself of a difficult responsibility and being perfectly unwilling to represent God at the point where he would have to join with the mighty Master of life in using soiled and imperfect instruments for the furthering of good in the world.

There is, then, this great intellectual valley of decision. Are we willing to approach the whole matter of the Christian philosophy of peace and war, brushing away all sentimentalities, clarifying all ethical misunderstandings, until we shall be safe from some other bitter period of appeasement twenty years after this war has come to an end? I think there is reason to believe we will, and because I think that, because I think a new moral clarity has come to civilized men, I count that as one of the reasons for gratitude on this Thanksgiving Day.

Then there is the political valley of decision. Inevitably, with all the terrific mass of political dreaming and planning and hoping and plotting which has been part of this great worldwide enterprise, the political valley of decision will be of the utmost importance.

I do not want to state the matter too strongly, but I hope you will agree with me that I am not stating it too strongly when I say that the Moscow Conference has given us such a hope for co-operation on the part of the forces engaged for democracy in this world as eight months ago the most optimistic of us would not have believed possible. I suspect that this Moscow Conference will go down as one of the great events of history. So often we fight well and then we do not plan well. It seems definitely true that at just the right moment, in just the right way, with just the right people participating in the Conference, the preliminary analysis of the political frame to be used as a basis of hope for common people the world over has been really worked out. Surely that is cause for gratitude so great that one could hardly find words to express the sense of how great that gratitude should be.

There is not only the military valley of decision, the intellectual valley of decision, the political valley of decision; there is also the moral valley of decision. In the long run a nation justifies its existence by the character of its citizens, by their capacity to look at an evil thing and turn from it because it is evil, to look at a treacherous thing and turn from it because it is treacherous, maintaining a strong and solid body of moral conviction as a basis for actual living.

Surely one would not want to take the hour when such tremendous groups of our own young people have risked life itself and more than life itself in the name of loyalty to that which they deeply believe to be right—it would surely be wrong to take that as a moment for a pessimistic utterance regarding the capacity of the young people of this Republic to respond to a great moral demand. They have responded, they will respond; but that is not quite all that one must say, because when the war is over and the tremendous reaction comes, especially to those who have endured that which is almost unendurable, the sheer nervous rebound, the sheer temperamental disintegration will produce, if one can prophesy from many another war, a temptation to masses on masses of our people to take the moral demands lightly.

There is an Italian picture of Saint George just after he has conquered the dragon. He has conquered it. The first time I saw the picture I was terribly disappointed; for, having conquered the dragon, Saint George stands there in stark reaction and lack of solidity and vigor. He has spent himself entirely winning the victory, so that you look on the edge of the canvas to see if there is any other dragon coming, for you feel that Saint George would need a great deal of help if he had to fight another dragon!

It is the hour after you have conquered the dragon which is the dangerous hour. That is the thing which this country has to learn morally. It will not be an easy lesson, but it will be a possible lesson, and it is a very important lesson. Saint George must not become morally limp the very moment after he has conquered the dragon.

Then there is one more valley of decision, and that is the spiritual valley of decision.

I have never been one of those who have what might be called a Messianic enthusiasm for psychopathic analysis of things that are wrong with human beings. But I think anybody who has given even a little attention to this sort of analysis, not to say a good deal of attention to a more penetrating sort of analysis, discovers something: we have to be right spiritually if we are to be safe from nervous disintegration. I am not saying that that is the loftiest motive for being right spiritually; but I am saying that it is a very practical motive.

We are built to be related to great and eternal spiritual experiences; and we cannot ignore them; we cannot turn from them; we cannot refuse them a place in our lives without having our own organism make a nervous protest which is likely to put us in a psychopathic hospital before we are through. As I say, there is a much loftier method of urging that spiritual decision, but I prefer for the moment to be rather bluntly realistic, and for this reason, that there are so many people who talk about the spiritual life as the one thing about which one cannot be realistic. As a matter of fact, it is the one thing about which one can be realistic. We were made for the spiritual serenity which comes only when we have made our peace with the great spiritual Source of all life.

Even in this year of a nation girded for mighty war, and even in this time of a world torn and broken, there is no matter more important than the analysis of this valley of spiritual decision, where people open their lives to the eternal glory. It all comes to this: you will never be broken by anything which happens *to* you; you will only be broken by something which happens *in* you. We have powers of standing up against circumstances which are simply incredible, but we have no power of standing up against inner disintegration. So the mighty mission of the Christian Church, to make it possible for us to find creative spiritual serenity through the glorious grace of our Lord Jesus Christ, to be thought of not as something which one refers to piously because it is expected, but as something of such terrific and dynamic importance that it is the most significant matter which one can discuss.

This Thanksgiving, as at every Thanksgiving, we can be grateful that the spiritual resources for creative living are ours if we will have them. "Multitudes in the valley of decision"—with military victory just beyond the horizon. "Multitudes in the valley of decision"—intellectually, with clear thoughts becoming the habit of people all over the Republic and all over the world. "The valley of decision" politically, with a surer hope for everyday people than it has been possible to hold for many and many a long year. "The valley of decision" morally, with some sense that this very courage which has given the strength to men's fighting arm can also give them imperial strength in the moral fight they will confront after the war. "The valley of decision" spiritually, with the grace and the glory of that fellowship with the perfect Person who, from the heart of His perfection, loves us in spite of our imperfections: that valley of decision which will set the trumpets blowing and fill our lives with music. So our gratitude captures from afar something of the gladness of the Hallelujah Chorus.

> PRAYER: *O God our Father, we thank Thee that Thy resources are greater than all our needs; and we doubly thank Thee because it is possible in some simple, human way to see the pattern of God's work for men in our time. As far as the decision is ours, may it be a right decision in every valley of decision; and this we ask in the name of Christ. Amen.*

What Alone Can Save Our Democratic Way of Life

Rabbi Abba Hillel Silver, D.D.
Rabbi, The Temple, Cleveland, Ohio

Born in Neinstadt, Lithuania, in 1893, Abba Hillel Silver came to this country at an early age. After studying at the University of Cincinnati and Hebrew Union College, he became a rabbi in 1915. During the years from 1915 to 1917 he served as rabbi of the Congregation L'Shem Shamayim, Wheeling, West Virginia. He then went to The Temple in Cleveland.

For his outstanding work in many fields, Dr. Silver has received honorary degrees from Western Reserve University and Hebrew Union College. He has served as university preacher at Harvard, Cornell, Chicago, Syracuse, Purdue, and New York Universities, and in 1940 he was Dudleian lecturer at Harvard. In France, during World War I, he was made an *Officier de l'Instruction Publique.*

His civic activities are numerous. He is a member of the Ohio Committee on Unemployment Insurance, an honorary chairman of the USO, a member of the National Child Labor Committee, and is active in the American Civil Liberties Union. A good deal of his time is devoted to such organizations as the Jewish Agency for Palestine, the United Jewish Appeal, of which he is national chairman, and the Zionist Organization of America, of which he is vice-president. Among his published works are *Democratic Impulse in Jewish History, World Crisis and Jewish Survival, Messianic Speculations in Israel,* and *Religion in a Changing World.*

Sermon Forty

WE ARE FIGHTING A WAR TODAY TO SAVE OUR democratic way of life. Why is the democratic way of life in need of saving today? What has endangered it? Surely not the scientific failures of our generation nor the breakdown in our technology nor the fact that we have not had enough schools, colleges, and universities. The tragedy of our generation has resulted not from our scientific but from our spiritual shortcomings, from the disas-

275

trous moral failures of our age, and from the failures of the last war and the last peace.

We could have built a better world after the last war, had we not lost the vision and scuttled our ideals. The victorious nations abandoned the promising structure of a peaceful organization of the world at the very outset, or betrayed it soon after. By their disunion, selfishness, and rivalry they destroyed the moral foundations of a peaceful world. They sent the world back to its cynicism and blackguardism. They paved the way for a whole crop of dictators and helped them to wax strong until their shadows darkened the whole earth. It is well that we should remember Pearl Harbor! But we should also remember Manchukuo and how we abandoned China and how we sent bursting cargoes of scrap iron and shiploads of oil and gasoline to help Japan kill the Chinese and bomb their defenseless cities. We should remember Spain and how we helped to strangle the Spanish republic by our embargo and our fraudulent policy of nonintervention. We should remember Ethiopia and how the democratic nations finally consented to her bloody subjugation. We should remember Munich and the brutal dismemberment of Czechoslovakia to which we all consented. We should remember the unheeded cries of the terribly wronged and persecuted minorities of Europe, especially the barbarously assailed and outraged Jewish minority, and how we made sure of their doom by announcing that their treatment was an internal political affair of the respective nations and not of our concern. We should remember all the handy slogans and catchwords of isolationism and neutrality, by which we and other nations sought to evade our share of the moral responsibility for maintaining order, decency, and justice in the world. It is true that our national sins were not so much sins of commission as of omission. We did not invade China or Ethiopia, and did not attack Czechoslovakia or Spain. We did not persecute any people. But we stood idly by the blood of our neighbors—and that is a grave and punishable sin in the sight of God!

What kind of a world did we build for our children after the last war? A world of wild inflation, bloated prosperity, disastrous panics, prolonged depression, and appalling unemployment. Millions of our young people were denied the opportunity to work, and were consigned to enforced and demoralizing idleness. Is this the kind of a world which we shall again build for the youth of the world after this war?

A cleansing memory is a rare prophylaxis. History is the teacher of life. A true knowledge and frank acknowledgment of our past will teach us to understand the present, and will help us to plan for a better future. It is we in the free countries of the earth who helped to undermine the democratic way of life in the world as much as the dictators, in that we lost our religious fervor and our crusading zeal for it. Democracy is either a religion or a clumsy political technique.

Friends of democracy have forgotten the religious origin of the democratic dogma in the modern world. Political freedom came as a result of the struggle of the peoples of Western Europe for religious freedom in the sixteenth and seventeenth centuries. They struggled first for the emancipation of the spirit of man from the shackles of ecclesiastical tradition and domination, in the name of a higher authority—the inner revelation of the spirit of God in the soul of man. They demanded spiritual liberty for man. As an inevitable corollary, there soon emerged the demand for political and economic liberty as well. This, too, was demanded in the name of the same higher authority which was revealed in a sacred religious book—the Bible—which declared that God created all men equal, that all men are His children, and that all men are therefore entitled to a fair share in the things which God created for the sustenance and enjoyment of all.

These doctrines were carried over from the continent of Europe and England to our own country, and they became the inspiration of the first attempts to establish a free society in the new world. The Founding Fathers of our Republic were motivated by them. The American Revolution kindled its torches at the flame of these great religious convictions. It is religion which is the arsenal of democracy.

Democracy has its roots in religion. Without its religious sanction and inspiration, democracy shrivels. Democracy has shriveled in our day precisely because our age has forgotten the great religious principles which must underlie all human rights and progress and, having forgotten or ignored them, it has sunk into the blood, muck, and horror of two world wars in one generation.

What are these great religious principles which were the foundations of the faith of our fathers, to which our age must deliberately return and to which all of our education must be deliberately redirected if the larger synthesis is to be achieved which will save man from being destroyed by his own handiwork? What alone can bind and hold together all the varied subjects of our educational program and give unity, power, and direction to the lives of the men and women of tomorrow?

First is the principle of the Moral Law. Just as the physical universe is governed by immutable and irrefragable law, so is the social universe of mankind governed by law which, if flouted, brings disaster on men and nations. Society must be governed by the authority of law and not by men. No man, no class, no fuehrer, no duce, no commissar, is above the law; and it is one law for the weak and the strong, for the rich and the poor, for the alien and the native-born, for the white and the black. All races, all creeds, all colors come within the sovereignty and the protection of God's eternal Moral Law. To deny this Moral Law is to strip man of his ultimate protection against all forms of tyranny and abuse of individuals, state, or society.

It is important that immediately following this war there be universally proclaimed anew and reaffirmed the Rights of Man under God— that complex of human rights which our country, first among the nations of the Western World, proclaimed more than a century and a half ago. The revolutionary heart of the Declaration of Independence is the proclamation that there are certain rights which belong to the individual by virtue of the fact that he is a child of God, and not merely a member of a society or a citizen of a state, and that therefore these rights are not subject to the veto power of the state or society. They are inalienable—the right to life, liberty, and the pursuit of happiness. In the last two decades dictatorships both of the Right and the Left have repudiated this basic American doctrine which derives directly from the great Judeo-Christian religious tradition and which is rooted firmly in the rich soil of Biblical doctrine. Their cynical repudiation has led to a very cataract of disasters, and finally plunged mankind into the world war which is now raging. There must be a return to those fundamental doctrines of the inalienable rights of man for, in the last analysis, all social stability and progress depend upon the acceptance of this prophetic dogma. It must be written into the constitution of every state. It must also be written deep in the hearts of men. It is not an easy thing to do. But we are not dealing here with things that are easy.

A second basic religious principle is that of Human Brotherhood. The classic religions of mankind declared that all men are the children of one God, and that "He hath made of one blood all nations of men to dwell on all the face of the earth." This proclaimed not only the equality of all men, but also their mutual dependability and their responsibility for each other's welfare. Our age rejected this principle of human brotherhood as a guiding factor in international relations. Democratic governments proclaimed a contrary principle of moral neutrality and isolationism. When they beheld injustice, aggression, and cruelty perpetrated in other lands, they absolved themselves of all responsibility by declaring that it was the internal affair of those countries, and that they could not intervene. The Nazi and Fascist states, of course, completely rejected the ideal of human brotherhood by offering the world a blown-up race philosophy which justifies the exploitation of one race by others, and the total extermination of others. The dikes of cruelty and bestiality were burst open. A vicious bloodcult, the like of which mankind has never seen, was established in our day in many parts of the world, and upon its altars some of the noblest and bravest of the children of men were sacrificed.

There will be great spiritual strains in our country after this war. Eras of reconstruction are dangerous eras. Passions, hopes, and fears run high. Demagogues and political adventurers hope to find in the very fluidity of the social forms their great opportunity. Orthodox and earmarked Fascist and Nazi doctrines and slogans will of course be discredited. Dogmatism, generally, of both a political and an economic character, is likely to suffer eclipse. But this will not preclude other attacks upon human rights and liberties under other guises and with other catchwords, nor will it prevent the recrudescence of bigotry and intolerance which, for the duration, have gone underground in our land. The Ku Klux Klan was launched on the ebb tide of the last war, and capitalized on the totalitarian patriotism which the war engendered. In the severe adjustment which will follow this war and which will probably entail periods of inflation, depression, and large-scale unemployment, everybody will be looking for scapegoats. Some have theirs already well tethered in their backyards. It is not too early to begin preventive educational measures to counteract the menace to come.

The third basic principle of religion is that of Economic Justice. The prophetic leaders of religion sought to deliver man from crushing slavery and poverty and to establish a just community in which men would be secure in their human and divine patrimony. "If thy brother wax poor, thou shalt surely help him." Unless there is social justice, there is civil strife. A reign of injustice is always followed by a reign of terror. Our age has given abundant evidence of this fact. The many, frightful social upheavals of our day, the violent swing of the pendulum between the extremes of Communism and the extremes of Fascism, are due in the last analysis to the struggle of the masses—a struggle often blind and misguided—for greater security and for a greater sharing in the economic goods of the earth. It is the latest phase of the immemorial struggle against economic degradation and misery, and the outreaching of the spirit of man for a condition in life where each man will live under his vine and under his fig tree with none to make him afraid.

We, the people of the United States, have learned under the hard exigencies of war that we must lend-lease to other nations in order that they may help us fight our foreign foes. Religion would have us lend-lease to our own fellow citizens so that together we may wage war upon our far more dangerous domestic foes—poverty, slums, unemployment, dependence, insecurity.

And there is yet another basic principle which religion has proclaimed and upon which the free rights of man can alone be built. All truly good and desirable things in life are established and conceived through sacrifice. Love and friendship thrive upon it. Honor and integrity cannot exist without them. Our freedom and liberties were won through sacrifice and were cemented in blood and tears. When men and nations no longer care enough about them to fight and die for them, they quickly lose them. Martyrdom and sacrifice are not necessary to prove that two times two are four. Scientific observation and logic are sufficient for that. But love and honor and faith and truth and freedom are valid only for men and nations if they test, exalt, and demonstrate them through sacrifice. Else they simply vanish from their midst, and hate, deceit, faithlessness, cruelty, and slavery come to take their places.

If, after this war, the nations of the world will not be prepared to make substantial sacrifices in terms of their absolute sovereignties, or their monopolistic control over the earth's resources, or their political domination of colonial or so-called backward peoples, then our age will be granted only a very brief breathing spell before it is summoned again to the bloody massacre of a third world war.

True patriotism calls not only for self-sacrifice in defense of one's country but for the sacrifice of all those preferences selfishly held by one's country which make peaceful international co-operation impossible.

Finally, the goal of all religion has been peace among men and the sublimation of man's belligerent instincts into fruitful and co-operative efforts for the common good of all—the beating of swords into plowshares.

One cannot forget that the last world war was fought for the very same objectives as this war, and against the same foe. The war was won, and yet following it, the world entered one of the most disastrous periods in its history—a breakdown and blackout period, culminating in this second world war.

Why did victory lead to defeat? Not because the Versailles Treaty was vicious. It was no better and no worse than similar treaties which are imposed by victors upon vanquished. The recognition of the independence of Belgium, Poland, Czechoslovakia, and Austria; the acceptance of the principles of the rights of minorities; and the establishment of the League of Nations marked definite forward steps. The failure of the peace was due first to a lack of economic foresight. Political self-determination was confused with economic self-sufficiency. The failure was also due to defects in the structure of the League. The League was not given military power to enforce its decisions. The right of secession was reserved to the member nations, and a unanimous vote was required for all important decisions of the Assembly and the Council. The failure of the United States to join the League was a nigh-mortal blow; and the failure of Great Britain, France, and the other principal signatories to live up to the letter and the spirit of the Covenant completed its ruin.

It was this last failure—essentially a moral one—the failure to assume responsibility for world peace, or having assumed it, to live up to it—which was principally responsible for the wreck of the first important and promising experiment in world pacification. Statesmen called national cowardice "nonentanglement," and the successive acts of betrayal of the League "appeasement," and so another world war was blunderingly concocted. Those nations which did not wish to intervene for peace are now intervening in war, and the peacemongers turned out to be the real warmongers.

What will come after this war? Will victory again lead to defeat? This will depend largely upon the moral attitude of the victorious United Nations toward a revived and revised world union. All the ethical promises of an Allied victory depend entirely upon it.

It will not be easy to build a peaceful world after this war. It is idle to assume that an era of peace and good will can set in right after the signing of the armistice. Europe and other parts of the globe will be ravaged after the war. Famine, poverty, misery, and hate will stalk over the face of the earth. There will be ruined economies, social collapse, and revolutions in every defeated country—just as after the last war. Millions of people will seek new homes in a world which will be inhospitable to immigration. The youth of half the world which has been indoctrinated with the racial and nationalistic mythologies of dictatorship will be spiritually lost and unsuited to a democratic way of life which they had been taught to hate and despise. There will also be resentments, rivalries, and recriminations among the victorious Allies—just as after the last war.

Under these conditions the attempt to build a peaceful and stable social order will tax the intellectual and spiritual resources of human statesmanship to the utmost. Only a revived religious fervor for peace— a world-embracing crusade for it—will provide the driving and sustaining power requisite for the difficult and protracted reconstruction of our world on a peace pattern.

It can be done!

If men and nations can be aroused—and if they will have the courage to face their own past and will recall in humility and contrition all that has gone before, then it may be that they will be reborn into a new life.

We should not listen to the cynic, the skeptic, and the scoffer. They are the dregs and the lees in the cup of life. There is nothing that man has made crooked that he cannot make straight. Behind every system is man. It *is* possible to banish war and eradicate poverty. It is possible, even though difficult, to reconcile the sharp and bitter contradictions of our day—nationalism with internationalism, the trend towards collectivism, hastened by our industrial technology and mass production, with the rights and liberties of the individual. It *is* possible to give men economic security without robbing them of their political freedom. What the world needs is inspired new leadership, and the welling-up from within of new faith and new courage. The dictators of our day are not in any

281

sense inspired new leaders. They are replicas of all the tyrants of old. They are as old as Nero and Caligula. They prate of a new world order. Actually they are reaching only after new boundaries and new empires, which can be laid only in blood and at the cost of the rights and freedoms of other peoples. To the youth of the world they offer nothing but chains and death. Their ideas reek of the dungeon and the charnel house. They have no faith in man or humanity, nor in the power of men to transcend themselves and, through their own initiative and experience, to achieve higher and nobler forms of a free and secure society. They are arrogant rulers with the instincts of slaves—and they are on their way out!

The democratic faith alone can provide the new leadership; for democracy has faith in man and mankind in an advancing human society and in a co-operative commonwealth of all free and equal peoples—only democracy can achieve this good and gracious life for mankind. But only the democracy which remains continuously and vividly aware of its religious origin and destiny, and of the underlying and indispensable spiritual principles of law, brotherhood, justice, sacrifice, and peace can sustain the free life of man and society.

God and the Hills of China

THE RIGHT REVEREND ANDREW YU-YUE TSU, D.D., PH.D.
Protestant Episcopal Bishop of Kunming, China

BISHOP TSU is one of the younger religious leaders of New China. Before assuming his present post in charge of Protestant Episcopal missionary work in Southwest China, he was for many years professor of Sociology at St. John's University, Shanghai. He did his graduate work in America and holds the degree of Doctor of Philosophy from Columbia University and of Doctor of Divinity from the University of the South, Sewanee, Tennessee. He has been active in war work and is a member of a government commission to study post-war reconstruction problems. His recent work before coming to the United States earned him the title of "The Bishop of the Burma Road."

This message by Bishop Tsu shows both the influence of the Orient and his complete understanding of the Christian faith. Leaders are more and more agreed that the problems of the Orient can best be solved by Christian principles, that missions are better than machine guns, the love of God more lasting than hate. When we conquer with love, everyone wins. The Orient watches the West.

Sermon Forty-one

TEXT: *I will lift up mine eyes unto the hills.* PSALM 121:1

HE ANCIENT PSALMIST LOVED THE HILLS OF HIS native land. They reminded him of the Creator who made heaven and earth. They stood for the everlasting presence of God and His providential care of the nation. The annual pilgrimage to the hills crowned by the city of Jerusalem, which every adult member aspired to make at least once in his life, and which our Lord Himself made for the first time when he was twelve, was symbolic of this inner faith. The 121st Psalm and a dozen others which have been preserved for us in the Book of Psalms are known as "Songs of Ascent," so-called because they were commonly recited by pilgrims as they made their way up the hills leading to Jerusalem, the center and citadel of their religious and national consciousness.

These psalms became familiar songs among young and old, as the great popular hymns are among us. A shepherd boy, guarding his sheep at night, scans the dim silhouette of the hills against the starlit sky, and in his lonely watch hums to himself, "I will lift up mine eyes unto the hills, whence cometh my help. . . ." A traveler, far away from home, dreams of his native land, lifts his eyes and sighs, "The Lord shall preserve thy going out and thy coming in. . . ." A busy wife burdened with the daily chore, throws wide the upper windows, catches a glimpse of the distant hills and returns to her work, refreshed in spirit. An anxious mother thinking of her absent son, whispers herself to sleep, "The Lord is thy keeper; the sun shall not burn thee by day, neither the moon by night. . . ." Even with the lapse of centuries, these lines of the Psalms have not lost their appeal to us, for in them are embodied the deepest hopes and aspirations of the human heart in all ages.

It has been said that the ability to lift up one's eyes is a truly human trait, distinguishing *homo sapiens* from the living brood of lesser nature. The question has been asked, in the slow process of evolution, when did the manlike ape turn the corner and become the apelike man? The whimsical reply is that the hypothetical moment came when, in some distant eon, the primordial creature first raised itself on its hind legs, gazed into the sky, and wondered! It might not have happened in just that way, but to lift one's eyes unto the hills does indicate a superior achievement, an awakening to the meaning of life beyond the merely animal, an awareness of spiritual presence. Someone has said it is the unique though gloomy prerogative of man to contemplate the meaning of his own death. Lifting his eyes unto the hills, man has been led to the most wonderful discoveries—the deepest apprehension of what is true, good, and beautiful, the highest idealism by which he lives, and the awesome awareness of the eternal source of being.

One summer I visited the home of a Christian Japanese friend in the foothills of Mount Fuji. Through the wide window of the house, the majestic panorama of the sacred mountain was clearly visible, its summit robed in eternal snow. The almost overpowering impression was fittingly conveyed by a pair of scrolls on the wall with the Chinese inscription:

> Awestruck I look up at great Fuji,
> Reverently I kneel to worship the Maker.

The fascination of the hills is irresistible. They challenge us ever to climb upward, even though we are exhausted in the effort. They point to far horizons which we must reach for perspective and clarity of view. Tantalizingly, they beckon us on to the unknown beyond, to catch a glimpse of Paradise Lost and Paradise Regained. The strength of the hills mediates a spiritual quality.

In the novel, *Hidden Years,* the boy Jesus was a lover of the hills. In the early morning early risers could see him slip out of the lowly cottage, climb the hill behind the village of Nazareth, his dog, Tobias, following him, reach the top, and with his arms outstretched and the morning breeze sweeping his garment around his youthful figure, sing the praise of the rising sun. Repeatedly it is recorded in Scripture that our Lord, in his busy ministry, was in the habit of retiring at the end of day into the mountain to pray, and when morning came he was back among men, full of radiance and grace. The beauty and serenity of the hills refreshes us with the consciousness of Divine Presence.

Thus the pre-Tang poet, Tao Yuan Ming, wrote in far-off China:

> I build my hut among the haunts of men,
> But the clangor of horses and chariots disturb me not.
> You ask, how can this be;
> I answer, because my heart is far away.
> Chrysanthemums I pick under the east hedge;
> In the distance I spy the southern hills.
> Birds circle around:
> How beautiful, day or night.
> There is deep meaning in all this,
> But to express it, I have lost the use of words.

We are living in a sorrowing world full of strife, bitterness, and bloodshed. To outward confusion is added inward insecurity. In material abundance we are tormented by spiritual hunger. The longing for peace is nullified by conflicting loyalties within. Materialistic philosophy is bankrupt. Only a return to the "Faith of our Fathers" can save us. We must overcome the prejudices which divide us by a larger perspective of human fellowship, replace self-interest by a higher responsibility, and regain our sanity by a clearer commitment to the mind of God, revealed in Christ.

Nothing in all these eventful years has heartened our people more than the knowledge that your country and ours are now allies-in-arms. We do not exactly rejoice that you too have been plunged into the holocaust of war, but we do rejoice over the fact that, whereas we had been fighting a lone war for a cause which seemed to us to be greater than mere self-preservation, we now have America with all her power and resources making common cause with us in the struggle for human decency and freedom. This new phase of our united front has been brought vividly to our people by the presence in our country of your magnificent air-fighters. It is our good fortune to know quite a number of these young men in our city of Kunming in Southwest China. We have had them in our home and in our church; I have preached at their Sunday services and visited their Army hospital. It is my special joy that in this trip to America, I have been asked by some of these men to look up their home folk, to bring a personal message, and to call upon the pastors of the churches to which they belong.

In China the Christian community is but a small minority in the total population, but out of all proportion is the leadership that has come out of the Christian homes, Christian churches, and Christian schools. You have an illustration of this in the presence of President Wu Yi-fang of Ginling Women's College, the only woman member in the Presidium of five, in our People's Political Council, prototype of the National Congress to come; and she is a Christian Chinese woman. A generation ago, higher education for Chinese girls was social taboo, and women in public and professional life were simply unthinkable. But the work of a few mission schools for girls has proved their worth, and the impetus thus given has opened the way for Chinese women to come forward and take their rightful place in society, in the Church, and even in councils of state. The influence of Christianity upon the social regeneration of our nation is unmistakable. Madame Chiang Kai-shek is herself the outstanding example of this, and her Christian leadership in turn has inspired millions of Chinese girls and women to devote themselves to service for their fellow men. Christian schools and colleges have made a great contribution to Chinese life and the up-building of the Christian Church in China. St. John's, Yenching, Oberlin-in-Shansi, and others, have occupied a position of strategic importance in the Christian Movement in my country.

The war has done great damage to Christian work in China. The economic strain caused by the long war, the impoverishment of Christian members, the destruction of churches, the disruption of hospital and school work, and the forcible evacuation of our missionary colleagues from large areas under enemy pressure are bound to affect Christian work in China for many years to come. But the hardships and trials of war have not put despondency into the hearts and minds of the Christian believers. Instead, they constitute a challenge to renewed consecration and new adventure for the spread of the Gospel.

What do Christian Missions mean? What are we aiming to achieve? What does Christian Faith offer to men and to nations? Probably a good way of answering the question is to give the testimony made by China's great leader, Generalissimo Chiang Kai-shek. It happened in the winter of 1938, at a dark hour in our national struggle against the invaders. The Central Government had to move again from its temporary capital of Hankow, farther west into the mountains of Szechwan. Canton had fallen, followed by Hankow. The country was plunged into gloom bordering on despair. The Generalissimo and Madame Chiang Kai-shek invited a small group of war workers and some of the cabinet ministers to their home for a Christmas Eve celebration. Before the group dispersed, the Generalissimo was asked to say a few words. In his usual quiet way, he told of his religious experience during his captivity in Si-an City two years before at the hands of his political enemies. Everything was taken away from him, but they acceded to his request to retain his Bible. The daily reading of the Bible was a source of comfort and peace of mind to him in those anxious days. Then he reviewed the events of the intervening years and concluded by saying, "Without faith, we could not have gone through these critical years." We too have gone through trying times, when only faith has enabled us to carry on. But faith in ourselves is not enough; faith in a just cause is not enough; only faith in God, in His divine justice, in His over-ruling sovereignty in the affairs of men and nations is able to sustain us in the day of trial and tribulation, and to give us courage and hope to tackle the difficult tasks of the morrow.

A new day is breaking upon us. A new world is seeking to be born out of the travail and bloodshed and tears of war. Pray God to strengthen the Christian forces already at work in your country, in my country, and in all lands, that they may exert their influence in the shaping of the future, that the new world will bear some semblance to the Kingdom of God, for the coming of which we daily pray. As we "lift up our eyes unto the hills," we shall have the assurance that "help cometh even from the Lord, who hath made heaven and earth."

Justice to the Nation

THE VERY REVEREND IGNATIUS SMITH, O.P.

Dean of the School of Philosophy, and Director of the Preachers' Institute,
The Catholic University of America, Washington, D. C.

FATHER IGNATIUS SMITH has trained many of the leading Catholic clergy in the United States in the art of preaching. As director of the famous Preachers' Institute, he seeks to raise the standards and effectiveness of Catholic preaching. A fine preacher himself, he has the respect and confidence of all who attend the Institute. He believes that sermons must be vital, dynamic, searching the human heart, touching the mind, and awakening the conscience; that texts and subjects should be selected with care; that texts should really fit the sermon; and that every sermon should be a coherent unit of spiritual power.

He entered the Dominican Order in 1904, was ordained in Washington, D. C., in 1910, and received his Ph.D. from Catholic University in 1915. For several years he was Pastor of the Church of St. Catherine of Sienna, New York City, and was National Director of the Holy Name Society and Third Order of St. Dominic, 1916-20. In 1919 he was appointed Associate Professor of Philosophy at Catholic University, and in 1936, became Dean of the School of Philosophy. In 1922 he was made Prior of the Dominican House of Studies in Washington.

As Dean of the School of Philosophy, he directs the studies of many of the graduate students, but he is best known to the public for his sermons in Catholic churches and before other important religious gatherings. Every year he is heard on certain Sundays on the Catholic Hour, a national program on NBC, and also on the local Catholic Hour on a Washington, D.C., station. Father Smith is primarily a preacher, averaging one hundred and fifty sermons a year in New York, Washington, and other cities.

"Justice to the Nation" was delivered on the anniversary of Pearl Harbor, December 6, 1943. It is Catholic, American, insists that men owe God and the nation more than the nation owes them, that God is the sovereign of life, and that each man has a dignity based on human personality that is God-given.

Sermon Forty-two

TEXT: *Render therefore unto Caesar the things that are Caesar's; and unto God, the things that are God's.* MATTHEW 22:21

HEN I SPEAK TO YOU ABOUT JUSTICE TO THE nation I have in mind this democracy of the United States. I have in mind, in speaking of justice, some of the debts that are owed to our nation and which must be paid.

There are consolatory foundations for the presentation of this question both in the life and teachings of our Master, the Divine Jesus, and in the facts and philosophy of our democratic nation. Our Lord Christ gave constant proof of His special love of, and interest in, His own people and His own country, liberty-loving and patriotic Galilee. He laid deep foundations for patriotism and the recognition of indebtedness to country when He told the questioner who sought to seduce Him into sedition, "Render therefore unto Caesar the things that are Caesar's; and unto God, the things that are God's."

The facts and philosophy of this incomparable democracy reveal that a great army of debtors to our nation has been created. I do not refer especially to the other nations of the world who during the last world war and this global war have become indebted to our government and our people. I have in mind the indebtedness of our own citizenry and of other residents of this nation to our country. These constitute a vast army of debtors, some native-born citizens, some adopted or naturalized citizens, some refugees hoping for citizenship, and some who are just temporary guests of the nation. All are debtors of this country because of the advantages conferred on our population. May I recall some of these advantages to you?

Our nation has given to us a government that recognizes two truths absolutely necessary for the achievement of the human happiness which individuals crave. The first of these truths is the sovereignty of God in the life of the nation. The second truth is the inestimable dignity of individual personality as the recipient of God-given inalienable rights. The recognition of these basic truths has given our citizenry advantages that cannot be enjoyed under atheistic or totalitarian governments.

Our nation has also made us debtors because of the opportunities for the development of personality it has offered to teeming millions. To the oppressed and persecuted peoples of the whole earth, to your ancestors and mine, it has offered sanctuary and an opportunity to find gainful employment, to possess the land, to erect their homes, to rear their families, progressively to advance their standards of living, to choose their rulers, and to enjoy a life which the old world could not

289

or would not give our forebears. These opportunities are precious and the conferring of them on us by the nation makes all of us debtors.

Our Country has also deepened our indebtedness to it by its generosity in guaranteeing to us manifold occasions for enjoying the freedoms which other nations have denied their people, which totalitarian governments say we are unworthy of, but which lie close to the dignity of human nature and the teachings of Almighty God. Let me flash before you, in quick survey, some of the freedoms which have been hard-earned and preserved by struggle in this nation, the enjoyment of which makes us debtors.

And, incidentally, you had better be on guard lest these American freedoms be so amplified as to be neutralized or destroyed. Some recent public utterances do not make clear the important freedoms which we in the United States of America enjoy, which other peoples want to enjoy, and which make us debtors to our nation.

The American way of living, founded on the Declaration of Independence, on the Constitution, and on the Amendments that were introduced through the Bill of Rights, grants native-born and adopted citizens precious privileges. I mention only the most sacred freedoms that constitute our American way of living. We must keep in mind and in our prayers that American citizens of every creed and of every national and racial ancestry have fought and died that these liberties might be a part of our national structure. And do not forget that it is our obligation to hand these liberties down to future generations unvitiated and entire. Here are some of these precious freedoms that make us debtors to the nation and for which payment should be made:

Our homes are free from unwarranted invasion. We Americans have liberty, through freedom of assembly, to satisfy the impulses of human, social, and sociable nature. We have the liberty of worship that pledges our nation to keep unobstructed the arterial highway between our citizens and our God. We enjoy freedom of speech, freedom of the press, freedom of radio, freedom of other means of communication, so important for the enlightenment of a self-governing people. We have the inestimable liberty of election, the freedom to choose those who, under God, will rule us. We possess freedom of labor, with the right to choose our profession or trade, the right to own, to save, and to bequeath. We glory in our freedom of education and our liberty of recreation, by which we freely choose the ways in which we use our leisure time. We are proud of the freedom which recognizes our right to trial by jury. These are some of the liberties which our American way of living gives us the chance to enjoy, which make us debtors to the nation.

The justice that is called patriotism demands that each and every citizen of the nation make payment for this kind of government, for this kind of opportunity, and for this kind of freedom, in proportion to his ability to pay. This is our American idea of patriotism. It is not based merely on emotion, bad or good. Our loyalty to this Republic is not founded on hatred of others, on fear of our authorities, on arrogant and overbearing pride, on lust for power or greed for gain. Neither is our American loyalty based on the mere sentiment of love, though love is the payment offered to the nation in the name of justice. Justice, intelligence, and service are the foundations of our patriotism: justice, because a debt is owed to the nation; intelligence, because we have a conscientious conviction of our indebtedness; and service, because the debt must be paid.

Peacetime and wartime payment of the debt we owe the nation may differ. In peacetime our patriotic debt is discharged largely by payment of taxes, by conscientious use of the ballot, by public service, and by cooperation in projects for civic betterment.

In time of war, and especially in time of total war, our patriotic services must assume a faster and more vigorous tempo. Tomorrow will be the anniversary of the perfidious attack made by Japan on Hawaii. Tomorrow will live in American history as Pearl Harbor Day. This year, today and tomorrow will honor the memories of those who died in that fiendish attack. And we pray God for all who have died this past year in the defense of the nation. We pray God in thanksgiving, that we have survived the first year of total war, for which we were unprepared. We ask God to continue to help us organize for the total defense of our nation on the military and on the industrial front. Fight, work, and sacrifice we must, if the debt we owe the nation in these critical hours is to be paid.

On the military front our men and women in the uniform of our armed forces—in the Army, Navy, Marine Corps, Coast Guard, and Merchant Marine—have accomplished miracles, not only in their victories but also in the induction and training of the millions who have joined them from civilian life. In this commemoration of Pearl Harbor Day our hearts thrill to the generosity of our peaceful American manhood, which has rushed to the defense of the nation against professional killers.

On the industrial front, with few exceptions, labor and management have given us a year of miracles of production and transportation. They have done magnificently and will do even better in the payment of the debt owed the nation along the industrial front.

The civilian front has been slower to organize, but it has shown a willingness to pay that is genuinely American and patriotic. Our Axis enemies have been organizing for from twenty to forty years for this total war. Along their civilian fronts they have organized by a complete upheaval of their homes, their schools, their economic life, their political institutions, their social life, and their religions. In the short space of a year we are catching up with them on our civilian front, and without the abolition of our basic freedoms or constitutions. God be thanked, and may we make a greater payment of those virtues without which neither the industrial nor the military fronts can carry on. May I tell you what these payments must be.

Pay the nation by patience. Pay the country by humble acknowledgment that we do not know as much about the strategy of war as trained experts. Pay the debt of patriotism along the civilian front by obedience to war laws, even though they restrict our traditional freedoms for the duration. Serve the cause of justice by showing courage in facing the casualty lists sure to confront us. Pay the debt of loyalty on the civilian front by action, action in civilian defense where there is a job for everyone. Wipe out the debt you owe the nation by generous and uncomplaining sacrifice for victory and peace. Cancel a part of your debt of patriotism by refraining from such criticism and defeatism as might aid the enemy and sever our national unity. Above all, remember the just debt of patriotism cannot be paid without prayer and religious devotion to the God to Whom this nation is dedicated, and by Whom alone it can be preserved.

In conclusion, let me suggest that justice to this nation demands justice to those nations which are our friends and which are united with us in this conflict. Justice to this nation demands that these countries pay us a debt at least of gratitude and of noninterference in our national affairs. Justice to this nation demands that our enemies be punished for their unjust disregard of international law, for their repudiation of natural decency, and for their barbaric assassination of American boys. Only by such vindication can justice and peace be restored. Fight! Work! Sacrifice! Pray!

The Catholic Church dedicated this Democracy to the protection of the Blessed Virgin and Her Immaculate Conception. The Catholic Hierarchy, at its recent meeting at the Catholic University of America in Washington, requested that concerted prayer for the success of our cause be addressed by all American Catholics to Mary in honor of the Feast of the Immaculate Conception, to be celebrated on Tuesday. Tens of millions of our Catholic people are in prayerful Novena Sessions and are pledged to dedicate each of the nine days before next Tuesday to Godly communication with God for the welfare of the Nation. Catholic men and women on the fighting fronts are on their knees in this tribute to the justice which Mary did to God and which America will make no mistake in doing in honor of this exemplar of American womanhood—at home, in shops, in hospitals, and on the battle fronts. We pray that Mary will ask God to guide and stiffen all Americans in their justice to their Nation. Let us know if you will join us in increasing our prayers for a Nation so living and acting as to be worthy of the victory, the peace, and the future life, which God alone can give.

NIHIL OBSTAT: Arthur J. Scanlan, S.T.D., *Censor Librorum*

IMPRIMATUR: ✠ Francis J. Spellman, D.D., *Archbishop, New York*

When the Lights Come on Again

REVEREND WILLIAM A. YOUNG
Minister, First Presbyterian Church, Peoria, Illinois

THE HISTORIC First Presbyterian Church of Peoria is now in its hundred-and-tenth year. Throughout the long span of its life, it has been served by only twelve ministers, of whom the Reverend Mr. Young has the distinction of being the youngest ever called to its pulpit. Under his leadership for the past ten years, the membership has more than tripled. In addition to his regular pastoral duties, his activities include a weekday nursery school for children from three to four years old, and a lecture-forum series entitled "The Pulpit," which brings to the city many outstanding speakers in contemporary religious life.

This sermon was preached as a result of a crisis in the community, and it had a profound effect. Conditions of immorality had nearly forced the Army—because of the proximity of one of its posts—to take over Peoria under the May Act. This sermon, together with others preached in Peoria pulpits during the same month, aroused the social and religious consciousness of the leaders of the community. Conditions were immediately improved and the "old, traditionally wide-open city was awakened to a new alertness." It is an inspiring example of what the leadership of the church and the ministry can achieve—and one good answer to those who ask, "Of what use is the church?"

Sermon Forty-three

TEXT: *Give not that which is holy unto the dogs.* MATTHEW 7:6

WHEN HISTORIANS OF THE FUTURE WRITE ABOUT our times, they can easily summarize the thinking and feeling of today's people by quoting our popular songs. All good tunes do not belong to the devil. Here's one that speaks of love, but it speaks also of every hope and aspiration we have:

When the lights go on again all over the world
And the boys come home again all over the world

Then rain or snow is *all* that may fall from the sky above.
A kiss won't mean 'good-by'—but 'hello' to love.

When the lights go on again all over the world
And the ships sail again all over the world
Then there'll be time for things like wedding-rings
And free hearts will sing
When the lights go on again all over the world.

Some wag has said that when the lights go on again, there will be many divorces when people really can see whom it was they married in the black-out. But it is well to remark in rebuttal that this need not be so. For the basic factors of love and trust and mutual honor that make for success-ful married life are just as much present in wartime as in peacetime. And so also are the dangers that make for unhappy marriage just as much present in peacetime as they are in wartime. Some of each are merely in-tensified in time of crisis.

And so I say, without any embarrassment, that when the lights come on again all over the world, you and I and the world will be as good or as bad as we have ever been—unless right now we deepen the portion of our spiritual lives that controls us and determines our growth of mind and of spirit. Tomorrow, as today, we can go straight or we can go wrong. Tomorrow, as well as today, we can be more smart—or we can be more foolish. It is eternally wise to heed the simple admonition of Jesus: "Give not that which is holy unto the dogs."

But let's take a look at Tomorrow. Have you wondered whether the postwar era will really be the age of the airplane, as the era after the last war was the automobile age? Listen then. If next year's production goals are reached, the airplane industry will be eight times as large as the automobile industry ever was even at its peak. The airplane industry today is already five times as great as the automobile industry.

Take another look at Tomorrow. A recent airplane advertisement, entitled, "How Far Is An Hour?" shows a horse and buggy jogging along into the sunset at the rate of four miles per hour. And overhead a modern airplane is roaring in the same direction at four hundred miles an hour.

When the lights come on again all over the world will be no time to decide where we belong. Unless now—even in the heat of battle—we have a firm foundation of character with some adequate understanding of our destiny in life, the material progress of the world will leave us miles behind.

And there are certain problems already present which demand our immediate attention, even if we are so foolish as to think these other problems of space and time can themselves wait. We need but mention the havoc as well as the joy that will accompany the sudden return to civilian life of ten million men and women now in uniform. Even before that happy time there will be another problem of equal magnitude. Principally because of war work, in the last three years, six million civilians have left their home states for employment in other states. And millions of others have changed residence within state boundaries. Worse still, from one standpoint, though it has partially been slowed, is the desertion of farm and town communities for large industrial areas. Almost two million additional people have moved into only 137 metropolitan counties of our nation in the last three years. Twenty-three million people are working in war plants. When the lights come on again in the United States, what's going to happen?

Again I say, without embarrassment, that unless the agencies which produce character and provide growth for individual personalities are not merely still functioning but have more on the ball than they ever had recently, we may well view the future with alarm.

I dare to speak of a problem full of social dynamite right here in Peoria. I have written these words lest there be any misunderstanding. Unless there is an immediate and a radical improvement in the vice situation in Peoria, General Hartwell, the Commandant of Camp Ellis, a hard-bitten Army man of real vigor, will seek to have clamped down on this city, under the May Act, a control so tight that an arm of the Federal government will take over. The May Act, in force in only two corrupt and low-standard areas in the nation, may soon be in a third area, and the third area is Peoria. And why? Because of no co-operation worthy of the title. The number of venereal infections contracted by Camp Ellis men and traced to individuals in this city increased last month almost five hundred percent over the reported cases so contracted three months previously. Six in July—forty in October. Will it be necessary for the Army to do what we Peorians, and our city officials, have not been willing to do? I know the old answers of those who would evade responsibility by passing the buck. It belongs to the police department, or it's a responsibility of the health department, or of the Mayor or of the Chief of Police or of the Sheriff or the Coroner or the State's Attorney. Any single one of these instrumentalities would have the backing of the majority of Peorians if they would act. Have you told them your wishes? Not on a petition. Not in a form letter. By a personal contact have you demanded that stewardship in public office that you wish? For, be very sure, the ones who stand to profit by traffic in vice make their wishes known.

Or, again, some answer, you must have commercialized vice in Peoria to keep the streets safe for women. Bosh! Long before this war, before Hamilton Boulevard's magnificent lighting, and while houses of ill repute were present in the city with far less restriction than now, there were three assaults reported on three different women in this very block. The fact is that, because of the indolence of many so-called respectable people even to exercise their single responsibility of the ballot, organized interests are the real governors of much of our city's life. I would almost say that I should like to see the government show this town what decent community life could be.

But I take pause. J. Edgar Hoover says that the alarming increase in the venereal infections of high school children is reaching astounding proportions. Sixty per cent of the crime in America today is by children under seventeen years of age, he says. Now, comparatively little of this is commercialized. The simple, but terrible, truth is that somebody's children are among the carriers of disease and somebody's children are indulging in practices not consonant with the highest ideals of American and Christian citizenship. And the children are usually not to blame. Their parents are the guilty, even if their sin has been one of omission of parental duty rather than the commission of an illegal violation. Some adults somewhere are guilty of an absolute failure to inform their children adequately about the facts of life. More are guilty of not having allowed their children to grow up from infancy with such trust in parental judgment, wisdom, and honesty that they could share every problem with every parent. For children naturally come to a father or mother first, for information or for confirmation of facts, and will continue to do so, so long as they are met honestly and naturally.

Have you felt that your church or your club had no business trying to entertain soldiers in decent surroundings, without cost to them? Because of some scruples against dancing or card playing, have you limited your church's or your club's recreational activity so that many —now literally thousands—of men and women in uniform who have wished for such recreation while on leave have had to dance in highly commercialized joints, or play cards with professional sharpshooters? If you have even said that such a program was all right for those who wished to support it, but that you were too busy to help out, and if by your failure to help you are making weak a program that should have been strong, then you are just as guilty of contributing to the total problem as any public officer you may accuse of negligence. You don't have to go very far from Peoria to find the highways full of young women coming into Peoria for the weekend from many farms or small communities these days. Have you, both throughout the countryside and in this city, so lived as a parent should have lived that you know where your children are, in whose company they are, in what recreational pursuit they are engaged? Have you so made your home their home that they and their friends are truly welcomed at your fireside? Do you still exercise a sympathetic but wise and disciplined control over those at least below college age? Have you been challenged by your children with the statement that other parents let their children do thus-and-so and have felt, therefore, that you should not discriminate unfairly against your own children? If so, have you let it go at that, or have you helped a parent-teacher organization or a neighborhood fellowship plan with the youth, a schedule of hours and places and means of recreation and dating congenial to all?

Have you in Peoria done anything at all about enlarging our recreational facilities for even our own youth? I can remember when the great Proctor Recreational Center was kept closed because there was no money to open it. It was a beehive of activity when I went by there last night. Yet, at Proctor, there is still the only outdoor public swimming pool available in this city. "What man is there of you, whom if his son ask for bread, will he give him a stone?"

One final indictment of many of us remains. It will be a shallow victory if, in keeping our factories running and our soldiers supplied with sufficient implements to win the war, we fail to keep the home fires burning—and I mean *home* fires. Until womanpower is drafted, there is no justification whatsoever—yes, there is failure to preserve that for which our courageous sons and fathers are fighting—if, in normal circumstances, a mother leaves children in formative years at home at any time alone in order that she may work. It was Jesus who said, "What shall it profit a man if he gain the whole world and lose his own soul?" And it was Jesus who also said, "Whatsoever a man soweth, that shall he also reap." May the Christian-minded mothers and fathers of this community look to their own households, now and constantly.

John long ago wrote a challenging letter about a great opportunity. In his letter he said: "I have written these things to you, young men, because you are strong." Men and women here today can well take that to heart. The tragedy can be overwhelming. But the victory can come —if men and women who have the initial strength of character to take time out for worship, as we are doing now, will face squarely the issues confronting us and our fellow men. In America, it is a call to Catholics, Jews, and Protestants. It can be solved by no one alone. It can be solved only by all strong men together. Clergy and laymen alike of every faith, while maintaining understandable pride in their denominational heritage, must, when the lights come on again, be found already doing something more than fighting battles of theological bigotry over issues no longer vital to victorious living. Andrew Blackwood puts it in these words—too often church people are busy mending nets that their fathers used in deep-sea fishing.

It is a difficult assignment, for even our little ideological differences have many generations behind them. But we have also behind us one of the greatest passages in our national history. As Walton Cole says: "The courageous spirit of the Pilgrims is gloriously recorded in William Bradford's *History of Plymouth Plantation*. Bradford tells us that when the idea of a journey to the New World was first announced, it 'raised many variable opinions—and caused many fears and doubts—it was a great design and subject to many unconceivable perils and dangers.' And then came the reply which is one of the noblest passages in the heritage of America. Here are words that sound a bugle to our era, words that stiffen our backbone, words that strengthen our morale:

" 'It was answered that all great and honorable actions are accompanied with great difficulties, and must be both enterprised and overcome with answerable courages. It was granted that the dangers were great but not desperate; the difficulties were many but not invincible.' "

And the battle is being won. The Jewish Educational Committee of New York recently gave its annual award for the most significant contribution to the promotion of human brotherhood to a Presbyterian Christian—Dr. Arthur H. Compton, the 1927 Nobel Prize winner in physics, for years chairman of the Protestant Laymen's Missionary Movement. In Cincinnati, Protestants, Catholics, and Jews are just completing a United Financial Campaign for the support of all churches of all faiths in that great metropolis. In Buffalo, Protestants, Catholics, and Jews have just formed a permanent committee on Public Decency. And 146 leaders of American religious life of all faiths, including many of the hierarchy of the churches not before so uniting, have just signed and issued a phenomenally penetrating outline of a Proposal for World Peace and Justice.

Out of our Jewish ancestral faith comes the historic pronouncement: "Unless The Lord build the house, they labor in vain who build it." And out of Christian teaching, from Him Who was himself a Jew and who became the head of the Christian Church, the great Rabbi, Master and Lord of both Protestant and Catholic faith, comes this solemn injunction about our opportunity to serve and about our strength to so build: "Give not that which is holy unto the dogs. . . ."

A Just Cause Wins

Rabbi Solomon B. Freehof, Ph.D.
Rabbi, Rodeph Shalom Congregation (Reform), Pittsburgh, Pennsylvania

Dr. Solomon B. Freehof was born in London and came to the United States with his parents at the age of eleven. After graduating from the University of Cincinnati and Hebrew Union College, he served during World War I as a chaplain with the A.E.F. After the war, he taught at Hebrew Union College for nine years, then became Rabbi of the Kehillath Anshe Maariv Temple in Chicago. He went to Rodeph Shalom Temple in Pittsburgh in 1934, and has served there ever since.

He is now the president of the Central Conference of American Rabbis (Reform) and a member of the Board of the Union of American Congregations. Among his published works are a Commentary on the Book of Psalms, *The Small Sanctuary,* and *Modern Jewish Preaching.* His fame as a scholar and speaker is nation-wide, and his "Book Review Sermons" are eagerly anticipated each year.

"A Just Cause Wins" was given on February 21, 1943. It was the first of a series of three sermons given at Rodeph Shalom Temple on "The Religion of Our National Anthem." In it Dr. Freehof asks whether we share the faith of the founders of our country, whether we believe in justice, whether we believe in God as the great Judge of man and the world; and he urges that we try to understand God's grand dimensions.

Sermon Forty=four

Text: *They that wait for the Lord shall renew their strength.*
Isaiah 40:31

NY AVERAGE AMERICAN CAN QUOTE FROM THE Declaration of Independence, yet almost all he can quote comes from the second paragraph, as, for instance, "... that all men are created equal; that they are endowed by their Creator with certain inalienable rights; that among these are life, liberty, and the pursuit of happiness." I call your attention to another phrase from that same paragraph. It is not an important phrase, yet it implies a revelation of the character and personality of the founders of our republic. These incidental words not often quoted are, "We hold these truths to be self-evident."

The way to judge a person's character is not by listening to the things he announces aloud—he may simply be shouting words—nor by listening to his arguments or debates—he may simply be belligerent. You can judge his character chiefly by the ideas which he thinks do not need to be asserted or require definition. A man's real beliefs are to be judged by those things which he believes to be self-evident, things that he takes for granted. For our founders there were certain truths which did not need expression, they took them to be self-evident. They believed it self-evident that liberty is better than slavery. To them it was inconceivable that if a nation had a choice between freedom and slavery, it would prefer to put its head under the yoke of slavery. It was likewise obvious to them that education is better than ignorance. They never debated that question. Jefferson took for granted that he had everybody's approval of his long-distance plan to have a school-house within walking distance of every farm community. They could not imagine that there would be men who would prefer ignorance to learning.

As much as they took for granted the superiority of liberty over slavery and the choice of culture over ignorance, they had another basic belief which they never debated. They just referred to it naturally at the end of the Declaration. They spoke of "Divine Providence" to which they pledged their life, fortunes, and sacred honor. They referred to the "Supreme Judge." They took for granted that there was a Judge in the world, a standard of justice, and an ultimate decision in favor of justice. It was obvious to them that there was a moral meaning and a moral direction to the universe.

When we judge ourselves by the standard of what the founders of our republic deemed to be self-evident, we might be astonished at the conclusion to which in honesty we might come. There are many people in the world who now doubt their political preference and who question whether it is at all better for people to be free rather than controlled by dictators. There is a question in many minds whether people really want to be free. They may actually prefer to have someone tell them, "You do this and just trust the Fuehrer." As for our cultural standards, we have seen a great country burn books and close colleges. We are not sure that it is an automatic human choice to prefer education over ignorance. The deepest question is with regard to the third hypothesis, that there is a justice in the world that will surely triumph. This question involves our entire philosophy of the universe, our complete view of the world. Do we share the faith of the founders in this regard or have we begun to doubt it? We are in the midst of a great world war in which we need to mobilize all our moral strength. We had better ask ourselves whether we still share that mighty conviction which was proclaimed by those who founded our republic. Can we still say we believe that "conquer we *must*, for our cause it is just?"

When the Talmud desires to express the extreme limit of religious skepticism, it uses a beautiful terse phrase which sums up the essence of disbelief. It is Aramaic: *Layss din, v'layss dayan.* It means "There is no justice, there is no judge." To rabbis the limit of possible skepticism is reached when we say, "There is no justice, there is no judge." It must be confessed that in recent years the average man has come very close to that ultimate skepticism. See what his eyes have beheld as to the actual, visible outcome of justice! Before the war we used to read books about the Scandinavian countries and we learned of the co-operative spirit in which these countries have been solving patiently and peaceably the problems of economic injustice. Which country had achieved the most complete and friendly economic justice? It was certainly Norway. Which country was more just politically than Czechoslovakia, which had people of different races and yet managed through all the storms of modern times to maintain even-handed, democratic justice without prejudice? Yet what happened to the economically just Norway and the politically just Czechoslovakia was precisely the reverse of the historic faith that justice always triumphs. As far as we could see, it is the just cause which collapses and the unjust cause which wins. Modern events seem to prove that "there is no justice, there is no judge."

We must, therefore, ask ourselves a question about the founders of our republic. How could they believe that there is a supreme judge who sees to it that good causes win? Did they perhaps have a happier experience than ours? No, they suffered as many disappointments as we. Reread the sad early history of the Revolutionary War. They lost battle after battle, abandoned city after city to the army that they considered the army of the oppressor. They suffered defeat and disappointment, and Valley Forge was the vivid symbol of their suffering. Yet in spite of their constant suffering, the defeat of the cause they believed just, they still held firmly to the faith that the just cause would yet win. What is the explanation of this stubborn faith? Were they different from us? Could they endure better?

Let us leave the question unanswered for a while for there is a greater question than that of how, in spite of tragic experience, they still could believe that ultimately justice would triumph. What about the people who actually introduced this whole idea to the world? The idea of a divine law of righteousness was introduced to the world by our ancestors. Nietzsche despised them for it and the Nazis hate them for it. The people of the Bible, the psalmists, the prophets were the ones who insisted that justice shall flow like water, and righteousness, like a mighty stream, shall sweep away injustice and all evil. They are the people who created the idea. Out of which background did they create it? Out of triumph and success? Just the contrary. They were the most miserably weak political power of which we have any continuous record in the whole history of the ancient world. Their military history was a succession of constant defeats. They believed their cause was just and yet they saw the just cause lost time and time again. Nevertheless they produced for the world the doctrine that there is a judge and a justice and that justice will surely triumph.

How did they do it? It is not to be concluded that we are wise and they were foolish, that we have more intelligence than they. It is safe to say that we may have misunderstood the meaning of the doctrine that a just cause wins. What it meant to the geniuses of the past is different from our popular meaning of the phrase. They were not so foolish as to ignore the contradiction between actual experience and the doctrine which they proclaimed, but the Biblical writers were different from modern people. They stood upon a different footing. We stand deep down in a dark valley and watch the little eddies on the bank of a stream. They stood on a high mountain and could see the vast horizon and the whole current of the stream of history. They were constantly on the mountain top in the presence of God. God was the companion of their thought, which is not true of us. Therefore they thought in a larger scope than we habitually think. They visualized the world in God's time, not in our time. They thought in the time dimension of Him to whom a thousand years are but a day. Therefore they did not speak of little skirmishes in the battles of every day. They were talking of the long sweep of history, the strategy of the universe, when they spoke of God's triumphant justice. We stand in our little years down by the river bank and all we see is the little backwater which gets nowhere. Stand on the high mountain and see the long sweep of time. Then you will know where the current of history is moving.

Their doctrine must be understood not in our little dimensions, but in God's grand dimensions. You may lose battle after battle, even war after war, but the great strategy of history flows in a certain direction, because tyrannies are such that by their very nature they contradict themselves and their false universe will surely collapse. No tyranny was ever permanent.

This same thought is beautifully expressed by an American woman:

The conqueror comes a-riding with flaunting flags and neighing nags,
And the echoing roll of drums;
But truth proclaims this motto in letters of flaming light:
No question is ever settled until it is settled right.

It is not a promise for every skirmish in life. It is not a promise just for today. It is an ultimate assurance. Yes, a just cause will win—if not today, if not the next day, then upon some great tomorrow. We may not live to see it, but here is a grand faith inherent in the Bible taken for granted by the founders of our great republic, a faith that requires the sweep of God's years. Our life is short and we get only the pain and only the disappointments. We often feel like crying out with the psalmist, "O God, make haste. Do not tarry." We are never granted sufficient years to see the far-off triumph of God's justice. Nevertheless, our forefathers believed that although the fulfillment is far off, the faith will irradiate the life of man.

A second question immediately arises: If it is a distant grandeur, what good is it to us? We are in wartime. The best answer is given by a military analogy. A soldier in his little section of the trench, in his foxhole, has a very plain, specific duty to perform. He must shoot his gun and take cover; he must keep on shooting and keep under cover until he gets the order to move. He gets the order from his sergeant, who gets it from the lieutenant, and so on up to the commander-in-chief. These men are trained to do their job and they will do it until told to do otherwise. The trained men keep on shooting and keep on taking cover day after day. Hidden behind the automatic skill of every sergeant and every lieutenant is the unexpressed confidence that the commander-in-chief knows what he is doing, that he has a plan, that he has a complete strategy, that all this shooting and this exposing of one's self to danger has a purpose. Although the simple soldier does not express himself, he relies upon his confidence in that far purpose. He may not have any inkling of what is in the marshal's mind, and the distance between them is almost infinitely large; but if it ever dawned upon a soldier, if the idea ever became widespread in any army, that the commander-in-chief has no plan, has no strategy at all, that he is hurling men into battle just to push them forward—as soon as it became known that there is no all-over plan, then the fighting heart would die even in the veteran soldier.

So it is with us. Since Biblical times the religious world has been teaching that there is a plan, a moral direction to the universe. The great Commander-in-Chief knows what He is doing; we rely upon it. Without that confidence in the plan, the heart would be taken out of our resistance. The best proof is Germany. Germany is governed by a party which claims to be anti-Biblical. It considers Christianity and Judaism as slave morality by which the Jews of Palestine have corrupted the world. The Government says, "Do not believe in justice, in mercy, in pity. The victorious race takes what it wants." This is the official doctrine, but when this doctrine is squarely before the German people, the Nazi propagandists know that the people have fifteen hundred years of Biblical heritage which must be overcome. So the people have to be told, "See, you are very important to the world. You are the sole bulwark against the flood of Bolshevism. You are the most important people to civilization. Your cause is just." The Nazis are compelled, against their own nihilistic and moral philosophy, to declare that there is justice and their cause is just and, therefore, they will win.

We do not need such indirections or such hypocrisy. We know it is necessary to be aware that our cause is just. We could not keep on fighting if we did not believe it. We must call upon our conscience to add strength to our courage. That does not mean that this sense of righteousness can allow us to dispense with the superiority of weapons, yet it is worth a thousand tanks and a thousand airplanes. We are just plain soldiers and there seems to be a large distance between us and the World Marshal, the Lord of Hosts. We do not understand His plans. It puzzles our human minds, yet as long as we feel there is some plan, some distant purpose, then we have the strength to stay in our foxholes and keep on fighting. We may be wounded and we may be crushed, but we hold on because we feel we shall win. So conscience, contrary to what Shakespeare implies, can make heroes of us all. That is the practical and inspiring worth of such a far-off moral doctrine in everyday human life.

Somebody ought to write a book about all the American correspondents who lived in Berlin during the rise of Nazi power. Many of them have written their own stories, yet someone should write a book about them as a group. They constitute a fascinating phenomenon. They remained loyal to democratic ideals in spite of the early Nazi victories. One after another grew miserable and had to leave. Shirer ends his book unhappy and helpless; others do the same thing. They called this depression "The Berlin Blues." What they meant was that they saw Hitler and his party triumph time and time again and it made them "blue" and depressed. They began to feel that good has no chance against evil in this world.

The practical question with us is to what extent we have been crushed by our disappointing experience in the modern world. We know what the doctrine of divine justice means. It is ultimate; it is useful; it would strengthen us. But can we still believe it? Can we convince the embittered modern mind that it is really true? We might as well know that it cannot be proved. No ultimate world doctrine can actually be proved. That justice will triumph and a just cause win cannot be proved until the millennium comes, and you and I will not be here to see it. The great principles of the world are an assertion, a proclamation, a choice: "Behold, I put before you life and death. Choose you life." A man must make his choice. Do I believe that there is no sense to the world or do I believe that justice will triumph? I must pick my side. That is the only way to live. We cannot live long enough to see proof. It ought to be enough if we can find some tentative proof to help us hold to our choice.

I suggest that there has been in recent months enough moral triumph to help us make a choice in our life philosophy. Hitler has been forced back onto his heels. It is an industrial and military achievement but there is a moral reason behind it. What has driven him back so far? He had plans for an absolute conquest. He knew that you cannot conquer everybody, but that you can win rapid victories and scare the rest of the people into helplessness and terrify them by remorseless brutality. You can break their hearts and thus build up your new Europe. That is why a third of Rotterdam, after the city had surrendered, was systematically wiped out from the air and fifteen thousand men, women, and children were killed. It was not senseless cruelty; it was purposeful cruelty. It was an assertion of an essential Satanism, anti-morality. But what happened? Hitler's very immorality, the very brutality defeated him. It was that systematic cruelty which convinced people that they will never live at peace with Nazi Germany and that they might as well begin their revolt now. What has defeated Hitler's attempt to organize all of Europe into one master-dominated nation is the fact that his moral wickedness created moral resistance and, therefore, a moral debacle for him. Thus did a moral law work out before our eyes.

Now consider an opposite phenomenon. We captured North Africa in quick time. The invasion was successful not only because we are such good organizers, but because the people wanted us. That was indicated two days later, after the settlement and after the surrender, when the President ordered food sent to the African civilians. The people believed us because we have a good reputation. We had fed Europe; we fed China and Russia. Out of our generosity in an offhand way, we are in the habit of performing ethical deeds. It has been so throughout our history. We have always helped the hungry and sick. Because of that fact, the people of Europe who hate the Nazis are waiting for our coming. Our moral acts prepare the way for our military victory.

We have each seen enough to be able to say: I have often seen evil triumph. I know that by military strength it can win victories. But it is only a temporary picture on the screen of the human story. The real light, which may take some time to shine in full noonday glory, is that truth and justice will surely triumph. We have seen evil wave its sword, but in our day we have already begun to see Him, the Eternal One, loose "the fateful lightning of His terrible swift sword," and "His truth is marching on."

All this the founders of our republic considered to be self-evident. The fact that we have to argue the question with each other shows that we no longer consider it self-evident. We have to convince each other that there is a justice in the world which leads to ultimate triumph. One hundred and twenty-nine years ago Americans said, "Conquer we must, for our cause it is just." They believed the words literally. They took the phrase to mean that it is inevitable that our cause in time will win because it is just. We find it a little difficult to have the same faith; we are not as strong as they. Let us then for our purpose take the text, "Conquer we must," to mean that to conquer is our *duty*, conquer we *should* since our cause is just. We wish we could believe that to conquer is our destiny, but we are content to say that to conquer is our obligation. If once we realize how just our cause is, how many millions of people all over the world are dependent for their freedom and food, for the very hope of life, upon our victory, we shall know that our cause is just and that we have no *right* to fail. We have to put all the energy that we can summon into this victory because the happiness of millions of all colors, all faiths, on all continents depends upon our doing that duty. Conquer we should and conquer we will. We are buoyed up by the resolution until not only the Star-Spangled Banner (for which the song was written) but every flag in every land shall wave over the home of the free and the land of the unafraid.

The Prince of Peace

Reverend Ernest Fremont Tittle, D.D.
Pastor, First Methodist Church, Evanston, Illinois

ERNEST FREMONT TITTLE has been minister of the First Methodist Church in Evanston, Illinois, since 1918. Ordained a minister in 1910, after completing his studies at Ohio Wesleyan University and Drew Theological Seminary, he held several Methodist pastorates in Ohio before going to Evanston. During World War I he served for eight months with the YMCA in France, and was in the St. Mihiel offensive. The honorary degree of Doctor of Divinity was conferred upon him by Yale University, Ohio Wesleyan, and Garrett Biblical Institute.

Active in the formation of the World Peace Commission of the Methodist Church in 1928, he has been a member or an officer of the Commission since that time. He is also a member of the Department of International Justice and Good Will of the Federal Council of Churches of Christ in America, of the Federal Council Commission on the Bases of a Just and Durable Peace, and of the Commission on the Church and the War. He is past president of the Chicago Council against Racial and Religious Discrimination and a member of the Board of Trustees of Northwestern University. He also managed to find time to take an active part in the Christian Mission on World Order of the Federal Council of Churches and in the Crusade for a New World Order sponsored by the bishops of the Methodist Church.

His eloquence makes him much in demand among the schools and colleges of the nation. He has given many foundation lectures, and preaches frequently at Harvard, Yale, Princeton, Cornell and the University of Chicago.

Sermon Forty-five

ESUS CHRIST HAS BEEN ACCLAIMED AS THE PRINCE of Peace. This title has been conferred upon him, and he can wear it without mockery—he alone of all the sons of men. His reign in the human heart brings peace. Those who consent to be ruled by him come to know "the peace of God which passeth all understanding." And there is reason to believe that human society under his rule would be delivered from war and established in peace. Indeed, this *is* the belief of many today, including sophisticated

308

persons like George Bernard Shaw, who has said: "We crucified Christ on a stick, but he managed somehow to get hold of the right end of it, and if we were better men we would try his way."

Peace on earth calls for human relations that are friendly and not hostile or strained. When people manage to get along with one another, in the home or outside of it, there is peace. When they do not get along with one another, there is war, actual or latent. If there is to be peace on earth, we must learn to get along with our neighbors. This, at least, is clear. Or is it? An American world-planner has come forward with a plan that says: "We are reluctant to extend our borders, but at last we must face realities, respond to no wave of mawkish sentimentality, no silly surge of unselfishness. We must take what we must have. The Pacific Ocean must become an American lake. Nor must we be content with fortifying the Pacific. We must turn to the Atlantic, and there again we must acquire by treaty or by occupation (that is, by force) such islands, such territories as we may think necessary to our safety." To the architect of this plan it is not, apparently, quite clear that we must learn to get along with our neighbors! One might almost suppose that the question for which he was seeking an answer was: What can we Americans do to make it impossible for our neighbors, any of them, to get along with us?

It is, however, a fact that we are "members one of another," as Paul said long ago. We are "made of one blood," as science also has said, refuting and putting to shame the prejudice that calls for separate blood banks. We belong to one world, as *events* in our time have most convincingly said. Let there be economic depression in any part of the world, and how much of the world can hope to remain unaffected by it? Let there be war anywhere on earth, and how many peoples can hope to stay out of it? We live on one planet. We are one race, one world; and we must learn to get along with one another if human society is not to descend to the level of the jungle.

This is no small undertaking, seeing that our neighbors today are all sorts of people, with different languages, different customs, different political and economic institutions, different historical and racial backgrounds, different traditions and religions. It is so great an undertaking that we may doubt our ability to go on with it, even though we know that to give up is to go down to certain and overwhelming disaster. But what if we should come to look at one another through the eyes of Christ?

Jesus had no illusions about human nature. "He knew what was in man," one of his biographers has said. And who reading the Sermon on the Mount can doubt that he did? No man can read the Sermon on the Mount without having his very soul laid bare. But Jesus, who looked deeper into the human heart than anyone else ever has done, believed in humanity. For he saw men as children of God, having within them divine possibilities. He saw men not only as they were but as they had it in them to become. Hence his attitude toward the "forgotten man" of his day—toward publicans and sinners—and toward all little children; and his parable of the Good Samaritan, which, no doubt, when it was first told, created as much of a furor as would today be created by any similar story about a good German or a good Japanese. What if we should come to look at one another through the eyes of Christ?

To be sure, not all God's children are easy to get along with—not even all his American children, if one may judge from the records of our divorce courts. From the fact that God is the Father of all men and that He cares for all, it does not follow that all men are pleasing. Some of us are not pleasing even to look at! But the habit of looking at people through the eyes of Christ makes a difference. Try regarding a Negro not merely as a man with kinky hair and a dark skin but as a child of God. Or try regarding a German or a Japanese not merely as a man whose country is at war with your country but as a child of God. Or—a crucial experiment—pick out the meanest man you know and start thinking of him not only as a mean person but as a child of God. If you think of a mean person as a child of God, you do not find it so easy to despair of him, to lose all patience with him, to conclude that he is utterly hopeless. If you recognize a Negro as a child of God, you do not find it so easy to subject him to cruel indignities, humiliations, and injustices. If you recognize a German or a Japanese as a child of God, you do not find it so easy to believe that all Germans or all Japanese are uniquely, incurably barbarous and wicked.

And what if you look at a backward people through the eyes of Christ? You may then think: This people is lacking in modern education, modern medicine, modern sanitation, modern industry, and in modern instruments of destruction such as tanks, flame-throwers, rockets, bazookas, bombing planes, submarines, and poison gas. This people has none of these things. It is a backward people! But all the same it may be potentially a great people. It may contain large numbers of gifted individuals who, if they were given the opportunity of self-development, might make important contributions to human culture as artists, musicians, writers, scientists, philosophers. And you may think: In any case, I have no right to rob this people of their rubber, their tin, their oil, their jute, their gold, their diamonds, or anything else that belongs to them. I have no right to subdue, police, and govern this people in such a way as to keep them a poor, illiterate, and backward people, and then regard them as inferior, order them about, bawl at and strike them if they are not instant in obedience, forgetting or denying that they, too, are children of God.

The habit of looking at people through the eyes of Christ makes all the difference between kindness and cruelty, between justice and injustice, between reason and prejudice, between the question: What can I do for you? and the question: What can I make you do for me? In a world where Christ's view of humanity prevailed, people still, no doubt, would sometimes get on one another's nerves. But there would no longer be the snobbery, the prejudice, the cruelty, and the exploitation that are now as a cancer in human society, causing it to suffer in bloody wars and revolutions and threatening to destroy it. In a world where people looked at one another through the eyes of Christ, racial prejudice would die out, human exploitation would come to an end, statesmen would be glad and proud to preside over the liquidation of empire, the administration of backward lands would be regarded as a sacred trust and carried on with a view to enabling the native population to advance as rapidly as possible toward complete self-government.

And what if we should come to care for people as Christ cared? "I have come," he said, "that they may have life, and have it to the full."* What if we should cherish any similar desire and ambition?

We of the West, during the past two hundred years, have acted on the belief that we have only to attend to our own business, and that our business is simply to look out for ourselves and our own families. Charles Dickens in a book published exactly one hundred years ago, his now famous *A Christmas Carol*, undertook to tell us something different. Old Scrooge, when he is visited by the miserable ghost of his dead partner, says, "But you were a good man of business, Jacob." To which Marley's ghost, wringing its hands, cries: "Business! Mankind was my business. The common welfare was my business. Charity, mercy, forbearance, benevolence were, all, my business. The dealings of my trade were but a drop of water in the comprehensive ocean of my business." But just about all that we learned from *A Christmas Carol* was that once each year, during the holidays, we ought to fill baskets for the poor.

At the turn of the century we did come, some of us, to regard philanthropy as an obligation. But we sharply distinguished between philanthropy and business. We said, "Business is business," that is, an undertaking in which you have only to pursue your own interest, with the understanding that if and when you make a lot of money, then but not until then, you are bound to go in for philanthropy, although not, of course, to the extent of making any real sacrifice. We did not come to regard the general welfare as our business—our *daily* business.

As it now is, we are prepared to make sacrifices when there is a war on. We will do anything to win a war in which we have become involved. We will live on short rations of butter, of meat, of fuel oil and gas—complaining a little, but not seriously, as we count, not our cash, but our coupons. We will surrender our "freedom of initiative," and submit to

* John 10:10 (Moffatt's translation)

311

regimentation. We will accept planned production and planned consumption. We will pay taxes—and how! We will give not only our money but our sons and our daughters. We do not stop to count the cost when there is a war on. "Anything to win," we say. But what do we say when the war is over?

Winston Churchill, writing of the situation that obtained at the close of the last war, says that up to eleven o'clock on the eleventh day of November, 1918, "a requisition . . . for half a million houses would not have seemed more difficult to comply with than those we were already in process of executing for a hundred thousand airplanes, or twenty thousand guns, or the medium artillery of the American Army or two million tons of projectiles. . . . But," he adds, "a new set of conditions began to rule from eleven o'clock onwards. The money cost, which had never been considered by us to be a factor capable of limiting the supplies of the armies, asserted a claim to priority from the moment the fighting stopped."*

When a war is on we will make any sacrifice needed to win it. But when the war is over how many sacrifices are we prepared to make to the end that our people, all of them, may have the opportunity of life to the full, and that human relations the world around may be infused with justice, good will, and hope?

It will be said, and it is of course true, that the reason we are prepared to make sacrifices in wartime is that we regard the winning of the war as necessary for survival. We have, however, to recognize that the winning of peace, a just and durable peace, is now become necessary for survival. Mr. George Sokolsky, no doubt, went too far when, having seen Walt Disney's screen version of de Seversky's *Victory through Air Power,* he wrote: "The world is actually coming to an end." But it may well be the case that our civilization will come to an end if science and technology are not employed for the common good, but are conscripted for war and made to produce ever more deadly instruments of destruction.

Mankind *is* our business. Seeing to it that people have enough to eat is our business, and that they have decent houses and adequate medical care and the chance of an education. Seeing to it that minorities are not discriminated against because of race or color or religion; that backward peoples are put in the way of self-government; that human beings the world around are given the opportunity to life to the full—all this is our business. And woe to us if we do not recognize it as such!

Well, of course, we *would* recognize mankind as our business if we should come to care for people as Christ cared. But are we capable of an enthusiasm for humanity such as would lead us to desire and seek for all

* Winston L.S. Churchill, *The Aftermath* (New York: Charles Scribner's Sons, 1929), p. 19.

men everywhere the opportunity of life to the full? We are slow to believe that we are. That some people are capable of working for the general welfare we do not, indeed we cannot, deny. There are, as we know, heroic missionaries, unselfish slum workers, faithful priests and pastors, selfless sisters of charity. But we, the rank and file of men, are made of different stuff. So we think. But are we right?

No! We are not right. We do ourselves a grave injustice. We try to make out that we are essentially small, selfish, greedy creatures, whereas essentially we are children of God. We try to make out that economic activity, at any rate, is bound to be influenced mainly, if not solely, by considerations of profitability. Yet there are men in industry and in business today who could not be induced to produce or sell shoddy, inferior goods, even though they were guaranteed a profit of a hundred per cent. And there are salaried workers today—many of them—who, rather than do something monotonous or something morally questionable, would prefer at less pay to do something interesting, inherently rewarding, and socially beneficial.

Note, too, the implications of the following quotation from the London *Times* of October 7, 1940: "Save when immediate tragedy comes their way, enormous numbers of ordinary, peaceable citizens are personally in this time of horror and trial extraordinarily happy. There is work to be done, now, in this island, by them." What does it mean, this fact that when London was being bombed, when the blitz was on, enormous numbers of ordinary people found happiness in helping one another and in finding themselves asked and expected to do something big, brave, and unselfish. Well, it does not, of course, mean that war is desirable or that it is enjoyable. War is neither. But it does mean that modern society has been wrong in its assumption that man is essentially a small, selfish, greedy creature who cannot be expected to put forth his best efforts unless there is set before him the lure and hope of large financial gain. It means that the rank and file of men are capable of greatness.

We need not live at the level of the jungle, stalking and killing one another like beasts of prey. We are made in the image of God. We are capable, we ordinary folk, of loving and helping one another and of gaining happiness thereby. We are capable of doing anything necessary for the making of a just and durable peace. Of course, we shall not, overnight, solve all the problems, the many and complicated problems, with which we now are confronted. But we are capable of solving them. We can carry on our economic life with a view primarily to the satisfaction of human needs. We are capable of subordinating private profit to the general welfare. We can create a world order in which all nations—large and small, victor and vanquished—shall have the opportunity of life to the full. We are capable of forgiving our enemies and seeking to do them good.

And, of course, we are not alone in this time of trouble. Losing sight of God and of the end to which we are born, we commit all manner of folly and suffer, in consequence, all manner of grief. That is the profound explanation of the mess we are in. We have now to repent of our sins, our prides, our greed, our cruel prejudices, and false ambitions. Also, we have now to recognize our inability to save ourselves by our own efforts alone. We must turn to God for guidance and help, in the conviction that He has not abandoned us to our fate but is working mightily for our salvation. And, indeed, it is true: God, who nineteen hundred years ago spoke and acted in Jesus Christ to the end that we might have life and have it abundantly, is now opening our eyes, putting new ideas into our minds, and inclining our hearts to do His will, in which is our peace.

Basic Principles of a Truly Christian Peace

THE MOST REVEREND JOHN T. McNICHOLAS, D.D.

Roman Catholic Archbishop of Cincinnati

THE MOST REVEREND John Timothy McNicholas, O.P., S.T.M., Catholic Archbishop of Cincinnati, was born in Kiltimagh, Ireland, on December 15, 1877. He was brought to the United States in 1881, and was educated at St. Joseph's College, Philadelphia, after which he went to Italy and entered Minerva University in Rome. In 1894, he entered the Dominican Order and was ordained at St. Joseph's, Somerset, Ohio, in 1901. From that time on he has held many important positions—National Director of the Holy Name Society, assistant to the Master General of the Dominican Order in Rome, Assistant to the Pontifical Throne, and Chairman of the Episcopal Committee on Motion Pictures.

The Archbishop is the founder of the Institutum Divi Thomas, a graduate school of science which was opened in 1935. He has recently invited the Home Missioners of America, a society which proposes to establish rural missions in neglected parts of the United States, to lay the foundation of their Institute in the archdiocese of Cincinnati. Most of his time is given to attempting to enlighten public opinion on the means of establishing a just and lasting peace.

This sermon is part of the Archbishop's campaign of enlightenment. In it he sets forth several specific conditions for a Christian peace, issues which affect all of us: the rejection of might as right, limitation of armaments, establishment of a regulating international institution, recognition of the just demands of nations, peoples, and minorities, and freedom of religion.

Sermon Forty-six

IN CONSIDERING PEACE IT WILL BE WELL TO examine the proximate and remote causes of war.

Global war is the evil business promoted by totalitarian governments. We know today the horrors of total war in a nation. We know the gruesome terrors, the inhumanity, and the mass murder of groups, peoples, and nations in this global war. Europe at many points has literally become a slaughterhouse of human beings, without any regard to the dignity of human personality and the sacred and divine value of an immortal soul.

Unparalleled in all history are the large-scale destruction and murder which are ruthlessly exterminating the Poles, the Jews, the Yugoslavs, to mention merely the most conspicuous examples.

That such little value should be attached to human life and that physical degradation should be brought about by monstrous rulers who have usurped the seats of authority would seem incredible if it were not a reality. This physical degradation we can, to some extent, understand, because we are witnesses of it. But it is more difficult to understand the intellectual and moral degradation which has made it possible.

What are the causes of this global war? The causes are acute and remote. Economic slavery and economic world crises, industrial and social injustice, in large measure, have been the proximate and acute causes. Uninformed and unsympathetic industrialists, capitalists, and legislators have contributed much to the global conflict. They have helped to maintain the false security of society by four inadequate measures which they assumed would maintain peace under all conditions. These measures are: First, adequate protection by police and armed forces; second, defense of private property; third, distracting recreations; and, fourth, the freedom of religion.

These are not adequate measures when teeming millions of persons throughout the world, constituting more than half of the population of the earth, undernourished, ill clothed, and poorly housed, are forced to expend all their efforts merely to eke out a miserable existence, unfavorable alike to body, intellect, and soul. These inadequate measures cannot long stand, because moral standards and spiritual values must demand more.

Modern means of travel, communication, transportation, and distribution have made the world a village. Evil report is flashed instantly to every part of the earth. Weapons of destruction move with lightning speed above and below the waters. These same means turned to construction instead of destruction could make every hamlet in the world a garden of plenty. In a short time they could transport all the things which potentially could supply the essential needs of mankind for shelter, clothing, food, medicine, and even for modest security.

Selfishness, ambition, injustice, legal but not moral monopolies of individuals, groups, and nations must be overcome before the fact is accepted that every human person on the face of the earth is entitled to live as a human being not by the favor of some one or by the privilege of government but by the native, inalienable, and imprescriptible right that is his as a human person.

A minority is found and will always be found in every nation, totally incapable of caring for itself physically and in the temporal order. These incapable and dependent persons, by whatever name they may be called, become the charge of each government. Until the essentials necessary to maintain the physical man in honor are accessible and can be earned by all, we shall have unrest, the beginnings of revolutions, and the acute and proximate causes of war. Mere palliatives will not do.

We who are public moral teachers, whose duty it is to promote harmony, good will, social justice, and love of all men because of God, must not betray the poor, the laborer, the dependent and incapable group, and those unjustly dealt with in our times. We must fearlessly say that some increase in wages, fewer working hours, a token of partnership by an annual bonus, and some protection by new and questionable forms of security in time of sickness and old age are not of themselves sufficient. These palliatives have no assurance of continuity and increase. Permanent peace cannot be established under them.

The Christian spirit only can change the mind and heart of employer and employee and make governments just to both. It is only Christian principles and Christian living that will make the employer satisfied with a just return on his investment and nothing more. It is only the Christian spirit that will make the worker a true crusader, insisting on his dignity as a human person, on his right to sit at the conference table with his employer to agree upon, or to readjust, the terms of the contract under which he labors. Christian principles, Christian living, and Christian labor can awaken and stimulate the creative spirit among workers, can insist that there be joy in one's work and a genuine sense of responsibility. This fullness of joy, enthusiasm, and responsibility in work are not possible if the profit motive dominates everything. These are not possible while mechanized slavery or the spy system of our industrial age pervades the shop or factory, or while regimentation, suspicion, unchecked ambition, and sharp and immoral practices rule employees and professional men.

The remote causes of war are those that make human beings intellectual and moral degenerates. One becomes an intellectual or moral degenerate who prostitutes his noblest faculties by accepting and acting on the following false propositions, either in whole or in part:

FALSE PROPOSITION 1:
    There is no personal and omnipotent God.
FALSE PROPOSITION 2:
    There are no eternal laws and no unchangeable laws of nature having their source in God.
FALSE PROPOSITION 3:
    There is no accountability to God, either by individuals or by nations.

FALSE PROPOSITION 4:

    Man is not free, is not entitled to enjoy freedom as a native right, and the human person is not invested with a dignity that gives it something of a divine character.

FALSE PROPOSITION 5:

    The family is not of divine origin. It is merely a convention of society. Family life can be entirely abolished by government.

FALSE PROPOSITION 6:

    All the sanctions under which men live today can be modified, changed, or abolished by human convention tomorrow.

FALSE PROPOSITION 7:

    There is no revealed or supernatural religion. There is no natural religion that imposes any obligation on man or on society.

FALSE PROPOSITION 8:

    Every person is not entitled to the minimum of sufficient food, clothing, shelter, and security to live according to the dignity of human nature.

All persons embracing these erroneous and degrading principles, and they are legion today, constitute a regiment that, consciously or unconsciously, promotes war.

Unfortunately, many in this unnumbered army are misled; they have never studied fundamental truths or basic principles; they know many of the wrongs and evils of society. Many have embraced these pernicious principles through the influence of university and college professors, through ephemeral literature, through attractive promises of atheists, who are often eloquent and right in condemning what is unjust but who cannot reasonably hope to put society in order by bringing about chaos and confusion, and by promoting strife, class hatred, and war.

Nations that have accepted these false principles have descended to the depths of intellectual and moral degradation. This apostasy of the nations has built a broad highway on which citizens are directed to move not truthward, not Godward, but to be indifferent to the Supreme Being— yea, even to turn against God and to wage war on Him! The division, the confusion, the hostility existing between religious groups, and the consequent decadence of faith among their followers, have advanced intellectual and moral degeneracy. Religious groups cannot avoid all responsibility of promoting remotely this unspeakable global war.

We have now been involved in two global wars. Those who study world economy and world politics insist that if there be a third global war, we cannot possibly escape involvement. It behooves us, therefore, to turn our thoughts from global war to global peace. We have made

318

unparalleled sacrifices for global war. We should be prepared, if necessary, to make great sacrifices for global peace. The best students of world affairs and of our own country are convinced that, as the most powerful nation on earth, we should exercise our influence in maintaining world peace by preventing global wars.

Two great Popes, especially Benedict XV and Pope Pius XII, have laid down the basic principles of a truly Christian peace. If world peace does not have its source in Christ and in the teachings of His Gospel, it cannot long endure.

The first condition of world peace is the rejection of might as right. The might of any nation, however powerful, cannot, in the court of God and in the court of true conscience, destroy the right of another nation, however small or weak, to life and independence.

Might will win the victory in this global war. Only right can win a true and lasting peace. Might may grant only a token sovereignty and independence to Poland, Finland, Lithuania, Estonia, Latvia, and the Balkan states. Might can refuse to be just to many of the weak nations throughout the world. Might can insist that the colonies remain after the war as they were before it, without insisting that they be given the responsibilities of national life and independence when they are prepared for them. Might can refuse to go beyond the mandates that were given after the First World War. These mandates were a promise of better things for colonial and backward peoples, but mere promises will not be sufficient after the present global war. The nations that have might on their side must, if they want a really peaceful world, strive above all things to do what is best for these colonial and backward peoples in the interest of global peace.

Might can ignore the interdependent economic life of the nations of the world, especially the weak nations. There is abundance and super-abundance, of everything that is necessary for all nations and peoples of the world, but, to supply it and to distribute it, might must divide the earth into regions and be just to the weaker nations and to the backward peoples, so that they can live according to the dignity of human beings.

We see then clearly what is the terrifying responsibility of the mighty nations—the United States of America, Great Britain, Russia, and China. The might of these nations will gain victory for the world. Their might of itself cannot win the peace. These four powers can establish global peace and maintain it only by justice and charity. They must recognize that there is not one law of justice and charity for individuals, and another law very different for the four nations that have won the war. The Christian duty of these four powers will be to exercise justice and charity, not only to the defenseless nations, peoples, and minorities, but even to conquered Germany, Italy, and Japan.

The second condition for global peace is that the four victorious nations in some way unite according to moral principles in listing the armaments of all the nations of the world. If this be done reasonably and justly, it can be done without violently depriving any country of its right to national life and independence. Each nation, in the interest of global peace, will be called upon to surrender cheerfully something of its sovereign rights in placing limitations upon its armaments. If a nation refuses to place these limitations, then the mighty peacemakers, the four great powers, must find some formula to restrict and restrain a government that wants to be an outlaw.

The third condition of world peace is a regulating international institution. The peace of the world will depend, in large measure, upon an international institution, which may be called the league or family of nations or world community. This international institution must not be a world government which will not and cannot long endure. The four great powers that won the victory must not control the world for their own interest or for the greater interest of any one of them, but for the justice and peace of the world.

This world organization must, if it is to succeed, continue and develop the humanitarian efforts of the League of Nations, but it must avoid the political mistakes that caused the League of Nations to fail. The four victorious powers must assume responsibility for whatever sort of international organization is set up to aid all the countries of the world. The four great powers can profit by the mistakes of the past. They may decide, in their wisdom, that it will be better to have several international institutions than to have one over-all world organization.

Certainly among these institutions there should be an international tribunal whose judge would interpret the terms of peace. These same judges ought to be given authority to make broad applications to conditions that could not possibly have been foreseen at the time of the peace agreement. The peace covenant ought to be a document incorporating basic principles, which international judges should be instructed to regard as something living and applicable to countries and conditions that are moving and developing. This juridical institution should give a living voice to the peace covenant and should, if conducted on the highest plane, inspire confidence, not only in our day but also in generations yet to come.

The fourth condition for a lasting peace is that the four great powers must catalogue the real needs, the just demands, of nations and peoples and also those of racial minorities. Colonial expansion, colonial government, and colonial exploitation have written black pages in the history of nations. Can the four great victorious powers be entirely fair in listing the imperialistic aims of the nations? Will they state fearlessly the truth about densely populated countries, the need of raw materials in many nations? Will they insist on fairness to groups constituting a large population, and likewise, will they demand that racial minorities be treated justly? Will they try to avoid grouping elements and racial minorities that cannot live in peace, such as was done in the Treaty of Versailles? Will they condemn the violation of the God-given rights of racial minorities, which violation has been a scourge of the world since the end of the First World War?

These are black and ugly spots that the four great powers must acknowledge and change if we are to have a world at peace.

The fifth essential condition for peace is freedom of religion. This freedom must be a true freedom. Religion must not be harnessed and hampered and made a tool of the state for merely civic and material ends. Religion must not be told that it is free and then denied liberty to carry on its mission. If the four great powers really want freedom of religion, they must insist on some measures by which unrestrained, unlimited, and vile attacks on religion cannot be carried on with assurance of state protection. If the four great powers really appreciate the salutary influence of religion, they will realize that it is the greatest support of a nation, and of all the nations of the world. They will realize that any encouragement they give to those who attack religion and destroy it will ultimately react on themselves, to their own great disadvantage and to the injury of world order and global peace.

If the four great powers have a comprehensive grasp of an ordered world and of nations living under the principles of justice and charity, they will realize that global peace is not merely a question of economics or of industry or of capital and labor but that it is basically a moral and religious matter, which must be settled by the principles of morality and religion. The great curse of the world for several decades has been the abandonment of the moral order and of the juridical order founded on the principles of religion.

Let us hope that the four great powers will not fail substantially in international co-operation and solidarity. If they do fail, it will be because they have rejected the moral order and the principles of religion. There is the possibility of the United States reacting to isolationism. There is the possibility that Great Britain will refuse to change anything of her imperialistic or colonial system. There is the possibility that Russia may want to control Europe, and force under her sway peoples and countries that can never really be united to her. There is the possibility that China may be left to her own resources despite all her sacrifices. If all these things happen, the world will be left in what seems to be a hopeless condition. But even if all this should happen, it seems clear that our country should take the practical measures, which can readily be done, to have

321

all the countries of North, Central, and South America live in perfect harmony, subscribing to international co-operation and solidarity. All the Americas can be an example and inspiration to the whole world.

We are all peacemakers, and in that sense are we all blessed. The peacemakers shall be called the children of God. We should, as peacemakers, do the most we can to influence public opinion for a just and lasting peace. We should offer our prayers incessantly for the authorities of the four great powers that must decide soon, either on the peaceful destinies of the world, or on an armistice that will mean preparation for a third global war. May God enlighten and guide these rulers and make them courageous to do what is best for the peace of the world.

from the Horns of the Wild Oxen

REVEREND ALBERT W. PALMER, D.D., LL.D.

*President of Chicago Theological Seminary, Congregational-Christian,
Chicago, Illinois*

DR. PALMER has traveled widely and has preached in Hawaii, California, Siberia, and many other interesting places. He was born in Kansas City, Missouri, in 1879, and was ordained as a Congregational minister in 1904. He was assistant pastor in Redlands, California, from 1904 to 1907; pastor of Plymouth Church, Oakland, California, from 1907 to 1917. He was also instructor of pastoral and social problems at Pacific Theological Seminary from 1911 to 1917. Then he became pastor of the picturesque Central Union Church in Honolulu, Hawaii, from 1917 to 1924. During World War I he was with the YMCA in California and in Siberia. He left Hawaii to be pastor of First Church, in Oak Park, Illinois, in 1924, and in 1930 he became Professor of Practical Theology and President of Chicago Theological Seminary, a position which he still holds, and in which he directs the training of ministers and future ministers.

He is the author of *Drift toward Religion, The Human Side of Hawaii, The New Christian Epic, Paths to the Presence of God, Orientals in American Life, The Minister's Job, The Art of Conducting Public Worship,* and *Come, Let Us Worship.* All these show the workings of imagination, his variety of interests, and deep concern for the work of the ministry and the church.

He received his training at the University of California (B.L., 1901), and at Yale (B.D., 1904). The Pacific School of Religion recognized his work by conferring the D.D. in 1922; Olivet College, Michigan, the LL.D., in 1931; and Boston University, the Litt.D. in 1939.

"From the Horns of the Wild Oxen" discusses answered and unanswered prayer in wartime. Dr. Palmer combines faith and reason in his discussion and shows the balanced judgment of a man of deep religious beliefs.

Sermon Forty-Seven

TEXT: *From the horns of the wild-oxen thou hast answered me.*
PSALM 22:21 (American Standard Revised Version)

HERE IS A NEW TENDERNESS AND CONCERN ABOUT religion today. I would not say that a great revival of religion is sweeping the country like a prairie fire. That would not be true. But there is a certain wistfulness and open-mindedness about spiritual things. People are wondering if they haven't lost out on something in this area of their lives, and are asking themselves how it might be regained.

One illustration of this awakening concern for religion is the better status of Army and Navy chaplains. I was an Army YMCA secretary in the other war, and saw army life from the inside. Things are decidedly different now. The chaplain has a chapel, a more dignified status, and works in a more receptive atmosphere than in the First World War. Note the quick passing of the superficial popularity of "Praise the Lord and Pass the Ammunition," and its replacement in popular attention by a chaplain's saying, "There are no atheists in foxholes."

Most impressive of all has been the impact on the public mind of the Eddie Rickenbacker stories and other similar accounts of heroic wartime adventure, most of them with a strand of religion, not added like the moral to one of Aesop's Fables but woven into the very fabric of the narrative itself. Millions of people have read and been impressed by Eddie Rickenbacker's simple, direct account of his little group of aviators forced down in the Pacific and adrift on their rubber rafts for many days. One man, Bartek, had a New Testament and was reading it. That struck Eddie Rickenbacker as a good idea, and so each morning and evening the rafts were gathered together in a rough triangle and in turn the men read passages from the Bible and joined in the Lord's Prayer. Some of them are reported to have become backsliders when the prayers did not seem to be answered at once, but others persisted. Then deliverance came. When they were starving, a seagull lit on Eddie's hat and they had food. When they were dying of thirst, a passing shower drenched them. When they seemed to lack strength to pull the last few hundred yards to shore, superhuman strength seemed to be given them. No wonder that the first thing they did on reaching the beach was to kneel down and thank God for their deliverance.

As a result of these widely publicized experiences, and others like them, a great many people, previously indifferent to religion or adrift from their spiritual moorings, have been called back to faith. "Perhaps there

324

is more in this religion business than I realized," they are saying to themselves. "I wish I knew more about how to pray."

Certain interesting reflections grow out of all this. First of all is the basic fact that human beings are "incurably religious." In the great crises and emergencies of life they cry out to God. Some one has said that if you take a dog out into the loneliest wilderness and let something happen to startle him, perhaps only the full moon coming over the horizon, he will bark. He barks not only by way of defiance at danger but because he is a gregarious animal. He belongs to a pack, and barking is his way of summoning the rest of the pack to his assistance. So, it may be argued, such experiences as we have been considering reveal that man, too, is a gregarious animal. When he is in deep trouble he summons the rest of the pack to his assistance—and the rest of the pack is God!

And not only that. God comes! Strength rises up within a man as he prays. Courage is rekindled, insights are quickened, power to endure and to survive is heightened. Out of this experience of released energy he comes with new faith: he has rediscovered God, he has learned the power of prayer, religion is reborn within his soul. This happens over and over again. It is the constantly recurring miracle that keeps religion alive in the hearts of men.

All this is good—but also dangerous. Superficially interpreted, and combined with a shallow mechanical theology, it may do harm rather than good. The more sophisticated minds who read the Eddie Rickenbacker stories may say: "Yes, that's all very well, but what about Amelia Earhart? She was forced down in that same part of the Pacific. Why didn't God save her? Didn't she pray? Or didn't she use the right formula? Or didn't she belong to the right church? Why did God pass her up in favor of Eddie Rickenbacker?" Sincere but highly intelligent Christians, as they meditate upon sermons which use these incidents as demonstrations of the power of prayer, may go on to ask very searching questions. At the church door, after a glowing sermon on "Faith and Prayer in the Pacific," or some such theme, the minister may have a thoughtful parishioner grasp his hand and say, "Yes, that was grand about Eddie Rickenbacker; I'm glad God saved him. But what about my boy who died at Guadalcanal or on the beaches at Salerno?"

Are we not driven by such questions to rethink our conceptions of God and of prayer?

Too many people still have a very crude anthropomorphic conception of God and prayer. Perhaps they have never quite crystallized it into words, but too often they are operating mature life on a boy's theology. In conceptions of law or business or art they have grown up, but in theology they may have done little constructive thinking since childhood. They assume that God is a superhuman figure or external ruler seated somewhere up in the sky, to whom Sandalphon, the angel of prayer, brings in the petitions of human beings somewhat as telegrams might arrive. And God sorts them over. "Grant this one," he says. "Deny that one." "Give this man fifty per cent." "Give that woman twice what she asks for." "Wait till this person joins the church," etc. All of which would, of course, be very external and arbitrary.

In order to understand prayer and how it operates, we need first of all a deeper understanding of God and our relationship to him. One of the best parables to explain in part how our lives are related to the life of God is, I believe, one which occurred to me some years ago when I lived on San Francisco Bay. Now the bay is very different from the ocean. It is limited, shallow, brackish, and often muddy and discolored; whereas, the ocean is almost boundless, thousands of miles wide, thousands of feet deep, salty, and clear as crystal. The bay never gets itself confused with the ocean. Yet there is something they have in common which unites them and that is the movement of the tides. Twice in every twenty-four hours the great flood tides of the ocean pour in through the Golden Gate and lift every nook and cranny of the bay to their highest levels. And twice in every twenty-four hours, at the ebb tide, the brackish, discolored waters of the bay reach out into the great deep.

So it is with our little, shallow, brackish souls and the great ocean of spiritual being which is God. We share something in common; and, if we can keep the golden gate of prayer open, God's power can sweep into our lives and lift them to higher levels. Or, in the ebb tide of our need, we can reach out and enter into communion with him.

Such a conception of God and prayer helps one to understand what Phillips Brooks meant when he said: "Do not pray for easy lives! Pray to be stronger men! Do not pray for tasks equal to your powers. Pray for powers equal to your tasks: then the doing of your work shall be no miracle. But you shall be a miracle. Every day you shall wonder at yourself, at the richness of life which has come in you by the grace of God."

I think it was some such conception of our relationship to God that underlay Josiah Royce's great definition of faith as "that something in the universe which enables a man to stand anything that can possibly happen to him."

Now one of the things that can happen to him is outward defeat. It is less likely to happen if he has a relationship to God that removes fear and tension, releases his utmost energy, and gives him alertness, courage, poise, and self-possession. And faith that this life is undergirded by the love and power of God does just those things for a man. But, even if defeat comes to such a man, it can be an outward defeat only, for he has already won an inner victory by his faith. He knows that his life is "hid with Christ in God." And in that assurance he can meet misfortune without being inwardly defeated or spiritually cast down.

There are two great examples of this in the Bible.

One example is Job. Here is a noble, God-fearing, evil-hating, upright man, just to his servants, kind to his family, devout toward God. But, blow after blow, disasters, came upon him. At last, bereft of flocks and herds, property and home, wife and children, bereft of health and any human sympathy, he sits upon his ash heap the victim of theological recrimination by three self-constituted judges. But, in spite of all these outward defeats, Job is not defeated within. On the contrary, his spiritual vision clears and his faith deepens in the very process of his trials, until at last he cries out: "Yea, though he slay me, yet will I trust him"; and "Oh, that I knew when I might find him—I would set my course in order before him—he would give heed unto me"; and "He knoweth the way that I take; when he hath tried me, I shall come forth as gold"; and "I know that my Redeemer liveth and at last he will stand up upon the earth—and mine eyes shall behold him, and not as a stranger." These are among the greatest words of spiritual faith in the world. And they were born not of success, victory, or outward deliverance but out of pain, defeat, and darkness. They represent an inner victory!

The other Biblical example is Jesus himself. In the garden of Gethsemane he prayed to be delivered from the Cross. That cup, however, did not pass from him. He drained it to the dregs on Calvary. And in the darkness of that afternoon he cried out words which we never can forget: *Eloi, Eloi, lama sabachthani?* (My God, my God, why hast thou forsaken me?) Were they words of defeat? Did God abandon Jesus on the Cross? Some have thought so. But not wisely, I believe, for we must always remember that these are not Jesus' words alone—they are the opening words of the twenty-second Psalm. Jesus undoubtedly knew the Psalms by heart. Now the twenty-second Psalm, if you will read it, is not a Psalm of despair but a cry of faith by an anguished soul in the face of suffering. And it comes to a magnificent climax in the twenty-first verse, where, after narrating all his troubles, the Psalmist cries out, "Yea, from the horns of the wild-oxen thou hast answered me!" Jesus was not physically delivered on the Cross. But he was spiritually triumphant. He could say at last: "Father, into thy hands I commend my spirit." It was an inner victory.

This, then, is religion: There is a God. Our lives are vitally related to him, as closely related as the bay to the ocean, the leaves to the tree, the tree to the sunshine, the receiving-set to the great central radio station— use whatever figure is most meaningful to you. And, because of this intimate relationship, we can open our lives to God in prayer. Thereby we come in tune with the Infinite, and new powers, peace and courage, poise and wisdom, creative imagination and capacity for endurance, are given to us. That is religion!

No, that is only one-half of religion! There is another side. Some one recently called my attention to the fact that, in one of Lloyd Douglas' novels, Dean Harcourt says to a troubled inquirer: "Don't worry so much right now about believing in God; first conduct yourself in such a way that God can believe in you!" That is the other side of religion—not only do you believe in God, but can God believe in you? God is trying to get some things done in the world, things like justice, good will, a co-operative world order, a sense of human brotherhood beyond all racial differences, a respect for the sanctity of human life. Within his own self-imposed limitations God cannot get these things done by divine fiat. He does not make us automatons. He depends upon our recognition and acceptance of his truth. To do certain things he has no hands but ours. In the darkness of this hour you have come to a new understanding of God. You believe in him and rely on him in life's critical emergencies. Good! But this must be an emergency for God! Can he rely on you?

The Windowsill of Heaven

REVEREND THEODORE FLOYD ADAMS, D.D.
Pastor, First Baptist Church, Richmond, Virginia

DR. THEODORE FLOYD ADAMS, one of the leading preachers in the Southern Baptist Convention, is pastor of First Baptist Church, Richmond, Virginia.

He has held just three pastorates—the Cleveland Heights Baptist Church, Cleveland, Ohio, from 1924 to 1927; Ashland Avenue Baptist Church, Toledo, Ohio, from 1927 to 1936; and First Baptist Church, Richmond, from 1936 to the present. The First Baptist Church—with a membership of over twenty-seven hundred—is one of the leading churches in the Southern Baptist Convention in missions and benevolences.

In "The Windowsill of Heaven," Dr. Adams touches prayer as it affects the life of the individual in his contacts with God and the world. There is a quietness and peace in his message that would be good for our warring world today. More hours in prayer and more millions for missions might make a more Christian world and prevent World War III. He shows Jesus' use of prayer.

Sermon Forty-eight

TEXT: *In the morning rising up a great while before day, he went out, and departed into a solitary place, and there prayed.* MARK 1:35

N A SUNDAY AFTERNOON SOME YEARS AGO I attended an outdoor vesper service in a small Wisconsin town. It was a beautiful day and we gathered in the shade of some old maples for a union service conducted by the local Episcopal rector. Together we sang the great hymns of the church, joined in the prayers, and listened to the sermon. As we left each of us was handed a card. I have long since lost mine, but I carry it still in my mind. It bore a picture of Jesus kneeling by a great rock in the wilderness. The trees about him seemed to join in worship as he prayed along with his Father. Beneath the picture was this verse:

> Every morning lean thine arms awhile
> Upon the windowsill of heaven
> And gaze upon thy Lord,
> Then, with the vision in thy heart,
> Turn strong to meet thy day.

"The windowsill of heaven." Here is a poet's description of the reality of prayer. His, however, is an enlarged concept of prayer; not that of the little boy who explained to the visiting minister that he didn't say his prayers every night because "some nights I don't want anything."

Many of us are guilty of such a limited view of prayer. We feel our own lack of spiritual power. We are troubled by weakness, doubt, and failure, largely because we miss much of the help that prayer might give us. We need to say with the disciples, "Lord, teach us to pray." They not only needed to learn to pray, but how to pray. How well Jesus knew is revealed in our text. The Master had just finished a hard, grueling day. Another awaited him. How could he be ready for it? Mark gives us the answer and with it a key to Jesus' power. "In the morning, rising up a great while before day, he went out, and departed into a solitary place, and there prayed."

Our little verse also suggests the wisdom of prayer: "Every morning lean thine arms awhile upon the windowsill of heaven." Prayer is a valid part of human experience, however men attempt to define it. "Prayer is the act by which man definitely tries to relate his soul and life to God." "Prayer is a cumulative life of friendship with God."

> Prayer is the soul's sincere desire,
> Unuttered or expressed;
> The motion of a hidden fire
> That trembles in the breast.

No matter how we try to picture or explain it, prayer is a real and vital factor in the life of the Christian. William James tells us, "We pray because we cannot help praying." Carlyle says, "Prayer is and remains the native and deepest impulse of the soul of man."

One summer morning in North Carolina I was awakened before dawn and with a group of young people climbed to the top of a nearby mountain. There we sat waiting, singing hymns, watching the rim of earth to the East made by a range of hills. Suddenly all were silent. We saw what we had been waiting for. The ball of fire that was the sun slowly crept into view above that distant rim of earth. We seemed literally to be at "The windowsill of heaven." It was a time for prayer and we were experiencing anew the reality of which our poet speaks, "And gaze upon thy Lord." Prayer can and does bring a daily revelation of God to man. As you pray you know that God is there. You see him with the eyes of the soul, you hear "the still small voice" within. The fact of communion with God is the great reality of true prayer.

When we pray something happens. "The vision in thy heart" comes as one result of prayer. How much that vision can mean! It was said of the disciples long ago that men "took knowledge of them that they had been with Jesus." What an effect it has on us to pray and see our Lord as he is and ourselves as we are. We realize in that moment of vision that all is not as it should be. A simple experience will picture what I mean. You are working about the house in old clothes, fitting garments for the dusty, dirty work you are doing. The bell rings and company comes. You stand at the door before a visitor freshly dressed. On the instant you become apologetic; you compare yourself with your guest. Clothing and dust that a moment before seemed all right now are evidently out of place and a source of embarrassment as you see yourself with new eyes.

Such is the vision and effect of prayer. We see ourselves as we are and as we ought to be. Humility, repentance, cleansing, and resolve follow naturally. If prayer can do that, and it can, how much we all need to pray.

Something does happen during prayer and as a result you do "turn strong to meet thy day." Power comes as we see ourselves surrounded by God's love and wisdom and strength. The weakest, humblest life can be made stronger spiritually. The greatest life is weakened without the constant refreshing afforded by the resources of prayer. Each of us, as we pray, is fitted to meet our own day. Was it not Martin Luther who said, "I have so much to do today that I could not possibly get it done without spending two or three hours in prayer"?

> Lord, what a change within us one short hour
> Spent in thy presence will prevail to make!
> What heavy burdens from our bosoms take,
> What parched grounds refresh as with a shower.
> We kneel, how weak; we rise, how full of power.
> Why, therefore, should we do ourselves this wrong,
> Or others, that we are not always strong,
> That we are ever overborne with care,
> That we should ever weak or heartless be,
> Anxious or troubled, when with us is prayer,
> And joy and strength and courage are with Thee.

331

How strange, how foolish that we should be content with so little prayer. We need to pray more, we Christians. "More things are wrought by prayer than this world dreams of," and many, many more could be wrought if we would pray more. A friend of mine, a Jewish rabbi, once said to me as we talked about the lack of power in the Christian church, "The trouble is that you Christians claim to have all the mechanics of salvation, but you don't act saved."

Contrast our own experience with that of Jesus. The incident related in our text was no unusual occurrence for him. He knew well "the windowsill of heaven." Jesus prayed and prayed often, for himself and for others. He took time for prayer before every great crisis of his life. He taught us to pray by precept and by example, for he knew from his own experience what it meant to talk with the Father.

How can we pray more effectively? I have been helped in my own thinking by some excellent suggestions of Dr. T. R. Glover as to the essentials of prayer in Jesus' mind. Let us always think of prayer as fellowship with God. Prayer is more than thanksgiving, petition, adoration, and intercession. Those are parts and forms of prayer. Think of prayer as Jesus did, as communion, conference, a personal realization of the very real presence of God. Sometimes when you pray, kneel down. It is not essential, but it does help to create the sense of humility and trust. Remember, too, that you can pray anywhere, in church, in the midst of the beauties of nature, in the stress of life, but that nothing can take the place of a moment alone with God in the morning and at night. Jesus knew the importance of this fellowship with God alone and told his disciples, "Thou, when thou prayest, enter into thine inner chamber, and having shut Thy door, pray to thy Father who is in secret, and thy Father who seeth in secret shall recompense thee."

As you pray, have faith in God. Believe that he can help, expect that he will help, realize that he has helped already. Believe and you will receive; in fact, you already have received much that prayer can give.

In true prayer there is identification with the purpose of God. We pray "Thy will be done." We identify ourselves with the needs of those we love, or ought to; with the world's sin and misery; with the plans and program of God in Christ for the redemption of the world. We cannot pray only for ourselves when we say with Jesus, "Thy will be done."

Such praying leads us naturally to a new dedication of self to God. A very real part of true prayer is our surrender to his will and our trust in his ability to change and use us. As you pray you build your life on God. All He has is yours, all you are is His. You and the Father are one in purpose and resources.

332

Such was the experience of Jesus. See Him on the cross. You marvel at His strength, at His forgiveness, His redeeming love. You can hardly understand it until you go back of the cross to a garden and a prayer and a Son at one with his Father.

Would you be like Jesus? Then pray and

> Every morning lean thine arms awhile
> Upon the windowsill of heaven
> And gaze upon thy Lord,
> Then, with the vision in thy heart,
> Turn strong to meet thy day.

Corpus Christi

The Most Reverend Robert E. Lucey, S.T.D.
Roman Catholic Archbishop of San Antonio

Archbishop Lucey is a fearless preacher, known and respected for the forcefulness of his sermons, especially those on labor and the rights of the workingman. Born in Los Angeles, California, he recognized the call to the priesthood and studied at St. Vincent's College and St. Patrick's Seminary. Then he took a four-year course in theology in the North American College in Rome, where he was graduated with an S.T.D. He was ordained to the priesthood on May 14, 1916.

In 1921, after serving as assistant pastor in several churches, he was appointed Director of the Catholic Welfare Bureau of Los Angeles. In 1925, he was appointed Pastor of St. Kevins Church, Los Angeles, and in 1929, he became Pastor of St. Anthony's Church, Long Beach, California. His leadership led to his consecration as Bishop of Amarillo, Texas, on May 1, 1934; and seven years later he became Archbishop of San Antonio, Texas, where he has won an enviable place in the community.

He is vice-president of the Catholic Conference on Industrial Problems, of the Catholic Association for International Peace, and is a member of the Texas State Committee on Postwar Planning.

His "Corpus Christi" sermon reveals his deep convictions on brotherhood, man's need of Christ the Saviour; the urgency of a truly Christian culture; his opposition to race discrimination; his insistence upon justice for labor and in international politics; and his appeal for collaboration with non-Catholics. The sermon was delivered in Corpus Christi, Texas, on March 18, 1943, on the occasion of the Golden Sacerdotal Jubilee of Bishop Emmanuel Ledvina. Archbishop Lucey is best known for his struggle for the rights of labor of all races and creeds. He demands security for the workers.

Sermon Forty=nine

TEXT: *Now you are Corpus Christi, you are the Body of Christ.*
I CORINTHIANS 12:27

ORPUS CHRISTI! WHAT PROFOUND SIGNIFICANCE is found in that title today! Corpus Christi is the body of Christ, and that phrase has two meanings in the language of our ancient Church. It refers to the Eucharist which is the Sacrament of Christ's body and blood; but it also refers to that great group of human beings in every part of the world who are members of the visible Church of Christ, united to God and to one another by the grace of Christ, vivified and directed by the Holy Spirit of God. Christ is the Vine, we are the branches; Christ is the Head, we are His members, as the Apostle of the Gentiles declared: "Now you are Corpus Christi, you are the body of Christ."

Through the centuries this original concept of the body of Christ as taught by St. Paul has been extended to include all who love God, all who are united in the bond of sanctifying grace to Christ and to one another. Thus the citizens of every nation who love our Father in heaven are sons of God, our brothers in Christ, and members of that Corpus Christi which is the Mystical Body of Christ.

Why do we say that this beautiful title, Corpus Christi, has a profound significance for our country and for the world today? Because our culture, our way of life, our civilization are predicated on the idea of human brotherhood in Christ. Our culture is not of the jungle, our way of life is not of the fang and the claw, our civilization is not of force and violence but of justice and of charity. We live by law, at worst by natural law, at best by divine revelation, but in any event, we recognize our fellow man for what he is—a creature of supreme dignity and surpassing destiny, a sublime personality upon whom Almighty God has bestowed certain rights which no man or government can take away, such as the right to life and liberty and happiness. To us, all men are children of God even when they deny Him, and all men are members of the body of Christ, and our brothers in Christ, if they truly love their Creator.

Through the centuries we of the Western world, under the influence of religion, built this magnificent structure of human brotherhood. But alas! the foundation of the structure has become impaired. The people of the West have not been true to their own ideals. God and religion, the Church and the home, have been neglected, and out of a welter of irreligion, immorality, and injustice forces of evil have risen up to challenge our whole way of life, making it abundantly clear that we shall practice what we preach or go down in ruin. We cannot enjoy the blessings of Christian culture and reject the Christ Who inspired it. We cannot expect peace and order in the Christian community if we forget that we are the body of Christ.

Do you wish to know the measure of the crisis that is upon us? Listen to the words of Our Holy Father, Pope Pius XII, in his last Christmas message addressed to all men of good will. The Pontiff speaks of "a world that is plunged in darkness by fatal errors"; of "the sons of Adam shackled with the chains of sin and guilt"; of "the tempestuous strife and hate of our stormy days"; of "embittered and exasperated mankind." His Holiness tells us of "this hour of unspeakable trial and strife"; of "the fatal economy of the past decades"; of "the worker who is or will be the father of a family, being condemned to economic dependence and slavery"; of "this war of material and moral disintegration"; and of "the need of contact with the eternal." The Holy Father deplores "the appalling catastrophe which the present upheavel brings to man and which portrays all the terrifying lineaments of a general judgment." He exhorts us "to realize fully the dreadful gravity of this hour." He tells of "the vastness of this universal disaster" and "the lack of moral fiber in the society of today." Finally the Pontiff speaks of "the ruins of a social order which has given such tragic proof of its ineptitude as a factor for the good of the people."

Surely the mind of the Holy Father is revealed in these quotations. All who are not blind must recognize that the Christian community, the body of Christ on earth, has collapsed. Our social order lies in ruins and all men of good will must join to build a finer one. The long-developing revolution has broken upon the human race and out of it shall come a better world or chaos.

What chance have we of restoring human brotherhood in a disordered world? Of rebuilding the broken body of Christ? In some ways the picture looks very dark. By common consent, and perhaps by default, the moral leadership of the nations, in political and social matters, has been confided to our own beloved country. In the field of spiritual things our ancient Church undoubtedly enjoys incomparable prestige. But will the nations of the West harken to the voice of the Holy Father and the President of the United States? Have our citizens in this country the capacity to assume leadership in building a new order founded on justice? For peace is a work of justice.

The Holy Father himself tells us that reconstruction must begin from within. The natural law must be observed at home if it is to be recognized abroad. A reign of law among the nations cannot be established by lawless peoples. Where do we stand in relation to law?

By the natural law all of our citizens here have a right to economic, political, and international security. Are we prepared, in so far as we are able, to give economic security to our fellow citizens who are our brothers in Christ and sons of God? Our record in that matter is not too good. It was Pope Pius XI who declared that "all of economic life has become hard, cruel, and relentless in ghastly measure." What have we done as Christians to give our brother in Christ economic security? Is it not true that many individuals among us still follow the path marked by greed of gold and lust of power? Is it not true that private citizens and associations would still deny to working people the right to form workingmen's organizations for their mutual protection and progress as allowed by the natural law and Papal documents? Do not many of our citizens insist that laboring people shall stand defenseless and alone in the awful struggle for existence? Do we not know that in normal times about a third of our citizens cannot live in decent and frugal comfort because they are victims of injustice and economic immorality?

Reconstruction begins from within. How can we practice justice in Europe if we cannot do justice at home? How shall we recognize Asiatics as our brethren if we cannot recognize our neighbor as our brother?

In addition to economic security every citizen has a right to political security and equality. Through the years we have held in honor the immortal words of Thomas Jefferson: "All men are created equal." The Founding Fathers began a revolution when they abolished rank and class leaving only citizens equal and free. Our pioneer statesmen were Christians, holding the belief that all men are brothers in the Fatherhood of God. But the men who succeeded the pioneers never completed the revolution. And even today many of our citizens cling to the empty myth of a master race. They feel that the man whose skin is brown or black is somehow inferior and must be held in subjection. Apparently all men are created equal if their skin is white. As though Almighty God were concerned with pigmentation!

Race discrimination is an insult to God and to His children. When St. Paul said to the Corinthians, "Now you are the body of Christ," he spoke to all men in all nations, through all the centuries of time, excluding no man who loved and served his God.

Race discrimination gives aid and comfort to the enemy. When we disfranchise native-born citizens because of color, the Axis radio announces to all the world that the American people are dishonest. And when, with bestial cruelty, we lynch colored boys without trial or hearing, that same Axis radio tells the world that Americans are a ferocious race; they will fight for freedom in Africa but they don't grant freedom at home.

Race discrimination inspires employers who have a poll tax mentality to hire white women in war industries while colored men cannot find a job. Thus juvenile delinquency increases, victory is delayed, and a large segment of good American citizens live in poverty and squalor. And these, the least of our brethren, are called, and are, the sons of God. If we are fighting to destroy the very idea of a master race, let us destroy that thing at home. Let us make complete the revolution of Thomas Jefferson: "All men are created equal."

A third security to which we are all entitled is found in the field of international relations. It is freedom from the constant danger of devastating war. There are some who tell us that we shall find security only in building up overpowering armaments which will discourage attacks from our neighbors. But this formula of security merely means a race for armaments and makes a mockery of peace. Others tell us that, because of original sin, war is inevitable and peace plans are utterly futile. One might remark in this connection that, because of original sin, death is also inevitable. Shall we, therefore, abolish hospitals and health departments? The point is that human relationships can be good without being perfect. Men can be just and still make mistakes. Long periods of peace are possible with men of good will, and war can be made remote if its causes are removed. Peace is not something that happens; it is a temple built by human hands in patience, in justice, and in truth. Peace must be studied and planned and organized. It is, indeed, a *work* of justice.

In these fateful days our beloved country is twice placed in jeopardy. We went on trial as a decadent nation unwilling and unable to fight. Our adversaries, very much to their discomfiture, have learned that we are both willing and able to fight. As a people we love justice and hate iniquity, but we did cling to the desperate hope that with all the world in flames we could have peace. Jolted out of that comfortable dream, we gathered up our tremendous power, and today, with faith in God, we are marching on to victory.

In the trial of force we are unconquerable. But as victory approaches we go on trial a second time to prove, not the strength of our arms, but the quality of our soul. When peace comes, will America have the grandeur to be great?

It is not merely that we shall be asked to feed hungry men and starving children when this war is over. That sort of charity is no challenge to us. Feeding the hungry is almost a habit with our people. The real challenge that peace will bring will probe deeply into the soul of America. We shall be asked to forgive our enemies and to love those who have hated us, while at the same time we support the moral order by punishing international criminals. We shall be asked to have patience with Europeans and Asiatics that they may grow to their full stature as children of God. It will be our privilege to help in the restoration of that spiritual beauty and charm and grandeur that once was Europe. It will be our duty to support the law of nature and of nature's God here and everywhere in the world. With the advent of peace we shall be asked to join with other nations in building a world government for the world community. We shall be expected to abandon our quaint idea of exaggerated national sovereignty and submit our disputes with other nations to a court of international justice. As the most powerful country in the world it will be our high privilege to lead the way in restoring to the common man his heritage of sublime dignity and immortal destiny. We shall be asked to repair the broken brotherhood of man, the mangled Corpus Christi, the shattered body of Christ. In simple language we shall be asked to live and act like Christians. And oh! what a challenge that is!

Again and again the question comes to our mind: Can America fulfill the responsibilities which are inherent in her power, her leadership, and her wealth? Can America rise to meet the challenge of this strange, new era in human history? Has America the capacity for greatness? If she has not, then indeed grey days have come upon the world. But, in spite of all our weakness and our folly, I hold the conviction that, God helping us, we shall in large measure fulfill the mandate of our destiny. We have never renounced the Christian traditions that surrounded our republic at its birth. We have broken the laws of God and man, but we never denied the validity of those laws nor their ultimate sanction in the hands of the living God. When we did evil we did not call it virtue, and when we worshiped the Creator we knelt before the God of heaven, not a strange deity of nation, of blood, or of soil. If some of our people have treated their neighbors unjustly, the majority have never praised them for it. In a word, our Christian heritage, weak and impaired at times, still lives in the hearts of our people.

That it will be possible for the world to repair our broken brotherhood and re-establish Christian standards of life is declared by no less an authority than the Vicar of Christ, himself. Listen to the words of Pope Pius XII in his Christmas message of last year: Charity and justice "elevate human life to that social atmosphere where, even amid the failings, the obstacles and the difficulties of this earth a fraternal community of life is made possible. . . . Today, as never before, the hour has come for reparation, for rousing the conscience of the world. . . . For a Christian who is conscious of his responsibilities even toward the least of his brethren, there is no such thing as slothful tranquillity, nor is there question of flight, but of struggle, of action against every inaction and desertion in the great spiritual combat where the stakes are the construction, nay the very soul, of the society of tomorrow."

The Holy Father then goes on to say that we are not to spend our time crying about the mistakes of the past but go into action at once to build a better world tomorrow. Here are his words: "The call of the moment is not lamentation but action; not lamentation over what has been, but reconstruction of what is to arise and must arise for the good of society."

The Pontiff then appeals to a very interesting group of people to join in a crusade for the re-establishment of justice and charity. He first summons "the best and most distinguished members of the Christian family to unite in the spirit of truth, justice, and love." This appeal is made not to Catholics only but to Protestants and all Christians. The Holy Father then addresses himself to "you, beloved children, who recognize and adore in Christ, your Saviour." Here again the appeal is made to all the followers of Christ. But the Pontiff goes even further and declares: "We turn to all those who are united with us at least by the bond of faith in God." Here, quite clearly, Pius XII includes in his crusade people who are not Christians but who believe in God. And, finally, the Holy Father calls upon those who, perhaps, know little or nothing about religion but are groping for the light. These are his words: "We turn, finally, to all those who would be free of doubt and error, and who desire light and guidance." All these, Christians and non-Christians, Catholics and Protestants, the Vicar of Christ invites "to unite and collaborate toward the renewal of society in spirit and truth."

There are some Catholics who, I fear, will not accept with good grace this moving appeal for collaboration with our non-Catholic friends. These brethren are contented individuals, serene and confident in the validity of their faith and the reality of their personal eternal salvation. They do not realize that Western culture is in jeopardy, that the Christian community, the Corpus Christi, the body of Christ, torn and broken, has collapsed. Enjoying truth in doctrine and grace in sacraments, they see no reason to collaborate with non-Catholics and non-Christians for any purpose whatever. Satisfied with their own spiritual well-being, contented with the gift of faith which they did not merit, they walk with unaffected poise through a confused and disordered world. Either they make the mistake of thinking that Catholics alone can build a better world, or they are too apathetic to engage in collaboration.

His Holiness is not dismayed by the presence in the Christian community of some who are given to apathy and lethargy. He speaks of those who cling "with childish stubbornness to things as they are." He speaks of the reluctance, cowardice, and selfishness of some who will not face the burning questions of the day. But he adds that "for a Christian who is conscious of his responsibilities to the least of his brethren there is no such thing as slothful tranquillity." It is the hour for struggle, for feverish activity, for a social and spiritual crusade.

And if you ask me what these crusaders are to do, I will answer that they are to battle for justice and human dignity; they are to renounce egoism and national isolation; they are to pledge themselves "not to rest until in all peoples and all nations of the earth a vast legion shall be formed bent on bringing back society to its center of gravity, which is the law of God."

My friends, all of you qualify for membership in this legion of God. Remember that the renewal of society begins at home; reconstruction starts from within. Treat your neighbor as a child of God equal to you in the sight of your Creator and destined for a blessed immortality. Treat all your fellow citizens with justice and love, not only the strong but the weak, not only the dominant majority but the persecuted minority, not merely the great and the powerful but the meek and the lowly. If all men who are upright and honest will join this crusade for God and man, we shall build a better world in justice and peace; we shall repair our broken brotherhood, our Corpus Christi, our body of Christ.

Human Neighborliness and Eternal Life

BISHOP FRANCIS J. McCONNELL, D.D.
Senior Bishop of the Methodist Church

FOR FIFTY YEARS, Bishop McConnell has preached for the people and the ministers of the Methodist Church. Since 1894, when he was graduated from Ohio Wesleyan, he has brought a current of new ideas to the Church. Believing that a minister must also be a scholar, he took his Ph. D. from Boston University in 1899. In 1909, he became President of DePauw University and in 1912 he was elected a Bishop.

He has always been a capable administrator and an inspiring preacher to the ministers of his Conferences. For a hundred years "a Bishop's sermon" has been something to talk about in the Methodist Church, and Bishop McConnell has never failed his Church. He has always been a stimulating speaker, with exactness of words, sharpness of wit, and the ability to hold men.

When he was Bishop of Pittsburgh, he became the spearhead for the movement that brought about one day of rest in seven for the worker. He is still interested in the affairs of the laborer, and is President of the American Association for Social Security.

Bishop McConnell has a profound philosophical and theological outlook. He has made a great contribution to the philosophy of religion, and has written many outstanding books, both theological and philosophical, including *Borden Parker Bowne, Is God Limited?*, and *The Diviner Immanence*.

In this sermon Bishop McConnell takes the old, old story of the Good Samaritan and shows how the social Gospel and Eternal Life go together. No one can read this sermon without finding new meaning in the tenth chapter of Luke. (For a different approach see Dr. Scherer's and Dr. Day's sermons.)

Sermon Fifty

TEXT: *And, behold, a certain lawyer stood up, and tempted him, saying, "Master, what shall I do to inherit eternal life?"* LUKE 10:25

E SOMETIMES MISS THE POINT OF SCRIPTURAL passages by not observing the context in which they are set. The Parable of the Good Samaritan is justly regarded as standing in its own right as a gem or a classic in itself. In vivid and unforgettable form it sets forth the attitude of our Master toward what we call the race problem, or the problem of any oppressed or distressed human being in need. The parable illustrates also the Master's idea of how we are to prove neighbors or "to get close" to those in need.

Referring now to the context of the Parable, we note that it was uttered upon the occasion of a lawyer's attempting to heckle Jesus. We have had occasion many times to note the passionate determination of the official classes in Jerusalem to get rid of Jesus. If they could have had their way, they would have carried through a plot of some kind to put Jesus to death, but they dared not do this because they feared the people. So their only recourse was to seek to break the hold of Jesus on the people, to destroy his popularity, and thus to overthrow his power. They therefore employed keen questioners to follow Jesus about, to enter into the groups of his listeners, and to put questions to him. The question might be something that would raise a laugh against Jesus and thus spoil his effectiveness by making him ridiculous. This was not tried often and when it was tried, it failed outright. The other method was to frame a question so that Jesus could be forced to take a stand on some problem or issue about which the people of the day differed. This was the plan followed by the lawyer in today's Scripture reading. He asked Jesus, "What shall I do to inherit eternal life?"—a question upon which the religious opinion of the time was divided.

This lawyer was of no ordinary mind. He asked a decisive question and he received and dealt with a decisive answer. Jesus in turn became the questioner and asked the lawyer, "What is written in the law? How readest thou?" This question showed in turn the keenness of Jesus, for the difference of opinion about the inheritance of eternal life turned largely upon the extent to which the Mosaic law was observed. Jesus forced the lawyer to tell what he thought essential. The lawyer unerringly seized the heart of the Mosaic system when he picked out one passage from Deuteronomy, "Thou shalt love the Lord thy God with all thy heart, and with all thy soul, and with all thy strength, and with all thy mind." Then he added to it a passage from Leviticus, "And thy neighbor as thyself." The lawyer had given the right answer and Jesus frankly commended him. "This do, and thou shalt live." Then there was a revelation of further keenness on the lawyer's part. This Mosaic law was a statement of general principle. The application came in the question, "Who is my neighbor?"

Then follows the inimitable Parable of the man who fell among the thieves and of the one of the three passers-by who proved neighbor to that man. Jesus began by saying a "certain man" fell among thieves. The man was just anybody. The question was not as to his worth himself in any of his particular relationships. He was in need and he was a man. That was as far as it was necessary to go in any inquiries of the stricken sufferer. By chance a certain priest came down that way. He was just a priest and he was taking a journey by chance. He was, however, supposed to do what any priest would do whether he was traveling under orders or by chance. All he did was to look at the man and pass on. Next came a Levite. He was a little better than the priest in that he went up to the sufferer and looked at him. I do not wish to be flippant about this passage, but this Levite was of the type that can make good church surveys. Their work often consists in looking at a situation and then passing on. Finally came the Samaritan who did not have a priest's credentials and may not have known what a Levite was, but who was greater than either of the other two in that he was essentially a human being and dealt with the wounded man in a human fashion.

We come back to the context. The Parable was begun in response to a question to Jesus by the heckler. It ends with the question directed to the heckler by Jesus. Which of these three thinkest thou was neighbor unto him that fell among the thieves? The lawyer had to reply, "He that showed mercy on him." Then followed the word of Jesus, "Go, and do thou likewise." Recall now the lawyer's question, "What shall I do to inherit eternal life?" The answer of Jesus was, "Act as did the Samaritan." This lifts the whole problem up to the realm of one's eternal destiny. We often hear deeds of human kindness referred to as something expected of us, to be sure, but without any great significance for larger issues. We may take all such matters in the day's work. From the point of view of Jesus, eternal life, whether here or hereafter, depends upon the degree in which we show forth the spirit of Christ. That spirit has to be intense enough to leap across all racial barriers or artificial barriers between man and man. The Priest and the Levite had around them the racial barrier, or at least enough of such a barrier to separate their lives from the Samaritan's. They had an artificial barrier also in the fact that they were officials of the merely official caste which prevented their getting very close to human suffering. Both sets of barriers could block the path of eternal life.

The parable has been made a theme for all manner of ingenious homiletic treatments. I remember hearing a sermon once which tried to justify the Priest and the Levite for passing by the wounded man on the plea that they were horrified and frightened by what they had seen. All such treatment obscures the main point. The Levite passed by because he was a Levite, and the Priest passed by because he was a priest. That is to say, their professional work had institutional-ized the humanity out of them. Personally they may have been very good men, at least in the normal round of conventional moral relationships. But from the point of view of Jesus, they were sinners imperiling their prospects of eternal life by the fact that the ordinary, common human feelings had been dried up in them. We do not know just what the expression "eternal life" meant to the heckler, but we may safely assume that it included a thought of eternal destiny. In the mind of Jesus eternal life meant something that begins here and now. In such a life death is but an incident, the main importance being placed on the quality of the life itself. Jesus was not given to laying down formal tests for entrance into the soul's existence after death, but we can be quite well assured that the destiny of the soul here and hereafter was in his mind to be determined by the quality of the life here and now. The parable means at bottom that neither the Priest nor the Levite were in adequate degree human beings.

The proof of Christianity is the Christian. The proof of divine life in a human being is the degree of humanity it possesses. Even in dealing with the Church we have to insist that the degree of divinity which it possesses is to be measured by the degree of humanity which it manifests. This is so obvious that it hardly needs statement, but I know that there are hearers to whom such a sentence will bring something of a shock. I repeat that we are likely to take the manifestation of human kindliness one toward another as a matter of course, and from one angle we can say that it is well that this is so. From another angle, however, we are in danger here, the danger of losing perspective. We may well question if there is any religion in existence which does not at times fall into the error of seeking for the salvation of men in something extraordinary. In any realm this is a serious mistake. One of the long steps ahead in the study of the earth in which we live was the realization by scientists of the part played in the shaping of the earth by ordinary and commonplace forces, such as the running of water, the falling of rain, the blowing of the wind, and the differences among locations in degrees of heat. Likewise in the study of society we have come to see that the struggle of men for bread and for clothing and for shelter has shaped the destinies of nations. Admittedly, the accumulation and culmination of such forces both in the material and social realms may bring about tremendous crises, but the essentials are the continuously working powers. So it is in the spiritual realm. The manifestation of brotherly and neighborly spirit is the shaping force in the determination of the eternal life of the soul.

The essential teaching of the Parable of the Good Samaritan is similar to that in our Lord's picture of the final judgment. Our Lord speaks of the nations of the earth as assembled before the King for judgment to receive reward or punishment prepared from the foundation of the world. Jesus seems to have had in mind a passage in an old Jewish book, the Book of Enoch, I think it was, which supplied the framework for his picture of the judgment. In that old book the point of view seems to be that of patriotism toward the Jewish nation. The virtues are of those who made extraordinary effort for the Jewish nation, the type of effort we ordinarily even today applaud most loudly in our devotion to our own country. The picture of Jesus is grand enough. It is an assembly of the nations. The reward is great, the inheritance of the kingdom prepared from the foundation of the world, but those to whom the reward was given had rendered services so insignificant in themselves that they could not remember when they had rendered them, and those who had not rendered the services seemed to suppose that they had. The test was human interest in one's fellow men. Again, the terrible word of Jesus about the unpardonable sin has something of the same bearing here. If a man has a wrong idea of God, that is to say, if his theology is wrong, the error is not fatal. If a man has a false view of the Son of God, his mistake is not irremediable. If however, a man thinks that a good deed done one's fellows is inspired by the devil, his sin is unpardonable, not because an arbitrary divine judge would pass an extreme sentence but unpardonable in the same sense that a disease may be incurable.

This particular sin of inhumanity we regret to say is quite likely to be caused by the institutional relationships of men. Now institutions are probably the most potent civilizing influences in human experience, but their degradation can cast men as far down as their exaltation can lift them up. All things considered, the family is probably the best institutional creation of the human race, but family lines can be so drawn as to make families centers of hatred toward one another. An educational system can be, and usually is, a fountain of light for human minds, but it can be perverted to propaganda purposes which soil all the relations of one group to another. Just about the beginning of the nineteenth century an English clergyman, Malthus by name, published a remarkable scientific statement showing the tendency of animal and human beings to increase in number beyond the limits of the earth to supply nourishment. This was accepted as an inevitable natural law. Forthwith, certain privileged classes in England hailed it as a divine law, and, justifying themselves through it, introduced inhuman horrors against humanity, especially against the lives of women and children, in the so-called Industrial Revolution. We have only to look around us today to see how nationalism, which evidently has incalculable possibilities for good, is an agency of destruction in producing wars in which all high human values are likely to be burned out.

In the parable before us, Jesus was clearly thinking of the Church of his time as an institution. If his message had been merely personal and individual, he would probably have said that a man was assaulted by thieves, and there came one man and then another who paid no attention to him. We would not have used the terms Priest and Levite. We sometimes say that Jesus made no attack on the outstanding social evils of his time. Well, Jesus worked publicly not over three years. In that time he devoted himself to an attempt to transform what, to the Jew, was the outstanding social institution, the Jewish Church. That was powerful enough to bring his efforts to an end in a few months. The sin of that institution was that the highest manifestation of humanity the world has ever seen could not exist for more than a few months in its presence. The heckler was probably related closely to that Church. The word of Jesus to him did not close in an attack upon the Church, but made to him a personal application which was really an appeal. We may trust that this lawyer who sought to entrap Jesus, himself saw the force of the parable and went away with a new realization of what eternal life means. It may be hard to define neighborliness, but we see it in the parable, and looking back in the light of the illustration to the lawyer's citation of the double commandment which Jesus made his own, we recognize neighborliness to human beings to be the means of access to the eternal life, which is the life of God himself.

Social Service and Social Reform

THE RIGHT REVEREND MONSIGNOR JOHN AUGUSTINE RYAN, D.D.
Professor of the National Catholic School of Social Service,
Washington, D. C.

ONE OF MONSIGNOR RYAN'S main interests is the abolition of the social and economic causes of poverty and dependency in America. He grew up in Minnesota and studied for the priesthood at St. Paul Seminary. Ordained a priest in 1898, he did post-graduate work at Catholic University of America, Washington, D. C., then returned to St. Paul Seminary as instructor in Moral Theology. He went back to Washington in 1915, teaching successively at Catholic University, Trinity College, and since 1921 at the National Catholic School of Social Service. For the last twenty-four years he has also served as director of the Department of Social Action, National Catholic Welfare Conference.

A pioneer advocate of minimum wage legislation, he wrote the Minnesota minimum wage law.

He was one of the founders of the Catholic Association for International Peace, and he is now serving as chairman of that Association's Ethics Committee. Among his published works are *A Living Wage, A Better Economic Order,* and *Social Doctrine in Action.*

Most of his sermons have been delivered on special occasions and have dealt with the moral aspect of social and economic problems. This sermon was given at the baccalaureate services at the National Catholic Service School on May 23, 1943. In it he urges co-operation between Catholics and non-Catholics in all efforts toward social betterment. He insists that this country has the resources to afford a decent living to everyone. He offers a challenge, the answer to which can profoundly affect our national life after this war.

Sermon Fifty-one

TEXT: *Concerning brotherly charity there is no need for us to write to you for you yourselves have learned from God to love one another. . . . But we exhort you, brethren, to make even greater progress.*
I THESSALONIANS 4:9,11

WO YEARS AGO, I HAD THE HONOR AND THE pleasure of delivering an address at the closing exercises of this school. On that occasion I urged the graduates to co-operate actively with non-Catholic as well as with Catholic groups in efforts and movements for social betterment. I reminded them that a large part of social distress and individual dependency is due mainly to social and economic factors, that prevention is better than cure, and that poverty, distress, and dependency should be attacked in their causes. Present-day social workers, I said, do not seem to be as actively interested in the economic causes of dependency or in the removal of bad economic conditions and practices as were the social workers of twenty-five or thirty years ago. A little more than two weeks ago, I asked the assistant director of the School of Social Work at the University of Minnesota whether this unfavorable judgment upon the social workers of today was correct. She answered affirmatively, but added that in very recent years there had occurred a reaction against neglect of the economic factors and toward greater emphasis upon social and economic reform.

Whatever may be the present attitude of the average social worker, there can be no question of the position that ought to be taken by Catholic social workers. The comprehensive programs of social reform and social reconstruction laid down by Popes Leo XIII and Pius XI, and reaffirmed by our present Holy Father, should make a stronger appeal to the Catholic social worker than to either her fellow social workers who are not of the Faith or her fellow Catholics who have not enjoyed her advantages of general education and special training.

In this address I shall bring to your attention an outline of reform measures which are not only in harmony with the Papal teaching but calculated to abolish the great majority of the social and economic causes of poverty and dependency in our beloved America. I mean the recently published *Report of the National Resources Planning Board*. This Report presents two programs: one for security; the other, for employment. The first could be made effective immediately if Congress saw fit to enact the appropriate legislation; the second could and should be legislatively implemented now as a measure of preparation, but it could not become fully operative until after the war. Unfortunately, the present Congress is not disposed to give serious attention to any part of the Report. The congressional comments, which made the newspaper headlines when the Report was received, were mostly to the effect that the Report was "socialistic." Legislative action upon it will probably have to await the Seventy-Ninth Congress, in January, 1945. What will happen to it then is at the present moment completely unpredictable.

THE SECURITY PROVISIONS

The principal recommendations of the Report with regard to social security may be conveniently summarized under the following heads:

Old Age and Survivor's Insurance, Unemployment Insurance, Additional Insurance Protection, and Public Assistance.

Under the first of these heads the Report would extend old age insurance to all employable groups and to their dependents. As we all know, the provisions of our present Social Security Act for old age insurance do not take in agricultural laborers, domestic workers, or the employees of very small industrial and commercial establishments.

Under Unemployment Insurance the most important recommendations are that the benefit payments should cover twenty-six weeks of unemployment; that they be uniform in all the states; that they cover employees of small firms; and that workers with dependents should receive additional benefits.

The Additional Insurance Protection, specified in the Report, comprises mainly insurance for wage earners and their dependents against wage loss caused by disability, either permanent or temporary; a federal system of public health services, medical care, and hospitalization. The Report also recommends more attention to preventive measures, with regard to unemployment and ill health, but it contains no proposals for a system of health insurance.

Under Public Assistance is recommended a program adequate to the needs of all persons not now covered by social insurance or by the special public assistances; also assistance for mothers of dependent children and for children dependent from any cause; finally, grants of federal money to the states for all these purposes, in proportion to the ability of each state to share the costs.

The foregoing description is only the barest summary. It is too condensed to convey an adequate idea of any one of the proposed additions to our present Social Security legislation, but it does give us some notion of their comprehensiveness, of the vast and varied province of human needs which they are intended to meet. Instead of discussing them further, I shall draw attention briefly to two of their implications. The first of these implications is that society, the State, is obliged not only to protect lives, property, and contracts, but also to promote the common good, the general welfare. This function of the State was never more comprehensively defined than by Pope Leo XIII, fifty-two years ago this month, in his great encyclical, *Rerum Novarum,* or "On the Condition of Labor." Here is the statement:

. . . Whenever the general interest or any particular class suffers, or is threatened with, evils which can in no other way be met, the public authority must step in to meet them.

This great principle not only repudiates what Thomas Huxley derisively called "the policeman theory of the State" and the silly slogan, "no class legislation"; it also carries an implicit rebuke to all those alleged thinkers who condemn necessary measures of social security on the ground of alleged paternalism. Pope Leo was opposed, as we all are, to real paternalism. Hence he wrote in the same encyclical:

. . . The first duty, therefore, of the rulers of the State should be to make sure that the laws and institutions, the general character and administration of the commonwealth, shall be such as to produce of themselves public well-being and private prosperity.

The social security program recommended by the National Resources Planning Board is in full agreement with this principle also; it recommends not public provision of a livelihood for everybody nor substitution of state care for individual responsibility, but "laws and institutions" to promote "public well-being and private prosperity."

The second important implication of the social security program is that social workers should become thoroughly acquainted with its provisions and strive to visualize the various ways in which it would affect their own tasks. Every intelligent social worker will be able to see that most of the measures recommended would exemplify the maxim that "prevention is better than relief," and illustrate the method of attacking dependency in its causes. Finally, social workers ought to promote, in whatever way they can, the translation of this program into law. The social worker who is indifferent to social legislation is only half-educated.

A few moments ago I discussed from the viewpoint of political philosophy the assertion that the security program is "paternalistic." Another aspect of that objection emphasizes the alleged bad effect of so much security upon the average individual. The comprehensive provision which the program makes for human needs and hazards, from the cradle to the grave, would greatly discourage individual thrift, industry, and responsibility! It would mean the death of "rugged individualism"! I have been under the impression that the poor, pallid thing, called "rugged individualism" had already "passed out," under the accumulated bludgeonings of ridicule. At any rate, the fear expressed in this objection is quite unrealistic; for the proportion of Americans who will become shirkers and wastrels because their wants are fully satisfied by the very modest benefits obtainable under any security system that is likely to be adopted by our Congress, is very small indeed. From the viewpoint of humanity, social welfare, and the common good, it is better that a few thousand malingerers be tolerated than that millions of decent citizens be compelled to live in a manner unworthy of creatures made in the image and likeness of God.

To organize and maintain an economy in which all who want to work can readily obtain jobs is more fundamental and more beneficial than to provide complete social security. In proportion as the first of these objectives is attained, the second will become less and less necessary. Full employment is a greater preventive than social security; for the latter prevents, or diminishes, only the necessity for charitable relief, while the former prevents, or lessens, the need for social security itself. In other words, full employment is a preventive of a preventive. It removes the primary cause of, perhaps, the greater part of social distress and dependency.

Of enormous significance, therefore, is the proclamation by the National Resources Planning Board of the right to work, usefully and creatively, throughout the productive years; our economy must provide work for all who are able to work. This declaration is not only remarkable but revolutionary. It is also morally right and sound. It deserves the first place in an industrial bill of rights. Against whom may this right be asserted? Against whom is it valid? Obviously, against the common guarantor of all rights, the State. This does not mean that the State should itself become the employer of men who cannot find private employment, but it does mean that the State is obliged to create the conditions in which jobs will be available for all. The greatest merit of the Report is that it endeavors to outline the public measures that will be adequate to effectuate this right to work, this right to a job.

The sections of the Report which deal with employment are of more immediate, as well as of more enduring, importance than those which treat of social security. When the war ends, ten million or more men will be seeking employment in our various industries and services. Will they get it within a reasonable time? "Yes," is the answer given by the wishful thinkers and the economically illiterate. The realists on the National Resources Planning Board are not so credulous. They believe that private industry should be given full and fair continuing opportunity and encouragement to do its utmost toward providing employment for all the returning soldiers and sailors, as well as for all others who seek jobs; but they do not believe that either group should place its whole reliance upon an act of faith in the ability of private industry to carry out its good intentions. Hence the Report recommends a large and varied program of public works, from housing to T.V.A.'s and Coulee Dams, in order to provide jobs for all whom private concerns will be unable to employ. Moreover, the Report insists that this device should be adopted as a normal and permanent feature of our economy.

Probably the most important of the other economic measures proposed

by the Report for postwar America is that concerning mixed corporations. These would be partly governmental and partly private. They
might operate in the field of housing, in some of the plants into which
the government has poured billions of dollars during the war, and in
some of the great monopolistic industries which have grown enormously
in concentrated power during the same period. This sort of partnership
between industry and government in the operation of government-owned
factories, at least temporarily, would be much more sensible than the sale
of these properties to private corporations at bargain prices, as occurred
after World War I. In the most dangerous of the monopolistic industries
it might well exemplify the declaration of Pope Piux XI, in *Quadragesimo
Anno:*

For it is rightly contended that certain forms of property must be
reserved to the State, since they carry with them an opportunity of
domination too great to be left to private individuals without injury to
the community at large.

In any case, the mixed corporation, or partnership device, avoids the
opposite evils of purely political operation and inadequate private
operation.

In the immediately preceding paragraphs I have discussed only what
I regard as the three most important proposals in the economic sections
of the Report. The others may be summarized as follows: a dismissal
wage for soldiers and for factory workers; government supervision of the
process of industrial reconversion to peacetime uses; the continuation
of some war plants and war contracts; government grants for plant rehabilitation; a new RFC or a Federal Development Corporation for stimulating investment in basic industries; low-interest loans to small business
concerns needing capital; government research for new processes out of
which may come new industries; the opening of channels of investment
opportunity, by governmental intervention where necessary; the temporary retention after the war of many of the war economic controls, including the allocation of scarce raw materials, priorities on construction
goods, the rationing of consumers' goods, especially durable ones, and the
price controls to avoid a postwar inflation; the expansion of peacetime
goods production; the guarding of labor standards and the strict enforcement of protective labor legislation and collective bargaining; the retention in government hands of the property and patents of enemy aliens;
the enforcement of anti-trust laws and the encouragement of competi-
tion; a set of fiscal policies providing a five-point program which will
"complement and supplement private enterprise"; and the initiation of
a large public-works program.

The National Resources Planning Board is confident that our industrial system can be reorganized to give us a postwar era of full employment and universal prosperity. One of its ablest members, who is also its chief economist, Dr. Alvin E. Hansen, thus describes the requisites and the process:

We have to make up our minds as a nation that we will not permit a postwar depression to overwhelm us. We do not have to take economic defeat after the military victory is won. We can, if we will, maintain business prosperity. We can sustain a continuing demand for goods. We can keep industry going at high levels. We can maintain substantially full employment. We can achieve a society in which everyone capable of and willing to work can find an opportunity to earn a living, to make his contribution, to play his part as a citizen of a progressive, democratic country. . . .
Private business can and will do the job of production. It is the responsibility of government to do its part to insure a sustained demand. We know from past experience that private enterprise has done this for limited periods only. It has not been able to insure a continuous and sustained demand.

Here is our situation. America has the resources—physical, moral, and mental—to produce the necessaries, comforts, and luxuries in sufficient quantity and quality to provide more than a decent living for all her inhabitants and to lay the material basis for a vastly greater equipment of health, education, and culture than was ever before within reach of any people. Our national income for 1943 will probably be upwards of 125 billion dollars. This amount is three times the national income produced a decade ago, in 1933, the year which saw the nadir of the Great Depression. In that disastrous year the volume of goods and services produced by our industries and our employed workers was only forty-one and three quarters billions. Shall we go back to that disgraceful figure after this war is over? In all probability, we shall, if our industrial leaders and our government adopt the economic and political policies which were dominant between 1929 and 1933. There is grave danger that we shall do that very thing if our postwar policies are determined by some of our most powerful and most vocal business leaders, and by a Congress which holds the same views as our present House of Representatives.

Members of the graduating class: your professional life begins in a very troubled and very uncertain world. The most destructive, if not the most cruel, war in human history is not yet finished. When the tens of millions of fighting men have finally stacked their arms, the amount of want, suffering, misery, and despair crying out for relief and assuagement will possibly be greater than the world has ever before witnessed at any one time or period. Because your lot is cast in this fortunate country of

354

ours, you will see at firsthand very little of all this wretchedness. But you will see enough and hear enough to challenge not only your Christian sympathy and charity but also your Christian faith and intelligence. You will need that faith when you are tempted to question the dispositions of Divine Providence; you will need that intelligence when you are called upon to make some contribution to the postwar social order envisaged and delineated by Pope Pius XII. Your Christian faith will enable you to view the world's misery in its proper proportions, to realize always that the earthly life of the most wretched individual endures but a few years, while his life beyond the grave is eternal. Moved by faith in God and love of God, your trained intelligence can help mightily to make the world a better and happier place for the beneficiaries of your services and ministrations.

NIHIL OBSTAT: Arthur J. Scanlan, S.T.D., *Censor Librorum*

IMPRIMATUR: ✠ Francis J. Spellman, D.D., *Archbishop, New York*

Deathless Dreams

THE REVEREND HOBART D. McKEEHAN, D.D.
Pastor of the Abbey Church, Huntingdon, Pennsylvania

DR. McKEEHAN was born on a Pennsylvania farm. He was educated at Franklin and Marshall Academy, Valparaiso University, the Lancaster Theological Seminary, and the University of Oxford. One of the youngest men ever to enter the ministry of the Reformed Church, he was ordained at the age of twenty-one. Since 1924, he has been minister of the Abbey Church, Evangelical and Reformed, in Huntingdon, Pennsylvania. Beginning in his early twenties when Newell Dwight Hillis sought to bring him to Brooklyn, Dr. McKeehan has repeatedly had calls to metropolitan centers, but for twenty years he has chosen to remain in Huntingdon.

Dr. McKeehan's literary contributions, including sermons and reviews, are to be found in the best known religious and educational journals of America and the British Isles. His sermons have appeared all over the English-speaking world. Among collections to which he has contributed are: *Best Sermons* (edited by Joseph Fort Newton); *The Message of the American Pulpit; The Minister's Annual,* 5 volumes; and *The Speaker's Bible.* He was editor of *Great Modern Sermons* and *Anglo-American Preaching.* His own writings include *The Patrimony of Life* and *What Men Need Most.* England's *Manchester Guardian* has called him "one of the greatest of America's younger preachers," and Dean Lynn Harold Hough of Drew University has described him as "a master of vital words."

Outstanding pulpits, college chapels, and religious conferences across the land are coming to know him as an increasingly familiar figure. Dr. McKeehan's ideal for preaching is that "a sermon should be suggestive, measure up to the test of timelessness, and be as relevant and preachable in A.D. 2,000 as it was in A.D. 1944." The following sermon was preached in Christ Church, Methodist, New York, and reveals Dr. McKeehan's dream of a world redeemed by faith in Christ.

Sermon Fifty-two

TEXT: *The name of the City from that day shall be, "The Lord is there."*   EZEKIEL 48:35

> A man must dream or a man must die,
> Not even the deep, clean blue of the sky
> Is as fair as the thing which only seems
> And feeds his life when a wise man dreams.

NE OF THE CHIEF GLORIES OF MAN IS HIS ABILITY to dream dreams and to see visions. By virtue of this ability he is more than a creature of clay. He is a son of the Most High and a citizen of eternity. And whatever progress he has made over his fast-flowing years has been the result of his ability and willingness to invest his life and influence under the command of his best dreams and visions.

One of the most amazing things about these insights of the mind and soul of man is the fact that they have usually come to him in days of darkness and in seasons of tragedy. And the most significant thing about them is the fact that, while beginning as a personal experience, giving a light and a lift to some solitary soul, they have managed to live on in the heart of the race with a power at once haunting, evocative, and creative. They have managed to move out across our world, disturbing the indifferent, challenging the careless, healing the wounded, and giving poise and purpose and power to good men and women everywhere. The secret, of course, is that man's best dreams represent the haunting presence of God, and his authentic visions are illumined by a light that never was on land or sea.

The truth is that only men who dream dreams and see visions are equipped to sense from afar that community of life and love for which God created man and in co-operation with which man rises from dust to divinity. To be sure there have been all sorts of noble dreams and visions, and none has been without its own significance. It is a long and enchanting road from Plato's *Republic* to More's *Utopia* and on to the world of the *Four Freedoms* envisioned by the spokesmen for the United Nations. And these dreams tell us much about the aspiring and inspiring qualities of the civilized mind. Nevertheless, it is not with these that I am now concerned. It is, rather, with those which have had their origin in some soul's experience of the living God, and in times and under circumstances strangely similar to our own. For it is from such dreams and visions of things too good not to be true that we, living under similar conditions of tragedy and darkness, may find the secret of a quiet heart in an unquiet world; a clue to the meaning and mission of our lives; and the divine grace to do as we dream and to live as we pray.

Something more than twenty-five centuries ago a man of God was living in a concentration camp. The camp was located in Babylon. This man represented but one of some eight thousand families that, before a ruthless invader, had been uprooted from their homes and driven across seven hundred miles of desert into an alien land. The long years of imprisonment reached their tragic climax when word came back to the camp that the oppressor had gone again and sacked Jerusalem, outraging its innocent people and leaving their holy temple a pile of rubble and ruin. Something of the deep fraternity of mental anguish, something of the sacrament of suffering finds expression in the words, "By the waters of Babylon there we sat down, yea we wept when we remembered Zion." In our own day many a Pole has been saying the same thing about Warsaw; many a Greek about Athens; many a Frenchman about Paris; many a Belgian about Brussels; many a Netherlander about Rotterdam.

But this man who lived in an ancient concentration camp did more than remember. He dreamed a dream. He saw a vision. He did not magnify the crimes of his oppressors—though they were without parallel in all the history he knew. And he did not minimize the sins of many of his fellow exiles—men and women who, lured by the easy ways of heathenism, had begun to accept the vices of Babylon and to forget the virtues of Mount Zion. Indeed, these things broke his heart, but they did not frustrate his faith. Like Isaiah and St. Paul, like St. Francis, John Bunyan, and George Fox, Ezekiel was a citizen of two worlds. And the spiritual world was no less real than the world of nature. Ezekiel was a seer and a prophet. He saw above the din and dust of time. He saw beyond the years. His faith rested upon invisible, yet everlasting, foundations. If his feet were in the mud of unhappy circumstance, his forehead touched the shining stars of imperishable truth and splendor. His faith was firm, his hope a shining lamp, and God his greatest certainty. And so he envisioned a new and better city, even better than Zion at its best: "The name of the City," said Eziekiel, "from that day shall be, 'The Lord is there.'"

The scene changes. It is the latter years of the first century of our era. An aged saint, living in exile, on a lonely island, looks out at the dark sins of the Roman Empire and forward into the growing tragedy and terror of the future. He remembers the sweet fellowship of the Beloved Community and all the radiant beauty of Christ and his friends. But, like Ezekiel, he does more than remember. He sees more than what is about and in front of him. He feels more than the obvious. He thrills with the thought of God—the God and Father of Jesus. He feels the pressure of the hand of the living Christ. And, above and beyond the lonely shores of Patmos and the darkness of his age, he sees something too good not to be eventually true: "And I saw the holy City, the new Jerusalem, descending from God out of heaven, all ready like a bride arrayed for her husband." And with the divine vision came a divine voice saying: "Lo, God's dwelling place is with men, with men will he dwell; they shall be his people, and God himself shall be with them; he shall wipe away every tear from their eyes, and death shall be no more—no more wailing, no more crying, no more pain."

Again the scene changes. It is the year of Our Lord, 410. The sins which the writer of the Apocalypse saw and predicted have had time to bear their dark and deadly fruits. The Church itself, more litigant than militant, was weakened by heresies and divisions, and the impossible was happening before the very eyes of men and their minds were dazed. The vast and proud empire of the Caesar's—the greatest empire the world had ever known—was falling to pieces. The Imperial City of Rome was in the hands of Alaric the Goth. It was as if the solid and familiar ground had given way beneath one's feet, or as if the fixed stars had disappeared from a friendly sky. And, as might be expected, such an unbelievable, yet undeniable, catastrophe caused good men to react in very different ways. Many were simply awe-struck and speechless. Others, like Jerome, gave way to bitter lamentation. But there was one man who was neither dumb nor hysterical. His name was Augustine, bishop of Hippo, in North Africa, and the most influential figure in Christian history since Paul of Tarsus.

Augustine had, by the grace of God, the preaching of Jerome, and the unwearying prayers of a saintly mother, been converted. His conversion rescued him from the futile gropings of a clever intellectual and united his vast and varied talents to the steady purpose of a divinely illuminated life. And so, in a time of tragedy and terror for the whole of the civilized world, Augustine had a dream and saw a vision. Lifting his eyes above the fair but fragile Community of Man he saw the impregnable Community of God. Above the bright but brittle City of Man, which was Rome, he saw the *City of God,* inevitable and eternal.

Although penetrated with the majestic sorrow of the Apocalypse, and touched with many a speculative fancy, the principles of *De Civitate Dei* are as ageless and relevant as its insights are authentic. If, as Bryce affirmed, the Holy Roman Empire was built upon its foundations, it must also be confessed that this classic into which the son of Monica spent thirteen years pouring his dream was more than an inspiring and stabilizing influence in a day of deep darkness and social turbulence. From it, as from an unfailing spring, such men as Anselm, John of Salisbury, Aquinas, and many another drew long and life-giving draughts of spiritual refreshment, while the Church universal, Roman, Greek, and Protestant, continues to find in it a treasury of wisdom. As the writer of Christendom's first spiritual autobiography—*Confessions*—Augustine is known best to the world as the author of the words: *For Thou hast made us for Thyself, and our heart is restless until it rest in Thee.* Nevertheless, it is to the dream and the vision of the City of God that our civilization, torn from pole to pole by global war, may look for light and guidance. We have no need greater than that of sharing the vision of the African saint— "the blessedness of the holy city which is above the holy angels. . . . In the eternity of God is its life; in the truth of God its light; in the goodness of God its joy."

Once again the scene changes. Twenty centuries come and go between the sight of the prophet-prisoner in a Babylon concentration camp and the sight of a kindred dreamer who was exiled from his native and beloved city. This man was one of the greatest poets of all time. In pardonably exaggerated language he has been described as "the voice of ten silent centuries." Someone has called Dante the Ezekiel of his age. Like Augustine, he saw a world falling to pieces. It was the world of the Middle Ages. The Holy Roman Empire was going the way of the Roman Empire. In Florence, the city of flowers and the flower of cities, civil disruption was hastening the process of dissolution. The factional struggles between the Whiteshirts and the Blackshirts in which he was unhappily involved, resulted in his exile. Leaving behind him a wife and four children, Dante went forth "in bitterness and the heat of the spirit." Salting his daily bread with tears, he wandered from city to city, through Italy and France, and, possibly, to England. Few men have ever suffered so intensely because few men have been so keenly sensitive. Children in the streets, pointing at him, shouted, "The man who has come back from hell!" And, in a sense and for a time, their description was accurate. But it did not remain accurate. To Dante came something of that ineffable joy by means of which the Galilean was able to endure the Cross, and he returned to his native land to sing of the love which moves the stars and of that "will of God which is our peace."

> I raised my eyes aloft, and I beheld
> The scattered chapters of the Universe
> Gathered and bound into a single book
> By the austere and tender hand of God.

Dante's vision came to him sacramentally. It came by revelation. It was a redemptive and healing dream. And it was no less so for other souls and ages than for his own. In substance it was this: God lives and loves and rules. The church may be worldly and the empire may be doomed, but God abides, and "in his will is our peace." Just as in Beatrice the poet had seen a beauty lovelier than all the beauty of the world, so in God's

360

overruling providence he saw the ultimate triumph of truth, justice, righteousness and peace. Five hundred years after the death of the great Florentine, Lord Byron visited his grave. With deepest reverence the English poet knelt down and wept in the presence of the dead. But Dante is not dead! His soul, with all its vision of truth, lives on, and, in the light of that truth, we who live today may stand and take courage.

One could easily be tempted to pause in the times and with the minds of others of God's dreamers—with George Fox, John Bunyan, and William Blake, to name no more. But the whole story cannot and need not be told. The truth for us is what it was for these men. God is, and God rules by means of holy love. The kingdoms of the world may shake and fall, but the Kingdom of God remains. The cities of man may dissolve, but the City of God, which is man's true home, gathers and grows.

> Ah, great it is to believe the dream
> As we stand in youth by a starry stream;
> But a greater thing is to fight life through,
> And say at the end, "The dream is true."

The dream of the men of God will not fade; it is a deathless dream. The inspired vision will never vanish from our earth. All about our wounded world, one here and one there, in high places and lowly, are men in whose hearts the dream abides and the vision gleams and glows.

What then is the substance and genius of this dream? The answer is that to each divinely inspired dreamer, with a gift and grace of his own, it has been given to see and show some true aspect of the deathless dream. To Ezekiel it was given to express that dream which has been the light and life of the world's one and only religious civilization. To the Seer of Patmos it was given to express a vision which not only gave courage to the victims of the Colosseum and a kindly light to the faithful in dark Numidian mines, but which will ever be the healing hope of mankind everywhere. To Augustine it was given to see and show what cannot be shaken in a shaking world—the City of God above, beyond, and yet within, the City of Man. To Dante it was given to see and reveal that life's true values are beyond the reach of human tragedy—safe and secure in the loving hands of the living God.

Such insights constitute the content of man's redemptive and imperishable dream. They are the builders of the home of hope in our world, inspiring alike the saint kneeling at an altar and the soldier bleeding and dying for the sake of something he considers better than life itself. Indeed, this is the dream which lifts our heavy and wounded hearts, evokes our best loyalties, illumines the darkness of our pilgrim pathway, and, in some finer fashion, strengthens us, not only to protect and enhance our spiritual patrimony, but also to keep our date with a moral and ethical destiny.

What does the deathless dream demand of those of us who would live and labor for its fulfillment? It demands our complete commitment to the intention of God in Jesus Christ. It demands our search and sacrifice for a world of justice wherein, as J. B. Priestley has put it, "nobody carries a whip and nobody rattles a chain." It demands our search and sacrifice for a world of freedom—not freedom from God, which means the direst kind of slavery, but freedom in and for God, which is the secret and glory of man's most perfect liberty. It demands the ethical dictatorship of an humble mind and an enlightened, sensitive and Christ-inspired conscience. It demands a world in which principles have mastered prejudices, and strong bridges of understanding and appreciation unite races, creeds, and continents. It demands a world of righteousness in which the will of God creates and bestows the gift of peace. "I dreamt," said Walt Whitman, "I saw the city invincible. It was the new city of friends."

The City of God is the City of Man rescued and redeemed by the living Christ. It is the "new city of friends," in which the relation of man to God is that of child to father, and of man to man that of brother to brother. Nay it is more; it is the communion and community of living and loving souls—one family in heaven and on earth.

It is the city invincible. It is the city inevitable. It is the city imperishable. And whether its realization comes soon or late, whether within the framework of time or only in perfection beyond our mortal years, of this we may be certain:

"The name of the City from that day shall be, 'The Lord is there.'"

Once again, like Ezekiel and John and Dante, millions of men are in exile or in prison. And once again, as in the days of Augustine, darkness has descended and the legions of all manner of barbarism are at the very gates of civilization. Whence shall our help come? Only from the living God and our sure grasp of those truths and values which are beyond the reach of time and tragedy. Meanwhile, we celebrate the lives of all the souls in which the deathless dream abides and gathers and grows—the signal of their faith a white service star above Judean plains, the sign of their cause and sacrifice a Cross, and the promise of ultimate fulfillment an open tomb and a risen Christ.

362